FRANKLIN LIBRARY
FISK UNIVERSITY
DATE DISCARDED_____

Setting
National
Priorities

Setting National Priorities

POLICY FOR THE NINETIES

Henry J. Aaron, editor

JOHN E. CHUBB

ERIC A. HANUSHEK

LAWRENCE J. KORB

ROBERT Z. LAWRENCE

THOMAS E. MANN

WILLIAM D. NORDHAUS

CHARLES L. SCHULTZE

JOHN D. STEINBRUNER

The Brookings Institution
Washington, D.C.

JK271
·S43
1990

Copyright © 1990 by
THE BROOKINGS INSTITUTION
1775 Massachusetts Avenue, N.W., Washington, D.C. 20036

ISBN 0-8157-0048-2 (cloth)
ISBN 0-8157-0047-4 (paper)
Library of Congress Catalog Card Number 90-081338

9 8 7 6 5 4 3 2 1

The paper used in this publication meets the minimum requirements of the American National Standard for Information Sciences—Permanence of Paper for Printed Library Materials, ANSI Z39.48-1984.

THE BROOKINGS INSTITUTION

The Brookings Institution is an independent organization devoted to nonpartisan research, education, and publication in economics, government, foreign policy, and the social sciences generally. Its principal purposes are to aid in the development of sound public policies and to promote public understanding of issues of national importance.

The Institution was founded on December 8, 1927, to merge the activities of the Institute for Government Research, founded in 1916, the Institute of Economics, founded in 1922, and the Robert Brookings Graduate School of Economics and Government, founded in 1924.

The Board of Trustees is responsible for the general administration of the Institution, while the immediate direction of the policies, program, and staff is vested in the President, assisted by an advisory committee of the officers and staff. The by-laws of the Institution state: "It is the function of the Trustees to make possible the conduct of scientific research, and publication, under the most favorable conditions, and to safeguard the independence of the research staff in the pursuit of their studies and in the publication of the results of such studies. It is not a part of their function to determine, control, or influence the conduct of particular investigations or the conclusions reached."

The President bears final responsibility for the decision to publish a manuscript as a Brookings book. In reaching his judgment on the competence, accuracy, and objectivity of each study, the President is advised by the director of the appropriate research program and weighs the views of a panel of expert outside readers who report to him in confidence on the quality of the work. Publication of a work signifies that it is deemed a competent treatment worthy of public consideration but does not imply endorsement of conclusions or recommendations.

The Institution maintains its position of neutrality on issues of public policy in order to safeguard the intellectual freedom of the staff. Hence interpretations or conclusions in Brookings publications should be understood to be solely those of the authors and should not be attributed to the Institution, to its trustees, officers, or other staff members, or to the organizations that support its research.

Board of Trustees

Louis W. Cabot
Chairman

Ralph S. Saul
Vice Chairman

Ronald J. Arnault
Elizabeth E. Bailey
Rex J. Bates
Yvonne Brathwaite Burke
A. W. Clausen
William T. Coleman, Jr.
Kenneth W. Dam

D. Ronald Daniel
Charles W. Duncan, Jr.
Walter Y. Elisha
Robert F. Erburu
Robert D. Haas
Pamela C. Harriman
Vernon E. Jordan, Jr.
James A. Joseph
Thomas G. Labrecque
Donald F. McHenry
Bruce K. MacLaury
Mary Patterson McPherson

Donald S. Perkins
James D. Robinson III
Howard D. Samuel
B. Francis Saul II
Henry B. Schacht
Donna E. Shalala
Robert H. Smith
Howard R. Swearer
Morris Tanenbaum
John C. Whitehead
James D. Wolfensohn
Ezra K. Zilkha

Honorary Trustees

Vincent M. Barnett, Jr.
Barton M. Biggs
Robert D. Calkins
Edward W. Carter
Frank T. Cary
Lloyd N. Cutler
Bruce B. Dayton
Douglas Dillon

Huntington Harris
Andrew Heiskell
Roger W. Heyns
Roy M. Huffington
John E. Lockwood
James T. Lynn
William McC. Martin, Jr.
Robert S. McNamara
Arjay Miller

J. Woodward Redmond
Charles W. Robinson
Robert V. Roosa
Gerard C. Smith
Robert Brookings Smith
Sydney Stein, Jr.
Phyllis A. Wallace
Charles J. Zwick

For *twenty-one years Joseph A. Pechman served as
director of economic studies at the Brookings Institution.
During his tenure, he not only helped establish the
Economic Studies program as a center for high-quality,
objective research on important questions of public
policy, but also maintained a prodigious scholarly output
of his own. He warmly supported his colleagues. He
participated zestfully in debates on issues of public
policy. He edited seven volumes of* Setting National
Priorities, *contributed to others, and enthusiastically
supported the series throughout his tenure as director.*

 *Joseph A. Pechman died on August 19, 1989. This
book is dedicated to him and to his enduring contributions to his colleagues, to Brookings, and to the
principle that knowledge and reason can elevate debate
on public policy.*

Foreword

WE LIVE IN tumultuous times. Unprecedented changes in Eastern Europe and the Soviet Union hold out great promise for the United States and the world, but they also require radical rethinking of American strategies. The growing economic prowess of other nations is both challenge and opportunity for the U.S. economy. Domestically, large budget deficits are now in their second decade, but familiarity has not diminished their long-term economic damage. Serious problems afflict U.S. schools, medical care, transportation, and the environment, yet the political system seems deadlocked.

Setting National Priorities: Policy for the Nineties provides the basis for informed discussion of budget policy, national defense, international trade, the environment, education, and health. It contains specific proposals in each of these areas and an analysis of why political obstacles to action are so formidable.

This volume resumes a series that Brookings began twenty years ago. The purpose was to fill a gap in public understanding of the policies set forth in the president's budget and the problems those policies were intended to address. A large audience of policymakers, scholars, and citizens came to rely upon this series. This new volume looks not just at the president's 1991 budget, but ahead to the problems and challenges of the 1990s.

All of the Brookings research programs collaborated on this study. The editor is Henry J. Aaron, a senior fellow in the Economic Studies program. The authors are John E. Chubb, Lawrence J. Korb, Robert Z. Lawrence, Thomas E. Mann, Charles L. Schultze, and John D. Steinbruner of Brookings; Eric A. Hanushek, professor of economics at the University of Rochester; and William D. Nordhaus, John Musser professor of economics and member of the Cowles Foundation at Yale University.

The editor wishes to thank Nancy D. Davidson, Caroline Lalire,

Venka Macintyre, Jeanette Morrison, James P. Schneider, and Theresa B. Walker for editing the book; Roshna M. Kapadia, Linda S. Keefer, Vernon L. Kelley, and Pamela Plehn for checking the book for factual accuracy; and Susan L. Woollen for preparing the manuscript for typesetting.

The views expressed in this book are those of the authors and should not be ascribed to the people whose assistance is acknowledged above, to those who assisted the various authors, or to other staff members, officers, or trustees of the Brookings Institution.

BRUCE K. MACLAURY
President

April 1990
Washington, D.C.

Contents

Text Tables

Text Figures

1

HENRY J. AARON

Policy for the Nineties

THE LAST DECADE of the American century has begun. The United States that emerged from World War II produced nearly half of world output and enjoyed uncontested military superiority because of its monopoly of nuclear weapons. It helped restore the economies of Western European countries devastated by war. It nurtured multilateral free trade to the benefit of all. It rearmed to neutralize military threats in Asia and Europe. For four decades the United States stood as the bulwark of the NATO alliance. And as the decade of the nineties begins, that military and diplomatic resolve has been rewarded by political and economic reform in once-hostile tyrannies around the world.

At home, World War II called forth the highest output that this or any other nation had seen. Three subsequent decades of rapid growth surpassed even that achievement. Until the 1970s, inequality fell as incomes rose. The long struggle for simple justice overthrew legal barriers to equal participation in American life by minorities, most notably African-Americans.

But as the new decade begins, the proud achievements of the preceding four decades cannot obscure a growing sense that the United States is faltering, at home and abroad. As the military threat diminishes, so too does the role of the United States as leader of its alliance. Other nations, recovered from the devastation of World War II, challenge American leadership in virtually all aspects of production. Japan continues a century-long saga of economic expansion. Other countries of the Pacific rim are entering and in some cases capturing markets from the United States, Japan, and other countries. European nations, putting behind centuries of bloody strife, are moving toward economic reform and political unity.

In contrast with this vitality abroad, the United States is paralyzed by a psychosis of poverty and helplessness in the face of problems at home and abroad. Possessor of the largest and deepest capital stock in the world, its saving rate is lower than that of any other developed

1

country and less than half its own rate during the first three postwar decades. Beneficiary for decades of a system of free trade, it now quails before economic competition and flirts with proposals to undermine free international markets. World pioneer of mass public education, its students now perform worse than those of virtually all other countries for which data are available. Underwriter of the world's most costly health care system, it leaves more than 31 million people uninsured and millions more inadequately covered or at risk of losing coverage. Richer than ever before, it has found no way to reduce the significant fraction of its population that is poor, a fraction that remains larger than that of other industrial nations with lower average incomes. Victor in the cold war, its response to pleas from the countries of Central America and Eastern Europe for help in rebuilding economies ravaged by central planners is to agonize over how to shift monies within an already shrunken foreign aid budget.

President Bush stated in his first inaugural address, "We have more will than wallet." But the United States is a nation blessed with the highest per capita income of any developed country in the world. Its national product is two and a half times larger than that of the second-largest economy. It is enjoying its longest peacetime expansion. The question is not whether America has enough wallet, but whether it has the will to use its abundant wealth to solve the problems that it faces.

The United States faces no imminent crises that demand decisive leadership. It confronts neither lethal threat from abroad nor economic crisis at home. Rather it faces nagging problems whose solutions require immediate and tangible sacrifice but offer deferred and diffuse benefits. From such burdens leaders in the White House and Congress can easily shrink. The nation can muddle through without absolute decline. Yet Americans cannot escape the reality that decisions taken during this decade will determine whether the chronicle of growth at home and influence abroad continues or flags.

What is at stake are the priorities that the nation sets for itself in the coming decade. For many years, successive presidents used the annual budget to shape debate about national priorities. No president controlled the outcome of the policy debate, but each determined its content. Since the early years of the Reagan administration, however, and especially since the introduction of the Gramm-Rudman deficit reduction process, the president's budget has ceased to be a force shaping national debate.

Each January since the early 1980s Congress has convened under the shadow of large and damaging deficits. Late in the month presidents have transmitted to Congress budgets typically based on overly optimistic economic assumptions. All have called for large cuts in domestic expenditures. Most have called for a few small tax increases, usually camouflaged. Most have used such ploys as asset sales to hide the deficit's true size. In the months that follow, members of Congress find they cannot agree on honest expenditure cuts or tax increases that will meet the official deficit reduction targets. And so they fashion, sometimes alone and sometimes with the aid of the administration, quaint and curious budgetary evasions. In the end, Congress adjourns after certifying compliance with the deficit reduction targets, when in fact little or no progress has been made.

As a result, the influence of the budget on political debate remains slight. In the absence of national leadership, the United States is avoiding national priorities rather than setting them, jeopardizing future success at home and abroad—economically, socially, diplomatically, and militarily. Earnings per worker have not grown for more than fifteen years, and the distribution of income has become markedly less equal. Growth of productivity is depressed. American businesses are losing competitive ground abroad. In the age of media hype, everyone has become jaded by exaggeration. But it is no exaggeration to say that what is done about national saving, investment, research, education, and health will determine whether America chooses excellence or mediocrity.

Throughout the 1970s the Brookings Institution published annual analyses of the president's budget entitled *Setting National Priorities*. The title reflected the judgment of successive editors and authors that the president's budget was the place to begin if one wanted to discuss the nation's economic, defense, social, and other policies. The series was discontinued after 1983, partly because the Congressional Budget Office had emerged as a source of prompt and thorough analyses, but largely because the annual budget exercise had degenerated into a process marked by posturing and gimmicks that did little to reduce the deficit and less to focus informed debate on the nation's problems.

This book resurrects the name and tradition of its predecessors, but this year's subtitle, *Policy for the Nineties,* reflects a longer perspective than the yearly focus of the presidential budget. We are concerned with the challenges that the United States will face during this decade. Our purpose is to explain the background of selected problems and to indicate the range of choices that the country faces. The authors of each chapter not only analyze problems and evaluate the suggestions of others but advance proposals for action that, in their judgment, will work.

The overriding message can be simply stated. The United States remains rich and strong. Its richness and strength reflect an inheritance from nature and from past generations of Americans: a temperate climate, abundant resources, public institutions supportive of growth, and most of all an environment that rewards hard work, skills, and innovation. These are not immutable gifts. The United States can sustain and build upon its inheritance, but only if it cuts short its national consumption binge, spends its wealth sensibly, and responds with imagination to the opportunities and challenges that are emerging at home and abroad.

Three themes echo throughout this book. First, fiscal mismanagement of the United States must end. Until the president and Congress take the necessary actions, progress on many national priorities will be hamstrung. Second, in the areas of national defense, education, international trade, and health care, obsolete approaches must be discarded and new avenues tried. And third, with major structural reforms progress can be made in such areas as education and transportation without large additional expenditures. Without such reforms, extra spending will do little good.

That the government finances of the United States are being mismanaged is not exactly breaking news. The federal deficit has been around long enough to seem normal—and boring. While the deficit has lost its capacity to shock, it has not lost its power to damage the economy by diverting roughly half of private saving from productive investments at home or abroad. Had the federal deficit risen because of a sharp increase in public investment, it would pose much less of a problem. In fact, net investment by the government has fallen.

The swollen deficit results from a series of steps taken in the early 1980s: increased defense spending and reduced personal and corporation income taxes that far exceeded cuts in domestic spending. If private saving had risen, increased federal borrowing might have been harmless; however, net private saving in the 1980s fell to less than half the rate of the preceding three decades. The United States is in the midst of an extended consumption binge. Current national saving barely exceeds the annual depreciation of the existing stock of capital goods. Depressed saving slows growth of worker productivity. It is conventional wisdom that because of the deficit the United States cannot afford to solve serious problems of health care, education, and infrastructure. In fact, failure to attack these problems and the deficit simultaneously stems from a deeper common source: American leaders have been unwilling or unable to try to persuade the people of the need to cut spending, to raise taxes, or to take other controversial actions.

Several chapters of this book sound the second theme—that traditional modes of addressing certain national problems must give way to new ones. Clearly, in the field of national defense, the political transformation of the Soviet Union and Eastern Europe has reduced the military force the United States requires to protect itself and its allies. Beyond that, however, these events offer an unprecedented opportunity to achieve increased security through cooperative defense arrangements involving not only the United States and its allies but also its former adversaries.

In education, the conventional view that the way to improve schools is to add educational "inputs"—to reduce class size, to raise teacher pay, to provide in-service training to current teachers—is simply unsupported by research. U.S. educational performance fell disastrously at the same time that educational spending rose sharply. More generally, no consistent relationship has been found between educational inputs and educational achievement. Without fundamental changes in the way schools are managed and in the criteria on which they are judged, more money is almost sure to be spent to little effect.

In international trade, the centuries-old debate between those who advocate free trade and those who would restrict trade to promote national interest now seems simplistic in face of the changing character of technological competition. Although free trade still promises enormous benefits, government intervention—to support research, to facilitate cooperation among domestic companies, or to penalize the anticompetitive behavior of other countries—may be required to sustain free trade.

In the area of health care financing, it is becoming clear that neither the extension of insurance coverage nor the control of rising costs can be achieved unless both problems are addressed simultaneously. In each of these areas, new conditions have rendered traditional approaches obsolete in the 1990s.

The third theme is that important progress can be made on some problems—education, transportation, and the global environment—without spending large additional sums if the nation is willing to reform several current policies. As just noted, there is no evidence that simply spending more money on education will materially improve educational outcomes, but giving individual schools more authority and incentive to improve could generate large gains. Large additional expenditures to expand the current highway and airport systems will do little to relieve congestion, because simply adding to capacity without changing incentives for use will result in both more facilities and more congestion. But congestion can be reduced and the quality of roads improved by changes in usage fees and in the way roads are built, neither of which requires a major increase in spending. Fear of global warming has led to calls for large outlays to curtail emissions of "greenhouse gases," chemical entities that tend to prevent the earth from radiating heat into space. But analysis shows these emissions can be modestly reduced at low cost, and the large additional expenditures necessary to achieve further reduction in emissions do not promise benefits that come close to estimated costs.

No book of manageable size can encompass the full range of problems confronting a nation as large and diverse as the United States. This book does not address such critical national problems as drug dependency, the underclass, and rising income inequality. These problems may recede if America grows rapidly at home, competes effectively abroad, and responds imaginatively to the changing military and diplomatic environment, if its children learn as much as children in other countries, and if its health care system serves everyone at reasonable overall cost. But millions of Americans will not share in these improvements. These problems are serious, but we think that a sustained, vigorous, and perhaps costly attack on them will be possible only when the American people as whole enjoy a rising standard of living and regain their faith that the nation can meet challenges at home and abroad.

America's problems threaten no crises. They are hard for a democracy to solve, for they require that its citizens, most of whom are prosperous, make current sacrifices for long-term gains. They require that people unaccustomed to failure forsake old ways of thinking for new ones. The task of mobilizing the American people to deal with such problems and persuading them to do what needs to be done calls for both skill and courage.

The remainder of this chapter briefly summarizes what the authors have to say about how to go about meeting this challenge.

The Budget

In chapter 2, Charles L. Schultze examines the budget deficit—how it came about, how it can be reduced, and why it is important to eliminate it. The deficit is important not because it threatens immediate economic crisis, but because it reduces national saving and because its continuing presence stifles political debate and action on other national problems. The United States as a nation now saves only a little more than is necessary to replace the capital used up in production. Its net saving rate in the 1980s fell to historic lows and remained much below those of other developed nations. The fall in national saving had two causes: a drop in private saving and an enlarged federal deficit that diverted from productive investment much of what was left. As a consequence, America invested less during the 1980s than in earlier decades and had to rely heavily on overseas borrowing to finance that smaller investment.

Schultze presents estimates of how much Americans would have to save to cover domestic investment without borrowing abroad and to build reserves to help future generations meet the added costs that a growing population of retirees will impose in the next century. To reach this target, the federal government should run a surplus of about 1 percent of national product, rather than its current deficit of about 2.5 percent. Reaching this goal would increase growth directly by raising capital accumulation. And by promoting lower interest rates, it would encourage American managers and investors to take a longer-term view of investment payoffs.

Schultze then traces how federal spending has evolved. Social security spending and the payroll taxes to finance it have grown steadily as a share of national product in the years since World War II. But, contrary to common perception, general operating revenues other than payroll taxes have actually fallen as a share of national output since 1960. On the other side of the ledger, general operating expenditures have remained roughly constant as a share of national output, although the composition has changed. The result has been a deficit in the overall budget, consisting of a large deficit in the general operating budget, offset in part by a growing surplus in the social security trust funds.

Schultze examines policies to convert the budget deficit into a surplus. The key to such a program is less spending on national defense, as explained by John D. Steinbruner and Lawrence J. Korb in chapters 3 and 4. These spending cuts, like all others, would reduce the deficit both directly and through reduced interest payments on the national debt. On the domestic side, some middle-class subsidies could be curtailed and marginal programs cut, or social security benefits could be lowered (directly or by increasing the taxation of benefits). The nation would greatly benefit, however, from increased spending in several critical areas—to improve highways, bridges, and airports, to support reform of education, to increase outlays on research and development, to extend medical insurance, and to advance national objectives such as lessening substance abuse. The needed increases are a good bit less than those proposed by enthusiasts for these programs, but significant nonetheless. The final step to a sound fiscal policy could be taken by increasing taxes or by instituting the health program outlined below. Altogether these measures would produce a surplus in the overall budget, including social security, of about $70 billion in 1995.

Foreign and Defense Policy

While the collapse of the military threat from the Soviet Union and its allies augurs budgetary relief for the United States, the far greater promise lies in the opportunity for all nations to enjoy enhanced security at a greatly reduced cost. This opportunity can be fully realized, John D. Steinbruner explains in chapter 3, only within new military and diplomatic arrangements that he characterizes as "cooperative security."

Since the onset of the cold war, the primary goal of U.S. defense policy has been to prevent a hot war with the Soviet Union and, should that catastrophe occur, to prevent the Soviets from winning it. In the past the Soviets maintained huge ground forces in Eastern Europe and a powerful strategic nuclear capability. They also tried to keep their full capabilities secret. While the Soviets also sought to avoid war, their military doctrine held that, in the event of war, Soviet forces should attack Western ground forces and try to achieve immediate victory.

Both the size of the Soviet forces and uncertainty about their exact capabilities forced the United States and its allies to maintain large conventional forces near the borders with Eastern Europe to resist and repel any Soviet ground attack. To avoid incentives to strike first during a crisis, the United States also maintained strategic nuclear forces that could absorb a strike from the Soviet Union and still deliver devastating retaliation. With the political transformation of Eastern Europe and the expectation that most Soviet forces will be returned to their home territory, the size and the readiness of Western forces required for deterrence diminish greatly, as does the possibility of an unintended confrontation.

Steinbruner argues that large additional gains are within grasp if the

United States and the Soviet Union, along with the other principal nations, enter into cooperative security arrangements. Under these arrangements all countries with national interests requiring significant military outlays would sharply reduce their forces and, simultaneously, keep their potential adversaries informed about the size and capability of the remaining forces. The approach rests on the fact that smaller forces are normally sufficient to defend or to deter than to attack. Furthermore, if each side keeps the other informed, both can manage without the extra forces all countries now think they need to deal with "worst cases"—that is, possibilities that cannot be excluded without reliable evidence on the true capability and intention of rival states. Based on such arrangements, U.S. defense expenditures can be cut heavily—on ground forces, by nearly half; on naval forces, by a quarter; and on air forces, by nearly a third. By the end of the decade the United States can cut defense spending by $100 billion to $150 billion (in 1990 dollars). The Soviets could reduce their forces commensurately. The result would be that all nations involved in such cooperative security arrangements would enjoy both improved security and reduced defense budgets.

Steinbruner argues also that cooperative security arrangements are necessary to align U.S. foreign policy with the new features of world politics. The ideological barriers of the cold war are collapsing. The political effect of military power has declined. Participation in the international market economy has become imperative for all countries, especially the Soviet Union. These changes have produced a demanding agenda: the design of internal economic reform in formerly planned economies, the reallocation of foreign investment, the defense of open international trade, the maintenance of the global environment, and the resolution of regional conflict. Cooperation among the major powers is vital to the effective handling of each of these issues. Forging that cooperation is the dominant task of U.S. policy.

The Defense Budget

In chapter 4, Lawrence J. Korb examines the U.S. defense budget and finds that current policy is not well designed to achieve the cooperative security arrangements described by Steinbruner. Korb traces the evolution of U.S. defense policy since the end of World War II, paying particular attention to recent defense policy, the backdrop for the current debate.

President Ronald Reagan continued and accelerated a defense buildup

started by President Jimmy Carter. Because of pressures from the budget
deficit and a sense that U.S. forces were strong enough, Congress stopped
the buildup in 1985. Real outlays in 1990 are projected to be about 14
percent below their 1985 peak. Upon taking office, President George
Bush asked for and got modest cuts in total defense spending. But the
administration failed to eliminate three costly systems, as Congress once
again showed that it is willing to slow down or stretch out orders for
new systems, but not to cancel them.

The 1991 budget contains plans for continued cuts in real defense
spending of about 2 percent a year. Korb notes, however, that the
administration has not yet explained the rationale behind its proposed
force structure, nor has it indicated how it would respond to the larger
cuts in defense spending Congress seems likely to enact. Furthermore,
the current budget reveals no thought on how to help the economy
negotiate the transition to reduced defense spending. While shifting
resources from tanks and planes to factories and machine tools promises
economic benefits in the long run, the businesses and workers who build
the tanks and planes may suffer hardships along the way that will deter
Congress from cutting at the right speed or in the right way.

Calling the administration's requests for 2 percent annual reductions
timid and unrealistic, Korb suggests policymakers could safely pare
defense spending nearly 5 percent a year until 1995 and more rapidly
for the rest of the decade.[1] How to apportion the funds is another issue.
The administration would distribute future spending among defense
activities in about the same proportions as current spending. Korb argues
that the transformation of international political and military relations
fully justifies large cuts in the procurement of new military equipment
and in operations and maintenance, but he would make only small cuts
in research, development, testing, and evaluation, thereby sustaining the
ability of the United States to produce sophisticated and technologically
advanced forces should a future military buildup become necessary.

Both chapters 3 and 4 conclude that events in the Soviet alliance
present the United States and its allies with enormous opportunities to
increase security while cutting defense spending, but that the administration, by failing to seize this opportunity, may doom the United States

---

1. These cuts are somewhat larger than those presented by Steinbruner because Korb
assumes that spending on modernization and readiness would be cut back more than is
implicit in Steinbruner's estimates.

to spend more than necessary on defense while remaining less secure than a more daring policy would accomplish.

Technology and Trade

With the decline of military confrontation between East and West, the struggle for technological preeminence and control of markets emerges as the new arena for world competition. In chapter 5, Robert Z. Lawrence analyzes how the economic position of the United States has changed in the decades since World War II. He pinpoints the threats that it faces and the actions that public and private leaders can take to help the United States compete effectively.

Technologically preeminent at the end of the war, the United States is now merely first among equals. The return to health of war-ravaged economies was bound to diminish America's relative advantage. But domestic budget policies during the 1980s caused further slippage by overvaluing the dollar and damaging the competitiveness of U.S. companies. The rapid advance of other countries was supported in some cases by national policies to encourage domestic companies and, on occasion, to obstruct the operations of U.S and other foreign competitors.

The apparent success of these tactics has led some observers to question whether the U.S. government is wise to support free trade and to leave technological development largely to private business. Even the United States has made exceptions to these principles. It has awarded patents to inventors, subsidized research important to basic science and national defense, and on occasion violated free trade when powerful domestic interests demanded protection.

Lawrence points out that actions by foreign governments to aid their own businesses can actually help the United States—by making available consumer goods or industrial inputs at low prices, for example. But some kinds of assistance may injure not only particular U.S. companies but U.S. interests as a whole. This situation arises when extraordinary profits can be earned on a sustained basis. If one company can satisfy world demand more cheaply than can two or more companies, monopoly profits can be earned indefinitely. By subsidizing their own companies or obstructing U.S. companies, foreign governments can divert these profits from the United States to resident companies.

Lawrence acknowledges that rigid adherence to laissez faire exposes the United States to losses when foreign governments use tariffs, other taxes, subsidies, or trade restrictions to injure U.S. interests. Officially managing trade could reduce this risk, but at the cost of jeopardizing open markets, from which the United States has profited enormously in the past and stands to benefit greatly in the future. Efforts to date to manage trade in the name of preserving domestic employment have been extraordinarily inefficient, costing $75,000 or more for each job saved.

Rigid laissez faire would also result in too little investment in research and development. As Lawrence points out, technological advance now depends more heavily than in the past on cooperative research and interdisciplinary skills. The United States should strive to promote technological diffusion through encouragement of collaborative ventures, of competition at home and abroad, and of research that can serve many users. But extensive sector-specific industrial policies would require the government to make choices it is poorly equipped to make. The best option, Lawrence suggests, is to promote innovation in the United States through broadly based direct subsidies and tax incentives and to punish countries or companies that violate the open-market principle.

The United States would lose an enormous asset if it sacrificed the principle of free multilateral trade for negotiated bilateral agreements, even if such agreements brought identifiable short-run advantages. U.S. policy should be based on the conviction that U.S. interests will be best promoted within a global market. The United States should not expect to dominate every sphere, as seemed almost natural in the years immediately after World War II; but Americans will enjoy a higher and more rapidly increasing standard of living within an open global market than they can possibly achieve through a system of managed trade.

Global Warming

In setting national priorities, policymakers have to know when to move slowly as well as when to move aggressively. William D. Nordhaus argues in chapter 6 that, given current knowledge, drastic and costly measures to arrest climatic change are not currently justified. After describing the evidence that worldwide climate is changing, he concludes that climate has warmed slightly on the average in this century and that further warming is likely. The cause is the emission of "greenhouse gases"—carbon dioxide, chlorofluorocarbons, methane, and nitrous oxides, principally from the combustion of fossil fuels. All these gases contribute to global warming by inhibiting the radiation of heat from the earth into space.

Considerable doubt surrounds estimates of how much damage climate change will do to the economies of the world. Contrary to common perception, warming will bring benefits as well as losses. About 87 percent of measured U.S. output comes from sectors that are not sensitive to climate. Losses in sectors producing the remaining 13 percent will slightly exceed benefits. Nordhaus's estimate is that, on balance, climatic change will reduce U.S. annual output about a quarter of 1 percent. Effects in other advanced economies are also likely to be small, although developing countries and low-lying regions such as Bangladesh and the Maldives are more vulnerable. Despite the small size of these estimated losses, the uncertainty surrounding them means that neither larger climatic effects nor larger losses from given climatic change can be ruled out.

The emission of greenhouse gases can be reduced, but at a steeply rising cost as the size of the reduction increases. Nordhaus's calculations show that imposing a modest tax on each source of greenhouse gases— for example, a tax equivalent to $5 per ton of carbon (which corresponds to a 10 percent tax on coal and much smaller taxes on petroleum products)—would reduce emissions about 13 percent a year and bring global net benefits of about $12 billion a year. The effects would come primarily from virtually eliminating the use of chlorofluorocarbons and from inducing electric utilities to replace coal with other fossil fuels or to switch to nuclear power. Such a tax would retard global warming only slightly, but Nordhaus argues that larger changes cannot be justified on the basis of current estimates of global warming and of the associated damages. In particular, a tax large enough to cut the emission of greenhouse gases almost in half would probably inflict annual net losses worldwide of nearly $100 billion.

Nordhaus finds the policies proposed by the Bush administration to deal with global warming to be reasonable. They call for modest efforts to reduce the net release of greenhouse gases and for expansion of research to narrow today's uncertainties. Ill-designed schemes, he warns, have the capacity to do enormous harm. More costly steps should be deferred until further research indicates a more aggressive posture is warranted.

Education

The prosperity of the United States today reflects past investments in capital, research, and the skills of its population. As John E. Chubb and

Eric A. Hanushek explain in chapter 7, the last of these assets is eroding. American children perform worse in standardized tests than did previous generations or than do children abroad. Roughly a fourth of students nationally—as many as half in some cities—drop out of school before receiving a high school diploma.

These facts are all the more disturbing because the collapse of educational performance happened despite a huge increase in educational spending. Real outlays per student have nearly tripled since 1960 and risen roughly 60 percent since 1975. The funds have been spent on all the good things most people think are necessary to improve schools— smaller classes, teacher training and education, and higher teacher pay, for example. Chubb and Hanushek show that there is no evidence that increasing any input over which school boards or local governments have control is associated with improvements in educational achievement. They conclude that simply spending more on schools as currently organized holds no promise that future results will be any better than past ones.

What explains this dismal record and prognosis? Schools, say the authors, are managed rigidly and are not held to account for their results. Instead, bureaucratic rules and procedures focus on "inputs" rather than on what children learn, or educational "output." Only if schools that do a consistently bad job are permitted to go out of business, and schools that do a consistently good job are tangibly rewarded and permitted to grow, is there any chance of breaking out of the current educational impasse. Resources must be related to performance.

Chubb and Hanushek suggest a variety of ways in which schools can be encouraged to focus on output. These approaches include administrative reforms, such as merit pay for teachers or schools that consistently do a better-than-average job educating children. The authors hold out most hope for market-oriented reforms, which force schools to compete with one another for the allegiance and attendance of students. These reforms include magnet schools, open-enrollment plans, and tuition tax credits. But they hold out greatest hope for voucher plans, in which students can attend any of a wide range of schools and carry a sum of money to the schools they select.

They evaluate the arguments for and against a market approach. It promises to reduce bureaucracy, promote more effective school organization, and strengthen the relationship between families and schools— all of which should improve educational achievements. They acknowledge certain risks: parents might have inadequate information for choosing schools wisely, a school with a local monopoly might exploit its position, or markets might exacerbate inequality or permit the inculcation of values in conflict with those of the community. They show that government regulation could be used to forestall these problems. And they conclude that despite potential shortcomings, market approaches are by far the most promising avenue of educational reform.

Because input strategies have failed so consistently to improve educational achievement, Chubb and Hanushek see no good case for a large increase in expenditures by any level of government so long as schools remain organized as they are today. In the meantime, they indicate how federal policy could be used to promote the kinds of reforms that hold out promise of success. Such policies include grants to school districts that institute market reforms or to people residing in such districts and measures to improve and to publish data on student performance tabulated by state, school district, and school. While the authors acknowledge that they cannot assure complete success for the reforms they advocate, they are confident that simply pouring more money into schools without changing their organization will accomplish little other than to drive up the cost of an unsatisfactory educational system.

Health Care

Although per capita health expenditures in the United States greatly exceed those of other countries, more than 31 million Americans are uninsured for the costs of acute illnesses, and virtually all lack coverage for costs of long-term care. Concern is also spreading that a distressing share of total health care expenditures goes for procedures that cost more than they are worth.

In chapter 8, I outline three broad strategies for dealing with these problems. "Voluntary incrementalism" would aim to extend insurance coverage for acute care through a basket of measures to improve the operation of the private insurance market and through a modest extension of medicaid, the federal-state program for providing health coverage for the poor. For long-term care, the strategy would rely on private insurance companies to develop and successfully market policies to insure against these costs. And it would count on competition in the medical marketplace and the spread of private cost-containment efforts to reduce low-benefit, high-cost care.

The results of pursuing this strategy, I conclude, will be disappointing. It will not materially increase the share of the population insured for acute illnesses. Moreover, evidence shows the majority of the U.S. population will not voluntarily buy private long-term-care insurance. Competitive forces and private cost containment will fail to reduce the growth of health care spending in the United States or squeeze out much of the high-cost, low-benefit care now being provided, because they do not reach the root cause of such expenditures. As long as most people are insured for most costs of significant illnesses—and no one has suggested exposing most people to a large part of the costs of serious illnesses—they will have every incentive to demand every useful service regardless of cost.

A second strategy, mandating employer-sponsored health insurance plans for all workers and their dependents, could achieve nearly universal insurance for acute-care illnesses, particularly if combined with some extension of federal programs for people not covered at work or by current federal programs. Employer-sponsored insurance for long-term care has had little appeal to either workers or employers, however. And the extension of health insurance, without effective cost control, would aggravate the problem of rising costs.

The final strategy, fundamental restructuring, can deal with coverage for both acute and long-term care and with cost control. Early versions of fundamental restructuring, based on publicly sponsored insurance, now receive virtually no attention because they would enormously increase government spending. Accordingly, I suggest that fundamental restructuring must consist of three main elements: a new federally sponsored program for long-term care; a new mechanism for paying providers; and mandatory employer-sponsored insurance for acute care. Employers would initially have the option of paying a tax instead of offering health insurance, but would be required to offer insurance after a transition period. The payment mechanism would involve several state or regional agencies that would receive all payments from insurers or individuals and take responsibility for paying hospitals and physicians. I propose further that these three functions be supervised by a federal department of health that would assume responsibility for all current health activities of the federal government as well as these new responsibilities.

These functions would be financed by current medicare payroll taxes and premiums; current state medicaid spending; taxes paid by employers who did not offer coverage; revenues from personal income taxes levied on health insurance worth more than a stipulated maximum; and a new 6 percent value-added tax. This plan would provide universal coverage for acute care, broad coverage for long-term home health service and nursing home care, and the potential for controlling growth of health care spending. By moving health expenditures now financed from general revenues to a new trust fund, and by instituting a new tax to make that trust fund self-supporting, this plan would also contribute about $67 billion to deficit reduction, roughly the deficit remaining if the other policies suggested by Charles Schultze in chapter 2 were implemented.

Politics

In the concluding chapter, Thomas E. Mann looks at the political context for debate about the issues addressed in this book. A variety of circumstances, Mann suggests, stand in the way of decisive action to deal with national problems. President Bush succeeds a president whose theme was the ineffectuality or impropriety of virtually all federal expenditures and regulations to deal with national problems other than defense and social security. He inherited a large budget deficit. He faces a Democratic Congress. The power of special interests, enhanced by their growing role in financing congressional campaigns, constrains effective action on urgent problems. Public opinion surveys report that the American people want the government to spend more for almost every function except welfare and foreign aid, that they want the deficit reduced, and that they oppose higher taxes of almost any kind (other than higher payroll taxes if necessary to support medicare and social security). President Bush presides over a nation confused and divided on the rather technical issues it faces, and he seems unprepared to try to force action where consensus is absent.

Mann characterizes public discourse at the start of the 1990s as "brain dead" and suggests that resuscitation is not likely in the absence of crisis, such as economic collapse or environmental disaster. Although the end of divided government—through Republican control of Congress or Democratic control of the White House—might help, neither is certain to produce decisive action because the other inhibiting factors would remain.

Mann sees nothing in President Bush's proposed 1991 budget to contradict the appraisal of a high congressional official who characterized it as "play it again, Sam." Long on rhetoric, but short on specific proposals, it does not ask the public to make any sacrifices for future benefits and it does little to close the deficit.

Mann sees little short-run political incentive for either party to alter its position. Some Democrats remain attracted to an economic nationalism that, as John Steinbruner and Robert Lawrence show, would damage the long-term interests of the United States. Others are tempted to try to seize the low-tax image from the Republican party by embracing Senator Daniel Patrick Moynihan's proposal to cut the payroll tax, regardless of the medium- and long-term economic damage that would result from a higher budget deficit. But few are drawn to the politically risky strategy of dealing directly with the party's presidential weaknesses and the country's problems.

No one in either party seemed prepared to make a concrete deficit reduction proposal based on honest accounting and reasonable economic assumptions until House Ways and Means Committee Chairman Dan Rostenkowski offered a bold plan in March 1990. Fashioning and fighting for passage of such a plan hold few short-run attractions, either for a president elected as a champion of low taxes and strong defense or for members of Congress anxious to minimize their political vulnerability. But it is time for the country's leaders to put long-term national interests ahead of short-term political concerns.

2

CHARLES L. SCHULTZE

The Federal Budget and the Nation's Economic Health

IN FISCAL 1990 the federal government will run its eleventh large budget deficit. Not since 1979 has the deficit been less than 2 percent of gross national product, and not since 1974 below 1 percent. In the early years of large deficits—1980 through 1983—they did little or no harm because the U.S. economy was in a recession or just recovering from one. Excess capacity was available to meet the demands of both the private economy and the federal government. Borrowing to finance the federal deficit neither crowded out domestic investment nor required large amounts of overseas borrowing. But since 1984 the nation has been running a string of substantial deficits in a fully employed economy.

A reversal of the buildup in defense spending in 1986 allowed the budget deficit to fall from 5.4 to 3.2 percent in 1988, but progress has been slow since then, and the 1990 deficit will still be 2.5 percent. This string of large deficits has dominated budget making for a number of years, sharply limiting new initiatives and the growth of most existing civilian programs—which some view as a major evil and others as a blessing in disguise.

Until recently all possible sources of maneuver to relieve the budget squeeze were apparently blocked. Presidents Reagan and Bush were able to prevent any significant increase in taxes except payroll taxes. The defense buildup was halted in 1986, but the subsequent debate about the defense budget took place within fairly narrow limits, producing neither sharp reductions nor large further increases. Congress avoided major increases in program spending but, with a few exceptions early in Reagan's first term, proved unwilling to enact the deep program cuts he repeatedly proposed. Meanwhile, the mounting federal debt and the

The author wishes to thank Bruce K. MacLaury, George L. Perry, and Alice M. Rivlin for their comments and Allen L. Sebrell for his research assistance.

high interest rates (caused mainly by the large budget deficits) kept pushing up federal expenditures for interest on the debt. Just the *increase* in interest payments on the debt during the 1980s accounted for the entire budget deficit in 1990.

The administration's budget for 1991, like all of its predecessors in recent years, forecasts a substantial reduction in the deficit, from $138 billion in 1990 to $63 billion in 1991. Such a deficit would meet, by a hair, the Gramm-Rudman targets and would amount to only 1.2 percent of GNP, the lowest share since 1974. The actual budget deficit in 1991 will almost surely be much larger than the administration's projections, which are based on a quite optimistic economic forecast and presume Congress will agree to a series of expenditure cuts it has repeatedly refused to enact. A twelfth successive year of substantial budget deficits is a virtual certainty.

In this chapter I argue that large deficits are significantly harming America's future growth prospects because of what they are doing to national saving and investment, and make the case for converting the deficits into surpluses over the next six to seven years. After reviewing recent trends in spending and evaluating costs and benefits of major federal programs, I suggest that a combination of reasonable cuts in defense and entitlement programs and a modest tax increase could finance both some needed spending increases and the conversion of the current budget deficit into the desired surplus.

How Large Are Budget Deficits Likely to Be?

The administration not only projects a rapid fall in the budget deficit in the coming fiscal year to $63 billion, it also foresees a gradual conversion of the deficit into a surplus starting in 1993. Moreover, this conversion from deficit to surplus would occur even as the large annual surplus in the social security trust fund was being removed from the calculation of the budget balance. And the administration projects the achievement of this objective with only modest cuts in the (inflation-adjusted) level of defense spending. These projections, however, are far too optimistic, both for 1991 and for the longer term, given the budget policies the administration is proposing.

The Congressional Budget Office (CBO) estimates that with unchanged budget policies the 1991 deficit is likely to be $134 billion, slightly above last year's $127 billion.[1] The CBO's deficit projection is higher than the

1. All the expenditure estimates for 1990 and later years cited in this chapter *exclude*

administration's partly because its forecasts of economic growth and interest rates for 1990 and 1991 match the average of outside economic forecasters, while the administration projects higher economic growth and lower interest rates for both years.[2] The administration's estimates also assume Congress will accept some $15 billion in proposed spending cuts, most of which have been repeatedly rejected. The administration further counts on raising some $5 billion in additional revenues from its proposed reduction in capital gains taxes, based on the assumption that stockholders will rush to sell appreciated assets once the tax is reduced. (Whatever this tax change does to revenues in the first year, it will lose money over longer periods of time.)

If recent history is any guide, Congress will cut defense spending modestly below the president's request. Some small cuts will be made in civilian spending, but these are likely to be nearly matched by increases elsewhere. For purposes of trying to meet the Gramm-Rudman deficit target for the year ($64 billion), Congress will probably agree to accept the administration's rosy forecast. But in the end, the actual budget outcome for fiscal 1991 may not be much below the $134 billion CBO projection.

The administration's long-term forecast of a budget surplus by 1993, achieved without counting the surplus in the social security trust fund, is based on economic assumptions equally as optimistic those used to estimate the 1991 budget. The CBO projection of the current services budget—that is, a budget with no changes in laws governing taxes or entitlement programs and with discretionary spending increasing only enough to offset inflation—shows much higher deficits (see table 2-1). By definition the CBO budget estimates do not include the civilian and military spending cuts that are incorporated in the administration's projections, which build up to more than $70 billion by 1995. But even apart from these conceptual differences, the CBO projects higher deficits. The major reason lies in the economic assumptions underlying the estimates. The administration assumes economic growth at an average of 3.1 percent a year between 1990 and 1995, despite the widely held

the net outlays (except interest) of the Resolution Trust Corporation, which is financing the bailout of the thrift institutions. As the Congressional Budget Office points out, "A clear economic case exists for excluding . . . all of RTC's net expenditures except payment of interest. . . . Such spending does not change the government's balance sheet and does not affect national saving in the way that most federal spending does." CBO, *An Analysis of the President's Proposals for Fiscal Year 1991,* March 1990, p. 199.

2. An average of private forecasts is given by *Blue Chip Economic Indicators,* Eggert Economic Enterprises, February 10, 1990.

TABLE 2-1. Congressional Budget Office Projections of Current
Services Deficit, Fiscal Years 1990–95[a]
Billions of dollars

Item	1990	1991	1992	1993	1994	1995
Outlays	1,194	1,271	1,345	1,425	1,488	1,557
Revenues	1,067	1,137	1,204	1,277	1,355	1,438
Deficit	127	134	141	148	133	119

SOURCE: Congressional Budget Office, *An Analysis of the President's Budgetary Proposals for Fiscal Year 1991,*
March 1990.
a. Excludes noninterest outlays of the Resolution Trust Corporation. See footnote 1.

view among economists that the capacity or potential growth of the U.S.
economy at the present time lies in the neighborhood of 2.5 percent a
year. The CBO accepts that view and assumes a 2.4 percent long-term
growth rate. This seemingly small difference between growth assumptions
produces a difference in national output and income that by 1995 yields
some $63 billion in additional revenues.

Along with higher economic growth, the administration projects a
large fall in interest rates: it foresees ninety-day Treasury bill rates at
4.4 percent in 1995, compared with a CBO projection of 5.8 percent
(itself quite optimistic relative to the 8.1 percent level in 1989). Each
percentage point of lower interest rates has a major budget impact, given
the $2 1/2 trillion federal debt.

Since taxable income and federal revenues will continue to rise in line
with real economic growth and inflation combined, why, in a growing
economy, does the CBO budget projection, allowing for neither new nor
expanded programs, continue to show such a large deficit? Table 2-2
provides the answer. In addition to increases needed simply to cover
inflation—which affects revenues and expenditures about equally—the
federal government has many entitlement programs under which the
number of beneficiaries grows each year. It has two large programs for
medical care—medicare for the elderly and disabled and medicaid for
the poor—in which prices are rising faster than general inflation and the
utilization of medical services per beneficiary is also growing. And, of
course, so long as the budget runs huge deficits, servicing that debt costs
more each year. Indeed, had the CBO not been somewhat optimistic in
its projections, the current services deficit would be projected at an even
higher level.

In the absence of major changes in budget policy, the deficit is likely
to remain near current dollar levels for the first half of the decade. This
would imply some decline in the deficit relative to GNP, from 2.3 percent

TABLE 2-2. Components of Increased Outlays, Fiscal Years 1990–95
Billions of dollars

Component	Increase
Inflation	199
Increased use of medical care in federal programs	61
Work load, number of beneficiaries[a]	60
Interest on the debt	29
Other	14
TOTAL	363

SOURCE: Congressional Budget Office: Testimony of Robert D. Reischauer before the Committee on the Budget, U.S. House of Representatives, January 31, 1990, table 6, p. 18.
a. Includes the rise in real benefits for new social security beneficiaries.

in 1990 to 1.6 percent in 1995. But this improvement is made possible only by the large and growing surplus in the social security and other retirement trust funds, and the budget, exclusive of these funds, should be moving toward balance.

Why Worry about the Budget Deficit?

Had a representative group of economists or other budget experts been told in 1980 that the federal budget would average over 4 percent of GNP for six years—as it did from 1983 to 1989—almost all of them would have predicted an inflationary boom, followed by a severe cyclical contraction as the Federal Reserve slammed on the monetary policy brakes. In fact, the U.S. economy experienced not boom and bust, but seven years of relatively steady growth, with falling unemployment and moderate inflation. And this stability was achieved in the face of unprecedented budget and trade deficits, huge swings in the exchange rate of the dollar, and a stock market crash second only to that of the Great Depression.

Why the Deficit Produced No Economic Crisis

The principal reason for the economic stability of recent years has been the monetary policy of the Federal Reserve. In 1981 and 1982 the Federal Reserve broke the back of the double-digit inflation of the late 1970s with a severe bout of tight money accompanied by a deep recession. But since 1982 the Fed has consistently followed two major policy guidelines. First, it will do whatever it has to do by way of tight money and high interest rates to offset the potential economic overheating generated by the huge federal budget deficits. Thus, beginning in May 1983, only five months into the fledgling economic recovery, the Federal Reserve encouraged and engineered a rise in interest rates of more than 3 percentage points as a means of keeping the growth of aggregate demand within reasonable bounds. Again, in early 1987, as the falling dollar set off an export boom, the Fed boosted interest rates sharply to prevent inflationary pressures from getting out of hand.

Second, the Federal Reserve will not pursue monetary restriction to the point of bringing on another recession in order to push inflation lower. Despite the stern rhetoric when they testify before Congress, the chairman and the members of the Board of Governors seem quite prepared to live with the 4–5 percent inflation that has characterized the economy for most of the recent past. And so, in 1985 and 1986, when the budget deficit was being reduced and the growth of aggregate demand was easing, the Fed engineered a sharp decrease in interest rates. It did the same after the stock market crash of October 1987. Figure 2-1 shows how truly large the fluctuations in interest rates have been in recent years as the necessary accompaniment to a monetary stabilization policy operating in an environment of large expansionary budget deficits and essentially deregulated financial markets.[3]

The result of the Fed's monetary policy has not been complete economic stability; both GNP growth and inflation have fluctuated over the past seven years. But recession and even temporary stagnation have been avoided while major inflationary pressures have been kept in check. The political freedom that the public and the politicians have given the Fed to raise interest rates sharply when necessary is a prerequisite for this success.

It is, of course, impossible to rule out another large oil shock. Barring that, the odds are high that the Federal Reserve can continue to manage the economy without a major cyclical crisis even if the federal budget deficit remains large, so long as it is free to raise interest rates when necessary. In the postwar period economic recoveries have not usually died from internal causes, but were killed either by outside shocks or by

---

3. Measured as deviations from a long-term (eight-year) moving average, fluctuations in long- and short-term interest rates were 3 1/2 to 4 times as large in the 1980s as they had been in the prior twenty-five years.

FIGURE 2-1. Change in Short-Term Interest Rates, Selected Periods, 1979–89ᵃ

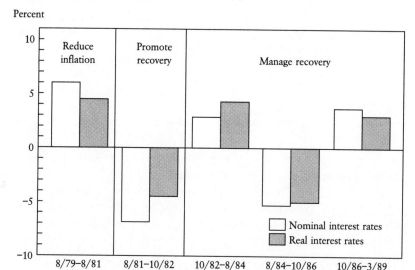

a. Change in rates for ninety-day Treasury bills during each period. Real rates calculated using two-quarters moving average of GNP deflator.

the severe monetary restrictions needed to reverse inflations that had been allowed to get under way. Only two of the seven postwar recessions were self-induced and those were quite mild. More important for the point at hand, however, even if a recession should occur, it will not be because the federal deficit remains at current levels.

Many of those who do worry that continuation of large budget deficits will lead to a cyclical crisis see that crisis coming in the form of a "dollar strike." Foreigners, observing that budget and current account deficits remain high, would suddenly lose confidence in the U.S. economy and desert the dollar in droves. The dollar's exchange value would plummet, import prices soar, and the U.S. price level rise sharply. To prevent the one-shot rise in the price level from turning into a persistent and possibly accelerating wage-price spiral, the Fed would have to tighten monetary policy severely, raise interest rates sharply, and put the economy through a recession.

This chain of events is possible, but unlikely. In the years ahead the dollar may well decline. But it is likely to do so precipitously only if international investors come to believe that the Federal Reserve would

TABLE 2-3. Net National Saving, Selected Periods, 1951–89
Percent of national income[a]

Item	1951–80	1984–86	1989
Private saving[b]	9.3	8.1	6.8
Minus government dissaving			
(budget deficit)	−1.3	−5.0	−3.6
Equals national saving	8.0	3.1	3.2

SOURCE: Author's calculations based on U.S. Department of Commerce, The National Income and Product Accounts of the United States (selected issues).
a. Net national product is used as the measure of national income.
b. Surplus in state and local insurance funds (mainly pension funds of state and local employees) classified as private saving.

lose its political freedom or its willingness to raise interest rates to neutralize inflationary effects of the budget deficit.

All in all, the wolf is not likely to appear at the door so long as the Federal Reserve continues to pursue a credible set of noninflationary policies—a quite reasonable assumption given recent history.

The Effect of High Deficits on National Saving and Interest Rates

That the nation can muddle through, sustaining large budget deficits without a cyclical crisis, does not mean that deficits do no harm and can be ignored. A successful economy ought not only to avoid recession and inflation, but also to provide for future growth. To that end it should save a reasonable fraction of its income to invest in increasing its stock of capital, which contributes to the growth of national living standards. In the past decade the national saving rate in the United States has fallen to an abysmally low level by comparison either with its own past (see table 2-3) or with the saving rate of other modern economies. The rise in the federal budget has been a major contributor to that fall in national saving. Its elimination, and indeed conversion into a surplus, may be the only sure way to restore a healthy level of national saving.

National saving is that portion of national income not consumed by governments or households. A corresponding portion of national output is therefore available to invest in the nation's future growth, through the construction of new housing or business plant and equipment or through investment in profitable assets abroad. National saving is equal to private saving plus the government surplus, or (more commonly) less the government budget deficit, whose financing absorbs some of private saving, leaving that much less available for private investment.

FIGURE 2-2. Financing U.S. Domestic Investment, Selected Periods, 1951–89

Percent of national income

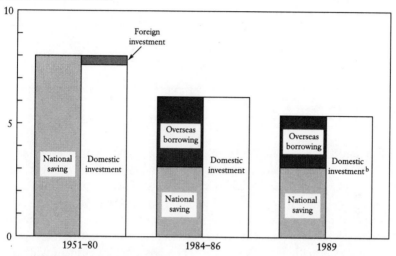

a. National income = net national product.
b. Includes 0.5 percent statistical discrepancy.

National saving in the United States fell from an average of 8 percent of national income in the thirty years before 1980 to 3.2 percent in 1989. Both elements of national saving contributed to the decline: private saving fell and the federal budget deficit increased.[4] The current U.S. saving rate is also quite low compared with those in virtually all other industrial countries. Except for the United Kingdom, other large industrial countries save more than the United States by a wide margin.

When a country's saving rate collapses, it can free up the resources needed to satisfy the rise in public and private consumption demand in one of two ways: by curtailing domestic investment or by importing more than it exports, borrowing from abroad to finance the excess of imports. The United States adjusted to lower saving partly by decreasing investment and partly by supplementing its shrunken national saving through borrowing from abroad (see figure 2-2). Although the trade

4. Robert Eisner of Northwestern University has argued that the official statistics overstate the size of the federal deficit and its role in reducing the national saving rate. Appendix A examines his arguments and concludes that they do not warrant any change in the conclusions reached here or elsewhere in this chapter.

TABLE 2-4. Average Real Interest Rates, Selected Periods, 1951–89
Percent

Period	90-day Treasury bills[a]	AAA corporate bonds[b]
1951–73	0.3	1.6
1974–82	0.5	2.2
1983–88	4.1	7.4
1989	4.0	5.0

SOURCE: Data from Federal Reserve Board; U.S. Department of Commerce; and author's calculations.
a. The nominal interest rate in one quarter minus the prior quarter's inflation rate in the GNP deflator.
b. The nominal interest rate in one quarter minus an "expected" inflation rate based on a weighted moving average of the prior twelve quarters' inflation.

deficit and the associated foreign borrowing forestalled an even larger drop in domestic investment, that approach has not been costless. The United States has abandoned its position as a net creditor abroad, is now a large and growing net debtor, and each year pays an increasing fraction of national income in debt service to foreigners.[5] The inflow of foreign saving into this country could conceivably continue for some time, but eventually it will taper off. Then domestic investment will have to be cut to fit within the limits of the shrunken national saving—unless in the meantime the problem of low saving has been solved.

Low national saving has led to high real interest rates. (Real interest rates, which represent the true cost of borrowing, are the difference between quoted or "nominal" interest rates and the inflation rate.) The rise in interest rates was the mechanism by which investment was reduced and foreign funds attracted into the United States to finance the spending binge. From 1983 through 1988 real short-term and long-term interest rates averaged, respectively, 3 1/2 and 5 1/2 percentage points higher than their earlier postwar averages (see table 2-4), a huge increase by any historical standard. Recently interest rates have fallen somewhat as the economy softened and some progress was made in 1986 and 1987 in cutting the budget deficit. But they remain well above their earlier postwar levels. Should the dollar decline and the U.S. trade deficit narrow further, the inflow of foreign savings into the United States would shrink and interest rates would rise again—unless, of course, steps are taken to raise national saving.

5. The current situation is not like the nineteenth century, when the United States also borrowed heavily abroad. In that case the proceeds were used to increase national investment in productive assets and to generate a stream of additional national income, out of which the debt service was paid. The country still ended up better off.

Lower national saving and higher interest rates had another more subtle but highly damaging effect on the U.S. economy. High interest rates particularly penalize *long-term* investments. When interest rates are 4 percent, for example, a one-year investment of $100 has to return $104 dollars to make it worthwhile; an increase in interest rates to 6 percent raises the required one-year return to only $106. But the return needed to make a fifteen-year investment worthwhile goes from $180 to $240, a rise of one-third, when interest rates go up from 4 to 6 percent. Any potential investments that paid off in the $180–$240 range would be ruled out after the interest rate increase.

A common explanation for America's loss of competitiveness and the slow growth of U.S. productivity is that this country's businesses are too interested in short-term payoffs and hence are reluctant to undertake many long-term investments to improve productivity. If the charge is true—and there is surely some truth in it—the explanation may not be simple shortsightedness, but a rational response to the extraordinarily high real interest rates brought on by the budget policies of the 1980s.

National Saving and the Social Security Surplus

As a result of legislation in 1978 and 1983 that boosted payroll taxes and restricted benefits, the nation's social security system of old age survivors and disability insurance (OASDI) is now collecting revenues far greater than future benefits. Moreover, these annual surpluses will rise from $66 billion in 1990 to $128 billion in 1995. This accumulation of reserves was intended to reduce the burden on future workers of supporting the social security benefits that will be collected by the large baby boom population, which will begin retiring in the early decades of the next century. The annual surplus in all the federal government's retirement funds will reach 2 1/2 percent of GNP by 1995.[6]

The mere accumulation of paper claims in a trust fund does not, of course, enable one generation to finance its own retirement and relieve the next generation of the burden. When today's workers retire, their consumption must come out of the production of future workers. To finance this generation's retirement, the nation as a whole must now add to its aggregate saving, accumulate productive wealth, and raise the

---

6. The other retirement funds in the federal budget include medicare, civil service retirement, and military retirement. The 2 1/2 percent estimate allows for some increase above the current schedule in payroll taxes to support medicare part A, which is actuarially underfunded.

income and productivity of the next generation so that real resources can be devoted to the consumption of retirees without placing an added burden on the generation that is then at work.[7]

But if the annual surplus in the social security funds is used to justify dissaving (a larger deficit) elsewhere in the budget, national saving and wealth accumulation will not have been increased. And that is exactly the posture of current federal budget policy. In fiscal 1990 the overall federal budget deficit is estimated at $127 billion. But that figure is the result of a huge $245 billion deficit in the general operating budget of the federal government, partially offset by a $119 billion annual surplus in the retirement trust funds. Even if the overall deficit of almost $120 billion in 1995 were eliminated, the operating budget would still show a deficit of some $182 billion (offset by a surplus of the same amount in the retirement trust funds).[8]

What Is a Reasonable Target for the National Saving Rate?

Because of the accumulating obligations to provide for retirement of the baby boomers early in the next century, the United States, now and for the foreseeable future, should raise its national saving rate, which includes both public and private saving.[9] The 2 1/2 percent of GNP that

7. One should be very careful about stating exactly how an appropriate current increase in national saving will ease or eliminate the burden of a large retired population on the then working generation. No matter what is done now through a surplus in the social security fund to put away additional saving, the next working generation will have to devote a larger fraction of its national income to paying retirement benefits than is now the case. What a current increase in saving and productive investment can do is to raise the future level of productivity and income. The higher proportion of income going to the retired will then be taken from a higher level of national income. But by, say, the third decade of the twenty-first century, no one except a few economic historians will realize that the level of national income is higher then because in the three preceding decades the country saved more. From a social and political standpoint, an increase in the "burden" of social security will appear to be occurring. (I am indebted to George Perry for this point.)

8. The problem is *not* that the social security surplus is being invested in Treasury bonds. Even if the rest of the budget were in balance, the trust funds would still be buying Treasury bonds. But in that case, since no new bonds would be issued to finance the operating budget, the social security reserves would be used to buy back government bonds now held by the private sector, making an equivalent amount of funds available for private investment. But now, when the social security funds buy government bonds, the proceeds simply go to finance the deficit in the remainder of the budget.

9. Even if there were no public social security system, the demographic projections imply the need for the nation to increase its national saving rate and raise its future

TABLE 2-5. Projected Saving Requirements and Availability, 1989–2000

Percent of national income

Net national saving	1989–2000
Targets	
To maintain a base level of saving	5.3
Additional saving needed for future retirement needs	2.5
TOTAL	7.8
Availability	
Private saving	7.0
Required federal budget surplus[a]	0.8
TOTAL	7.8

SOURCE: Charles L. Schultze, "Of Wolves, Termites, and Pussycats, or, Why We Should Worry about the Budget Deficit," *Brookings Review*, vol. 7 (Summer 1989), p. 32.

a. The unified budget, which includes retirement trust funds such as social security, medicare, and federal employee retirement.

will soon be accumulating each year as surpluses in the federal government's various retirement funds is a pretty good measure of how much that extra saving ought to be. But what is the base level to which the extra saving should be added? Table 2-5 represents an effort to provide a rough answer.

Output per worker in the United States is now rising at about 1 percent a year. To maintain that relatively sluggish growth of productivity, the nation must invest enough to replace the capital that depreciates each year, equip new additions to the labor force with today's average amount of capital per worker, and increase that stock of capital per worker by about 1 percent a year for all workers. Providing that much new investment—over and above depreciation—without continuing to rely on an inflow of borrowed funds from abroad would require a net saving of 5.3 percent of national income. Adding to that base saving the extra 2.5 percent saving needed to deal with the accumulating obligations for retirement benefits, as roughly measured by the surpluses in the retirement trust funds, yields a target for national saving in the 1990s of almost 8 percent of national income. If the private saving rate continues at roughly its current 7 percent of national income, achieving

---

national output and income. The consumption of retirees, whether publicly or privately financed, must come from future production.

an 8 percent national saving rate would require an overall *surplus* in the federal budget of 1 percent of national income.[10]

It will take time to convert the present large budget deficit into a surplus. Occasional recessions or economic slowdowns will sometimes cause the budget balance to fall below target. And so, to achieve a reasonable accumulation of national saving in the 1990s as a whole, budget policy should probably aim for a gradual transition to an overall surplus of about 1 1/2 percent of national income for the last half of the 1990s. It would probably make political sense to move to this target in two stages: first balance the overall budget by fiscal 1993 and then move to the 1 1/2 percent surplus over the next three to four years. Given continued moderate economic growth and the current inflation rate, that would imply a surplus of almost $110 billion in the *overall* budget by fiscal year 1996: a $200 billion surplus in the retirement trust funds and a deficit of $90 billion in the general operating budget.

How Deficit Reduction Would Improve the U.S. Economy

Reducing the budget deficit will require some combination of tax increase and expenditure reduction. The tax increase would reduce private income. Precisely where the cuts occurred in private spending would depend upon the nature of the tax increase, but most of the cut in income would be translated into reduced consumption. Cutting federal outlays would, of course, directly lower public spending. The accompanying reduction in the budget deficit and the decline in federal borrowing would reduce interest rates, but those interest rate cuts would not be large enough to produce a fully offsetting increase in other forms of spending. Taken by themselves, the fiscal actions needed to cut the budget deficit would reduce aggregate demand for goods and services in the economy and produce lower output and employment, at least for a substantial period. And so, when the budget deficit was being slashed, the Federal Reserve would have to ease monetary policy, providing additional bank reserves and driving interest rates down still further, in order to stimulate enough additional private spending to take up the

10. This assumes aggregate balance for the operating budgets of state and local governments. As noted in appendix A, the operating budgets of those governments do not on average run a surplus—indeed they are now in deficit. And the large surpluses of state and local governments in pension funds for their own employees have been reclassified as private saving, matching the treatment of the pension funds of private employers. As indicated earlier, net national product is used as the measure of national income.

slack. (This would be exactly the opposite of what the Fed did to avoid excessive aggregate demand when the budget deficit was ballooning in the 1980s.)

The record of the Federal Reserve in recent years gives no reason to doubt that it would pursue the appropriately accommodating policy. Thus a deficit reduction would leave the U.S. economy with output, employment, and inflation roughly unchanged but interest rates substantially lower. And the composition of national output would be altered. Public and private consumption would fall, while spending of the kind favored by low interest rates—business investment, housing construction, consumer durables, and exports—would rise. A slightly greater fraction of the country's demands would be met from domestic production and a little less from imports. In short, the nation would consume less and save more, and the higher saving would lead to some combination of more domestic investment and less borrowing from abroad.

The direction of the change in interest rates can be projected with a good deal of confidence, but estimating its magnitude involves a great deal of uncertainty. In one attempt to analyze this question, a number of prominent economic models were used to estimate the effects of a cut in federal spending phased in over four years and amounting to 1 percent of GNP ($70 billion) by fiscal year 1994, offset by a Federal Reserve easing of monetary policy sufficient to keep GNP from falling.[11] While the estimates varied across the different models, on average the results suggest that interest rates would fall by some 1 1/2 to 2 percentage points. Other estimates of the effects on interest rates of across-the-board tax increases gave about the same results. The interest rate effects of deficit reduction are not significantly determined by whether the reduction is accomplished by spending cuts or tax increases.

A substantial reduction in interest rates would be a major tonic for the U.S. economy. It would generate a substantial saving in interest

11. These calculations were performed by Ralph Bryant at the Brookings Institution as part of a project devoted to comparing the performance and characteristics of a large number of econometric models. The spending cuts were assumed to take the form of a reduction in federal purchases of goods and services. The simulation proceeded in two steps: first Bryant calculated, model by model, how large an expansion of the money supply would be needed to offset the demand-depressing effects of the deficit reduction, and he averaged those results. He then estimated, model by model, the interest rate (and other) consequences of the stipulated 1 percent of GNP fiscal action combined with this particular monetary expansion.

payments on the debt.[12] Further interest savings would arise from the fact that the deficit reduction would lower the projected federal debt itself. According to the average result from the model simulations, a phased-in reduction of federal spending or an increase in taxes amounting to 1 percent of GNP (approximately $75 billion by fiscal 1995) would save an additional $45 billion through lower interest payments on the debt, for a total deficit reduction of $120 billion. A cut of this size would eliminate the overall budget deficit, although the federal operating budget would still show a deficit of $180 billion and national saving would remain well below the target level of 8 percent of national income.

Reducing the overall budget deficit would change the composition of GNP. If deficit reduction came from tax increases or a cut in federal transfer payments to individuals, private consumption would tend to fall; reduced spending by the Defense Department or other government agencies would lower public consumption. But the accompanying fall in interest rates would tend to increase housing construction, business investment in plant and equipment, and exports. The effect on home construction and business investment is obvious. Lower interest rates encourage exports by reducing foreign demand for dollars, and when the dollar falls, U.S. exports rise.

As a general proposition, the fall in interest rates would spread its benefits widely. Workers laid off in defense or consumer goods production would have opportunities for good jobs elsewhere, principally in construction, machine building, and exports. The decline in the budget deficit would raise national saving by roughly an equivalent amount. Living standards would begin to grow faster because the country would be investing more at home in productivity-improving projects, management's attention would more likely be focused on longer-term payoffs, and the United States, borrowing less from abroad, would face a reduced burden of foreign debt service.

Where Does Federal Spending Go?

Converting the current budget deficit to a surplus, as a way to lift the national saving rate to a reasonable level, would substantially improve

12. With the federal debt currently at $2.3 trillion, a 1 percentage point decline in interest rates would ultimately lower interest payments on the debt by $23 billion. But since some of the debt is in long-term issues, these savings would not be realized all at once. This 1 percentage point lower interest rate would produce $10 billion in savings at the end of three years and $22 billion after six years.

the long-run prospects for U.S. economic growth and competitiveness. But wishing will not make it so. As noted earlier, a "standstill" budget policy—with tax laws unchanged and spending keeping pace with increases in prices and work loads under existing legislation—would leave the country with a $140 billion deficit in each of the next three years. The deficit would then drop slightly, to about $120 billion, by 1995. To convert that deficit into a $120 billion surplus by 1995 or 1996, a $240 billion swing, would require very large tax increases, spending cuts, or both.

The inherently difficult problem of getting political consensus on what painful deficit reduction steps to take has been exacerbated by the prevalence of inconsistent views about the social worth of government programs. There is a widely held view that federal spending in general had been "getting out of hand" before 1980, and that Ronald Reagan succeeded in halting but not reversing the upward trend. Particular programs, however, command substantial support, some from small groups of powerful beneficiaries but others among the broad public. Indeed, in the last few years there has been a growing perception, even among some conservatives, that budget austerity has shortchanged several important areas of public spending, especially on human and physical investment, sometimes called "public infrastructure." And both liberals and conservatives have often banded together to protect a number of ongoing programs from the deep slashes proposed by the Reagan and Bush administrations.

The general belief that the government is overspending has made it impossible to raise taxes, but both substantive and political pressures have limited expenditure cutting. The result is a political impasse. To assess the merits and feasibility of alternative deficit reduction proposals, it is necessary first to put government spending in perspective and to look more closely at specific categories.

Defense Spending

There is virtually unanimous agreement across the spectrum of politicians and defense analysts that the recent political developments in the Soviet Union and Eastern Europe enable the United States safely to reduce its armed forces and its military procurement programs. But how much and how fast remains controversial. In chapters 3 and 4, John Steinbruner and Lawrence Korb argue the case for a sizable restructuring and reduction in U.S. military forces and a substantially larger cutback in defense spending than the administration has so far requested. In one scenario, defense spending could fall over the next ten years by 4 percent a year, from the current level of almost $300 billion to about $200 billion (in dollars of today's purchasing power). An alternative and more ambitious cutback in military spending could be achieved if the down-sizing of the forces was accompanied by a reduced rate of weapons modernization and a lower level of readiness. In that case, military spending could fall to $150 billion at the end of the decade. By 1995 the constant-dollar value of defense spending could be some $45 billion to $65 billion below the CBO's "standstill" projections, depending on which alternative is chosen.

The administration's current plans for reducing the military budget are somewhat less ambitious, calling for cuts in the real value of military spending of some $30 billion by fiscal 1995.[13] To the extent the budgetary saving from these cuts are not offset by increased spending on other federal programs or through tax reductions, the resultant fall in interest rates and lower federal debt would, as explained above, generate additional deficit reduction.

Federal Spending for Civilian Programs

Table 2-6 traces the development of the federal budget (as a share of GNP) over the past thirty-five years in two major parts: the social security trust funds and all other federal programs, called the general operating budget. Three basic facts stand out. First, both the outlays and revenues of the social security funds have increased steadily relative to GNP throughout the postwar period.[14] The rise mainly reflects growth in the number of beneficiaries, but also a rise in the level of benefits relative to average per capita income and an associated rise in dedicated payroll tax revenues. The American people, rightly or wrongly, have repeatedly displayed their willingness to pay steadily higher payroll tax rates for the higher benefits.

Second, federal outlays for all purposes other than social security—the general operating budget—have been virtually flat as a share of GNP over the past thirty-five years. There was a temporary peak in 1985 at

13. Translated into the higher prices that are expected to prevail in 1995 (which are incorporated in the CBO deficit projection), the Korb-Steinbruner cuts would amount to $55 billion to $80 billion a year and the administration's reductions to $35 billion a year.

14. I include in "social security funds" only those financed by payroll taxes, that is, the old age and survivors, disability, and hospital insurance (OASDHI) trust funds.

TABLE 2-6. Budget Outlays and Revenues as a Share of GNP,
Fiscal Years 1955–90

Percent unless otherwise specified

Budget components	1955	1960	1965	1970	1975	1980	1985	1990	Value in 1990 (billions of dollars)
Total budget[a]									
Outlays	17.7	18.2	17.6	19.8	21.8	22.1	23.9	21.9	1,194
Revenues	16.9	18.3	17.4	19.5	18.3	19.4	18.6	19.6	1,067
Social security[b]									
Outlays	1.1	2.2	2.5	3.5	4.7	5.3	5.9	5.7	310
Revenues	1.4	2.1	2.6	4.2	5.1	5.3	6.2	7.2	391
General operating									
Outlays	16.7	16.2	15.2	16.5	17.4	17.0	18.2	16.8	915
Revenues	15.6	16.3	14.9	15.6	13.5	14.2	12.7	12.9	706

SOURCES: All data for 1955–85 from *Historical Tables of the Budget of the United States Government for Fiscal Year 1990*. For fiscal 1990, here, and throughout this chapter, the Congressional Budget Office (CBO) estimates and projections of outlays and revenues are used as control totals for fiscal 1990 and later years. (Congressional Budget Office, *The Economic and Budget Outlook: Fiscal Years 1991 and 1995*, January 1990.) The various budget components for fiscal 1990 in tables 2–6 through 2–15 are also CBO estimates where those are available in sufficient detail. Where CBO does not provide sufficient detail, the current service estimates of the Office of Management and Budget for fiscal 1990 are substituted. (*Budget of the United States Government for the Fiscal Year 1991*, various tables.) Since the OMB current service estimates of expenditures for fiscal 1990 are quite close to those of the CBO, the data in the tables should be consistent.

a. Total outlays and revenues are smaller than the sum of the two components because intrafund transactions such as interest payments from the general fund to the social security fund are netted out in the total.

b. Includes outlays and revenues of the old age and survivors, disability, and hospital insurance trust funds.

the height of the Reagan defense buildup and a low in the mid-1960s before spending on the Vietnam war or Lyndon Johnson's Great Society programs had gotten under way. Otherwise their share of GNP fluctuated between 16 and 17 percent. Social security apart, the historical pattern of spending in the federal operating budget does not support the notion that U.S. political institutions caused federal spending to grow relentlessly or to absorb an increasing share of the national economy.

There are indeed biases in the budget process. Pork barrel politics do influence congressional budget making. But, contrary to widely held opinion, the amounts of money involved in such practices do not bulk large in the aggregate and they explain neither the evolution of total federal spending nor the large budget deficits of recent years. Congressional budget politics produces inefficiency in the small rather than in the large.

The third basic fact is that general operating revenues—all federal taxes except the payroll taxes dedicated to social security—have fallen as a share of GNP, most notably in the early 1980s following enactment of the Economic Recovery Tax Act of 1981. Table 2-6 also displays starkly how the budget deficits developed in the 1980s. In the first half of the decade, the defense buildup raised the GNP share of federal operating outlays (the nondefense outlay share actually fell), while large tax cuts sharply reduced the flow of general revenues relative to GNP. By 1990 defense spending and total outlays in the general operating budget had fallen back to their 1980 share of GNP, while general revenues remained depressed. While federal operating spending relative to GNP is only slightly above the average of the quarter century before 1980, general revenues are some 3 percentage points of GNP below their historical level. Except for payroll taxes supporting the social security program, Americans now pay a lower federal tax rate than at any time in the past four decades.

Government Spending in Other Countries

The relative size and role played by central, provincial, or state, and local governments differ widely among countries. France, for example, concentrates much responsibility for spending in the central government. The German federal system more closely resembles ours, but uses the taxing power of the central government to collect and redistribute large amounts of revenues to its states (Länder). Because of this variety, meaningful comparisons of spending can be made only by combining data from all levels of government, as is done in table 2-7. The United States and Japan stand out with government spending at least 10 percent of GNP below that of other countries. If defense spending is excluded, governments in the United States spent a smaller share of GNP than any other country including Japan. Finally, the government spending share rose in all countries, but less in the United States than elsewhere.

The Major Components of General Operating Outlays

Table 2-8 divides the federal government's general operating outlays into three major components: defense, net interest, and civilian programs. The share of GNP devoted to defense spending has been declining since the mid-1950s, except for an increase during the Vietnam War and a lesser one during the defense buildup of the early 1980s. An increase in other spending, initially for civilian programs and more recently for interest payments, roughly offset the decline in the defense share. The growth of civilian spending on the operating functions of the federal government slowed in the late 1970s and was reversed after 1980.

TABLE 2-7. Six Countries' Government Spending as a Share of GNP, Selected Years, 1965–86[a]

Percent

Country	1965	1970	1980	1986
United States				
TOTAL	27.83	32.20	34.07	37.16
Excluding defense	20.72	24.86	28.79	30.54
Excluding defense and social security	17.45	20.26	22.09	23.37
France				
TOTAL	n.a.	44.45	46.99	52.85
Excluding defense	n.a.	41.24	43.69	49.71
Excluding defense and social security	n.a.	27.41	28.03	32.29
Germany				
TOTAL	36.94	38.99	48.77	47.18
Excluding defense	n.a.	36.06	46.04	44.52
Excluding defense and social security	n.a.	27.18	34.25	33.08
Sweden				
TOTAL	n.a.	43.72	61.95	64.90
Excluding defense	n.a.	40.41	58.90	62.29
Excluding defense and social security	n.a.	37.74	51.82	53.86
United Kingdom				
TOTAL	35.86	39.54	45.23	46.02
Excluding defense	n.a.	n.a.	40.28	41.21
Excluding defense and social security	n.a.	n.a.	33.85	34.45
Japan				
TOTAL	19.05	19.10	32.09	33.03
Excluding defense	n.a.	18.34	31.23	32.09
Excluding defense and social security	n.a.	14.81	23.08	22.20

SOURCE: Author's classification of data from Organization for European Economic Cooperation and Development (OECD), *National Income Accounts*, pt. 2 (available on computer disc from OECD).
n.a. Not available.
a. All levels of government.

Charles L. Schultze

TABLE 2-8. Federal General Operating Outlays as a Share of GNP,
Selected Fiscal Years, 1955–90

Percent unless otherwise indicated

Category	1955	1960	1965	1970	1975	1980	1985	1990	Value in 1990 (billions of dollars)
TOTAL	16.7	16.2	15.2	16.5	17.4	17.0	18.2	16.8	915
Defense	11.1	9.5	7.5	8.3	5.7	5.0	6.4	5.4	297
Net interest	1.4	1.5	1.4	1.6	1.8	2.1	3.4	3.7	202
Civilian programs	4.2	5.2	6.3	6.6	9.9	9.9	8.4	7.6	416

SOURCE: See table 2-6. Figures are rounded.

The pattern of federal spending before 1980 hints at a set of underlying forces governing budget outcomes. Although Congress raised payroll taxes to pay for social security, it never raised the general tax burden except for gasoline taxes to support highway construction.[15] The fear of large budget deficits kept general operating spending from getting seriously out of line with general revenues. Before the introduction of inflation indexing in the personal tax, which took effect in 1985, periodic tax cuts kept the ratio of income taxes to personal income from rising despite the tendency of inflation and economic growth to push people into higher tax brackets. With the total general operating budget kept in line by a combination of unwillingness to raise taxes in peacetime and a fear of large budget deficits, the civilian spending share expanded only as the defense share came down.

These implicit budgetary rules were broken in the 1980s. Taxes were cut and defense spending was increased without a commensurate cut in spending elsewhere. Although federal spending on civilian programs was pared significantly—from 9.9 percent of GNP in 1980 to 7.6 percent in 1990—this was not enough to offset the fall in the share of GNP going to general operating revenues. As a result, the operating deficit rose sharply, causing the federal debt to rise and generating an increase in interest rates. Interest payments on the debt consequently rose as a fraction of GNP by almost as much as civilian spending fell. And so, in the end, the budget policies of the 1980s, heralded as an all-out assault against excessive or wasteful federal programs, ended up by replacing spending whose benefits may have been smaller than its costs with spending that provided no benefits at all.

15. Taxes were raised to pay for the Korean and Vietnam wars, but were quickly reduced when hostilities ended.

TABLE 2-9. Federal Civilian Programs as a Share of GNP,
Selected Fiscal Years, 1965–90[a]

Percent unless otherwise indicated

Category	1965	1970	1975	1980	1985	1990	Value in 1990 (billions of dollars)
TOTAL	6.29	6.64	9.95	9.90	8.43	7.62	416
Payments to individuals[b]	2.47	2.96	4.89	4.89	4.68	4.80	262
Discretionary programs	4.70	4.55	5.95	5.76	4.25	3.35	183
Investment	1.69	1.76	1.85	2.07	1.68	1.43	78
Work load	0.62	0.62	0.73	0.69	0.62	0.68	37
Other	2.39	2.17	3.37	3.00	1.95	1.25	68
Undistributed receipts and special items	−0.88	−0.87	−0.89	−0.75	−0.50	−0.53	−29

SOURCE: See table 2-6.

a. Federal general operating budget excluding defense and net interest; see table 2-8.

b. Excludes hospital insurance (included in social security) and assistance to college students (included in investment outlays).

Where Does the Civilian Operating Budget Go?

The largest, and until 1975 by far the fastest growing, component of the civilian budget is the category "payments to individuals" (see table 2-9).[16] These are often called entitlement programs, since in most of them the eligibility to receive benefits is specified by law; the amount of annual spending is not controlled by the appropriations process. Total payments to individuals in the form of cash, food stamps, medical care, and other "in-kind" benefits grew much more rapidly than GNP until the late 1970s, when their share stabilized. Federal payments for medical care continued to grow rapidly; the rise in spending under most other benefit programs slowed. Table 2-10 shows how the major components of payments to individuals, measured in dollars of 1990 purchasing power, have changed since 1980.

Medical care. Two major medical care programs are financed out of general revenues. Medicaid provides acute and long-term care for the poor. Part B of medicare provides physician care for the elderly and

16. The high fraction of GNP going to individuals in 1975 is somewhat misleading. It was a year of deep recession. In recessions GNP falls more than federal spending. Payments to individuals actually rise above their long-run trend, since this category includes unemployment compensation. Had it not been for the recession, "payments to individuals" would have been about 4.3 percent of GNP in that year.

TABLE 2-10. Federal Programs of Payments to Individuals,
Fiscal Years 1980 and 1990[a]
Billions of 1990 dollars

Category	1980	1990
TOTAL	208	262
Medical care[b]	52	97
Welfare-like programs[c]	66	76
Federal employees' retirement[d]	63	72
Unemployment insurance	27	17

SOURCE: See table 2-6.
a. Excludes hospital insurance (included in social security) and assistance to college students (included in investment outlays).
b. Deflated with the same price index as the other components (the personal consumption deflator).
c. Principal components are aid to families with dependent children, food stamps, supplemental security income, earned income tax credit, and veterans' non–service-connected pensions.
d. Includes railroad retirement ($7 billion in 1990) and veterans' service-connected compensation.

disabled and is included here because, unlike the rest of social security, it is paid for not by the payroll tax but by a combination of premium payments from the beneficiaries and appropriations from general revenues. The continued growth of the medical care programs after 1980 occurred despite increasingly strenuous efforts to hold down medicare costs and restrictions on eligibility for aid to families with dependent children, through which many people gain access to medicaid. Spending grew because the price of medical care rose more rapidly than the general inflation rate and because of the increasing use of ever more expensive types of medical procedures.

Rapidly rising health care prices and steadily increasing use of expensive medical technology are common in all the developed industrial countries. But the share of GNP now going to health care (public and private) is larger in the United States than elsewhere. The United States is also distinctive in another respect. A much smaller fraction of the nation's medical bills is paid for by the government than is true anywhere else in the industrial world (see chapter 8 for a discussion of U.S. health care).

Other payments to individuals. Real growth in the other types of payments to individuals has slowed sharply, and payments for unemployment insurance have declined. Unemployment compensation payments fell in the 1980s both because unemployment dropped sharply after the 1982 recession and because many states tightened up on eligibility and other standards. More generally, the fraction of the unemployed receiving unemployment compensation has fallen since

TABLE 2-11. Federal Investment Spending, Selected Fiscal Years, 1965–90

Category	1965	1970	1975	1980	1985	1990
As a percentage of GNP						
TOTAL	1.69	1.76	1.85	2.07	1.68	1.43
Physical investment	1.19	0.97	1.03	1.14	0.91	0.75
Nondefense R&D (excluding space)	0.34	0.36	0.39	0.42	0.37	0.31
Education	0.16	0.43	0.43	0.51	0.40	0.37
In 1990 dollars						
TOTAL	48.4	60.6	59.8	78.1	76.3	78.1
Physical investment	31.2	30.5	31.7	39.4	41.1	40.7
Nondefense R&D (excluding space)	11.7	14.2	13.7	18.0	17.1	17.1
Education	5.5	15.9	14.4	20.7	18.1	20.3

SOURCE: See table 2-6.

1980; less than one-third of the unemployed drew unemployment compensation in 1989.

Spending for the means-tested programs for the poor and near-poor—cash assistance, food stamps, and housing subsidies—has grown quite slowly since 1980, except for housing assistance, which has risen sharply. Although budget authorization for new subsidized housing units dropped sharply, housing payment subsidies rose as housing units that had been authorized earlier were built and added to the stock of subsidized housing. Other assistance payments changed little. Both average benefit levels and numbers of recipients remained roughly constant.

Discretionary Federal Spending

In contrast to the entitlement programs, spending under the discretionary programs can be varied from year to year by congressional appropriations actions. Table 2-9 distinguishes three major categories: investment spending, the costs of supporting the federal government's many services (labeled "work load items"), and a residual category of miscellaneous spending programs. Real federal spending for investment purposes stopped growing during the 1980s, and as a share of GNP it fell. Three major forms of civilian investment spending—physical investment, education, and research and development—declined as a share of GNP; one of them fell in absolute value (see table 2-11).

Physical investment. The federal government supports physical infrastructure investment in two ways. It directly invests in physical assets, such as in the large water resource projects of the Corps of Engineers and the Bureau of Reclamation, as well as in office buildings, computers, autos, and trucks for its own use. It also provides grants-in-aid to state and local government for infrastructure investment such as highways, airports, waste treatment control facilities, and urban rehabilitation projects. Directly and indirectly, the federal government finances about 40 percent of the nation's total public investment in physical infrastructure, the rest being provided by state and local governments.

Infrastructure investment by all levels of government in the United States reached a peak in the 1960s as state and local governments spent heavily on highways, school buildings, and sewer and water systems. Starting in the early 1970s, investment declined, reaching a trough in 1982. It then began to recover, climbing back to the levels of the late 1960s by the end of the 1980s. As a result of this investment pattern, the stock of public capital grew faster than GNP in the 1950s and 1960s; the ratio of public capital to GNP reached a peak in the early 1970s and then began a decline that has continued until now. One recent study has argued that the declining stock of public infrastructure relative to GNP bears much of the responsibility for the fall in national productivity growth that began in the early years of the 1970s.[17] In a similar vein, others have called for a substantial expansion of federal investment expenditures, even at the cost of a higher federal budget deficit. These arguments are examined below in an analysis of future spending priorities.

Investment in education and R&D. Federal investment in civilian research and development outside the space program has always been small relative to GNP and the importance of technological advance to national productivity growth. And even that modest amount was hard hit during the 1980s, when real R&D spending fell slightly and its share in GNP was significantly reduced (see table 2-11).[18]

The federal government has never provided more than a modest

17. See appendix B for an analysis of why this study by David A. Aschauer overstates the productivity-raising effect of public investment.

18. These numbers exclude R&D outlays on the federal government's space program. While some spillovers for national productivity do stem from this activity, on balance outlays for the space program do not seem to belong in a measure designed to gauge how the federal government is investing in technological advance that contributes to productivity growth. And including the outlays on the space program ($6.8 billion in 1990) would not change the basic pattern of small federal support for civilian R&D relative to GNP.

fraction of the nation's public spending on education—a little less than 10 percent in 1988. About half the federal government's $20 billion in educational assistance went to state and local governments, providing only 6 percent of what those governments spent for that purpose. Most of the remaining federal funds were spent for aid to college students in the form of loans and grants. The federal share of educational spending declined during the 1980s as federal budgets were squeezed and critics questioned the efficacy of some earlier federal educational programs in support of elementary and secondary education.

In recent years evidence has accumulated that the quality of U.S. education at the elementary and secondary level has slipped well behind that in other advanced countries. There is also growing evidence that the deficiencies in the education of those entering the work force are harming U.S. productivity and competitiveness. Just as in the case of infrastructure investment, a number of groups are now arguing for a substantial additional infusion of federal money into the educational process (see chapter 7 for a discussion of how to improve the quality of U.S. education).

Work load items. The federal government provides many services that are essential to the operation of a modern society. They include operation of the air traffic and air safety system; the federal prison system; maintenance and operation of the national parks, national forests, and federal resource projects; the services of the Coast Guard and the Internal Revenue Service; and a number of other similar items. Only the operating budgets of the relevant agencies are included here; investment and R&D spending is classified in the previous category. Total spending on such activities is not large, $37 billion in 1990. In the first five years of the 1980s, real spending for these work load activities was roughly constant despite a growing economy. But in the next five years budgets expanded, and these activities' share of GNP returned almost to their earlier level (see table 2-9). However, the work loads facing many of these programs are growing faster than the economy as a whole. Air traffic is increasing more rapidly than GNP; the war on drugs has severely burdened the Coast Guard; sharp growth in the prison population has crowded federal prisons well beyond capacity. And the demands on the government's environmental control operations continue to mount as more stringent environmental laws are enacted. Looking to the future, many of these work load activities will have to expand faster than the rate of general economic growth.

Other federal spending. The final category is a miscellany of federal

TABLE 2-12. Federal Spending on Miscellaneous Programs,
Selected Fiscal Years, 1980–90
Billions of 1990 dollars

Category	1980	1985	1990[a]
TOTAL	126.2	92.6	68.2
Major "losers"	63.4	23.5	13.8
Energy excluding R&D	10.9	1.8	0.1
Community and regional development	17.8	9.2	6.4
Training and employment	16.2	6.0	5.3
Revenue-sharing general-purpose fiscal assistance	13.6	7.7	1.8
International financial programs	3.8	−1.8	−0.3
Education and training of health care workers	1.1	0.6	0.5
Farm income stabilization	11.7	28.5	13.8
Remainder[b]	51.1	40.6	40.6

SOURCE: See table 2-6.
a. Amounts in baseline budget.
b. Important components include: mortgage and housing credit, energy (excluding R&D), international security and economic assistance, community and regional development (except physical investment), veterans' housing assistance, and space programs (except physical investment).

expenditure programs that do not fit any of the earlier categories. Spending on this group of programs (virtually constant in nominal dollars) has been cut in half as a fraction of GNP over the past ten years (table 2-12). There has been a wide diversity of experience within the group. However, the Reagan administration was successful in dramatically scaling back real spending on one group of programs (labeled, in lieu of a better term, the "losers"), which fell by 80 percent, accounting for half of the decline in federal civilian spending as a fraction of GNP over the past ten years. Two of these programs were abolished: the public service employment programs and general revenue sharing with the states.

The two other large programs in this category developed in a different way during the 1980s. Spending on farm price supports, responding mainly to developments in world agricultural markets, rose sharply in the middle of the decade but by 1990 fell back to about its 1980 share of GNP. The space program (included in remainder) followed the opposite pattern, languishing during most of the 1980s and then expanding sharply in the last few years as shuttle activity expanded and the development of a manned space station began.

How Can the Deficit Be Turned into a Surplus?

Under the CBO current service projections of federal spending that I have been using, current laws specifying various payments to individuals are assumed to remain unchanged, and in the other programs, where spending can be changed from year to year through the appropriations process (such as the investment, R&D, and work load budgets), spending is assumed to be held constant in real terms. Since real GNP will be expanding over the period, the projected federal spending share for discretionary programs will fall, continuing the trend begun in 1980. Table 2-13 sets forth the pattern of spending that would occur by 1995 if civilian outlays followed the rules set forth above.

The civilian spending share would be lower than at any time since the early 1970s (compare with table 2-8). Payments to individuals would remain at slightly under 5 percent of GNP, but the discretionary spending programs would fall by 1995 to levels well below anything in the postwar period: 3.1 percent of GNP, compared with an average of about 4.5 percent in the thirty years before 1980. The proposals for expenditure increases and decreases discussed below represent changes from these current service levels.

In formulating budget policy for the 1990s, a number of often competing goals have to be weighed against each other: deficit reductions that will bring large economic benefits; expansion of federal spending in a limited number of areas where significant benefits could be demonstrated; further cuts in low-priority spending; and keeping the tax burden low, both to avoid unwarranted reductions in disposable income and to minimize the supply-side consequences of high taxes (often overstated but nevertheless real).

Differences in value judgments, ideologies, self-interest, and the way the evidence is read strongly influence the relative importance people give to each of these goals. But analysis of the evidence, although itself sometimes in conflict, can make an important contribution to the debate.

Candidates for Increased Spending

Four major components of federal spending are most frequently cited as areas for significantly enlarged spending: investment in physical infrastructure, education, civilian R&D, and health insurance for more than 30 million uninsured Americans. A fifth candidate for additional

TABLE 2-13. Federal General Operating Outlays for Civilian
Programs, Fiscal Years 1990 and 1995

	1990		1995	
Category	Billions of current dollars	Percent of GNP	Billions of current dollars	Percent of GNP
TOTAL	416	7.6	562	7.5
Payments to individuals	262	4.8	366	4.9
Discretionary programs	183	3.4	231	3.1
Offsetting receipts	−29	−0.5	−35	−0.5

SOURCE: See table 2-6. Figures are rounded.

spending encompasses many of the routine "work load" elements of
federal programs.

Investment in physical infrastructure. As noted earlier, the stock of
public physical infrastructure in place has steadily declined as a share of
GNP since the late 1960s. Moreover, projection of current budget policy
to 1995 implies that investment in federal infrastructure would continue
to fall relative to the size of the economy. Modest increases in public
outlays for highways, bridges, and airports may well be desirable. But
recent claims that additional public investment on physical infrastructure
would strongly boost national productivity and output are substantially
overstated. In any event, few are calling for a major expansion of the
traditional federal water resource projects or a surge in the construction
of public buildings or sewer and water pipelines. Rather, attention has
been focused on the transportation infrastructure: roads, bridges, and
airports.

A recent task force report of the National Governors' Conference
calls for outlays of $1 trillion to $3 trillion over the next twenty years
to build and make major repairs to roads and airports. But recent studies
cast serious doubt on the need for such massive sums.[19] In fact, they
argue that if the nation simply spends more on highways and airports
without altering the current planning of highway investment and doing
something to discourage congestion, it will end up spending more money
on highways, bridges, and airports that will soon clog up again with
congestion, and, in the case of highways, deteriorate too rapidly.

19. See Kenneth A. Small, Clifford Winston, and Carol A. Evans, *Roadwork: A New
Highway Pricing and Investment Policy* (Brookings, 1989); and Clifford Winston, "Efficient
Transportation Infrastructure Policy and Deregulation," *Journal of Economic Perspectives,*
forthcoming.

The authors of these studies propose, therefore, that the government change the way it charges for the use of highways and airports. Currently gasoline and diesel taxes pay for highway construction and maintenance. In the proposed system, drivers would pay charges scaled to the degree of congestion on the highways over which they travel. Inexpensive devices are now feasible that could register and identify the passage of vehicles, and monthly bills could then be sent.[20] With this approach, congestion could be quickly reduced and revenues raised to finance the necessary transportation investment. Over the longer run, such charges would reduce congestion further by providing improved incentives for firms about where to locate and for individuals about where to live. Congestion fees on airplane landings and takeoffs would similarly reduce congestion at airports. Unlike highways, however, there is a national need for additional airport runways, or conceivably whole airports, even after the imposition of congestion-reducing fees. The imposition of congestion-related charges to pay for airports and highways would generate benefits worth $12 billion a year (in 1990 dollars), principally by reducing the time wasted in traffic jams and airport delays.

Another important recommendation of these studies is a change in the way taxes are levied on trucks in an attempt to remedy road deterioration. Road wear is closely related to truck loading per axle. The incentive of the present gasoline tax is perverse because the use of additional axles on a truck requires larger engines and more fuel per ton carried. Thus truck taxes should be based on axle loading. In addition, if highways were significantly thickened as they underwent major repairs and reconstruction, the resultant reduction in future highway maintenance and wear and tear on trucks would generate handsome returns on the initial investment. An optimal program of investment in highway thickening and in airports (principally in more runways), coupled with the recommended change in truck taxes, could generate about $18 billion a year in national benefits.

Highways can only be reconstructed gradually, or inordinate delays would be imposed on travelers. The estimated gains could be achieved by a fifteen-year program of highway reconstruction and a ten-year program of airport building that would add about $4 billion a year to what is now being spent for those purposes. If highway responsibilities continue to be split as they now are among federal, state, and local

20. See William S. Vickrey, "Pricing in Urban and Suburban Transport," *American Economic Review*, vol. 53 (May 1963, *Papers and Proceedings*, 1962), pp. 452–65, for an early discussion of possibilities.

governments, the federal budget would have to absorb perhaps 50 percent of the added outlays. Most airports are owned by state or local authorities or by airlines. While the federal government might provide some up-front (but repayable) investment to induce changes in airport pricing policies, the federal budget share of an airport investment program should be small.

Education. A national awareness has formed that the quality of U.S. elementary and secondary education has deteriorated, especially in comparison with other countries. Similarly, evidence has been accumulating that there is a noticeable connection between the poor school achievements of workers with a high school education or less and their performance on the job. Many observers now blame low educational quality at the elementary and secondary level for an important share of America's sluggish productivity performance.[21]

Unfortunately, diagnosis is not cure. And finding a proper role for the federal government in improving elementary and secondary education is harder still. The federal government for several decades has provided financial assistance to college students. But it has never been a big player in elementary and secondary education, either as standard setter, policymaker, or financial supporter. The federal government has provided relatively modest financial support to schools dealing with high concentrations of disadvantaged children and to state and local school authorities to promote various educational reforms. Evaluations of these federal programs have not been able to identify major results in terms of better educational performance (see chapter 7).

The evidence that low-quality education is a barrier to high national productivity and the fact that Americans work far from the state or local jurisdiction that paid their public school bills might be reasons to enlarge the role for the national government in financing and influencing policy at the elementary and secondary education level. *If* there were wide consensus on how to improve educational quality, and *if* those improvements required increased spending, there might be a rationale for the federal government to provide a large share of the additional funds, perhaps through a special educational tax.

Unfortunately, consensus does not exist on what to do. And as John

21. John S. Bishop, "Incentives for Learning: Why American High School Students Compare So Poorly to Their Counterparts Overseas," in Commission on Workforce Quality and Labor Market Efficiency, *Investing in People: A Strategy to Address America's Workforce Crisis,* Background Papers, vol. 1 (Washington: U.S. Department of Labor, 1989), pp. 1–85.

Chubb and Eric Hanushek argue in chapter 7, evidence is lacking that more money for education spent in traditional ways would help much. Research has been unable to demonstrate educational payoffs from reducing the number of students per teacher, from longer school years, or from higher teacher pay that is unaccompanied by other reforms. One reform, though not guaranteed, has promise: more policy independence for individual schools and reduction in central control and bureaucracy. While this reform does not require extra money, modest extra funds for the newly enfranchised local school authorities might help gain acceptance for difficult changes in various school policies and practices.

In sum, given the present state of knowledge, increased federal spending on education, other than modest financial inducements for those school districts that decentralize control over educational policy, has low priority compared with other spending needs and deficit reduction.

Civilian research and development. The case for substantially increased federal support for civilian research and development is overwhelming. The highly specialized space program aside, federal support for civilian research and development is pitifully small. At $17 billion, real outlays are less than they were ten years ago. At only one-third of 1 percent of the nation's GNP, they are a smaller share than that provided by governments in other advanced countries. Two-fifths of that amount is for medical research at the National Institutes of Health. This is by far the largest government-sponsored program of biomedical research in the world and essential, among other things, for the rapidly growing biotechnology industry. But there is precious little left for other purposes. Moreover, the defense research budget will be shrinking over the coming years, and although military research is not an efficient way of supporting civilian science and technology objectives, lower spending on defense R&D will erode the nation's scientific base.

Successive economic studies have confirmed that, on average, research yields business firms a return well above that on conventional investments. The payoff to society as a whole is even higher. Because new knowledge cannot be hoarded or fully protected with patents, many of the gains from successful R&D spill over into the public domain.

While federal spending on R&D has begun to edge up in the last several years, much of the increase is for the space flight program and for the expensive supercollider, and the magnitude of the remaining effort is still paltry for a nation with a GNP of $5 trillion. A long-term program to boost the federal research support merits high priority.

Such a program should observe three basic principles. First, it should speed up the output of scientists and researchers from the nation's universities and colleges, which means increasing assistance to graduate students and research teams. Second, it should push but not outpace the scientific establishment's ability to absorb the increases, to avoid unneeded wage and price increases. And third, federal expenditures for research and development should be concentrated toward the research end of the R&D spectrum. Carefully selected assistance for commercial R&D ventures may sometimes be warranted, but organizational support and seed money should be the main instruments of policy. The government should resist becoming the principal financial backer of commercial projects; it has a bad history with such investments.[22]

Medical care. More than 30 million Americans lack health insurance. The cost of health care is rising sharply. In chapter 8, Henry Aaron examines how the nation might deal with these problems. He notes that the United States relies heavily on employer-sponsored health insurance. Whether the system is optimal or not, it is too late to unravel it and begin again. And so he proposes the federal government mandate the extension of this approach to cover all workers employed more than a minimum number of hours, with backup public coverage for everyone else. This system would require increased national expenditure for health services for people now lacking access to care. Part of the increased expenditure would show up on the federal budget, roughly $40 billion a year for acute care (and as much as an additional $25 billion if long-term care benefits are increased). Aaron proposes that these health care activities and current federal health programs be brought together under a single trust fund that would receive payroll taxes currently dedicated to the hospital insurance trust fund, a dedicated 6 percent value-added tax (VAT), and certain other revenues. By 1995 this 6 percent VAT would raise some $75 billion more revenues than needed to offset the additional health care spending that Aaron proposes; it would also help pay for some existing health spending.[23] The tax would thus contribute to deficit reductions and is discussed further in that context below.

Other national priorities. In addition to increasing its investment in human, physical, and technological resources and extending health insurance to those who are not now covered, the United States faces

22. Linda R. Cohen and Roger G. Noll, *The Technology Pork Barrel* (Brookings, forthcoming).

23. A VAT of 1 1/2 percent would provide the extra revenue required simply to pay for the Aaron proposal without deficit reduction.

other social challenges. While drug use appears to have been declining generally, drugs and drug-related crimes are an increasing scourge in the central cities. Quite apart from drugs, the crime rate remains tragically high. And the growing number of the homeless in the city streets are a visible reminder of major social distress.

To make progress against these problems will require, in varying degrees, some form of collective action and undoubtedly some provision of public expenditures. At the moment, however, there is no consensus on exactly what government should do, what level of government should take principal responsibility, and how much money might be required.

There is, however, a link between the recommendation for deficit cutting presented below and the social problems outlined above. So long as the federal government continues to run large budget deficits, it is almost certain that nothing but token actions will be seriously considered to attack such problems. In an era of "normal" budgets, when real military spending is not increasing and large deficits are not driving up interest payments on the debt each year, the annual growth in revenues tends to be a little larger than the growth in spending on existing programs. In such an environment it would be possible to have a serious debate about the merits of particular proposals to deal with social problems, either in terms of their relative priority or compared with a tax reduction. But until the problem of large and persistent deficits is dealt with, this sensible approach to deciding how the nation's resources should be allocated at the margin is foreclosed. In that sense, dealing with budget deficits will make an indirect, but nevertheless important, contribution to a rational debate about how to attack some of the country's social problems.

Candidates for Budget Cutting

After the early years of the Reagan administration, when Congress accepted a number of deep cuts in several federal programs (see the "losers" category in table 2-12), it has remained penurious about increasing spending but has repeatedly rejected other large program reductions repeatedly proposed by Presidents Reagan and Bush. The prospect of significant further deficit reductions through such budget cutting is quite small. And even if Congress enacted all the spending cuts proposed in the administration's 1990 budget, there would still be deficits over the next five years, instead of a transition to the surpluses advocated earlier in this chapter. Finally, as the history of the 1980s makes clear, the continuation of high budget deficits inexorably raises interest payments on the federal debt, making the job of deficit reduction increasingly hard as time goes by. Continued refusal to consider a tax increase, on grounds that the existence of large deficits and the pressure of the Gramm-Rudman deficit reduction targets will eventually force Congress to make deep expenditure cuts, simply guarantees that the deficits will continue.

While the budget cannot be balanced by spending cuts, it is equally clear that it cannot be balanced by tax increases alone. Budget balance, and eventually budget surplus, will never come about without some "grand compromise" between liberals and conservatives that includes more spending cuts than Congress now seems willing to accept. Some variant of across-the-board spending restraints could be used. But, as the experience of the 1980s amply demonstrates, this practice eventually undermines the capacity of the federal government to provide needed services and restricts the public investment outlays needed to foster growth. Far better, but much more difficult politically, would be an agreement on priorities that would concentrate cuts where they would not have such unwanted effects. Four approaches (which are not exclusive) can be identified.

Approach 1. Continue the recent practice—which administrations have proposed and Congresses have partially accepted—of putting caps and limits on reimbursement to hospitals and physicians under the medicare and medicaid programs. The administration's 1991 budget proposes another $5 1/2 billion of such cuts. However desirable fundamental reforms in the medical delivery system might be, the practice of putting the regulatory hand on the spigot by capping medical reimbursements in federal programs simply causes upward cost pressures to "squirt out" in the private sector, as hospitals and physicians make up there what they cannot get from the federal government. Making significant deficit reductions by this route would be politically unfeasible and substantively harmful.

Approach 2. Cut "middle-class" subsidies. Presidents and OMB directors of both parties have tried for years to get Congress to cut a long list of benefits for particular industries and middle-class individuals. The following is a list of examples of such cuts, with estimated savings for 1991 and 1995 shown in parentheses.[24]

24. The estimates of savings are from Congressional Budget Office, *Reducing the Deficit: Spending and Revenue, A Report to the Senate and House Committees on the Budget*, pt. 2 (February 1989 and February 1990).

—Eliminate school lunch and related subsidies to middle-class children ($360 million, $520 million).

—Eliminate disability compensation to veterans with low disability ratings, using half the saving to raise compensation to severely handicapped veterans and saving the rest ($1,350 million, $1,700 million).

—Eliminate annual operating subsidies to U.S. merchant vessels, including the requirement that all military cargo and a high percentage of other government cargo be carried on U.S. flag vessels ($390 million, $370 million).

—Charge fees closer to commercial levels for grazing and other commercial activities on federal lands ($65 million, $160 million).

—Liberalize, without eliminating, the Davis-Bacon Act, which in effect requires the federal government to pay union wage rates at journeyman levels or higher on federal construction projects ($190 million, $680 million).

—Tighten up the rules relating to the maximum price support payment one farmer can receive; by dividing ownership of one farm among relatives, farmers now can substantially stretch the maximum payment limits (0, $500 million).

—Raise the interest rate for rural electrification loans to the rate on Treasury securities (which would still be lower than that paid by other utilities) and put lower limits on the annual loan amounts ($70 million, $500 million).

These reforms, or something like them, have been blocked by opposition from the lobbies of the affected groups for over thirty years. Not even a grand budget compromise is likely to change things. In any event, when fully in effect the cuts would save only $4 billion a year. Although other such cuts might be included in this group, the total would still not be sizable.

Approach 3. Eliminate programs with low or questionable benefits. Value judgments differ on which federal programs belong in the list. My favorite candidates are given here, with estimated savings for 1991 and 1995 shown in parentheses.[25]

—Eliminate NASA's planned space station; it is a very expensive way to get modest scientific benefits and squeezes out more scientifically important unmanned space launches ($900 million, $2.05 billion).

—Cut the capital grants for mass transit to a 50 percent federal cost share and eliminate the operating subsidy. The program has done little

25. CBO, *Reducing the Deficit.*

to relieve congestion, and much of the subsidy goes for the benefit of middle-class suburban commuters. If local jurisdictions wish to provide such subsidized transit, let them do so with their own funds; there are few benefits for the nation as a whole, and it is surely not an effective way to aid the poor ($610 million, $1.55 billion).

—Eliminate the loan and loan guarantee program of the Small Business administration except for assistance to minorities and disaster victims. Financial markets are now more efficient and less susceptible to market failures than they were when the loan program was begun many decades ago. The sums provided are a drop in the bucket compared with the annual flow of private credit to small business firms and have no effect on the health of the small business segment of the economy ($-40 million, $310 million).

Except for the NASA space station, these programs—and those that others might choose as favorite candidates—have withstood repeated assaults for years. The potential savings again are not large. Moreover, hinging deficit reduction on getting agreement to eliminate whole programs usually means that the deficit is not reduced.

Approach 4. Cut social security benefits or tax social security benefits like other retirement income. If a comprehensive program to convert the budget deficit into a surplus includes a broad-based tax increase, a powerful case can be made that all nonpoor segments of the population should make some contribution, including those who receive non–means-tested federal benefits. And in fact, when in March 1990 Representative Dan Rostenkowski advanced such a deficit reduction proposal, a spokesperson for the elderly stated that they would be "willing to make sacrifices" as long as "everyone is making sacrifices on the same basis."[26]

The social security trust fund, however, is already accumulating reserves. Reducing benefits without changing payroll taxes would add to reserve accumulations, increase the degree to which the payroll tax is being used to support the general operations of government, and draw strong opposition. But if social security benefits and payroll taxes were cut equally, and income taxes raised, the deficit could be reduced without having increased the overall tax burden on the country. A reduction of benefits by withholding 1 percentage point of the cost-of-living allowances in all non–means-tested programs for each of the next five years would

26. Steven Mufson, "Rostenkowski's Proposal Gets Surprising Response," *Washington Post*, March 21, 1990, p. D1.

lower the budget deficit by about $9 billion in fiscal 1993 and $16 billion in 1995.

While a benefit reduction is harder on the poor than on the rich, taxing social security benefits more nearly like other retirement income would raise substantial revenues for deficit reduction while making the tax system fairer and sparing those with low incomes. Currently, social security benefits are taxed only to the extent that they raise income above $32,000 for couples ($25,000 for single persons), and then only half of those benefits are subject to income tax. There is no logic to the threshold; the income tax itself provides a threshold for low-income households through exemptions and a standard deduction. And the apparent logic of the 50 percent assumption is also spurious, since the workers' payroll taxes paid during their working life typically cover no more than 15 percent of the value of the benefits.

Removing the special threshhold and, conservatively, taxing 60 percent of social security benefits would bring in some $13 billion a year by 1995. If social security benefits were treated the same as similar benefits from private pension funds, taxes would be levied on 85 percent of their value, and the 1995 revenue yield would be $24 billion. (Accompanying the higher taxes on social security benefits with a 1 percent reduction in non–means-tested entitlement programs outside social security would add another $6 billion in 1995 spending cuts.)

Planning for a Budget Surplus: A Summary

The target for national saving set out earlier in this chapter implied the need for an overall surplus in the federal budget of about 1 1/2 percent of national income by the latter half of this decade. As noted, that surplus target for the overall (or unified) budget is less than the surplus in the social security and other retirement funds. There would still be a modest deficit in the federal government's operating budget.

Movement to the target should be expeditious, but gradual enough to avoid transition problems. Cutting the deficit by something like 0.6 percent of GNP each year would reduce the deficit to $25 billion by fiscal 1993 and produce a budget surplus of $70 billion in 1995 (on the way to attaining the full surplus target of nearly $110 billion by 1996). As noted earlier, the CBO projects deficits of $148 in 1993 and $119 billion in 1995 under current budgetary policies. To meet the 1995 target, a large package of expenditure reductions and tax increases will

TABLE 2-14. Deficit Reduction, Stage 1: Defense Cuts,
Fiscal Year 1995
Billions of dollars

Item	1995
Budget deficit with no policy change	−119
Defense spending cuts	+65
Interest bonus	+39
Resulting deficit	−15
Budget target	+70
Remaining to be cut	+85

obviously be necessary. But the opportunities opened up by the winding down of the cold war and the magic of the interest "bonus" that accompanies large deficit reductions both reduce the size of the job.

Decisions of three major kinds will be involved in achieving the budget target. First, the defense budget can and should be reduced. The alternative programs for defense cutbacks developed by Korb and Steinbruner would produce gradually increasing spending cuts below the CBO projections of $55 billion and $80 billion in fiscal 1995, in dollars of then current purchasing power. For purposes of developing a long-range deficit reduction package, I have assumed a defense spending cut of $65 billion, roughly halfway between the two alternatives (see table 2-14). Taking into account the interest bonus, the budget deficit would be reduced to $15 billion in 1995, a major improvement but still short of the target by $85 billion in 1995.

The second aspect of planning for an eventual budget surplus involves consideration of civilian spending priorities: where should spending be increased and where decreased? The analysis above identified a limited number of areas where federal spending should be increased and some where it should be cut. With reforms in investment and pricing policies for highway and airport investment, the nation's infrastructure needs can be met for additional federal outlays of only $2 billion or $3 billion a year. Federal spending for civilian R&D should be increased very sharply, but almost doubling that support could be done with an addition of only $15 billion a year to federal spending in 1995.

A case can be made that the nation should extend health insurance to all citizens. Aaron argues that the costs should be financed independently of the general budget with a special earmarked tax. A large increase in federal spending on elementary and secondary education is unwarranted at the present time, although educational grants, costing perhaps $6 billion a year (about $150 per elementary and secondary public school student), might be used to encourage the kind of reforms that Chubb and Hanushek propose. Finally, some modest increases in federal spending on certain "work load" items are called for to make up for the penny pinching of recent years. But the sums involved would not be large; $7 billion a year would provide a 20 percent increase across the entire category.

In total, all these outlay increases, converted to prices prevailing in 1995 (assuming a 4 percent annual inflation rate), would add $37 billion a year to the 1995 budget. If agreement could be reached either to tax social security benefits more fully or to make a modest reduction in cost-of-living adjustments (in all non–means-tested programs), the savings by 1995 should amount to about $17 billion a year. And if, in the rest of the civilian budget, a "grand compromise" could produce modest expenditure cuts growing to $10 billion a year by 1995, then $27 billion, or almost three-quarters of the additional $37 billion in outlays on high-priority programs, could be offset with outlay reductions elsewhere. The net addition to spending would be only $10 billion.[27]

The final step in the decisionmaking is the tax increase needed to close the remaining gap. If the spending reductions discussed above were enacted (including cuts in social security benefits or the equivalent amount of additional taxes on social security benefits), the required tax increase would be relatively modest—$67 billion in 1995, 1 percent of national income (see alternative A in table 2-15). Almost three-quarters of that amount could be raised, for example, by changing the 15 and 28 percent personal tax brackets to 16 and 30 percent and raising the corporate rate to 35 percent. All of it could be raised by an 8½ percent surcharge on all personal and corporate taxes; or by a gasoline tax of sixty-five cents a gallon; or by some combination of both. It could also be reached by a package that eliminated the bubble in the personal income tax,[28] taxed capital gains by constructive realization at death, and added fifty cents to the gasoline tax. Aaron's proposal to create a

---

27. If the reduction in non–means-tested benefits cannot be achieved, the net addition to spending would be $27 billion, not $10 billion.

28. When tax rates were cut in 1986, the top bracket rate was set at 28 percent. However, taxpayers with incomes between $82,000 and $218,000 (for a family of four) pay 33 percent. On higher incomes the rate drops back to 28 percent. The proposal above would keep the 33 percent bracket rate in effect for those higher incomes.

TABLE 2-15. Deficit Reduction, Stage 2: Tax Increase,
Fiscal Year 1995
Billions of dollars

Item	1995
Alternative A[a]	
Deficit reduction needed after	
defense cuts	85
Additional civilian spending (net)	10
Deficit reduction required	95
Tax increase	67
(Percent of national income)	(1.0)
Interest bonus[b]	28
Alternative B[c]	
Deficit reduction needed after	
defense cuts	85
Additional civilian spending (net)	27
Deficit reduction required	112
Tax increase	84
(Percent of national income)	(1.3)
Interest bonus[b]	28

a. Assumes reduction in means-tested payments.
b. The interest "bonus" is smaller, relative to the size of the deficit reduction, than the one shown in earlier tables. The econometric models on which the calculations of interest rate reductions were based imply that the second $50 billion of deficit reduction would yield the same fall in interest rates as the first $50 billion, and that the third $50 billion would yield an additional reduction as large as the second, and so on. But this is clearly unrealistic. It implies that after time interest rates could become negative, which clearly cannot happen. And so the 1995 estimate of the interest bonus for the second slice of deficit reductions (after the defense cuts have already been taken) was scaled down to equal 50 percent of the initial budgetary action, in comparison with the 60 percent bonus that comes in the first tranche of deficit reduction.
c. Assumes no reduction in means-tested payments.

new trust fund for the government's health care expenditures financed, in part, by a new 6 percent value-added tax would, as explained earlier, generate extra revenues for deficit reduction that would generate more than sufficient revenue to produce the target surplus ($75 billion versus $67 billion).

Alternative B in table 2-15 repeats the calculations under the assumption that the cuts in social security benefits, or their equivalent, are impossible. The necessary tax increase by 1995 would be some $17 billion larger, amounting to 1.3 percent of national income by 1995.

From both an economic and a political standpoint, achieving the budget targets should not be done piecemeal, year by year, with no overall strategies or broad budget compromise. Enactment of a phased multiyear budget plan would be highly desirable. Both the tax increase and the changes in the social security COLAs could be enacted at the beginning of the period but come into effect gradually. And while one

Congress cannot bind its successor, multiyear appropriations—at least for the next two years—could launch both the additional spending and the expenditure reductions on track toward the five-year target.

A Final Thought

For the past seven years a political impasse has prevented the country from dealing with its budget deficit and its low national saving rate. But as Western Europe reinvigorates itself by forming a true common market and opening economic ties with Eastern Europe, and as Japan continues to grow in productivity, technological capability, and market power, one has to hope that the United States will finally take the painful steps to end its own decade-long consumption binge and restore its national saving, investment, and productivity growth to levels worthy of a modern industrial power. The one sure way of doing this is to convert the current federal budget deficit into a significant surplus by the middle of the decade. For both substantive and political reasons, a program to do so will have to include large cuts in defense spending, reductions in middle-class subsidy and benefit programs, and a tax increase.

Appendix A: Do the Official Accounts Overstate the Size of the Federal Budget Deficit?

Robert Eisner of Northwestern University and some others argue that the official accounting measures normally used exaggerate the size of the federal deficit and substantially overstate its contribution to the decline in national saving.[29]

First, Eisner holds that the budget deficit should be adjusted downward to recognize the fact that inflation reduces the real value of the federal debt. Some part of the interest payments received by government bondholders—equal to the inflation rate times the public debt—has to be considered not as income to be consumed, but as an asset transfer needed to restore the real value of the bondholders' principal and consequently to be saved. This part of the deficit does not lower the national saving rate and should be excluded from the deficit calculation. If it were, the 1990 deficit would equal about 0.8 percent of GNP, not

---

29. Robert Eisner, "Budget Deficits: Rhetoric and Reality," *Journal of Economic Perspectives,* vol. 3 (Spring 1989), pp. 73–93; and Robert Eisner and Paul J. Pieper, "A New View of the Federal Debt and Budget Deficits," *American Economic Review,* vol. 74 (March 1984), pp. 11–29.

the 2.3 percent commonly cited. By the mid-1990s the inflation-adjusted deficit would disappear.

In assessing the effect of the budget deficit on private spending and saving, it may make sense to subtract the inflation adjustment as Eisner suggests. But the whole question is irrelevant to the measurement of national saving. If the inflation adjustment is subtracted from the budget deficit because part of government interest payments are not truly income to bondholders, then current statistics overstate not only the budget deficit but also the income and the saving of those same bondholders. The Eisner adjustment simply reallocates national saving among its components: less private saving, less government dissaving, with no net effect on national saving itself. Moreover, the inflation adjustment as a share of national income has recently been about the same as its average during the 1970s. Hence the increase in the budget deficit, and its contribution to the decline in national saving, is just about the same whether the inflation adjustment is made or not.

Second, Eisner argues that some of the federal deficit finances net investment in public capital, which adds to the nation's productive wealth. Hence government spending, and the deficit, should exclude that investment. In fact, however, making such an adjustment at the present time would not significantly modify the size of the deficit. Net investment equals gross outlays on capital goods less depreciation. In recent years federal outlays on capital goods (excluding military weapons) have been only slightly higher than depreciation: federal net investment in recent years has been running at only about $4 billion a year.

Third, Eisner and others say that the budget deficit for total government is much smaller than the deficit for the federal government alone because state and local governments are running a large surplus. In fact, the operating budgets of state and local governments are now in deficit. Their overall budgets are in surplus according to the national income accounts because that accounting system includes in state and local budgets the large annual accumulation of reserves in their employee pension funds. Were these same employees in the private sector, those pension fund surpluses would be considered as part of personal saving. The data in table 2-3 have been reclassified to shift this pension fund accumulation from public to private (personal) saving. In any event, wherever these pension fund accumulations are classified does not change the measure of national saving one whit and in no way diminishes its recent collapse.

Appendix B: The Productivity Payoff from Public Infrastructure Investment

In a widely cited work, David Aschauer argues that the rate at which public physical infrastructure increases can explain an important part of changes in the rate of growth of business productivity, including the fall in productivity growth since 1973.[30]

The Aschauer study regresses the rate of growth in human output, relative to a weighted index of labor and private capital inputs, against the rate of growth in the stock of public infrastructure, relative to the same weighted input index. His regression results imply, for example, that a $1 increase in the stock of public infrastructure adds about as much to productivity as a $4 increase in the stock of private business capital.[31] Those same results also imply that a one-time increase of $10 billion in the net stock of public infrastructure would yield a permanent increase of $7 billion in the annual level of GNP. While not a free lunch, this would be a very cheap banquet.

What the study actually demonstrates is simply that the time pattern of national productivity growth and the time pattern of the growth in public investment are similar. The growth rate of public capital peaked and began to decline at about the same time as productivity growth began to sag. This correlation tends to generate grossly inflated estimates of the returns to infrastructure investment. To be sure, carefully selected public investment in infrastructure can improve national productivity and output—the building of the interstate highway system, for example, was undoubtedly a major contributor to the rise in national productivity during the 1960s and early 1970s. But the kinds of payoffs promised by this study are not to be had.

30. David A. Aschauer, "Is Public Expenditure Productive," *Journal of Monetary Economics,* vol. 23 (March 1989), pp. 177–200.

31. According to Aschauer's regression, a 1 percent increase in the stock of public infrastructure raised the level of output—everything else held constant—by 0.39 percent during the period from 1949 to 1985. By virtually all estimates that increase was larger than the gain in output from a 1 percent increase in the stock of private business capital. Yet the stock of business capital (in 1987) was 3.3 times the size of the stock of public capital.

3

JOHN D. STEINBRUNER

Revolution in Foreign Policy

IF HISTORY were a personality truly able to speak, it could hardly have been more eloquent or more forceful than the events that closed the 1980s. As remarkably disciplined street demonstrations swept away authoritarian regimes in Eastern Europe, the overriding power of political legitimacy was dramatically revealed and a new Soviet respect for that principle was convincingly documented. As the Berlin Wall ceased to be either the prime symbol of confrontation or an effective human barrier, the once distant abstractions of German reunification and general European reconciliation became practical issues of immediate policy. As Poland embarked on a drastic, politically dangerous economic reform and appealed for relief from debt burdens at least as serious as Mexico's or Argentina's, the magnitude of the international economic agenda was ominously signaled. As the U.S. defense secretary projected a sharp budget decline for the first time in fifteen years, the underlying tension between established security policy and new economic priorities was revealed.[1] Not even the invasion of Panama—a successful unilateral projection of military power in stark exception to the noninterventionist principles on display in Eastern Europe—could obscure the prevailing message: the world is changing and so also must U.S. foreign policy.

The author wishes to acknowledge the collaboration of Ethan Gutmann in preparing the figures and tables and doing the underlying analysis. He is also grateful to Richard K. Betts, Raymond L. Garthoff, Ed A. Hewett, Nora Lustig, and Michael K. MccGwire for comments, to Steven E. Siesser for research assistance, and to Charlotte B. Brady for manuscript preparation.

1. The U.S. defense budget increased in real terms every year from 1976 through 1985 and then began a consistent decline. The reductions from 1986 through 1989 were imposed on the annual budget, however, against the projections of the underlying defense plan, which called for a continuation of the previous pattern of real annual increases. The projected increases allowed the U.S. armed services to commit themselves to weapons programs increases that were consistent with the plans but not with the actual annual budget. The Defense Department did not officially admit to this inconsistency until the late autumn of 1989, when the planning projections were reversed and consistent decreases against the base of the previous plan were mandated for a five-year period.

The problem, of course, is that the specific implications of the message are less apparent than the message itself. In fact, the swift dissolution of so many seemingly immutable features of ideological confrontation has evoked considerable astonishment and no little confusion in the United States. The driving problems are no longer the familiar ones of resisting calculated aggression or distributing some portion of a once decisive economic advantage. These efforts have produced accomplishments to be preserved, but few believe they can plausibly remain the cutting edge of policy. The dominant issues are now different in character. They emerge more from the spontaneous evolution of events than from the formulation of government policy. They have to do with the international diffusion of advanced technology, the surge of international capital markets, the rapid transformation of industrial organizations and resulting shifts in trade patterns, the emotional dynamics of diverse cultures driven into intense interaction, and many other matters that are not controlled by any small group of decisionmakers whose behavior can readily be made an organizing focus. Without a defined opponent or imminent threat to compel consensus, the diverse elements of American opinion exercise their carefully protected rights, and the United States has difficulty forming, as it is frequently said, a coherent vision, an agreed strategy, or a clear sense of direction.

The natural bewilderment produced by rapid and dramatic change is not likely to endure, however. There is an inherent logic to the emerging era that is probably powerful enough, over time, to channel American opinion and to bring U.S. policy into workable focus. In the first place, the basis of security is being altered by a natural historical progression. The prevailing confrontation between alliances is being transformed by its own side effects: most notably, the surge of long-suppressed nationalist sentiment in Eastern Europe, the accumulating fiscal pressures on defense investment, and the necessity of managing technically advanced, widely dispersed military operations. These circumstances virtually mandate that a cooperative security arrangement be implemented in central Europe and extended to worldwide military operations. That will require a profound change in U.S. policy, but the incentives, both positive and negative, are commensurately strong. The implied outcome offers better security at lower cost—a politically compelling proposition once it comes to be understood. The alternative, moreover, is not the smooth continuation of traditional deterrence and forward defense of allies as practiced over the past four decades, but serious erosion of the legitimacy and hence of the feasibility of global military deployments. Again, the choice is compelling once the situation is grasped.

Similarly, a substantial transformation of the international economic posture of the United States will predictably be forced by powerful circumstances. As the centrally planned economies shed their dogmatic ideologies and strive to emerge from economic isolation, a policy of positive engagement will have to be devised to replace the dominant pattern of sanctions and restrictions that accrued during the cold war period. The increasing internationalization of economic activity has decisively eroded the effectiveness of political barriers and has made domestic economic performance turn on international competition. All countries are being driven into assertive international engagement as a general matter, and none can afford to make large, ultimately unrealistic exceptions. For all their immediate difficulties, the centrally planned economies represent a major international opportunity over the longer term. The Soviet Union and China in particular are large, integrated, underdeveloped markets. Their renowned inefficiencies offer the occasion for highly productive investment if they can manage to adopt sufficiently encouraging internal rules. The East European economies are positioned to act as gateways or experimental stations for this very demanding reform process in the larger economies.

Success of this general reform effort would be the best apparent means for civilizing international political relationships; failure of it would be the most likely cause of dangerous political turbulence. For international economic policy, no less than security, opportunity and threat have aligned to compel a dramatic shift in the fundamentals of U.S. policy.

Beyond these two central imperatives of cooperative security and economic engagement, the inherent logic of events appears less decisive in practical terms but is still usefully instructive. With the power of all national governments declining relative to that of the world as a whole, international standards of equity are acquiring much greater practical significance as a means of inducing coordinated policies. Refinement of those standards is likely to be a consequence. It is reasonable to expect therefore that the new economic claims of the centrally planned economies will trigger a more general reconsideration of the balance of international capital flows and of the viability of prevailing development strategies. In the end, the integration of Eastern Europe cannot be accomplished at the expense of Africa or Latin America. It is also reasonable to expect that more cooperative approaches to regional conflict will emerge among the major powers because of their mutual interest in controlling civil violence, and similarly that looming problems of environmental management will force more sophisticated coordination. Although it is perhaps too early to proclaim the exact character of the new international order, nonetheless the outlines of a global alliance are visibly emerging. The relevant international political competition is for leading roles in forming it.

Cooperative Security

Strategic Origins

The idea of cooperative security has a lengthy history, most of it consigned by recent generations of political officials to the category of unrealistic idealization—material for speeches but not a reliable basis for serious business. As Soviet security policy has evolved under Mikhail Gorbachev, however, the status of the idea has been transformed from rhetorical aspiration to a central organizing principle for strategic reasons of overriding practical weight. The Soviets have focused on a new dimension of threat, encountered the necessity of more efficient force deployments, and relinquished direct political control in Eastern Europe— thereby mandating, from their perspective, some new basis for political stability. All three considerations have driven them into assertively promoting a cooperative security arrangement, and they are rapidly discovering the very substantial political advantage that the idea offers them. The impetus given by their policy, by the reinforcement of surrounding events, and by the undeniable resonance of Western security interests is making cooperative security the ascendant theme of international politics.

Indirect threat. Because nuclear weapons pose a potentially lethal threat to any industrial society, the prevention of full-scale war has inevitably been the dominant foreign policy commitment of all the major powers since the earliest deployment of these weapons and will continue to be so as long as they remain deployed. Traditionally that objective has been addressed by maintaining protected, immediately available strategic weapons capable of devastating retaliation in response to nuclear attack—the familiar posture of deterrence. The United States and the Soviet Union both developed arsenals directed to this purpose comprising more than 10,000 available weapons. The composition of each is roughly similar and their overall postures are equivalent.

The conventional weapons deployments of the two countries, however, have reflected a very different strategic calculation. Because there has been no significant threat of a direct invasion of U.S. territory, U.S. conventional forces have been deployed forward along the periphery of the Soviet Union to protect major allies and to discourage more limited engagements that might grow into a global war. The United States has attempted to give these conventional forces the ability to withstand attacks that might develop with as little as two weeks' warning—a very expensive aspiration never completely realized but approached closely enough to signal unmistakable resolve. These forward deployments have been supplemented, moreover, by shorter-range nuclear weapons integrated into their operations. The entire posture has been designed to deter a carefully calculating opponent—assumed to be the Soviet Union—from any attempt to conduct an effective surprise attack; that is, one that emanated warning signals too ambiguous to be useful.

Soviet conventional forces were originally deployed on a different theory. They were also positioned forward in Eastern Europe, but were instructed in the event of war to conduct an immediate offensive against the inherently superior coalition of NATO countries. Conceding that they were bound to lose a lengthy war against superior economies,[2] Soviet military planners concluded that they would have to stage a decisive forward offensive before NATO's superior economic and technical assets could be bought to bear. In support of that conclusion, they maintained a larger number of ground force units and preserved, with force on occasion, direct political control over the governments of Eastern Europe.

These respective commitments institutionalized alliance confrontation in central Europe and perpetuated it long after the original ideological motives had become relatively dormant. Despite the dangers inherent in heavily armed confrontation, global warfare was prevented for more than four decades but at a cost and a risk that have been disproportionately burdensome to the Soviet Union. Apparently for that reason, Soviet leaders initiated a series of doctrinal adjustments beginning in the 1970s.

---

2. In the 1960s the Soviets, despite considerable skepticism, came to accept the possibility that war in Europe might possibly occur against their will and without the use of nuclear weapons. Since they would not have been willing to initiate the use of nuclear weapons, eventual defeat was probable once the productive capacity and manpower reserves of the United States and its European allies had been mobilized. That in turn posed a problem in deterring such a war, since NATO members could make the same calculations.

These have developed rapidly under Gorbachev into a fundamentally different security policy.

A primary motive for this shift emerged from a recognition that the configuration of conventional forces in Europe intermingled with nuclear weapons would produce highly volatile, potentially unmanageable interactions under crisis conditions. The swiftness and destructiveness of nuclear weapons has meant that the coherence of military organizations could not survive the initial stages of warfare and thus critical missions had to be accomplished immediately, if at all. When translated into operational reality, this fact put the standard doctrine of retaliation—the essential feature of a deterrent posture—into severe practical conflict with imperatives to respond rapidly, even preemptively, if deterrence should fail and an unintended war should occur. The Soviets recognized that their force was designed to undergo a more elaborately controlled and probably slower-paced transition from their normal peacetime state to actual war, and yet their conventional forces in Europe were doctrinally committed to a preemptive victory in central Europe based on a superiority of initially mobilized firepower. They came to appreciate that alert procedures of the two alliances that were intended to be protective precautions would create instead an explosive atmosphere in which any random spark might trigger the war they were committed to preventing.

This assessment radically altered the Soviet conceptions of threat. They could presume that with the maturation of their strategic forces in the 1970s, their deterrence was compellingly strong and therefore deliberate Western aggression was effectively prevented. The possibility of an inadvertently catalyzed war was unacceptably high, however, particularly given the fact that underlying political dynamics in central Europe offered all too plausible grounds for a political crisis the Soviets might not be able to control. This assessment was strengthened, moreover, by Soviet sensitivity to the projected development of conventional weapons technology. They recognized that, primarily as a result of information-processing technology, conventional weapons could acquire some of the rapidly decisive effects long associated with nuclear weapons—particularly if used against the command system infrastructure that would be critical in executing the rapidly decisive counteroffensive their established doctrine required. Targeting information and long-range precision guidance could in principle compensate for the much lower explosive power of conventional weapons and could give NATO conventional forces dramatically enhanced offensive capabilities that might be decisively debilitating if used preemptively. Because this technical trend was produced largely by the application of microelectronic circuits, an area where relative Soviet disadvantage was probably the most serious and enduring, the situation represented a major strategic danger.

The conclusions derived from this assessment have emerged with increasingly clarity and specificity over recent years. Official Soviet policy declarations have given the objective of preventing war explicit precedence over the objective of preparing to fight it, thereby accepting some risk regarding the ultimate outcome in order to increase assurance that it will be prevented. The intention to transform Soviet forces into a defensive configuration has been repeatedly declared. In the initial phases of training exercises, Soviet forces are assigned the primary task of holding territory, and the imagined timing of a counteroffensive is sufficiently delayed to make its preparation less likely to affect crisis operations.

The size and location of Soviet forces are being aligned, moreover, with these fundamental doctrinal shifts. The removal of intermediate-range nuclear weapons agreed in the 1988 Intermediate-Range Nuclear Forces (INF) Treaty was explicitly represented in Soviet policy as the first step toward complete disengagement of conventional and nuclear weapons, and the Soviet political leadership is clearly attempting to expedite a supplemental reduction of strategic nuclear forces, as envisaged in the draft strategic arms reduction talks (START) treaty. The unilateral conventional force reductions that Gorbachev announced in December 1988 and began to implement in the spring of 1989 precluded a rapidly mobilized surprise attack against NATO. The additional highly disproportionate reductions the Soviet foreign minister first proposed in March 1989 as a negotiated agreement would further diminish the scope for any successful offensive by equalizing the basic firepower available to the two alliances and by introducing extensive inspection arrangements that would make operational surprise very difficult. The studied tolerance and subliminal encouragement with which the Soviets subsequently handled the revolutionary changes of government in all their East European allies added a strong political element to the pattern. These political decisions made it even more apparent that Soviet forces are not being postured to stage a decisive westward offensive, and that their physical defense perimeter is being realistically drawn at the borders of the Soviet Union.

The policy of military disengagement embodied in these measures is a rational, systematic response to a refined conception of threat. Although it has emerged under Gorbachev and has been connected to his policy of economic reform, it stands on its own in strategic terms and would be equally valid under any plausible variant of Soviet policy or any internal form of government. It can be expected to endure and to attract international support, particularly since it offers major benefits for all countries in terms of efficiency and political reassurance.

Improved efficiency. Even when designed against the traditionally conceived threat of deliberate aggression, military forces can be safely deployed in lesser numbers, their readiness states held lower, their technical development rendered less burdensome, and their operations committed to reaction rather than initiation, if uncertainty is reliably reduced about the size, location, and timing of attacks they might encounter. A calculating opponent denied the advantage of surprise is more readily deterred. Moreover, this reduction of uncertainty becomes even more important if the security problem is that of controlling crisis interactions. Uncertainty itself, combined with the fears it generates, is the most likely root cause of unintended warfare.

Force reductions and geographic disengagement reduce uncertainty to some extent, but are not considered reliable unless underlying intentions can be accurately judged. To instill the necessary confidence, there must also be an exchange of information about deployment plans, production schedules, and operational practices of military forces. Access to this information is the single most significant source of improved efficiency for current military establishments. It offers the possibility of performing legitimate defense missions more reliably with reduced force levels and lower costs. For that reason, exchange of information is the central mechanism of a cooperative security arrangement.

This basic fact offers the Soviet Union appreciable comparative advantage to compensate for inherent deficiencies in its technical development. The Soviets have successfully protected their planning systems from direct Western scrutiny and have also made substantial, presumably successful, investments in observing the more open planning, production, and deployment process of Western governments. By revealing more of their own operations and allowing direct inspections, they can have a substantial effect on Western defense postures, making them considerably more efficient and thereby achieving greater efficiency themselves. The Soviets' increasing willingness to use this inherent advantage is likely to be an enduring trend. The efficiency of their own security policy is clearly a preoccupying problem. They will probably discover that international political influence developed on the basis of mutual interest in defense efficiency is stronger than that based on the projection of threat.

Political stabilization. The emerging Soviet policy of military disengagement is both a contributing cause and a major consequence of the radical political transformation under way in Eastern Europe. In relinquishing direct political control over the governments of their Warsaw Treaty allies, the Soviets have almost certainly rendered the organization incapable of initiating an assault on Western Europe and have removed some forty-eight Eastern European divisions from the forces that can be imagined to participate in such an exercise. That development has probably rendered the standard calculus of a NATO–Warsaw Treaty engagement so improbable that it cannot indefinitely serve as the organizing focus for NATO's military organization. Military commitments to NATO and its very existence have become open political questions, and domestic consensus in the NATO countries probably cannot be sustained on traditional grounds.

At the same time, long-suppressed nationalist emotions have been released in central Europe, and several countries with very little relevant experience have committed themselves to forming governments through competitive elections. Political uncertainty has risen dramatically with the release of Soviet control, and no one can yet judge what the consequences will be against the background of economic hardship and the surge of national sentiment. Under these conditions, the indirect, silent functions of the two alliances in providing some degree of international organization of military power in central Europe have become more important as their traditionally acknowledged purposes dissolve.

This situation encourages rapid emergence of the idea of cooperative security as a means of defining and justifying the politically necessary transformation of the two alliances. Simply by proceeding with the conventional forces agreement that has been already reasonably well formulated in the Conventional Forces in Europe (CFE) negotiations, the basic structure of a cooperative security arrangement can be created. The agreement is designed to impose force ceilings and some operational restrictions on the members of the two alliances and is being formulated in the Conference of Security and Cooperation in Europe (CSCE) forum that includes all the European states. By specifying national force ceilings under the alliance aggregates, adding a supplementary rule that the CSCE states can not increase their current force levels and must disclose what they are, and including all parties in the inspection arrangements worked out to enforce the agreement, a cooperative arrangement can be formed without designing fundamentally new proposals or creating new organizations. Such an arrangement provides the natural model for yet deeper reductions that will inevitably be demanded and for the extension to global deployment that appears likely, given the domestic fiscal pressures besetting all major governments.

Support for this outcome is the most predictable track for Soviet policies and the course of least resistance for U.S. accommodation. Among its several virtues, the arrangement could be developed soon enough to provide at least part of the international context necessary to accompany German unification.

Design and Implications

If cooperative security is accepted as the apparent mandate of events, then its basic principles and implications for force structure can be advanced as likely components of a revised U.S. foreign policy. In broad outline these are not difficult to identify.

The basic idea of a cooperative security arrangement is that all countries are on the same side and their forces are not directed against each other. That being the case, military establishments should be modest in size, their operations should be defensive in character, and full disclosure rather than internal secrecy should be the prevailing norm. Standardized criteria for setting force ceilings would ensure that no state faced a decisive disadvantage against any other single state, and the residual alliances would offer protection against the formation of aggressive coalitions. If these principles were to be implemented systematically, not only would security improve but budgets could also be reduced dramatically. As a practical matter, however, there are some problems in implementing these principles, given that prevailing defense programs have been designed with traditional deterrence and alliance confrontation in mind. Dealing with these problems seems likely to be the dominant security business of the coming decade.

Ground forces. The disposition of ground forces should in principle be the least of the problems. The draft CFE agreement provides the basic outline of a cooperative security arrangement that will equalize the combined conventional firepower available to members of the two alliances. Equalizing that ratio is the most significant step required to produce a defensive configuration of forces, since it is widely accepted that a substantial advantage is required at the point of attack to be able to seize territory against a competently prepared defense. In the movement required in offensive operations, conventional ground units must expose themselves and therefore suffer a higher rate of attrition that must be matched by an initial margin of advantage if they are to win. The transparency of operations that cooperative inspection would enforce, and the inherently slow rate at which ground units can move, enables secure defensive positions at equalized force ratios. Absolute levels of deployment can be reduced in relation to the extensiveness and reliability of mutual inspection.

In ensuring that this impending arrangement between the two alliances meets the requirements of cooperative security, the main problem is devising an equitable criterion for matching the relative capability of individual states in a manner consistent with the overall alliance outcome. The best candidate for this criterion is a common standard of ground force density—that is, the amount of conventional firepower available to protect a given amount of territory. Plausible results emerge if density for the European states is defined in terms of national boundaries—the perimeter that each state would be committed to protecting (see figure 3-1). The prospective CFE agreement would allow each member of the two alliances residual forces sufficient to guard fifty kilometers of its total national boundary, on average, with a single brigade of standard size. That average figure, of course, allows denser concentrations in more threatened areas and lighter ones in more protected regions. It is generally believed that a standard brigade would have to be concentrated in less than a five-kilometer segment of front in order to produce the shock effect required to overcome well-prepared, competently positioned defenses. Producing such concentrations from average densities ten times less—the CFE standard—would be very risky for a potential aggressor: the unusual concentration would be relatively easy for the defender to recognize and would leave weaknesses in the aggressor's own perimeter exposed to counterattack. Reducing the average density to seventy-five kilometers of perimeter per standard brigade, as shown in figure 3-1, . would enhance this effect, making offensive force concentrations all the more difficult to achieve, particularly with expanded capacity for monitoring ground force movements. A standard of seventy-five kilometers per brigade would impose large reductions on the large German and Soviet force concentrations in central Europe while requiring ceilings but not substantial reductions for the states not currently involved in those concentrations. The residual balances would grant each state a secure defensive potential. This logical result and the common standard it would create have at least a decent chance of inspiring the necessary consensus in Europe.

FIGURE 3-1. National Ground Force Deployments in Europe
with Reduced Densities

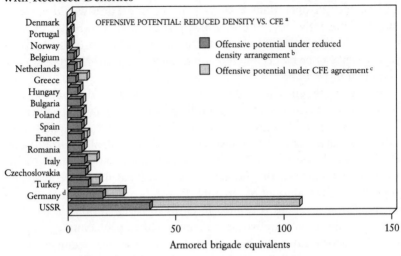

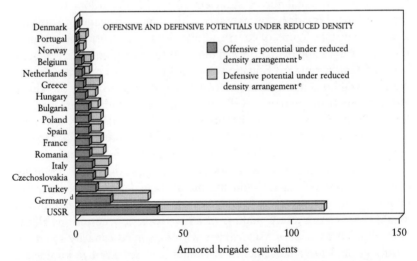

Armored brigade equivalents

SOURCES: For national boundaries, Central Intelligence Agency, *The World Factbook 1989* (Government Printing Office, 1989). For ground weaponry and armored division equivalent scoring, Joshua M. Epstein, *Conventional Arms Reductions: A Dynamic Analysis* (Brookings, 1990), especially app. C. For defensive weaponry scoring, U.S. Army Concepts Analysis Agency, *Weapons Effectiveness Indices/Weighted Unit Values III (WEI/WUV III)*, Study Report CAA-SR-79-12 (Bethesda, Md., November 1979).

a. Offensive potential measures tank, armored vehicle, and artillery WEI/WUV scores.

b. Seventy-five kilometers of national perimeter per armored brigade (forty tanks, forty-one artillery pieces, and fifty-six armored vehicles).

c. Fifty kilometers of national perimeter per armored brigade.

d. Combined West and East Germany.

e. Includes offensive potential plus WEI/WUV scores for small arms and antiarmor systems and mortars less than 100 millimeters.

Air interdiction forces. For tactical aircraft, accurate long-range artillery, and similar systems, force reduction poses more difficulties. When used for deep interdiction missions, these systems are already somewhat threatening to the command and supply infrastructure necessary to organize even a defensive military operation. Further technical improvement promises to make them even more so. A systematically developed cooperative security arrangement would have to constrain these systems disproportionately: not merely equalizing their deployment and technical modernization schedules, but restricting them in terms of absolute mission standards.

If ground force units were reduced to half the levels envisaged in the conventional forces agreement, then tactical aircraft would presumably have to be reduced by significantly more than half. Figure 3-2 displays a plausible result. Since tactical aircraft for deep interdiction missions are particularly high-prestige elements of the current military establishments, assigning them the disproportionately reduced allocations implied in such an outcome is likely to be a major problem. The balance of national government assets within the alliance allocations is likely to complicate the problem even further, at least on the NATO side.

Strategic forces. In pure theory, strategic forces—long-range nuclear weapons systems—would be entirely eliminated under a cooperative security arrangement. If military forces are to be restricted to the defense of national territory and to supporting the preservation of international order primarily through major power cooperation, then threat of massive destruction would be neither necessary nor legitimate. In fact, Gorbachev and President Reagan seemed to contemplate such an outcome at the Reykjavik summit meeting in October 1986, which inspired a chorus of objections for exactly that reason. The hard practical problem reflected in these widespread objections is that nuclear weapons are extremely difficult to eliminate entirely. The knowledge of how to make them cannot be surgically removed from the body of modern science, and the objects themselves have strategic significance in small numbers all too readily hidden from even the most intensive inspection. The degree of trust required to believe that nuclear weapons have been eliminated appears to exceed realistic aspirations for the foreseeable future; therefore their presence must presumably be accepted in numbers tailored to legitimate requirements. Although there is as yet no agreed definition of a legitimate requirement, the guiding principles are fairly obvious if still somewhat controversial. Moreover, there are stark physical facts to give them specific definition.

FIGURE 3-2. National Air Force Deployments under Alternative Densities

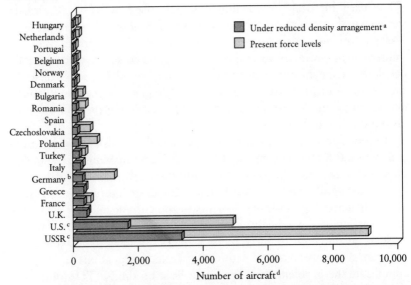

SOURCE: National perimeters are defined by the sum of national land boundaries and national coastlines; source for both, Central Intelligence Agency, *The World Factbook 1989*. Aircraft numbers and missions were taken from three sources: Institute for Defense and Disarmament Studies, *Cutting Conventional Force 1: An Analysis of the Official Mandate, Statistics, and Proposals in the NATO-WTO Talks on Reducing Conventional Forces in Europe* (Brookline, Mass.: IDDS, July 1989); International Institute for Strategic Studies, *The Military Balance, 1989–1990* (London: Brassey's, 1989); and John W. R. Taylor and Kenneth Munson, eds., *Jane's All the World's Aircraft* (Surrey, U.K.: Jane's Information Group, 1988). IDDS was used in preference to other sources.

a. Density falls from 11 kilometers of national perimeter per plane to 29 kilometers per plane.

b. Combined West and East Germany.

c. Perimeters and agreements are global.

d. Aircraft were separated into three categories: "attack aircraft" (fighter-bombers and ground attack), "defense aircraft" (fighters and air defense or alternately, "nonattack aircraft" as the Soviets have defined it), and "special-purposes aircraft" (reconnaissance and naval/antisubmarine warfare). No category could exceed 3,600 aircraft, and national holdings were based on the length of their perimeter compared with the overall ceiling within each category.

Under a practical cooperative security regime, the United States and the Soviet Union, as the major strategic powers and historical alliance leaders, will have to concede to each other the right to maintain a retaliatory threat against national assets, including military forces, sufficiently valuable to preserve an unquestionable deterrent effect. But that concession cannot be extended to threatened attacks on strategic weapons themselves, since any meaningful capability to perform that mission creates a commensurately strong incentive to initiate attack. The high priority that has traditionally been given to efforts to retaliate against opposing nuclear weapons would have to be abolished under a fully developed cooperative security arrangement. The adjustment of this principle promises to be difficult for the strategic organizations on both sides that have long considered the opposition's nuclear weapons to be the most compelling focus of attack.

A related problem concerns the intense political desire for a strategic security posture based on defensive technology rather than on retaliatory offensive threats. Were such a posture to be technically feasible, it would indeed fit the principles of cooperative security much better than mutual concessions of deterrent capability. The prospects for such technology, however, are far too remote to be a responsible basis for strategic security, particularly since partial unilateral commitments to it are self-defeating. Unless the performance of a defensive system is literally perfect and indisputably accepted as such, unilateral introduction would have the perverse effect of driving the opposing offensive force from a retaliatory to a preemptive operational doctrine in order to ensure coverage of deterrent targets.[3] As a practical matter for the foreseeable future, mutual concession of deterrent capability is the only available strategic rule for a cooperative security arrangement, and any gradual evolution of defensive technology would have to be mutually agreed upon under the requirements of this rule.

The implications of this situation for strategic force deployments are closely determined by the explosive power of nuclear weapons and the concentration of industrial societies. In both the United States and the Soviet Union, roughly 75 percent of the industrial capability and a comparable proportion of the military infrastructure are contained in a set of circular areas that could be effectively destroyed with about 2,000 nuclear weapons actually exploding at the intended locations. Beyond that level, damage against more widely dispersed targets is more difficult to achieve and much less significant in its net consequences. That means that a reasonable deterrent requirement would probably be fixed at or below the ability to reliably deliver 2,000 weapons in retaliation. Suitably designed and operated, strategic forces could be reduced to 25 percent of their current deployments, or about 3,000 warheads, and still meet this criterion with an ample margin of safety.[4]

3. This effect occurs because the ability to penetrate a defensive system would be much greater for an attacking force initiating with optimum coordination than it would be for a damaged, poorly coordinated retaliating force.

4. See Michael M. May, George F. Bing, and John D. Steinbruner, *Strategic Arms Reductions* (Brookings, 1988), chaps. 2, 3; and John D. Steinbruner, "The Effect of Strategic Force Reductions on Nuclear Strategy," *Arms Control Today*, vol. 18 (May 1988), pp. 3–5.

The composition of strategic forces presents more of a problem of adjustment because the major efforts at technical improvement, particularly in the United States, have been directed to increased offensive capability, which directly contradicts the principle of conceding the legitimacy of the opponent's deterrent capabilities. Whatever is said about them in rhetorical justification, the MX, Trident II, and B-2 bomber programs in the United States and the latest version of the SS-18 program in the Soviet Union all project an apparent intention to improve the effectiveness of attacks on strategic weapons installations, a mission that must be accomplished preemptively in each instance in order to be meaningful. These programs undermine the objective of efficiency by forcing increasingly demanding investments in methods of protecting their presumed targets. They also undermine crisis stability by encouraging operational practices that lean away from strict retaliation.

The advanced strategic programs are technically successful and politically popular. Given the commitment to them within the military planning systems on both sides and the impulse for increased strategic offensive capability generally, the arms control negotiations conducted to date have not formulated any significant restriction on technical improvement programs. Nor have official policy channels yet acknowledged the need to do so. Such restrictions are ultimately necessary for a cooperative security regime, however, to channel strategic investment more selectively into methods of protecting deployed forces and to distinguish a strictly retaliatory operational posture from one that threatens preemption. The development of qualitative restrictions on strategic weapons is one of the major problems of policy adjustment.

Tactical nuclear weapons. Under the provisions of the INF Treaty ratified in 1988, nuclear-armed ballistic missiles and ground-based cruise missiles with a range of 500 to 5,000 kilometers are being removed from the deployed forces. That will leave, however, some 3,600 nuclear weapons launchers deployed by NATO forces and 3,040 deployed by the Soviet Union for "tactical" use in support of ground force engagements and air interdiction missions.[5] These weapons have traditionally been considered necessary to compensate for the perceived disadvantages in ground force deployments and to bolster an allegedly questionable extension of U.S. strategic deterrent capability to cover NATO members

5. International Institute for Strategic Studies, *The Military Balance, 1989–1990* (London: Brassey's, 1989), p. 214.

and other allies. The former argument has been effectively removed, and in the new political context the long-standing technical incoherence of the latter argument is almost certain to be exposed.

Tactical nuclear weapons deployed in well-known forward positions on the crowded European continent and subjected to cumbersome alliance decisionmaking procedures are inherently vulnerable to interdiction, even by conventional aviation and sabotage operations. Because operational vulnerability is the single most significant factor affecting credibility of use, these weapons certainly do not diminish an opponent's assessment of any weakness in the U.S. strategic guarantee. Quite the contrary, these tactical deployed weapons encourage special preemptive operations and therefore threaten stable handling of crisis circumstances. Their complete removal is one of the clearest and most compelling elements of a cooperative security arrangement.

The United States has consistently made vigorous efforts to defend tactical nuclear weapons deployments, particularly in the wake of the INF Treaty and in the face of strong Soviet suggestions that this entire category of weapons be eliminated. In early 1989 an initiative was made to replace the 75-kilometer Lance missiles deployed in Germany with an updated 400- to 450-kilometer variant explicitly for the purpose of demonstrating NATO's resolve to sustain this class of weapons despite Soviet objections. Reflecting overriding domestic opposition to any new nuclear weapons deployment, however, the West German government rejected the initiative and a compromise was reached by postponing the final decision until 1992. That date sets a test case for the U.S. defense planning system, forcing it to balance its well-entrenched commitment to the traditional conception of tactical nuclear weapons against the predictable evolution of German political sentiment.

The impending process of German unification has effectively removed any serious prospect for European deployment of a new Lance missile, whose range largely confines it to operations within German territory. It is less immediately evident, but nonetheless probable, that tactical nuclear weapons installations will be a leading edge for broader questions about the appropriateness of a foreign military presence in Germany and that efforts to defend the traditional posture will collide with the necessity of revising the political rationale for NATO's operations. This will be another major problem for the U.S defense planning system, which historically has had great difficulty integrating technical and political considerations.

Naval forces. In terms of prevailing security concepts and public political discussions, the alliance confrontation in central Europe and the strategic interaction of nuclear weapons have been the most prominent instances of U.S.-Soviet military engagement during the cold war period. In terms of daily military operations, however, the two navies have provided an extremely prominent arena of contact, the dominant element of what might be called operational engagement. The two powers have regularly encountered each other in international waters, practicing search and tracking operations that closely resemble those that would presumably be undertaken in a major war. The two navies have learned to train each other in these spontaneous exercises in a manner well enough regulated by explicit and informal rules to be acceptably safe under peacetime circumstances.

The lessons derived from this experience strongly support the judgment that neither navy could comprehensively attack the other's deployed ballistic missile submarines in any short period. In the absence of that strategic threat, their direct engagement has entered calculations of the overall balance of military power largely as it affects the assessed U.S. ability to ship military supplies to Europe or Asia. The Soviet Union has maintained in its inventory large numbers of attack submarines that might in principle be used to interdict the sea lines, but it has not extensively developed the open ocean operations that would project a strong intention to do this. They have primarily dedicated their navy to guarding the sea approaches to the Soviet Union; particularly within range of their very extensive land-based naval air assets, they have a very good capacity to accomplish that. During the past decade, the U.S. Navy has assertively advertised an intention in the event of war to attack the Soviet Navy in its home waters and at its land installations within the Soviet Union. However, that would be such a flamboyant risk of naval assets so clearly insufficient to accomplish the task that the "strategy" is heavily discounted as domestic political bravado. As a practical matter, the major realistic commitments of the two navies are legitimate and compatible: protection of open ocean sea-lanes for the United States and protection of close sea approaches for the Soviet Union. A global cooperative security arrangement could readily accept these missions and need not require reductions in fleet sizes significantly larger than those that domestic fiscal measures are likely to impose.

Fully developed cooperative security, however, is likely to require very explicit arrangements for regulating naval operations under crisis circumstances. The regular engagement of forces is safe in peacetime because of a clear understanding that no weapons are to be fired. Under crisis circumstances, which would weaken that normal understanding on one side or the other, these engagements are potentially quite dangerous, particularly those involving submarines or tactical nuclear weapons. By their very nature, most naval operations cannot be monitored or directed by central authorities. A great deal of discretion must be placed in the hands of immediate commanders, who are quite aware that between ships in direct contact, initiative is very likely to decide the outcome. Moreover, these commanders also realize that a ship can be attacked with no collateral damage and often with no external observation to sort out whether the action taken was in self-defense. In light of these conditions, clearly specified arrangements for mutually agreed naval disengagement are a natural element of cooperative security, as is the ultimate removal of tactical nuclear weapons.

U.S. policy to date has rejected Soviet suggestions for discussions of naval arms control under the argument that the U.S. Navy enjoys a comparative advantage with no incentive to bargain it away. This well-established attitude, reinforced by the renowned institutional autonomy of the U.S. Navy and its strong political support, clearly poses a substantial problem for the U.S. planning system in developing the implications of cooperative security. Impending budget pressures and international political attitudes, however, are likely to be highly corrosive of traditional navy orthodoxy. Defense budget reductions and higher ship retirement rates in the 1990s will force the Navy to maintain its commitments with a fleet size reduced by some 25 percent (see table 3-1 and discussion in chapter 4). Perhaps even more significant, the preservation of worldwide basing rights is almost certain to require a less confrontational, more cooperative rationale for U.S. naval presence. The U.S. Navy seems destined to discover in the course of the 1990s that cooperative security is very much in its institutional interest and not merely the onerous imposition of a larger national security policy.

Overall outcome. The complete development of cooperative security arrangements would bring active U.S. and Soviet forces to much lower levels and would impose corresponding reductions on at least some other major military establishments and presumably ceilings on all of them. Table 3-2 displays potential results for U.S. forces. These changes would improve performance of military missions accepted as legitimate under cooperative security principles. Basic deterrence would be as decisively strong as it now is, and the overall threat of war would be substantially reduced by virtue of the improved control over force interactions under crisis circumstances. The territorial defense of Europe would be so

TABLE 3-1. Alternative Reductions in U.S. Naval Combat Forces[a]

Forces	Present levels				25 percent reduction				33 percent reduction				50 percent reduction			
	U.S. ships	U.S. SCETT[b]	USSR ships	USSR SCETT[b]	U.S. ships	U.S. SCETT[b]	USSR ships	USSR SCETT[b]	U.S. ships	U.S. SCETT[b]	USSR ships	USSR SCETT[b]	U.S. ships	U.S. SCETT[b]	USSR ships	USSR SCETT[b]
Aircraft carriers	13	1,220	4	160	10	938	3	120	9	844	3	120	7	657	2	80
Principal surface combatants	215	1,148	273	905	161	860	205	679	142	758	180	597	108	577	137	454
Attack submarines	100	1,291	302	2,367	75	969	227	1,779	66	853	199	1,559	50	646	151	1,183
Support forces ships	81	390	50	269	61	294	38	204	53	255	33	177	41	197	25	134
Amphibious warfare craft	64	735	185	33	48	551	139	24	42	482	122	21	32	367	93	16
TOTAL	473	4,784	814	3,732	355	3,611	612	2,807	312	3,192	537	2,475	238	2,444	408	1,868

SOURCES: The SCETT method was created by Michael MccGwire. See Michael MccGwire, "Building Blocks" (Brookings,1982). Ships' mission definitions and their tonnage from: Norman Polmar, *The Ships and Aircraft of the U.S. Fleet*, 14th ed. (Annapolis, Md.: Naval Institute Press, 1987); Polmar, *Guide to the Soviet Navy*, 3d ed. (Annapolis, Md.: Naval Institute Press, 1983); Defense Intelligence Agency, Directorate of Research, "DIA Unclassified Naval Order of Battle: Soviet Union and Communist Eastern Europe," DDB-1200-124-89 (Washington, June 1989); and *Jane's Fighting Ships 1988–89* (London: Jane's Publishing Co., 1989). For U.S. mission updating: *Department of Defense Annual Report, Fiscal Year 1990*, pp. 141–54, 232. Figures are rounded.

a. Training ships not included.

b. Surface combatant equivalent thousand tons.

markedly improved that it would probably no longer be considered an immediate policy problem. The military establishments would have a more accurate, elaborated understanding of corresponding military organizations, and the expanded flow of information supporting this improved mutual assessment would enable better coordination on the problems of weapons proliferation, terrorism, and communal violence that are expected to replace superpower confrontation as the most troublesome international security issues. Coordination on these issues is not guaranteed by policies of disclosure, but is not likely to occur without them. Presumably the United States and the Soviet Union in particular must mitigate the historical background of deep mistrust before they can expect to engage in sophisticated cooperation.

With all these results achieved, defense budgets required to maintain a much improved worldwide military equilibrium would be substantially lower in real terms. As summarized in table 3-2, the reduction in force levels alone would reduce the U.S. defense budget by $100 billion (fiscal 1990 dollars) a year even if current levels of force readiness and current rates of technical improvement are maintained. If, in addition, the rate of technical improvement were to be reduced by 50 percent and the rate of readiness by 25 percent, then the defense budget could be reduced by $150 billion a year. This promise of a better outcome for a reduced cost now appears strong enough to drive defense planners through the many difficult adjustments necessary to establish cooperative security.

Economic Engagement

The integration of the centrally planned economies into the industrial world is a policy problem very different in character from the transformation of security. Since economic opportunity is involved, the energies of the private sector can, in principle, be engaged, and government policy does not need to carry the burden of directly delivering the objective, as it does in the case of military security. In pursuing economic integration, moreover, the positive use of incentive can replace the negative use of threat as the dominant method of policy; this promises effects that are not only more constructive but also more visible. Economic activity can be measured, whereas the results of a prevented war remain, mercifully, a calculated abstraction, as are the effects of economic sanctions.

The connection between intention and result is nonetheless a more uncertain matter in economic policy, and effective design is therefore more difficult to determine. It is generally agreed on both sides that the

TABLE 3-2. Cost and Structure of U.S. Forces: Current Conditions and Future Alternatives

Forces	Fiscal 1989 force levels	Fiscal 1989 cost per year (billions of dollars)	Fiscal 1999 force levels	Fiscal 1999 cost per year (billions of dollars)[a]	Fiscal 1999 cost with reduced investment and replacement rates (billions of dollars)[b]	Fiscal 1999 cost with reduced investment, replacement and O&S (billions of dollars)[c]
Army						
Active divisions	18	49.8	10	26.9	23.2	18.3
Independent brigades	8	7.9	8	7.9	6.8	5.4
Reserve divisions	10	13.0	5	6.5	5.6	4.4
Fixed costs	. . .	7.2	. . .	7.2	7.2	7.2
Total (divisions)	31	77.9	18	48.5	42.8	35.3
Navy						
Surface combatants	373	53.5	271	39.3	31.4	25.5
SSNs	100	8.8	74	6.4	4.6	3.9
SSBNs	35	15.0	17	7.3	5.8	4.7
Other ships and craft	283	4.0	213	3.0	2.4	1.9
Marine divisions	4	8.8	4	8.7	7.2	5.8
Fixed costs	. . .	6.3	. . .	6.3	6.3	6.3
Total (ships and craft)	791	96.4	575	70.9	57.7	48.2

Air force

Tacair squadrons	78	31.3	38	16.8	13.8	11.1
Tacair support squadrons	44	10.8	20	4.7	3.9	3.1
Strategic bombers and support squadrons	37	18.7	10	4.1	3.3	2.7
ICBM squadrons	20	4.0	20	17.3	13.4	11.0
Aircraft and refueling squadrons	72	14.2	34	5.6	4.5	3.7
Reserve squadrons	149	13.3	73	6.4	4.8	4.0
Fixed costs	...	5.1	...	5.1	5.1	5.1
Total (squadrons)	400	97.4	195	60.0	48.8	40.7
Total						
Army, navy, air force	...	271.7	...	179.4	149.4	124.2
OSD/JCS/other	...	18.6	...	12.4	12.4	12.4
Defensewide	...	0.7	...	0.7	0.7	0.7
Atomic energy	...	8.1	...	8.1	8.1	8.1
Defense-related	...	0.6	...	0.6	0.6	0.6
Total defense budget	...	299.7	...	201.2	171.2	146.0

SOURCES: Cost estimates were derived using a method developed by William Kaufmann, as described in Barry M. Blechman with Ethan Gutmann, "A $100 Billion Understanding," in Simon Serfaty, ed., *The Future of U.S.–Soviet Relations: Twenty American Initiatives for a New Agenda* (Washington: Johns Hopkins Foreign Policy Institute, School of Advanced International Studies, 1989), pp. 364–74 and sources listed therein. The same method was used to derive total budget figures, but the estimates of current capital costs of weaponry may differ due to different program assumptions and updating and refining of the capital cost estimates of new systems. In addition to sources cited in figures 3-1 and 3-2 and table 3-1, these sources were used: Congressional Budget Office, "Total Quantities and Costs of Major Weapon Systems Procured, FY 1974–1987" (April 1986); U.S. Air Force, Deputy Comptroller, Cost and Economics, *The United States Air Force Summary, Fiscal Years 1988/1989 (Amended)* (May 15, 1988), table D-2; and U.S. Air Force, Directorate of Cost and Management Analysis, *Aircraft Cost Handbook* (December 1982). Figures are rounded.

a. Fiscal 1999 force levels correspond with the agreements presented in this chapter. The fiscal 1999 cost per year ($203.7 billion) assumes a stable rate of modernization and replacement (investment rate and operations and support both 100 percent of current rates).

b. Assumes an investment rate of 50 percent and operations and support rate of 100 percent of current rates.

c. Assumes an investment rate of 50 percent and operations and support rate of 75 percent of current rates.

productive incentives for individuals and enterprises that appear to underlie the superior performance of market systems must be introduced into the planned economies, but this involves a transformation that has never before been accomplished. The current designs for reform are theoretical projections largely unleavened by experience.

The explicit intention to forge reliable connections to the industrial economies is well advanced in the Soviet Union, Eastern Europe, and China for reasons that appear to guarantee its endurance. It reflects a realization that isolation from the increasingly integrated global economy guarantees inferior performance. This fact probably will prevent any full resurgence of traditional socialist ideology or the extreme economic autarky that emerged from it. However extensively and significantly the details may vary, all the socialist countries can be expected to make access to the world economy a major priority.

Within the industrial democracies, a corresponding intention has been articulated to support the internal reform and international emergence of the socialist states.[6] Since this commitment is less consequential for the industrial countries in economic terms, its practical meaning is more of a question. Strong initiative is unlikely, particularly in the United States, but fundamental interests do appear powerful enough to sustain a constructive response. It is one thing to reinforce an economic isolation the socialist states were imposing on themselves and quite another to resist their efforts to integrate. The overriding concern for the prevention of war, the positive interest in common prosperity, and the lure of eventual commercial benefit are sufficient to make economic engagement a prevailing theme of Western policy in response to the socialist states' initiative. As such, it is a natural supplement to the principle of cooperative security.

The Problem of Design

There are a number of recognized principles that are widely presumed to be necessary conditions for good economic performance and therefore the natural focus of any economic reform effort. State subsidies for consumer commodities and industrial products should be minimized to permit production to match buyers' preferences. Wage increases should be proportional to productivity gains to prevent inflation so that workers

6. Excerpts from Bush-Gorbachev news conference following the Malta Summit, *Washington Post*, December 4, 1989, p. 22.

TABLE 3-3. Economic Growth and Consumer Welfare in Eastern
Europe, OECD, and United States, End of 1988

Country	Average purchasing power (percent of U.S. purchasing power)	Net foreign debt per person (U.S. dollars)	Average GNP growth 1980–88 (percent)
Romania	21	50	0.0
Poland	28	930	0.7
Soviet Union	28	120	1.9
Bulgaria	29	670	1.2
Hungary	33	1,500	1.0
Czechoslovakia	39	320	1.3
East Germany	47	460	1.8
OECD	74	a	2.9
United States	100	a	3.1

SOURCES: "Plan Econ Report: Developments in the Economies of the Soviet Union and Eastern Europe," vol. 5 (Washington: Plan Econ, November 3, 1989), pp. 7, 55; and CIA, Directorate of Intelligence, *Handbook of Economic Statistics, 1989*, CPAS 89-10002 (September 1989), pp. 30, 33.
a. Comparable figures not available.

are encouraged to move to occupations in which they are most productive. Capital should be invested in assets yielding the largest net returns. To promote managerial efficiency, decisions about production, pricing, and employment should be made by producers who reap the benefits of wise decisions and bear the consequences of mistakes. National markets should be open to all producers to capture the discipline of competition. No country fully honors these principles, but the socialist states violate them massively. Out of conviction that a planned economy would operate more efficiently and equitably than a market economy, they centralized pricing, production, investment, and employment decisions, but are now admitting they were wrong. Economic growth and consumer welfare in the socialist states have lagged behind world standards (table 3-3). No gains in equity could compensate for this disparity. In order to connect to the international flows of technology and investment and to benefit from the momentum of product markets they cannot independently match, the socialist economies are forced to align with standard economic principles. Failure to do so dictates increasing disparity in basic economic performance and the risk of social convulsions.

The problem, of course, is that internal adjustment is not simply a matter of economic design. State bureaucracies developed to formulate and execute basic economic decisions must divest power. Enterprises accustomed to externally arranged supply and marketing relationships must absorb that responsibility themselves and develop practical alternatives that give them the flexibility demanded by standard economic principles. Employees must accept the risk of low wages or being fired for poor performance in exchange for a chance at higher pay and greater opportunity.

Such adjustments have sweeping political implications, and it is far from clear that they can be accomplished by popular consent. Although the decline of state authority is generally welcomed, the economic austerity inevitably associated with such a massive adjustment is not. Because subsidies for food, housing, transportation, and education will come down long before the gain in economic efficiency will be realized, standards of living for many people will fall for an extended period. Such austerity was accepted and successfully overcome by the populations of Germany and Japan in the wake of World War II, but the shock of the war, the imposing power of occupying armies, the fact that national identity was not a question, and prior experience with standard economic principles all contributed significantly to the process. The socialist economies have few if any of these circumstances to assist them and probably cannot prevent the process of economic adjustment from having wrenching political and social implications. The adjustment is fundamentally necessary and powerfully driven, but inherently dangerous.

Differing Reform Strategies

Different patterns in handling these inherent problems are rapidly emerging in the socialist countries, reflecting significant differences in their circumstances. China successfully initiated its reform effort in the agricultural sector, which included at the time more than 80 percent of its labor force. Chinese agriculture was largely based on relatively small plots using labor-intensive methods in densely populated areas. A simple revision of rules, not requiring any major reorganization of land holdings or infrastructive investment, gave Chinese peasants effective control over the land they had been working and the ability to market their products in nearby urban areas. The incentive of direct control produced an immediate productive surge throughout the economy, thereby validating the reform program with palpable benefits. In dealing with the industrial economy, however, the Chinese have been notably less successful, producing inflationary pressures, state budget deficits, and ultimately popular political demands that the leadership was not prepared to accommodate.[7] Cycles of economic retrenchment and political repression culminating in the June 1989 civil violence have damaged their carefully developed pioneering strategy of outward integration and have left Chinese policies in a presumably unstable state of considerable tension.

Poland, by contrast, operating from an extremely weak economic base, has depended upon political reform. Using the assets of strong national identity and the legitimizing history of the Solidarity movement, Poland has formed a broad coalition government and is attempting to marshal national consensus behind a rapid shift to standard economic principles. With a per capita GNP roughly one-third that of the United States, an average annual growth over the 1980s of less than 1 percent, an average annual inflation over the same period of more than 30 percent, and a large external debt ($40 billion), the case for drastic action is strong enough to inspire consensus, but the immediate consequences are another matter.[8] It is conceded that the standard of living is likely to decline from its already depressed level by 20 percent over two years before the productive incentives of the reform plan can be expected to produce positive growth. That process will be a severe test of Polish political cohesion and will be accompanied by truly urgent appeals for international assistance. Since Poland has very little immediate comparative advantage to offer, it will depend heavily on international political responsiveness and thus will be a test case for the policy of economic engagement.

East Germany represents yet another situation. Its economic performance has been the best of the centrally planned economies, producing a per capita national product that is roughly twice that of Poland's, and is statistically comparable with the European Economic Community average.[9] Average annual growth over the 1980s was 1.9 percent, roughly 1 percent below EEC growth levels, but consumer price inflation was

---

7. Ed A. Hewett, "Economic Reform in the USSR, Eastern Europe, and China: The Politics of Economics," *American Economic Review,* vol. 79 (May 1989, *Papers and Proceedings, 1988*), pp. 16–20; and Robert F. Dernberger, "Reforms in China: Implications for US Policy," ibid., pp. 21–25.

8. CIA, Directorate of Intelligence, *Handbook of Economic Statistics, 1989,* CPAS 89-10002 (September 1989), pp. 24, 25, 33.

9. The CIA *Handbook of Economic Statistics, 1989* measures East Germany per capita GNP at 63.1 percent of the (world-leading) U.S. level and the average for the EEC member countries at 63.3 percent of the U.S. level. Private analysts have discounted the figures for East Germany and the other centrally planned economies to account for stark differences in the qualities and availability of consumer goods. See "Plan Econ Report: Developments in the Economies of the Soviet Union and Eastern Europe," vol. 5 (Washington: Plan Econ, November 3, 1989), table 3.

1.5 percent a year, compared with 5.9 percent for the EEC.[10] As revealed in the dramatic collapse of the political system in late 1989, however, this economic performance did not confer political legitimacy and was not even considered favorable against the observably higher standard in West Germany. Denied its coercive apparatus, the East German state was unable to establish a basis for authority, and rapid integration into West Germany became the universally anticipated result.

From its explosive origins in October 1989, the East German reform process was driven by the spontaneous engagement with West Germany, uniquely enabled by a common language and culture and the special access built into the West German legal system. This spontaneous process was manifested in a continuing westward emigration of more than 2,000 people a day, in the eastward insinuation of the West Germany currency, and in large-scale interaction among industrial and political professionals. This process emerged as the dominant East German reform strategy, and it imposed itself on the policies of both German governments. Beyond that, it became a driving mechanism for the international process of economic engagement. With a well-trained labor force and decent industrial capability, East Germany provided the strongest national magnet for private-sector investment among the centrally planned systems, and with political or bureaucratic resistance collapsing very rapidly, the international entrepreneurial response has been particularly strong.

But the Soviet Union presents, of course, the largest and most demanding case. With a GNP of $2.5 trillion, the Soviet economy is the second largest in the world, half the size of the U.S. economy in absolute terms and about 45 percent in per capita terms.[11] It has supported a military establishment of comparable size and technical scope. It has sustained the industrial and agricultural capacity necessary to operate a large society substantially independent of the rest of the world, producing in combination with its East European economic partners just over 20 percent of the total world product. Throughout the 1960s and 1970s, average annual growth of the Soviet economy closely matched the Organization for Economic Cooperation and Development average, with

10. Again the statistical measurements should be discounted for the different state of consumer markets. The statistics reflect the fact that basic commodities—food, housing, transportation, education—have all been subsidized in East Germany and prices held low and stable by that means. According to informal reports from East German sources, the percentage of the state budget devoted to these subsidies has doubled from roughly 10 percent to 20 percent over the 1980s.

11. CIA, *Handbook of Economic Statistics, 1989*, pp. 12–13, 24–25.

lower rates of inflation and much lower net external debt. During the 1980s, however, the average annual Soviet growth rate (1.9 percent) fell one-third below even the rather sluggish world standards (2.9 percent), and the segment that was weakest in the Soviet economy—consumer goods and services—became for the world as a whole the principal engine for technical development.

In the global economy, consumer products, commercial organization, and basic industrial processes have been revolutionized even more rapidly than military power, and civilian markets rather than military programs have come to provide the dominant impulse for the underlying technical developments. Since the Soviets invested heavily in monitoring Western technical developments, they presumably became aware of this fundamental shift as it was happening. They explicitly recognized the implication that their own economy was not only dangerously isolated from these developments, but was also internally misallocated, that is, disproportionately invested in military programs.

In terms of strategic conception and political initiative, their response to this recognition has been forceful and bold, providing the strongest impetus for reform among the socialist states and for corresponding changes in global policy. *Glasnost* and *perestroika* have become household terms sufficiently embodied in changes in Soviet policy and procedure that even the most committed skeptics have to take them seriously. Political dialogue has been dramatically opened and direct political participation substantially extended. Both have been used to diminish the detailed authoritative control of the state bureaucracies and the Communist party apparatus, but effective political power nonetheless remains centralized in the hands of a leadership that appears to be energetic, visionary, decisive, and flexible—not a textbook model of democracy, but potentially an effective arrangement for handling the massive economic adjustment required.

The Soviet leadership's political decisions have already produced decisive, almost certainly irreversible, effects in Eastern Europe. Although the spontaneous popular movements that have so rapidly altered the East European governments could not and would not have been designed by Russian politicians, the disengagement of Soviet power that allowed these movements to succeed certainly was. That disengagement was motivated by economic reasons as well as by the new security calculus. The unwelcome exercise of political control over the East European governments was not accomplished by military means alone. As a more positive inducement, the Soviet Union has subsidized the East European economies at the rate of $10 billion to $20 billion a year by providing price advantages in their trade with these economies.[12] These subsidies will probably be rapidly reduced and eventually terminated as Soviet political control is withdrawn, not only reducing income for the East European countries but also removing protected markets for manufactured goods that do not meet international quality standards. Both effects will drive the East European economies into international markets and thereby energize the process of economic engagement.

In terms of the internal substance of reform, however—the business of implementing standard economic principles—the Soviet Union has evolved into an ambiguous and potentially dangerous intermediate state. Its leaders have weakened the planning apparatus but still rely upon it for macroeconomic control and product allocation. Particularly in the critical mediating service of transportation, bottlenecks once actively circumvented by lower party officials have begun to accumulate. The Soviets have allowed entrepreneurs to operate in service and commodity markets—particularly for food—alongside the standard state-subsidized arrangement. This has produced sharp disparities in prices, based more on convenience of access than product quality, that in effect release some of the underlying inflation long suppressed by product rationing. Moreover, it has induced hoarding of primary commodities and a lengthening of the queues for those sold at subsidized prices, with a resulting sense of shortages and inequity that has stirred popular resentment. Soviet planners have also attempted to induce foreign investment but have not yet revised property rights or the currency exchange rate system sufficiently to make it profitable. The Soviet economy therefore remains substantially isolated. And, of course, as a presumably unintended consequence, the more open political process has released divisive nationalist sentiments that have little to do with economic reform and threaten internal political cohesion.

Because of its size, its inherent importance, and the strength of its political initiative, the Soviet Union is the inevitable center of the reform processes in the socialist economies. The outcome within the Soviet Union will ultimately determine the success or failure of economic engagement.

12. Michael Marrese and Jan Vanous, *Soviet Subsidization of Trade with Eastern Europe: A Soviet Perspective*, Research Series 52 (University of California at Berkeley, Institute of International Studies, 1983).

U.S. Reaction

On the whole, the current state of the socialist economies' reform efforts is still presenting significant barriers to international investment. These economies are not producing goods of sufficient quality or price advantage to support a large volume of international trade. They are only beginning to revise their laws and regulations enough to attract direct foreign investment. The powerful productive mechanisms of the international economy are not yet available to drive the process of economic engagement, and government policy has yet to set the conditions. East Germany has emerged, however, as a major exception where spontaneous interactions appear capable of setting the terms and the timing for the development of policy. German unification has such significant political, military, and economic consequences that it creates a strong immediate demand for the elaboration of policy on economic engagement that otherwise might take considerably more time.

Beneath the recent declarations of constructive intent, there is an institutionalized structure of law and accrued policy in the United States designed to impose economic isolation on the Soviet Union and its allies, in part to deny technical and economic support for their military establishments and in part to express opposition to objectionable policies such as human rights violations and interference in other countries. The Trade Agreement Extension Act of 1951 imposed prohibitively high tariffs on all trade from all communist countries, setting isolation as the basic presumption. An attempt was made to reverse that presumption by the U.S.-Soviet Trade Agreement of 1972 during the initial period of détente, but the implementing legislation in the United States specifically made tariff concessions contingent upon changes in Soviet emigration practices, a requirement to which the Soviets originally took sharp exception as a violation of the agreement.[13] Despite the extensive liberalization of Soviet emigration in recent years, the United States has not yet issued the necessary waiver or certification of compliance, and general tariff barriers on Soviet imports remain.

In addition, U.S. exports are controlled by a variety of mechanisms, most notably the Export Administration Act and an informally organized international control arrangement in cooperation with U.S. allies that

---

13. Barry E. Carter, *International Economic Sanctions: Improving the Haphazard U.S. Legal Regime* (Cambridge University Press, 1988), p. 118ff.

restricts trade in specified products and technologies deemed to have military value (COCOM).[14] Despite the increasing commercialization of many of the technologies listed under these restrictions and despite their increasing availability in international markets, the United States conducted an intense effort throughout the 1980s to tighten these restrictions in response to extensive Soviet efforts to monitor and acquire Western technology. The United States also supplemented these national security restrictions with broader export controls, protesting the Soviet invasion of Afghanistan, and has generally resisted tentative Soviet efforts to gain standing in the major international economic institutions, the World Bank and the General Agreement on Tariffs and Trade.

Under the rationale of "differentiation," the United States has made exceptions to this basic pattern of economic restriction for other socialist countries that were judged to have adopted policies independent of Moscow. Poland was granted most favored nation (MFN) tariff concessions in 1960, although denied them from 1982 to 1987 in reaction to the suppression of the Solidarity movement.[15] Romania, Hungary, and China were given waivers from the emigration condition and were granted MFN status in the late 1970s. As U.S.-China relations progressed in the 1980s, special rules were worked out to enable the export to China of some dual-purpose and direct military technology.

By segregating the discordant cases, these specific sequential exceptions preserved the basic machinery of trade restriction and maintained economic sanctions as the dominant element of U.S. policy toward the socialist economies throughout the 1980s. The simultaneous political revolutions throughout Eastern Europe, however, particularly the spontaneous interaction developing between East and West Germany, have given a shock to the export control arrangements that could collapse the entire process. U.S. zeal in the 1980s carried export restrictions to impractical lengths, imposing controls on many items, particularly in the computer and telecommunications industries, where extensive international markets have developed and internationally integrated firms are strenuously competing for strategic positions. Although the United States has been able to preserve nominal compliance in the international coordinating process, significant disparities in national implementation have emerged, creating strong suspicions that the export controls cannot deny access to military technology but are being manipulated to serve

14. Carter, *International Economic Sanctions*, p. 65ff.
15. Carter, *International Economic Sanctions*, pp. 118, 121.

national comparative advantage in commercial markets. It is doubtful that the consensus on which international coordination depends can survive the pressures that the emergence of Eastern Europe will impose upon it. Since existing U.S. legislation prohibits unilateral export controls except in a declared international emergency, the failure of international consensus would weaken the legal authority of U.S. export regulations.[16]

However, the natural corrosion of trade restrictions and of other forms of sanctions does not constitute a constructive policy of economic engagement, and the content of such a policy is yet to be determined. Moreover, since the history of U.S. policy has been so systematically negative, there is very little conceptual tradition or political consensus on which to build any significant initiative. It seems most likely, therefore, that a constructive U.S. economic policy will evolve in reaction to a series of questions posed by the assertive efforts of the socialist states to enter the world economy.

Should any special trade restrictions be directed against the Soviet Union? Although that question still implies a negative economic policy, it is nonetheless important in that it sets limiting conditions for a constructive response. Obviously there are items relating to the manufacture of modern weapons, for example, where any international trade is inappropriate except under carefully controlled conditions, but control of such items is not specifically directed against any particular country. If fully implemented, the principles of cooperative security would remove the presumption that the Soviet Union is a potential enemy and would establish reasonably extensive collaboration in regulating military power. The commensurate economic principle would presumably grant the Soviet Union unqualified status as an economic partner and eliminate any special trade restrictions.

Should the United States make capital investments in the process of economic engagement? It is reasonably clear that in important instances, most notably that of the Soviet Union, the internal reform process is not sufficiently developed to engage the international capital markets or to enable significant direct investments. Even if external trade barriers are removed, internal regulation is rapidly diminished, and currency convertibility is established to allow repatriation of profits, the personnel training and the development of supply and marketing relationships necessary for successful business ventures will take time and entail

16. Export Administration Amendments Act of 1985 (99 Stat. 132); and International Emergency Powers Act of 1977 (91 Stat. 1626–28).

substantial risk. Initial capital from public sources will be required to absorb some of the risk and to signal the seriousness and likely endurance of a constructive economic policy. Against the background of cold war history, international investors are likely to require reassurance that their ventures will not be declared treasonous at some point in their development and will not be used to exercise political sanctions.

At the end of 1989, EEC members formed plans to institute a European Bank for Reconstruction and Development (EBRD) to issue development loans to the East European countries, to organize technical assistance in specifying the requirements of private-sector development, and in general to act as a catalyst for international capital flows—much as the International Monetary Fund does for developing countries. In January 1990 a capital allocation of $12 billion was tentatively projected, an amount conceded to be short of the ultimate requirements but nonetheless a significant start.[17] With the Soviet Union and East European governments as well as the United States, Japan, and other non-EEC industrial countries holding shares, the EBRD will provide an institutionalization of investment in economic engagement, supplementing the arrangements already worked out for China through the IMF.

Soviet eligibility for loans has been the central issue for the EBRD, reflecting the fact that investment in the Soviet Union is the test condition for an overall policy of engagement. With the Soviet Union excluded, the traditional U.S. policy of differentiation could be said to reign in triumph, virtually all other countries having been detached from the Soviet economic orbit, at least in aspiration. With the Soviet Union included, differentiation would be replaced by the principle of integration.

With an unusually low net external per capita debt, the Soviet Union currently has more access to international capital than it appears disposed to use. Moreover, the Soviet economy still lacks the institutional means for the accumulation and productive investment of domestic savings. Under these conditions, international public investment is likely to be made contingent on completed reforms, which may minimize investment for an indefinite period of time. A third policy question therefore arises: should investment in the Soviet Union be assertively encouraged as a means of accelerating internal reform?

There are some objectives that might motivate an assertive policy—for example, the management of global environmental and energy

17. Vlad Sobell, "The Founding of a European Bank for Reconstruction and Development," *RFE/RL Daily Report*, Munich, January 18, 1990.

balances. The Soviet Union has been extremely inefficient in both the extraction and use of its relatively abundant internal energy supplies and extremely neglectful of the environmental pollution generated. If global environmental balances become a driving concern, the outside industrial world may have sufficient reason to hasten improvements beyond what the Soviets by themselves are likely to manage. The possibility of political disintegration within the Soviet Union might also be considered serious enough to motivate more assertive investment. Under the prevailing ideology of the cold war, it was assumed that such an event would be a desirable victory for the United States and for Western political values, but its imminent prospect would now be likely to inspire other thoughts. If the principles of cooperative security are taken seriously, and if the violence that might accompany the breakup of the Soviet Union is also taken seriously, then Soviet political stability might become an urgent objective. In that case, international investment in the Soviet transportation and telecommunications infrastructure would take priority.

Policy discussion within the United States is currently well short of resolving these questions and does not as yet even display any major interest in resolving them. Over the course of the coming decade, however, the pressure of events appears likely to force some greater resolution and at least induce a fundamental shift from negative to positive in the basic U.S. economic posture toward what was once known as the Communist bloc.

International Equity

Whatever their ultimate fate, whatever degree of success or frustration they eventually achieve, the emerging ideas of cooperative security and economic engagement signal enduring changes in the character of international politics. The threat of military power no longer has either the intimidating or galvanizing effects that inspired the confrontational politics of the cold war period. The effective use of force is largely confined to the defense of legitimate political jurisdictions and of inherent interests so deeply and obviously established that they are unlikely to be challenged. There are some important potential exceptions, particularly in the Middle East and in Southeast Asia, but the perceived strategic significance of these volatile regional situations clearly has diminished. At the same time, as widely noted, economic activity has been internationalized, sharply diminishing any one country's inherent leverage and authority. The United States is and will indefinitely remain the largest single national economy, but it has declined in size relative to the world as a whole. Even more significant, the driving elements of economic activity—capital markets, technical innovation, corporate organization, and trends in consumer demand—have crossed national boundaries so extensively that they exceed governments' control. Power is more diffuse and the traditional unilateral instruments of influence are much less effective. The circumstances that are forcing changes in the substance of U.S. policy also affect its methods.

The management of technically advanced military operations and the oversight of economic activity will require more sophisticated forms of international coordination, but the traditional methods of achieving coordination cannot be relied upon. The standard bargaining dynamics— in which national governments have traditionally attempted to coerce agreement by negative leverage or to induce it by positive incentive— produced useful but distinctly limited results even when national power was much more concentrated. That process is not likely to be the primary mechanism of coordination under the emerging new order. It is just as unlikely, however, that the basic instruments of national government can be developed on an international basis as fast as economic engagement and cooperative security will apparently require. Even in Western Europe, where the most advanced experiments in international government are taking place, national identity remains quite decisively the dominant basis for political legitimacy. In working out robust processes of political competition, conducting legitimizing elections, and establishing policy through freely formed consensus, the cohesion produced by national identity appears to be vital, as strongly suggested by the unfolding events in Eastern Europe and the Soviet Union. Therefore some innovation is needed in the methods of foreign policy that fall between the emanation of national power and the formation of international government.

Under these conditions, standards of equity, principles of law, and ideas of fundamental human rights are likely to acquire much greater practical significance as sovereign states struggle to achieve more sophisticated coordination of policy. The results that can be achieved by consensual coordination will almost certainly have to be derived from principles that can inspire support across differing national perspectives without a formally organized vote. Like axioms in mathematics, such principles offer points of departure that can plausibly stand on their own. Like articles of a constitution, they establish agreed rules useful in regulating national policies.

Selection among the many such rules that can claim significant standing across diverse cultural traditions is not an easy matter. One can surmise, however, that the ubiquitous pressure for access to the international economy and the need for coordination in managing it might encourage particularly relevant rules to emerge. These principles are likely to preoccupy U.S. foreign policy and ultimately to form the basis for exercising influence.

Principles of Inclusion

A rapid and successful development of cooperative security and economic engagement would be quite threatening to countries not involved in the traditional alliances unless it were accompanied by principles of inclusion allowing any country to qualify. An arrangement centered exclusively in central Europe but involving, by practical necessity, the United States and Japan would include such a large proportion of the world's economic and military capability that everyone not included would have legitimate cause for concern. An exclusive arrangement of this sort that is actively hostile to the rest of the world is quite unlikely, but indifference is imaginable and also quite worrisome. Disruptive actions have been motivated in the past by fears less likely than these. Fear of exclusion from a dominant global coalition is actually a very promising means of disciplining states whose politics are considered repugnant, but even that requires a constructive alternative to be specified, that is, a basis for inclusion that is broadly comprehensive and acceptable.

Stating clear and consistent standards for the international community is a difficult problem for the United States. There are a few expressions of basic values that command virtually universal support—"freedom," "democracy," "self-determination," "human rights"—but their operative meaning is subject to considerable ambiguity and dispute. There is a natural American skepticism about the abstractions involved, and the political system is designed to make specific practical decisions rather than authoritative declarations. Moreover, the specific decisions made in reaction to circumstances and domestic debate are not perfectly consistent.

Nonetheless, in a series of treaties, legal actions, and more informal coordinating arrangements, the United States has established a network of international relationships that embody its standards. Formal security treaties have been signed with 28 nations, all of which would presumably be encompassed in cooperative security arrangements. Principles of trade are embodied in the General Agreement on Tariffs and Trade with 96 participating states and principles of economic management in the International Monetary Fund with 151 members and in the OECD with 25 members. Special support is extended to 107 recipients of economic and military aid. Coordination of military planning has been routinely conducted within the 16-member NATO alliance, and for particularly significant matters there is an informal group within NATO involving the United States, the United Kingdom, France, and Germany. For international financial coordination Japan is added to this group to form the G5, Italy and Canada to create the G7, and Belgium, the Netherlands, and Sweden to create the G10, all of which are regularly used. These inner circles are implicitly defined in terms of inherent interest, fundamental harmony of policy, and compatibility of political systems.

The United States has also defined standards for the international community in negative terms by imposing export controls for political reasons on 17 countries other than those of the opposing Warsaw Treaty Organization. For some the rationale has been their perceived involvement in terrorist activities (Cuba, Iran, Libya, Syria, and Yemen); for others, human rights violations (Afghanistan, Albania, Laos, Mongolia, Namibia, and South Africa); and for a few, reasons that amount to a fundamental objection to the entire form of government (Cambodia, Cuba, Nicaragua, North Korea, and Vietnam).[18]

This entire network of relationships and the criteria that underlie it have been established in the context of alliance confrontation with the centrally planned economies and economic isolation from them and will have to be significantly revised as a new international order emerges. Conflict among the underlying criteria will create difficulties for the process of revision. These will be most sharply and most significantly posed in the case of the Soviet Union.

If inherent interests in the substance of security and economic policy are the driving consideration, then the Soviet Union would have to enter the inner circles of coordination. That development would radically alter the pattern of international politics and would offer substantially increased potential for controlling terrorism and other forms of international civil violence. It would require much greater presumption of a harmony of purpose, however, and even under optimistic projections of Soviet political reforms would demand much greater tolerance of differences between political systems than the United States has been willing

18. Industry Coalition on Technology Transfer, "Presentation for the National Academy of Sciences and Engineering Panel on Export Controls" (Washington, January 18, 1990).

to grant. Comparably radical adjustments were made for China in the course of normalization, but they were motivated by a common sense of Soviet threat. In the wake of the Tiananmen Square incident, moreover, the adjustments are also being reconsidered from the perspective of human rights and may not stand as a precedent.

The case of Japan is only slightly less central. Although the United States has clearly established with Japan the political mechanisms and the habit of close coordination, the scope of concern has been strictly limited and the United States has monopolized the initiative. Expanding the scope of coordination and sharing the initiative with Japan would also alter the pattern of world politics and potentially add to the power of policy coordination. Conversely, the possibility of confrontation with Japan over issues of economic competition could seriously disrupt the existing methods of coordination.

As a practical matter, relationships with the Soviet Union and Japan, both of which seem destined to evolve constructively or otherwise, will have profound effects on the influence the United States can be expected to exercise on international standards. Some flexibility in defining standards within the context of these relationships would be prudent in order to increase their effect on the world as a whole. It will nonetheless be difficult either to focus American political dialogue on such a calculus or to derive an agreed conclusion from a well-focused debate. Since there is no guarantee that events will cooperate in focusing attention, the political basis for coordination is one of the major uncertainties affecting prospects for a new international order.

Balance of Investment

To the extent that the process of economic engagement takes hold, it will concentrate international economic investment on Eastern Europe and at least potentially on the Soviet Union, with some portion inevitably diverted from other parts of the world. That prospect is a distinct threat to struggling economies in Latin America and Africa that are laboring with their own economic reform efforts against a background of unmanageable debt and the international disillusionment that accompanies such a situation.

Throughout 1989, third world debt instruments were trading at average prices 65 percent below their nominal values, an indication of the degree of capital market skepticism these countries were encountering. Nonetheless, under an agreement that emerged after nine months of negotiations with Mexico—the leading case in the debt relief effort U.S. Treasury Secretary Nicholas Brady launched in March 1989—the net reduction of Mexico's public debt in terms of discounted present value was only about 25 percent of its nominal value, and the net cash flow reduction of $1 billion in annual debt servicing was only a 10 percent reduction from the previous $9.6 billion in interest payments.[19] Because of the relatively small amount of money available for guarantees, Mexico was not able to capture a nominal discount closer to the 60 percent rate in the secondary market for Mexican debt. The result of the negotiation provided relatively little *direct* benefit for the effort expended. It also sent a strong signal to other debtors that the United States and other creditor governments are not yet prepared to offer the amount of support required to eliminate the debt overhang.

It is doubtful that this degree of economic stringency could be imposed on the developing countries at the same time that investment is encouraged in Eastern Europe without inciting highly divisive political reactions. The sense of equity necessary to organize and sustain a cooperative international order presumably would not tolerate gross disparities in standards or radical shifts in priority that effectively abandoned major population concentrations. Nor are the magnitudes of debt so overwhelming that they justify such a result. At current secondary market discount rates, the entire current third world debt could be guaranteed with long-term bond issues at a nonrecurring cost of slightly more than $100 billion. The release of defense investment resources associated with a shift to cooperative security arrangements would compensate for that cost within a few years, and that fact is bound to be noticed.

In advancing the Brady plan for debt relief and in providing active political sponsorship for the negotiations with Mexico, the United States has documented a general sensitivity to the problem of third world debt. Through aid programs and sponsorship of the World Bank, it has demonstrated some concern for the broader issues of international equity. However, it has steadfastly rejected the major action that would convey seriousness of purpose—an increase in national savings. As widely noted, in the course of the 1980s net national savings declined in the United States by 6 percent of GNP, an effect produced by a large increase in the government's fiscal deficit and a comparable decline in private savings. In the face of this savings decline, the United States used a large

19. Nora Lustig, "Agreement Signed by Mexico and its Commercial Banks," Testimony before the Subcommittee on International Development, Finance, Trade and Monetary Policy of the House Committee on Banking, Finance and Urban Affairs, February 7, 1990.

inflow of foreign capital to prevent the otherwise radical drop in investment that would have been imposed. This produced a $750 billion debt accumulation by the end of the decade.[20] That drain on international capital is far greater than anything Eastern Europe and the Soviet Union are likely to command. It could be reduced if the United States took steps either to raise taxes or to cut government expenditures, steps that are not only quite feasible but economically prudent. That also is bound to be noticed.

The fact that the United States has so far refused to undergo an internal fiscal adjustment, for familiar domestic political reasons, seriously undermines its ability to advance international equity standards as the basis for a new international order. Without such a step it has neither the capital nor the political credibility nor the moral authority required. Fiscal adjustment is the price of international leadership—another choice not yet fully clarified in American political discussion.

Open Trading

There is some chance that the global implications of cooperative security and economic engagement might be derailed by confrontations among major U.S. allies over commercial trade practices. Intense political resentment of protective foreign trade practices and a strong instinct for organized retaliation have emerged from a number of underlying economic conditions. These include the extensive penetration of the U.S. market, the development of a strong comparative advantage in many foreign firms (particularly Japanese) in several advanced industries, the rapid growth in direct foreign investment inexorably driven by the decline in U.S. national savings and the resulting influx of foreign capital, and the large trade deficits sustained throughout the 1980s.

The official policy response has been reasonably effective as far as the traditional mechanisms of trade policy are concerned. A series of formal negotiations and more informal political discussions with the Japanese government and with members of the EEC and GATT have made reasonably steady progress in reducing tariffs and quotas. As the EEC has developed the many directives associated with its attempt to remove all internal market barriers by 1992, the United States and other outside countries have been able to deflect the options that would be most

20. Ralph C. Bryant and Gerald Holtham, "The U.S. External Deficit: Diagnosis, Prognosis, and Cure," in Ralph C. Bryant, Gerald Holtham, and Peter Hooper, eds., *External Deficits and the Dollar: The Pit and the Pendulum* (Brookings, 1988), p. 69.

discriminatory against outside trade. Moreover, the relative value of the dollar has declined from the high levels in the early 1980s that were almost entirely responsible for a surge in the U.S. trade deficit.

It is increasingly apparent, however, that these traditional mechanisms do not provide a complete set of measures to ensure effectively open international markets and to enable an expansion of U.S. exports—the only graceful means of bringing the U.S. economy into more stable alignment with the rest of the world. The principle of open markets—clearly a necessary complement and indeed a precondition for the process of economic engagement—needs more assertive support than simply the gradual reduction of traditional barriers. That is particularly true since the idea of managed trade—basically the political negotiation of market shares by threatening retaliatory trade restrictions—has become an alternative policy with some considerable political support. That idea discounts the facts of reduced national leverage that have encouraged the promotion of international equity standards. It nonetheless has strong emotional and therefore political appeal, in part, one can surmise, because it resonates with the familiar combative politics of the cold war period.

The principles of open trade are likely to become increasingly important and demanding as market conditions evolve, and there might be some unusually strong interactions with the process of economic engagement. The underlying process of international integration is being powerfully driven by advances in the technology of processing and transmitting information that are likely to become a prominent focus of policy. Over the past two decades, the cost of information-processing capacity has been reduced at a rate of 25 percent a year. That trend will apparently continue for at least another decade, continuing what is by far the most radical sustained decline in the cost of a fundamental economic commodity in economic history.[21] Similarly radical progress is being made in the cost of transmitting information, and this combination of developments will dramatically affect patterns of economic activity on an international scale.

The potential resonance with the process of economic engagement is strong because of the critical role that telecommunications presumably will play in this overall development. Telecommunications is a particularly underdeveloped area of the centrally planned economies, and the shift

21. Kenneth Flamm and Thomas L. McNaugher, "Rationalizing Technology Investments," in John D. Steinbruner, ed., *Restructuring American Foreign Policy* (Brookings, 1989), p. 119.

in policy opens up perhaps the strongest potential for international investment. Because initial position has powerful implications in an industry of this sort, which has many of the classic features of a national monopoly, and because the industry also forges a strong link between economic and military capability, critical issues for emerging international relationships are likely to be posed well before policymakers are prepared for them.

The design and management of an open trading system is probably an imperative for the United States of much greater consequence than has yet been appreciated. Trade policy will be a central element of the impending adjustment of U.S. foreign policy.

The State of Adjustment

The changes in U.S. foreign policy being compelled by fundamental economic and military trends, radical changes in policy among former adversaries, and spontaneous reactions throughout the world are largely happy ones. The principles of democracy, personal expression, and market economic operations that the United States has long espoused are sweeping the world and are offering, in principle, much better forms of international organization. The pace and scope of change have clearly exceeded the reach of prevailing American opinion, however, invalidating or transcending basic features of the post–World War II consensus long before most Americans are prepared to replace them.

Skepticism and caution remain the dominant themes of the politically popular Bush administration. The administration has conceded substantial initiative to the Soviet Union and to the spontaneous process of German unification, but has prepared constructive responses within the framework of traditional policies. It has offered increased reductions of conventional forces in Europe to the minimum level believed necessary to preserve NATO's military infrastructure. It has agreed to a schedule for discussing German unification in the postwar four-power forum and has advanced a proposed outcome that is also designed to preserve the traditional alliance organization. Completion of the long-negotiated strategic weapons reduction agreement is now considered imminent, reversing considerable initial reluctance. That agreement is also designed to preserve all strategic weapons modernization programs, and the reductions will not significantly affect any of the underlying strategic missions. The defense budget is projected to undergo marginal real reductions—slightly less than the trend of reductions since 1986—but virtually all major weapons programs are to be continued. Most favored nation status for the Soviet Union is anticipated in connection with the summit scheduled for June, the export control list is being liberalized for Eastern Europe, and some $20 billion in new international financial commitments is being projected for Eastern Europe; but these actions are not yet cast in a context of policy that would embody the idea of economic engagement.

There has not yet been any major political objection in the United States to this pattern of polite caution; it is always difficult to quarrel with what is perceived as prudence. There is an inherent possibility, however, that excessive caution in circumstances of rapid change might be the greater danger, particularly given the rapidly evolving integration of East and West Germany. That process does force decisions about the rules for handling military power in central Europe, and neither of the initially suggested formulas seem likely to survive truly serious reflection on that question.

The U.S. position is that a unified Germany must remain within NATO's diminished but essentially intact military organization. This strongly implies that the East German army would switch sides as a practical matter—an outcome bound to be considered grossly irresponsible within the Soviet Union. It is one thing for the Soviet leaders to arrange a negotiated strategic disengagement and quite another to do it unilaterally, leaving a security vacuum across the traditional invasion routes into the Soviet Union. Those are matters over which even the strongest government could fall. Stubborn U.S. adherence to that position on the theory that the spontaneously unfolding process gives the West decisive bargaining leverage is one way that the Soviet policy of disengagement might be reversed.

The alternative that had been suggested in some Soviet statements and widely asserted in the West to be their posture—that of a neutral unified Germany—is at least as irresponsible, even from a Soviet perspective, if the word *neutrality* is taken literally. That would imply that security in central Europe is to revert to national military organizations essentially unregulated by external connections. Presumably no one, least of all a unified German government struggling with the considerable economic and political demands of internal integration, would want the dynamic of mutual suspicion that would inevitably flourish under these conditions. Whatever labels are used and however the details are worked out, the only responsible way to handle the unification of Germany and the future of central Europe is a cooperative security arrangement in which there are no neutrals but rather a single organization, to which all states belong, that regulates the conditions of military deployment for everyone. If East Germany joins West Germany and thereby NATO as well, then so must the Soviet Union and all the other neighboring states, thus transforming the character of NATO. An alternative route would be a unified Germany accepted as a member of both the residual alliance organizations, symbolizing the agreed commitment to cooperation that would have to accompany such a step.

It is understandable that official policy has not yet articulated the larger consequences of German unification or those of many other events. The events are recent. Conceptual change is difficult. Consensus on conceptual change is even more so. But the caution of the moment is a warning of adventures yet to come. U.S. foreign policy is in for much more drastic revision than has yet been understood.

4

LAWRENCE J. KORB

The 1991 Defense Budget

THE DECISIONS made in the annual defense budget process are among the most critical ones in the U.S. political system. For five reasons, "dollars are policy" for the Department of Defense.

First, the defense budget is the linchpin of U.S. defense policy. Planning is irrelevant and operations impossible if the budget process does not result in the correct mix of manpower and material. For example, if planners postulate that deterrence against a strategic nuclear attack by the Soviet Union requires the United States to have x number of land-based warheads capable of surviving a Soviet preemptive strike, then the administration must ensure that funds for sufficient hardening or mobility of the U.S. land-based missiles make it through the defense budget process. In the early 1980s the Reagan administration claimed that too few land-based missiles, then all in fixed sites, could survive a Soviet first strike. But the administration was unsuccessful in persuading Congress to buy the mobile MX missile, with the result that its strategic nuclear plans became suspect.

Dollars determined policy even more notably for President Ronald Reagan's strategic defensive initiative (SDI), or Star Wars. In March 1983 Reagan announced he had decided to revolutionize U.S. strategic policy by challenging American scientists to develop an impenetrable strategic defense that would make nuclear weapons obsolete. At the time of Reagan's speech, the Defense Department had $14 billion in its fiscal 1985–89 defense program budget allocated to research on strategic defense.[1] Despite five years of unprecedented rhetorical efforts by the president and his key national security advisers, Congress appropriated only $17 billion for SDI during 1985–89, well below what Reagan had

The author wishes to thank Jacqueline P. Mildner and Marlene C. Perritte for secretarial assistance and Ethan Gutmann and Vernon L. Kelley for research assistance.

1. Unless otherwise indicated, all years referring to defense budgets or to the defense program are fiscal years.

111

sought. Star Wars thus remained a research program, and U.S. strategic policy was unchanged.

Second, defense budget decisions are important because they have long-term consequences. The B-2 Stealth bomber, for example, received initial funding in 1978, but the first B-2 did not fly until 1989. The procurement of all 132 planes will not be completed until the late 1990s. Once built, these planes will remain in the U.S. strategic arsenal well into the twenty-first century, some fifty years after the initial funding of the project. About 150 B-52 bombers, procured in the 1950s, still remain in the strategic arsenal and are likely to do so for the rest of the decade.

Third, the size of the defense budget sends important signals to the domestic and international community. In 1977 the Carter administration and the NATO allies decided to show their resolve to the Soviet Union and its Warsaw Pact allies by increasing defense spending by 3 percent a year (an interesting decision, since at that time NATO was already outspending the Warsaw Pact). In 1979 the Joint Chiefs of Staff and Senator Sam Nunn, chairman of the Senate Committee on Armed Services, conditioned their support for the SALT (strategic arms limitation talks) Treaty, then before the Senate for ratification, on President Jimmy Carter's agreement to support 5 percent increases in real defense spending. In the 1980 presidential campaign, Reagan pledged to make America number one again by increasing the defense budget by 5 percent.

Fourth, the defense budget powerfully affects the domestic economy. In 1990 defense outlays will consume about one-fourth of the federal budget and more than 5 percent of GNP. They will represent slightly more than 14 percent of net public spending. The 3.1 million Defense Department employees constitute more than 60 percent of the total federal work force and, together with the 3.3 million defense industry employees, more than 5 percent of the total national labor force. It is not surprising, therefore, that economic factors drive defense budget decisions much as strategic factors do. For example, when Secretary Dick Cheney revealed in late 1989 that dramatic changes in Eastern Europe were causing the Defense Department to reduce its projected defense budget for 1992 through 1994 by $180 billion, many commentators focused not on the changing international environment but on whether the U.S. economy could absorb such a dramatic reduction in the projected level of defense expenditures and on how the United States would spend its peace dividend.

Fifth, defense expenditures are the largest source of realistically controllable expenditures in the federal budget. The Office of Manage-

TABLE 4-1. Requested and Actual Budget Authority for Five-Year Defense Plans, Fiscal Years 1986–90

Billions of current dollars

Plan	1986	1987	1988	1989	1990	1986–90
Administration request, February 1985	314	354	402	439	478	1,986
Administration request, February 1986	281	312	332	354	375	1,654
Administration request, January 1987	281	282	303	323	344	1,533
Actual authorized	281	279	284	290	291	1,425

SOURCES: *Department of Defense Annual Report, Fiscal Years 1986, 1987, 1988, 1989, 1990.* Figures are rounded.

ment and Budget (OMB) estimated that the 1987 budget contained $263 billion in relatively controllable outlays, of which $175 billion, or 67 percent, were in the defense budget. Since 1987 was the first full year of the Gramm-Rudman-Hollings deficit reduction law, it was not surprising that Congress slashed the 1987 defense budget request of the Reagan administration by $30 billion, or 10 percent. Indeed, Congress has cut actual defense budget authority by more than $500 billion, or almost 30 percent, since Gramm-Rudman was enacted (table 4-1).

The Defense Debate

Because of the importance and impact of the defense budget, debates over defense programs are among the fiercest within the U.S. political system. Within the Pentagon, the four armed services and the dozen or so defense agencies struggle with one another over the allocation of defense dollars, often by deriding the capabilities of their sister agencies.[2] Within the administration, the secretary of defense and the director of the OMB argue about the percentage of the federal budget that should be allocated to defense, with the former focusing primarily on the threat to the United States and the latter concerned about the size of the deficit.

Furthermore, the administration and Congress debate the size and allocation of the defense budget, a debate that is exacerbated when the

2. See, for example, the comments of Marine Generals John J. Sheehan and Charles E. Wilhelm about Army contingency forces, in Michael E. Gordon with Bernard E. Trainor, "Army, Facing Cuts, Reported Seeking to Reshape Itself," *New York Times*, December 12, 1989, p. 1.

executive and legislative branches are controlled by different parties. Generally the debate on each budget lasts well over two years from start to finish. The original strategic guidance for the 1992 budget, for example, was issued to the armed services in October 1989. That budget will be presented to Congress in January 1991 and enacted into law in the fall of 1991.

Unfortunately, the quality of the debate surrounding the defense budget has often not matched its strategic and economic importance. Proponents of high defense spending will often point out that, even during the Reagan buildup, defense spending did not consume as high a level of GNP as it did in the 1950s and 1960s. Though true, this line of reasoning says more about the performance of the U.S. economy than about what the nation should be spending on defense. Moreover, it ignores the significant real growth of defense spending since the 1950s, 1960s, and 1970s. In 1990 defense budget authority was $291.4 billion, or 32 percent higher than the real spending of $220 billion a year in the nonwar years from 1951 through 1979. Finally, when confronted by the prospect of reductions in defense spending, proponents of high defense spending will quickly point to the large cuts defense has already taken, conveniently ignoring that these were reductions from projected increases rather than from actual outlays.

The logic of defense cutters is often equally sloppy. They point to the increase in defense authority between 1987 and 1990 from $279 to $291 billion (an increase of $12 billion, or 5 percent), neglecting an inflation in the defense sector of about 12 percent that reduced the buying power of defense spending by 7 percent.

The Context of the 1991–95 Defense Program

The debate over the size and distribution of the 1991 defense budget and the 1991-95 five-year defense program promises to be among the most contentious since the late 1940s. Important events in 1989 destroyed the threat of Soviet military expansion, the rationale behind the defense strategy and budgets of the United States for four decades. In February 1989 the Soviets withdrew the last of their 110,000 troops from Afghanistan, ending deployments that had begun in 1979. The Soviets also announced a unilateral reduction of 500,000 people in their own armed forces. Throughout the spring, summer, and fall of 1989, the Soviet East European empire collapsed suddenly and swiftly. In April Solidarity, the Polish independent trade union, was legalized, and by

August Poland had a noncommunist prime minister. In October Hungary renounced Marxism and proclaimed itself a free republic. That same month the long-time, hard-line communist leader of East Germany, Erich Honecker, was arrested and in November the Berlin Wall was torn down. November also witnessed the ouster of hard-line communists in Bulgaria and Czechoslovakia. By year's end Nicolae Ceausescu of Romania, the last Stalinist-type dictator, was dead, and Bulgaria and Czechoslovakia had announced they would hold free elections in 1990. More important, all the Eastern bloc nations in one way or another made clear their wish to see the 600,000 Soviet military forces withdrawn from their territories. It became apparent that a unified Germany would soon emerge, that the cold war had ended, and that the Brezhnev doctrine of intervention had given way to the "Sinatra doctrine" of letting former satellites "do it their way." It was hardly surprising that the collapse of the Soviet empire and of the threat of Soviet expansionism would elicit calls for sharp reductions in defense outlays and increased spending to address pressing domestic problems.

The debate will also be intense because it is mathematically and politically impossible for President George Bush to keep his April 1989 pledge to seek $1.3 trillion in defense authority and spend $1.25 trillion on defense for 1991–94,[3] to honor his 1988 campaign commitment not to raise taxes, and to meet the Gramm-Rudman target of eliminating the federal budget deficit by 1993. To meet that target, the Bush administration has already accepted congressional decisions to cut projected defense spending in 1990 by about $14 billion below the president's original projection. Because so many one-time gimmicks were used to meet the Gramm-Rudman target in 1990, defense will clearly have to contribute even more in 1991 than in 1990 if the deficit is to be reduced by another $35 billion.

President Bush, like his predecessors, did not inherit a blank slate for national defense. Decisions by his predecessors constrain his flexibility to change the size and distribution of the defense budget. Presidents Carter and Reagan spent more than $25 billion to develop and produce 15 B-2 Stealth bombers. President Bush can either cancel the program at 15, which means paying almost $2 billion per plane, or move to produce 117 additional planes, as originally planned, at a cost of about $300 million for each new plane.[4]

3. Office of the Assistant Secretary of Defense (Public Affairs), "Amended FY 1990/91 Department of Defense Budget," News Release 174-89 (April 25, 1989).
4. Unit costs of individual weapon systems are calculated by dividing the total cost of

Background

The roots of the 1991 budget and the 1991-95 defense programs reach back to the late 1940s. Since then, the defense programs have been designed primarily to deal with the Soviet threat of military expansion. Although the United States demobilized after World War II, defense spending did not fall to anywhere near prewar levels. Defense spending fell 90 percent from 1945 to 1948 but remained six times greater than in 1939.[5] Moreover, whereas in 1939 the active duty force was about 400,000 and employment in defense industry 300,000, in 1948 the active duty force had grown to 1.5 million and defense industry employment had jumped to almost 1 million.

The United States reinstituted military conscription and began to increase real defense spending in 1949. It took these actions as it embarked on a policy of containment, primarily in response to Soviet expansion in Eastern Europe and the triumph of the Communist party in China. In 1950, on the eve of the Korean War, defense spending had climbed to 54 percent above the 1948 level and consumed 27 percent of the federal budget and about 4.4 percent of GNP.[6]

Defense spending rose markedly during the Korean War, reaching a post–World War II peak in 1952 of $395 billion (table 4-2). In that year it consumed 60 percent of the entire federal budget and 12 percent of GNP. The armed forces increased to 3.6 million people, and defense-related employment jumped to nearly 4 million. Total defense employment (active duty military, defense civil service, and defense-related industry) in 1952 accounted for almost 15 percent of the total labor force.

After the Korean War the defense budget fell once again, despite President Dwight D. Eisenhower's recognition that the United States had

---

researching, developing, testing, and producing the system by the number of units purchased. Since the research, development, and testing costs must be paid regardless of how many units are procured, unit costs drop throughout the production run as the up-front costs are amortized.

5. Unless otherwise indicated, all figures for defense are expressed in 1991 dollars and refer to budget authority for the Department of Defense (budget category 051).

6. To supplement the information given here and in the rest of this section, see the three appendix figures. Figure 4A-1 shows the relation between the defense budget and the federal budget from 1950 through 1995; figure 4A-2, the relation between the defense budget and GNP; and figure 4A-3, defense-related employment as a portion of the labor force. Sources are given in the figures.

TABLE 4-2. Trends in Defense Budget Authority, Fiscal Years
1951–90

Billions of 1991 dollars

Year	Authority	Year	Authority
1951	296	1971	242
1952	395	1972	234
1953	379	1973	224
1954	233	1974	215
1955	203	1975	208
1956	207	1976	216
1957	216	1977	227
1958	212	1978	224
1959	225	1979	224
1960	217	1980	228
1961	218	1981	257
1962	251	1982	292
1963	254	1983	309
1964	243	1984	329
1965	233	1985	351
1966	279	1986	335
1967	305	1987	322
1968	309	1988	316
1969	298	1989	311
1970	269	1990	303
Nonwar-year average			
1954–60	216	1973–80	220
1961–65	240	1981–90	310

SOURCES: Office of the Assistant Secretary of Defense (Comptroller), *National Defense Budget Estimates for FY 1989–1990*, pp. 61–66; Lawrence Korb and Stephen Daggett, "The Defense Budget and Strategic Planning," in Joseph Kruzel, ed., *American Defense Annual, 1988–89* (Lexington, Mass.: Lexington Books, 1988), p. 45; *Department of Defense Annual Report, Fiscal Year 1991*, p. 69; and author's calculations for nonwar-year averages.

to maintain a large standing military even in the absence of a shooting war and that to do so would require large and unprecedented peacetime expenditures on defense. During his administration defense spending averaged $216 billion a year, more than twice the 1946-50 average and fifteen times more than the average in the 1930s. In the Eisenhower years defense consumed 8.5 percent of GNP and almost half the entire federal budget. The 2.7 million people on active military duty and 2.7 million people "permanently employed" in private defense-related industries, plus the 1.5 million defense civil servants, accounted for about 10 percent of the total labor force in the 1950s. It is not surprising that on leaving office, President Eisenhower warned of the power residing in what he called the military-industrial complex.[7]

President John F. Kennedy came into office convinced that defense spending under Eisenhower had been too small to support adequate conventional and special operations forces or to allow the United States to keep pace with the expansion of Soviet strategic forces. Accordingly, between 1961 and 1965 defense spending budget authority was increased to an average of about $240 billion, some 11 percent above the average level of the Eisenhower administration. Because of strong economic growth and a rising federal budget, however, defense spending fell to less than 7 percent of GNP and 40 percent of federal outlays. During the 1961–65 period the armed forces averaged 2.7 million people, defense civil servants 1.2 million, and civilian defense employment 2.5 million— in all, about 9 percent of the national labor force.

Shortly before Kennedy died, he and his secretary of defense, Robert S. McNamara, concluded that the gaps in the Eisenhower defense posture had been filled and that real defense spending could safely decline. Indeed, the 1964 and 1965 budgets did decline slightly in real terms. But beginning in July 1965, the United States became massively involved in Vietnam, and defense spending increased rapidly. Real defense authority climbed 31 percent in the succeeding two years, peaking at about $310 billion in 1968. Defense spending reached 10 percent of GNP and 46 percent of the federal budget. Active-duty military manpower peaked at 3.5 million, civil servants at 1.4 million, and defense-related employment at 3.2 million—just over 10 percent of the total labor force.

Defense spending grew rapidly during the Vietnam War, but much less than during the Korean War. In real terms defense spending more than tripled in the Korean War and at its height took 57 percent of the federal budget and nearly 12 percent of GNP and accounted for 15 percent of the labor force. During the Vietnam War defense spending increased in real terms by only one-third. Moreover, at its height, spending for Vietnam never went above half the federal budget or 11 percent of GNP or accounted for more than 11 percent of the labor force.

Defense spending dropped rapidly as disillusionment set in over the conduct of the war in Vietnam and as the United States began to withdraw from Southeast Asia. Between 1968 and 1975, during the Nixon-Ford years, defense spending fell 33 percent in real terms. By the

7. The term was actually coined by C. Wright Mills.

mid-1970s the defense share had fallen to below 5 percent of GNP and to less than 22 percent of the federal budget, lower than since before the Korean War. During this same period the armed forces dropped by about 1.5 million, defense civil servants by 0.4 million, and defense-related employment by about 1.5 million, the total falling to less than 5 percent of the labor force, the lowest level since before World War II.

Although everyone expected defense spending to fall after the end of the war in Vietnam, few expected the decline to be so rapid or so deep. The incremental costs of the war in Southeast Asia never accounted for more than 27 percent of the defense budget.[8] Yet before defense spending bottomed out in 1975, it was not only one-third less than 1968 but also 14 percent below the level of 1964, the last prewar year.

For several reasons this decline could not have come at a worse time for the U.S. military. First, between 1965 and 1976 Soviet military expenditures grew 61.5 percent measured in rubles (41.2 percent measured in constant 1985 dollars).[9] By 1976 the Soviet Union's defense budget, measured in dollars, was 41 percent higher than that of the United States. Second, the U.S. military emerged from the Vietnam War in very poor shape. To hold down the defense budget during that war, the federal government had postponed the modernization of the force structure and had drawn down worldwide stocks of ammunition. Moreover, the switch to the all-volunteer force required larger military salaries, pushing up personnel costs from 41 percent of the defense budget in 1963 to almost 52 percent by 1976.

Jimmy Carter, who had come into office in 1977 pledging to cut defense spending, held defense spending level during the first three years of his presidency. Because Soviet military spending continued to grow, the military balance deteriorated further. The American people, confronted with the Soviet invasion of Afghanistan, the seizure of American hostages in Iran, and the hollowness of their own military forces, supported increases in defense spending of 13 percent for 1981. Even

8. Department of Defense (Comptroller), *The Economics of Defense Spending: A Look at the Realities* (July 1972), p. 149; and Lawrence J. Korb, *The Fall and Rise of the Pentagon: American Defense Policies in the 1970's* (Westport, Conn.: Greenwood Press, 1979), p. 38.

9. Abraham S. Becker, *Sitting on Bayonets: The Soviet Defense Burden and the Slowdown of Soviet Defense Spending*, JRS-10 (RAND/UCLA Center for the Study of Soviet International Behavior, December 1985), pp. 4, 13; and *Allocation of Resources in the Soviet Union and China—1986*, Hearings before the Subcommittee on National Security Economics of the Joint Economic Committee, 100 Cong. 1 sess. (Government Printing Office, 1988), pt. 12, p. 131.

so, Ronald Reagan accused Carter of being soft on defense, pledged to increase real defense spending by 5 percent a year, and won the 1980 elections.

President Reagan did better than that. By the end of his first term in office, real defense spending had increased 53 percent, an average of over 12 percent a year, a higher rate than during the war in Vietnam. In fact, real defense spending in 1985 was 13 percent higher than peak spending in the Vietnam War (1968). It is no exaggeration to say that in the Reagan years the Defense Department enjoyed a wartime buildup without a war. Defense outlays rose to 27 percent of the federal budget and 6.3 percent of GNP, their highest shares since the war in Vietnam. Active duty manpower grew 8 percent and civil servants 10 percent, while defense-related employment doubled between 1976 and 1986, reaching 3.3 million, the highest level since the peak of the Korean War buildup in 1953. Nonetheless, defense employment in the Reagan years never exceeded 5.6 percent of the total labor force.

The massive military buildup of the first Reagan administration could not be sustained. Because it took place simultaneously with a big tax cut, the increases in the defense budget contributed to large and increasing federal budget deficits that in turn inspired the Gramm-Rudman-Hollings deficit reduction law. Moreover, no overall strategy guided the buildup, and management was ineffective.[10] As a result, the American people and their elected representatives felt that much of the money spent during the buildup was wasted. Also, growth of Soviet military expenditures, which had averaged over 4 percent a year from the mid-1960s to the mid-1970s, slowed to less than 3 percent a year between 1977 and 1982, less than one-half the U.S. rate for that period.[11]

Not only did defense spending in Reagan's second term stop growing as fast as in the first, but it declined in real terms. By 1990 real defense spending was 13.6 percent below its 1985 peak. More significant, President Reagan's $2.0 trillion projected defense program for 1986–90 was cut sharply. The Defense Department actually received $1.4 trillion, or about 30 percent, less than Reagan had sought in 1985. In 1990 the share of GNP and the federal budget devoted to defense dropped to 5 percent and less than 25 percent, respectively. Active duty manpower,

10. See, for example, the comments of the chairmen of the House and Senate Armed Services Committees, quoted in Lawrence J. Korb, "Spending without Strategy," *International Security*, vol. 12 (Summer 1987), p. 169.

11. Becker, *Sitting on Bayonets*; and William W. Kaufmann, *Glasnost, Perestroika, and U.S. Defense Spending* (Brookings, 1989), table 2.

TABLE 4-3. Reagan's Final Five-Year Defense Plan and the Bush Amendments of April 1989, Fiscal Years 1989, 1990–94
Billions of current dollars

Item	1989	1990	1991	1992	1993	1994	1990–94
Budget authority							
January 1989 budget	290.2	305.6	320.9	335.7	350.7	365.6	1,678.5
Reductions	...	−10.0	−9.9	−13.7	−14.8	−15.8	−64.2
Amended budget							
(April 1989)	290.2	295.6	311.0	322.0	335.9	349.8	1,614.3
Outlays							
January 1989 budget	289.8	293.8	304.7	316.2	329.3	343.4	1,587.4
Reductions	...	−4.0	−6.9	−9.4	−11.9	−13.9	−46.1
Amended budget							
(April 1989)	289.8	289.8	297.9	306.8	317.4	329.5	1,541.3

SOURCE: Office of Assistant Secretary of Defense (Public Affairs), "Amended FY 1990/91 Department of Defense Budget," News Release 174-89 (April 25, 1989). Figures are rounded.

civil service manpower, and defense industry employment all declined slightly, as did the percentage of the national labor force dependent on defense.

Although Reagan left a sizable defense budget to his successor, it was not large enough to pay for all the programs he had initiated, because he and his advisers had originally refused to recognize that budget pressures would force cuts in defense spending in the late 1980s. President Reagan accommodated the yearly declines primarily by stretching out programs. Thus President Bush and Secretary of Defense Cheney inherited a $400 billion program but only a $300 billion budget. It is estimated that more than $1 trillion in programs are now in the defense pipeline and that the 1990-94 defense program presented to Congress in January 1989 by President Reagan was underfunded by $300 to $400 billion.[12]

The 1990 Debate

President Bush inherited a five-year plan from the Reagan administration that called for $1.7 trillion in defense budget authority, $1.6 trillion in defense spending, and spending growth of about 2 percent a year (table 4-3) over 1990–94.[13] Bush recognized that he could not

12. William W. Kaufmann and Lawrence J. Korb, *The 1990 Defense Budget* (Brookings, 1989), pp. 9, 20.

13. Though large, the final Reagan plan was considerably smaller than the $1.9 trillion in budget authority Reagan planned to request before the stock market crash of October 1987. His precrash projection for the 1990 budget authority was $344 billion, $38 billion (or 12 percent) above his actual request.

spend that much on defense without violating his no-tax pledge if he wanted to meet legislated targets for deficit reduction. He quickly trimmed the Reagan plan. By April 1989 the president and the new secretary of defense cut $64 billion in budget authority and $46 billion in outlays out of the five-year plan. As part of an agreement with Congress, the 1990 request was cut 3 percent, from $306 to $296 billion. This meant that real defense authority for 1990 fell almost 3 percent rather than increased by 2 percent. Although Congress appropriated the $296 billion for the Defense Department, failure to meet the Gramm-Rudman deficit reduction targets triggered sequestration on October 1, 1989. For the department, sequestration lasted 130 days, bringing budget authority for 1990 down to $291 billion and outlays to $287 billion.

While Bush and Cheney were relatively successful in achieving their goal for the size of defense budget authority and outlays, their attempts to shape defense priorities were disastrous. In modifying the Reagan budget, Secretary Cheney proposed to keep all the main Reagan strategic initiatives including such controversial programs as SDI and the B-2 Stealth bomber, but to cancel three major conventional programs: the Navy's F14-D aircraft, the Marine Corps V-22 tilt rotor Osprey aircraft, and the Army's AHIP helicopter.

Members of Congress from the areas that would be affected by the proposed cancellations challenged them vigorously. Cancellation of the F-14D would have meant that Grumman, a big Long Island corporation, would not be building any more naval aircraft for the first time in fifty years. Unfortunately, Cheney had no convincing strategic rationale for his proposed cutbacks. Instead, he fell back on cost-effectiveness analyses, admitting that if he had more money, he would fund the V-22, F-14-D, and AHIP.

Thus, rather than examining the role of the Marine Corps or naval aviation in a postcontainment world, the debate focused on comparing the V-22 with the CH-53E and the F-14D with remanufactured F-14As. Eventually Congress diverted $1.1 billion from SDI, just over $0.4 billion from the B-2, and just under $0.4 billion from the Trident II missile (D-5) to fund the AHIP, F-14D, and V-22.

Although most analysts feel that Cheney lost in his first important budget confrontation with Congress, the real losers in the 1990 defense budget battle were the American people. The Bush administration developed no coherent plan with which to defend its priorities. Congress is institutionally incapable of developing such a rationale but is adept at protecting the interests of its constituents. And if the administration has no strategy to frame the debate on its budget, these parochial interests will normally prevail.

The 1990 battle therefore committed U.S. taxpayers to pay $1.6 billion for eighteen F-14Ds and thirty-six AHIPs that the Defense Department says the country does not need and another $0.3 billion on research and development for a V-22 that the department is still trying to cancel. True, Congress "saved" some $2.0 billion in strategic programs. But that is a short-term saving. At $3.6 billion, SDI is too big to be a research program and too small to be moving toward deployment. Cutting one B-2 Stealth bomber "saved" $400 million but drove up the unit cost of the planes scheduled for purchase out of 1990 funds from $1.3 billion to $1.8 billion and added about $5 billion to the total program cost. Similarly, almost $400 million was saved by cutting twenty-one Trident II missiles, but the unit costs of the 1990 purchases rose 20 percent, from $288 million to $347 million.

The 1991–95 Problems

In justifying its 1991 budget and the 1991–95 defense program, the Bush administration faces short- and long-term challenges that fall into four categories.

A rationale. The president and his advisers need to develop a convincing rationale for a significant military force tailored to an era in which the Soviet threat is sharply reduced. They should have developed this rationale in the new administration's first year. Like the Nixon administration in 1969 and the Carter administration in 1977, the Bush administration did in fact undertake a strategic review upon taking office.

This review, however, came to nothing, in large part because neither the president nor his top national security advisers provided a clear vision of how the United States should respond to the changing international environment. Bush's national security team contains no conceptual thinkers like Henry A. Kissinger or Zbigniew Brzezinski. The absence of a secretary of defense throughout the transition and the first three months of the Bush administration further hindered the strategic review by depriving the defense department of senior representation in the review. Without authoritative input from the department no significant changes could realistically be made to existing national security policy. Even with a full team of strategically minded planners, formulating a coherent vision in the face of changes in the international system would have been a daunting task. With a team without conceptual thinkers, the result was an inadequate strategic review that did little more than respond to fast-moving events.

During the Reagan administration there was, as Senator Nunn and Representative Les Aspin, chairman of the House Armed Services Committee, observed on more than one occasion, an Army strategy, a Navy strategy, and an Air Force strategy but no overall national strategy to guide the massive buildup that took place between 1980 and 1985.[14] The lack of a coherent strategy during the Reagan buildup bred waste. If the Bush administration does not develop a strategic vision such as the one outlined by John Steinbruner in chapter 3, reductions in defense will be inefficiently planned, and the United States will not get the most out of whatever funds are appropriated to defense. The danger is clear and present that defense could be cut too much and too fast or in the wrong places as America "comes home" after the cold war.

Limits. The Bush administration must reconcile its 1991–95 defense program to the budgets it is likely to receive. Even if real defense spending authority grows at 2 percent a year, as projected by the Reagan administration, spending will fall more than $100 billion short of what is needed to implement the five-year program Bush inherited from Reagan. If the budget declines by 5 percent a year in real terms, as seems likely, that shortfall could approach $300 billion.[15]

Sustainability. The Bush administration must develop sustainable targets for defense spending. During the second Reagan administration, budget authority and outlay projections for the succeeding five years were radically revised every year. The 1989 budget was projected at $439 billion in early 1985, $354 billion in 1986, $323 billion in 1987, and $291 billion in 1988. In just one year the Bush administration reduced the 1990–94 defense program three separate times, by $45 billion on February 9, 1989, by another $20 billion in April, and by yet another $180 billion in November, for a total of about $250 billion, or 15 percent.

No organization can change that much so quickly without becoming disorganized, especially if it lacks a coherent strategy. Outgoing Secretary of Defense Frank C. Carlucci knew in January 1989 that expectations of 2 percent real growth in the defense budget were unrealistic. Bush and Cheney had to know in April 1989 that the need to meet deficit reduction targets made it impossible to attain even 1.5 percent real

14. Korb, "Spending without Strategy," p. 169.
15. Kaufmann and Korb, *1990 Defense Budget*, p. 20.

growth. Whatever President Bush might want, prudence requires that the Defense Department present a strategic vision to guide defense budgets in which real spending falls perhaps 5 percent a year. Congress would probably support such a gradual sustained cutback and is unlikely to spend more.

Economic transition. The administration needs to develop a plan to help the economy adjust to reduced defense spending. The defense cut can be an enormous gain, a true peace dividend, but only if the resources once used for defense are shifted smoothly to civil use. Also, careful attention to the adjustment problems generated by demobilization will improve the efficiency with which remaining defense dollars are spent. Had Secretary Cheney presented a plan to Congress to help Grumman adjust to its demise as a major defense supplier, Congress might have agreed to cancel the F-14D. Congress in effect provided its own adjustment plan: eighteen unneeded planes over the next three years at a cost of about $1.5 billion. Similarly, without an adjustment plan Cheney will not receive congressional permission to close the fifty-five bases he has designated.

The Solutions

The Bush administration has many advantages in dealing with its short- and long-term budget problems. The U.S. armed forces are well staffed and supplied because the Department of Defense enjoyed a wartime buildup without a war. The four services have enough modern equipment and their warehouses are full of ammunition and other supplies. The department has 10 percent more tactical aircraft and 18 percent more ships than it did in 1980.[16] In addition, the quality of personnel is at an all-time high. Over 90 percent of the new recruits have high school diplomas and score average or above average on the armed forces qualification test. Retention of qualified people is also at record high levels. Thus, even if the military threat from the Soviet Union were unchanged, defense spending could fall briefly without jeopardizing national security.

The diminishing military threat to U.S. national security is a second advantage in planning for reduced defense spending. More than half the defense budget goes to pay for the conventional defense of Western Europe. The United States is committed to providing 10 divisions, 100

16. *Department of Defense Annual Report, Fiscal Year 1991*, p. 76.

tactical air squadrons, and a Marine Corps expeditionary brigade to Europe within ten days after a warning of a Warsaw Pact mobilization.[17] Whatever else the events in Eastern Europe signal, they mean that NATO will have a much longer notice, perhaps as much as six months, of any impending invasion. Because of this extra warning time, the United States can keep a smaller force on active duty and increase its reliance on reserves as well as reduce the amount of material it must keep on hand.

Furthermore, the United States and the Soviet Union have agreed on an arms control regime that will reduce the strategic and conventional threat to the United States. At the strategic arms reduction talks (START), the two superpowers have agreed to cut countable nuclear warheads to 6,000 and delivery systems to 1,600, a reduction of about 50 percent in warheads and 30 percent in delivery vehicles. At the Conventional Forces in Europe (CFE) negotiations, NATO and Warsaw Pact nations have agreed to greatly reduce the number of troops, tanks, armored personnel carriers, and aircraft on each side and to move their forces away from the East German and Czechoslovakian borders.[18]

Even before these agreements are signed, the Soviet Union has begun to cut its military spending and armed forces. In May 1989 the Defense Department, citing a consensus in the intelligence community, told President Bush that President Mikhail S. Gorbachev had reversed a twenty-year pattern of growth in Soviet military spending and force structure to boost the civil economy and Soviet foreign policy. The intelligence community predicts that Gorbachev will keep his public promises to cut Soviet military forces by 10 percent, total defense spending by 15 percent, and weapon outlays by 20 percent over the next two years.[19] The House Armed Services Committee reported in August 1989 that Gorbachev had already completed approximately half the unilateral reductions of troops, combat divisions, tanks, and aircraft in Eastern Europe that he had promised in December 1988.[20]

17. *Department of Defense Annual Report, Fiscal Year 1990*, p. 171; and Patrick E. Tyler and R. Jeffrey Smith, "Study Finds NATO War Plans Outdated," *Washington Post*, November 29, 1989, p. A1.

18. For an analysis of the positions of both sides in the START and CFE talks, see Kaufmann, *Glasnost, Perestroika, and U.S. Defense Spending*, tables 20, 21, 22, 24, 25. Because the ordnance carried by bombers is discounted, the actual number of weapons allowed under START I will be more than 6,000.

19. Patrick E. Tyler and R. Jeffrey Smith, "Bush Alerted in May to Soviet Military Cuts," *Washington Post*, December 11, 1989, p. A1.

20. Council for Livable World Education Fund, *The Soviet Threat: 14 Ways It Has Declined* (Washington, January 1990), p. 1.

In formulating the 1991–95 five-year defense plan, the Bush administration had to make a number of choices about force structure. From a strategic point of view, it had to decide whether to emphasize maritime forces or Army and Air Forces for power projection. Emphasizing maritime forces would mean a large Navy and Marine Corps. Emphasizing the Army and Air Force would require a much smaller Navy and Marine Corps. As regards the size of the armed forces, the administration could emphasize investment in a comparatively small active duty force equipped with the latest, most sophisticated weapons and backed by a robust technological base. Or it could choose a comparatively large force armed with less sophisticated weapons but capable of going into action quickly and fighting for sustained periods. Each of these strategies has its advantages and disadvantages.

The 1991–95 Program

The Bush administration is requesting $295.1 billion in budget authority and $292.1 billion in outlays for national defense in 1991 (table 4-4). Although larger in nominal terms than the 1990 budget, the proposed 1991 budget would result in a real decline of 2.6 percent in authority and 2.2 percent in outlays. The proposed cut in budget authority is slightly smaller than last year's cut.

For the 1991–95 period Bush is requesting authority of $1.52 trillion and outlays of just under $1.5 trillion. If the Bush five-year plan is approved, defense authority will reach $312 billion and outlays $305 billion in 1995, increases of 5.7 and 4.3 percent over the next five years. In real terms, however, authority will drop by 10 percent and outlays by 12 percent over the five-year plan. Compared with his predecessor's approach to defense spending, Bush's proposal is remarkable. Reagan always asked for real increases in his five-year defense plans. Even in his second administration, when the defense consensus had collapsed and Congress was warning him that the best he could hope for in defense was zero real growth, Reagan requested real increases ranging from 2 to 7 percent. Moreover, with his 1991–95 program, Bush becomes the first president since John Kennedy in 1963 to call for real reductions in the baseline defense program, the part of the budget not affected by an ongoing shooting war. For example, in 1969, 28 percent of the last defense budget request of Lyndon B. Johnson was attributed to the incremental costs of the Vietnam War. In his five and a half years in office, Richard M. Nixon requested total budgets showing real decline,

TABLE 4-4. The Bush Administration Five-Year Defense Plan,
Fiscal Years 1990, 1991–95

Billions of current dollars unless otherwise specified

Item	1990	1991	1992	1993	1994	1995	1991–95
Budget authority							
Current dollars	291.4	295.1	300.0	304.4	308.0	311.8	1,519.3
Constant fiscal 1991							
dollars	302.9	295.1	289.2	283.4	277.7	272.1	. . .
Real growth (per-	−2.7	−2.6	−2.0	−2.0	−2.0	−2.0	. . .
cent)							
Outlays							
Current dollars	286.8	292.1	296.9	299.0	302.3	304.8	1,495.1
Constant fiscal 1991							
dollars	295.4	292.1	283.6	277.4	270.5	263.4	. . .
Real growth (per-	−5.5	−2.2	−2.9	−2.9	−2.2	−2.5	. . .
cent)							

SOURCE: Office of Assistant Secretary of Defense (Public Affairs), "FY 1991 Department of Defense Budget Request," News Release 29-90 (January 29, 1990); and author's calculations.

but his baseline budget request showed real increases as he reduced the incremental costs of the war by withdrawing troops. By 1973 the incremental costs of the war had dropped to 5.2 percent of the budget.[21]

The Bush proposal also decreases the burden of defense on U.S. economic resources. If his 1991–95 defense plan is adopted and the economic assumptions hold up, defense outlays will drop to 4 percent of GNP, the lowest share since 1950, when it took 4.4 percent. Defense outlays will drop to 21 percent of the budget, the smallest share in fifty years, 1.5 percentage points below the 1978 low of 22.5 percent and down 6 percentage points from the Reagan administration peak of 27 percent in 1987 (figures 4A-1 and 4A-2).

In the light of events in Eastern Europe, however, the Bush reductions seem rather timid and unrealistic. Although, as discussed, it is impossible to calculate the exact proportion of the U.S. defense budget attributable to defending Western Europe from a Soviet–Warsaw Pact attack, at least 50 percent of the budget is driven by that threat.[22] Not even the most rigid hard-liner now argues that the Soviet Union and its Warsaw Pact allies pose a serious military threat to Western Europe. As CIA Director William Webster told the House Armed Services Committee on March

21. Korb, *Fall and Rise of the Pentagon*, p. 38.
22. For a complete discussion on measuring U.S. contributions to NATO, see Lawrence J. Korb, "Measuring U.S. Contributions to NATO Defense," in Stanley R. Sloan, ed., *NATO in the 1990's* (Pergamon-Brassey, 1989), pp. 193–208.

TABLE 4-5. Defense Budget Authority for Fiscal Years 1990–94,
April 1989 and January 1990 Plans
Billions of current dollars

Item	1990	1991	1992	1993	1994	1990–94
April 1989 plan						
(0%, 1%, 1%, 2%, 2% real growth)[a]	295.6	317.5	332.4	351.0	369.4	1,665.9
Reduction	−4.2	−22.4	−32.4	−46.6	−61.4	−167.0
January 1990 plan						
(−2% annual real growth)	291.4	295.1	300.0	304.4	308.0	1,498.9

SOURCE: Office of Assistant Secretary of Defense (Public Affairs), "FY 1991 Department of Defense Budget Request," News Release 29-90 (January 29, 1990), table 2.
a. Adjusted for final economic assumptions.

1, 1990, with or without Gorbachev the Soviet Union has made a historic turn away from militarism.[23] Real cuts in defense spending of more than 10 percent over the next five years are reasonable and prudent. If the Bush plan is approved, U.S. defense spending in 1995, in constant 1991 dollars, will be 6 percent higher than in 1981, when the Soviet Union was at the peak of its military power, and higher than the average nonwar-years defense budget of the 1950s, 1960s, and 1970s (table 4-2). The decline the president projects over the next five years—10.1 percent—is smaller than the actual drop of the past five years—13.6 percent. Finally, the plan reneges on Secretary Cheney's own promise to reduce the 1992–94 program by $180 billion. It shows reductions of only $140.4 billion from the 1992–94 program projected in the spring of 1989 (table 4-5); moreover, these are not program reductions. According to a General Accounting Office audit of the Pentagon's most recent five-year plan, the Defense Department must trim $138 billion more in programs by 1994 to bring its spending in line with the Bush administration's plan.[24]

Events in Eastern Europe and the current excellent condition of the U.S. armed forces would permit holding nominal defense spending constant over the next five years without undermining national security.

23. Patrick E. Tyler, "Cheney Finds CIA Director Is No Comrade in Arms," *Washington Post*, March 6, 1990, p. A21. See also the testimony of Richard Perle, former assistant secretary of defense for international security, to the Senate Armed Services Committee on January 24, 1990 (Perle's testimony is summarized in *Defense Daily*, January 25, 1990, pp. 124–25), and that of James Schlesinger, former secretary of defense, to the same committee on January 30, 1990 (Schlesinger's testimony is summarized in R. Jeffrey Smith, "Schlesinger Urges Radical Cuts in Europe," *Washington Post*, January 31, 1990, p. A12).
24. Mark Thompson, "Pentagon Cuts Fall Way Short," *Fort Worth Star-Telegram*, February 27, 1990, p. 1.

TABLE 4-6. Defense Budget Authority for Fiscal Years 1989–95,
by Program and Function
Billions of current dollars

Item	1989	1990	1991	1992	1993	1994	1995	Change, 1991–95 Amount	Change, 1991–95 Percent
Military personnel	78.5	78.5	79.1	80.5	81.8	82.8	83.9	4.8	6.1
Operations and maintenance	86.2	86.8	90.1	91.7	93.2	94.4	95.6	5.5	6.1
Procurement	79.4	82.6	77.9	78.9	79.8	80.7	81.5	3.6	4.6
Research, development, test, and evaluation	37.5	36.8	38.0	38.6	39.2	39.7	40.1	2.1	5.5
Military construction	5.7	5.3	5.6	5.7	5.7	5.8	5.9	0.3	5.4
Family housing	3.3	3.2	3.5	3.5	3.6	3.6	3.7	0.2	5.7
Other	0.9	−0.7	2.3	2.3	2.3	2.4	2.4	0.1	4.3
Offsetting receipts	−0.7	−1.1	−0.9	−1.0	−0.9	−0.9	−0.9	...	...
Allowances	...	...	−0.3	−0.3	−0.3	−0.3	−0.3	...	...
TOTAL	290.8	291.4	295.1	300.0	304.4	308.0	311.8	16.7	5.6

SOURCE: _Budget of the United States Government, Fiscal Year 1991,_ p. 157. Figures are rounded.

And Congress is unlikely to allocate more than that to defense. A nominal freeze would reduce real spending by about 25 percent over the 1991–95 period, about twice the size of the cut proposed by the Bush administration. The resulting defense budget of about $227 billion in 1990 dollars by 1995 would match average real spending on defense from 1950 through 1980 (see table 4-7 below).

Distribution

All categories of the defense budget would rise slightly in nominal terms from the year before under President Bush's 1991 budget except procurement, which would fall by $4.7 billion, or 5.7 percent (table 4A-1). The rest of the budget would rise by $8.4 billion, or 2.8 percent. Real spending in all the major accounts would fall slightly, except for procurement, which would decline 9 percent. This pattern continues trends begun in 1986. Between 1985 and 1990 the procurement account fell 29 percent in real terms, from $121 billion in 1991 dollars to $86 billion. For the period beyond 1991, President Bush seeks to allow all categories of the defense budget to grow at about the same rate (table 4-6).

The Bush plan reflects neither a manpower nor an investment strategy. This indecision is not surprising, since the budget was submitted before the administration completed its review of strategy and programs, which is now expected in April 1990. The 1991–95 plan still supports systems and forces that are cold war relics and are unsuited to the risks the United States will confront in the postcontainment era or the impending arms control regime. If those systems were canceled and forces eliminated, real defense authority could easily be cut by 5 percent a year without jeopardizing national security.

Strategic Forces

For 1991 the Bush administration plans to spend about $17 billion on six major strategic programs: the B-2 Stealth bomber, the MX rail garrison and Midgetman mobile land-based missiles, the Trident II submarine and Trident II (D-5) missile, and the strategic defense initiative. These six systems are programmed to consume over $80 billion during 1991–95 as the Bush administration seeks to modernize sea-launched missiles, land-launched missiles, and manned bombers (the strategic triad), as well as to develop a comprehensive defense against ballistic missiles.

Procuring all these systems at this rate does not make sense at this time. Over the last decade the United States has modernized the strategic triad and added more than 4,000 warheads to its strategic nuclear arsenal, an increase of 45 percent. The number of warheads that could survive a Soviet attack and remain deliverable has risen 16.4 percent.[25] More important, however, the United States and the Soviet Union are on the verge of agreeing to reduce the number of warheads and delivery systems significantly. The agreed limits at the START negotiations are 6,000 warheads and 1,600 delivery systems for each side, and the sublimit is 4,900 warheads on missiles. Why would the United States spend scarce budget dollars to add to its arsenal while simultaneously signing an agreement to manage with fewer than it already has?

Secretary Cheney argues that the Soviets, while cutting their conventional forces, are still modernizing their strategic forces.[26] U.S. strategic programs must be continued, presumably as bargaining chips. The argument is absurd. If Soviet strategic modernization is a problem, the United States can conclude the START treaty expeditiously. In early February 1990 the Soviets cleared a major hurdle by accepting the

25. Kaufmann and Korb, *1990 Defense Budget*, pp. 23, 30; and *Department of Defense Annual Report, Fiscal Year 1991*, p. 75.

26. *Department of Defense Annual Report, Fiscal Year 1991*, p. 31.

American position on SDI.[27] The main current obstacle to concluding the treaty is the failure of the Bush administration to resolve internal disagreements on several issues, most important the question of how many mobile missiles will be permitted in START. The national security adviser, Brent Scowcroft, wants no mobile missiles. The secretary of defense, Dick Cheney, favors the rail garrison MX. The secretary of state, James A. Baker III, leans toward the Midgetman. The president's own views remain a mystery.[28] Meanwhile the Bush administration has given first priority to concluding the agreement on reducing conventional forces in Europe; in early 1989 its national security team decided that the superiority of Warsaw Pact forces, which then seemed formidable, posed more of a threat to United States interests than Soviet nuclear forces did.

At this point, the administration should not only promptly conclude START I but also develop a framework for START II that will reduce the number of warheads to 3,000 on each side, more than enough firepower to destroy the targets outlined by John Steinbruner. Indeed, the Soviets are already pressing the Bush administration to do just that. Recent testimony of the three officers who have served as chairman of the Joint Chiefs of Staff over the last twelve years indicates that Soviet forces do not now threaten the U.S. deterrent, nor will they do so in the near future. These retired flag officers, one from each of the services, noted that even with the Soviet Union's modernization programs, its forces do not threaten the U.S. second-strike posture.[29] In short, the administration could slow the modernization of all three legs of the triad without risk to U.S. security.

Through 1990 the Defense Department will have received budget authority of more than $25 billion to develop and build 15 B-2A Stealth bombers. Procuring the remaining 117 planes in the current plan will cost at least an additional $50 billion. The B-2 is an unnecessarily expensive way to guard against the remote possibility that other systems— land- and sea-based missiles, cruise-missile-carrying B-52s, and pene-

27. Warren Strobel, "Soviets Drop SDI Link to Treaty," *Washington Times,* February 9, 1990, p. 1.
28. R. Jeffrey Smith, "Scowcroft Seeking Ban on Some Mobile Missiles," *Washington Post,* January 15, 1990, p. A1.
29. R. Jeffrey Smith, "2 Missiles Unnecessary, Ex-Chiefs Say," *Washington Post,* February 3, 1990, p. A5; and Smith, "Soviets Press U.S. for Deeper Reductions in Strategic Weapons," *Washington Post,* February 25, 1990, p. 14.

trating B-1 bombers—would be unable to launch a successful second strike. Former Secretary of Defense Carlucci calls it a plane without a clearly defined mission.[30] The United States would be far better off to cancel the B-2 program and use a small part of the $50 billion saved to test (and deploy) the 15 B-2s it has purchased and equip the B-1 with advanced cruise missiles as the remaining B-52s are phased out. (Fifteen hundred advanced cruise missiles with stealth characteristics can be bought for $7 billion.)

The Defense Department is requesting almost $3 billion to place the first twelve MX's on railroad cars and $202 million to keep research and development going on another small missile, the mobile Midgetman. As the three former chairmen of the Joint Chiefs noted, neither mobile missile is needed. Nevertheless, research and development on the Midgetman should continue pending successful conclusion of the START agreement.

To date, the Navy has received funding for 17 Trident submarines. (Eight are already deployed and one is undergoing sea trials.) For 1991 it is requesting $1.5 billion for full funding of an 18th Trident and advance procurement for a 19th and 20th. The 17 Tridents already authorized would carry 192 warheads each for a total of 3,264, more than the entire number allowed under the projected figure for START II and two-thirds of the number allowed under START I. Placing so many warheads on so few platforms is a risky policy, since an enemy could destroy U.S. second-strike capacity by sinking a few submarines. The Trident program should be terminated and research begun on a new, smaller submarine that would be a less profitable target.

In 1991 the Defense Department seeks to purchase 52 Trident II or D-5 missiles for $1.7 billion. This missile is highly accurate and gives the Navy the capacity to destroy hard targets such as reinforced missile silos. To date, the Navy has spent about $17 billion to develop and purchase 195 D-5s, enough to equip 8 Trident submarines. The Navy plans to spend another $18 billion to purchase enough missiles to arm 20 Tridents, 8 of which are already at sea, armed with the Trident I or C-4 missile. It would make sense to allow the Navy to purchase only the 52 D-5s requested in this year's budget. This would permit the Navy to arm the 9 Trident submarines purchased but not deployed, but not to replace the C-4 missiles for the unneeded submarines requested in this year's budget. Canceling the D-5 program after 1991 would save about $18 billion in this decade.

The administration seeks $4.5 billion, or a 22 percent increase, for SDI, looking toward eventual deployment of a space-based ballistic missile defense designed to destroy a large portion of incoming missiles. The increase may appease the Reagan legacy, but it lacks any strategic rationale. The strategic defense initiative is both technically and fiscally impossible. Moreover, deploying a space-based system would violate the Antiballistic Missile (ABM) Treaty. Congress should and probably will reduce SDI to a $3-billion-a-year research program for the 1991–95 period. Such a research program will allow the Defense Department to guard against any expected breakthroughs on the Soviet side and bring strategic defense back to the level that existed before Reagan's March 1983 speech challenging the department to make nuclear weapons obsolete.

Conventional

A strategic vision is no more apparent in plans for conventional forces than in the budget for nuclear forces. Particularly for the Navy and the Air Force, the administration is clinging to a cold war mentality.

Army. The Army, which would have borne the brunt of any war in central Europe, is wisely cutting some forces dedicated to that threat. In 1991 it will complete its purchase of 8,000 M1A1 Abrams Main Battle Tanks, freeing $6.2 billion over the next five years. It will eliminate two divisions in 1991 and is considering eliminating another three by 1995. Overall, its real budget authority for 1991 drops 6 percent, and its procurement account 28 percent.

The Army should also consider eliminating two other expensive systems that are oriented primarily toward the central front: the Patriot air defense missile and the Bradley fighting vehicle. The 1991 budget requests $1.6 billion to buy 817 Patriots and 600 Bradleys, even though the Army inventory already contains thousands of these weapons. The Army should also drop its requests for $112 million (up 239 percent from 1990) for research on a new short-range nuclear missile to replace the Lance and for $193 million for the procurement of 377 army tactical missile systems (ATACMS). The nuclear replacement for the Lance is designed to be deployed in West Germany to attack East Germany and Poland. With German reunification imminent, this contingency is remote, to say the least. Similarly, ATACMS, a surface-to-surface conventional missile with a range of about 100 miles, is designed primarily to break up the second echelon of Soviet forces launching a blitzkreig on Western Europe. With Soviet troops heading home as former satellites ask them to leave, such an attack is another implausible scenario. Finally, the Army should cancel once and for all the light-armed scout attack helicopter (LHX), which continues to experience delays (it will not be operational until 1997), rising costs (unit costs for 2,100 are $20 million), and technical problems.

Not only can the Army safely eliminate five active divisions between now and 1995 (assuming the success of negotiations with the Soviets), it should also be planning to eliminate at least five more divisions by the end of the century as the U.S. military presence in Europe drops from 300,000 to about 50,000, and in Korea to 10,000. That would leave the Army with a force of eight active and ten reserve divisions in the year 2000.

Navy. The Navy budget for 1991 is virtually the same as for 1990. The Navy does propose to retire or deactivate 12 older ships, and it has reduced its force structure slightly, from 551 to 546 ships. However, the Navy still plans to maintain 14 carrier battle groups, a number consistent with the maritime strategy of carrying the battle toward the Soviet Union. The Navy seeks $3.7 billion for 5 Aegis-equipped Burke-class destroyers (DDG-51),[31] designed primarily to protect the fleet from attacks by Soviet naval aviation and Soviet missile firing ships, and another $3.7 billion for 2 Seawolf submarines (SSN-21), designed to attack Soviet fleet ballistic missile submarines in their home waters (in addition to the 18th Trident submarine). Not only do these vessels lack a clear mission in the postcontainment era, but they also would consume 80 percent of the Navy's $9.2 billion shipbuilding budget in 1991. This allocation permits the Navy to build only 14 ships. Since Navy ships last an average of about twenty-five years, this shipbuilding program would lead to a 350-ship Navy, one too small even for the postcontainment era.

A reasonable force goal for the Navy in the mid-1990s would be approximately 500 ships centered around 12 carrier battle groups, a number that the five presidents who preceded Ronald Reagan found adequate, during more perilous times than the 1990s, to protect the sea-

---

31. Aegis is the code name of a sophisticated air defense system deployed on cruisers and destroyers. The system is designed to shoot down incoming missiles and airplanes that threaten a carrier task force.

lanes and project U.S. power. The Navy could then retire 5 older carriers, saving $800 million per carrier on the "service-life extension" program. Such a goal would also allow the Navy to cancel the SSN-21 and to cut the number of air wings from 15 (13 active and 2 reserve) to 13 (11 active and 2 reserve), thereby relieving pressure to rush the advanced tactical aircraft (ATA) and the Navy version of the advanced tactical fighter (NATF) into production. And the Navy should retire both remaining battleships, because they are expensive to operate ($1 billion over 1991–95) and inappropriate for the changing international environment.

In addition, the Navy should develop a less expensive and less sophisticated frigate than the costly DDG-51 and a new small submarine to replace the Trident. Finally, because the changes in Eastern Europe mean that the West will have much more mobilization time to deal with an unexpected Soviet breakout, the Navy should begin developing a fast sealift program to replace current reliance on airlift. For example, fast sealift could deliver more tons to Europe (in two weeks) than airplanes can, for about 5 percent of the cost.[32]

For the long term the Navy should be aiming toward a force of 9 carrier battle groups, with 7 active and 2 reserve air wings and 400 ships. This force should be adequate to protect the sea-lanes and support flexible deployments to various areas of the world in the next century.

Air Force. The 1991 Air Force budget increases in nominal terms by $1.9 billion, or 2 percent. Its procurement budget increases by 4 percent. And no wonder. Besides the plethora of strategic programs mentioned earlier, the Air Force wants to purchase 6 C-17 cargo planes for $2.7 billion and 1,250 AMRAAMs (advanced medium-range air-to-air missiles) for $0.9 billion; continue full-scale research on the advanced tactical fighter (ATF), which eventually will cost at least $100 million each for 750 planes; and buy 186 additional F-15s and F-16s for almost $5 billion. The service leaves its conventional force structure virtually intact.

Since the C-17, AMRAAM, and ATF are oriented primarily toward a European contingency, they can easily be canceled. As discussed, with more mobilization time, fast sealift is a much better buy than the C-17. Thus the program for the new cargo plane, which would cost about $42 billion for the 211 planes envisioned, should be terminated now. The AMRAAM continues to have problems in identifying enemy aircraft

---

32. Kaufmann and Korb, *1990 Defense Budget*, p. 44. In 1990 Congress appropriated $600 million for fast sealift, but Secretary of Defense Cheney reprogrammed the funds.

beyond visual range, and its costs continue to rise (at $700,000 a missile and rising, its costs are already 22 percent above the level the secretary of defense certified to Congress as the absolute limit in 1986). Moreover, its primary mission—engaging sophisticated aircraft in a complex air battle—is far less likely to be needed than it was when planning for the missile began. Rather than continue to throw good money after bad, the Air Force should kill the AMRAAM right away. The ATF, which suffers from similar development and cost problems, should be canceled, especially since there is little need now for a long-range Stealth plane to fly deep behind Soviet and Warsaw Pact front lines. In its place the Air Force should develop a new combat air support plane as a follow-on to the A-10. Any high-technology missions can be handled by the two existing squadrons of Stealth fighters (F-117A).

The size of the Air Force should decline. There is no need in the postcontainment era to maintain 35 tactical air wings whose primary mission is to wage high-intensity combat in Europe. Indeed, under the now outmoded NATO plans, 100 of the 116 squadrons in these 35 wings were to be in place in Europe within ten days after a war began. To reflect the new environment, the Air Force could cut 5 active wings, or 17 squadrons, by 1995 and another 7 wings by the end of the century.

Conclusion

The security interests of the United States would be adequately protected by a 1995 defense budget of $227 billion and a 2000 budget of $152 billion (in 1990 dollars), distributed as shown in table 4-7. In 1995 the Army and Marine Corps together will have 27 active and reserve ground divisions, the Air Force 30 active and reserve wings, and the Navy 12 carrier battle groups and 500 ships. This force would be augmented by 6,000 nuclear weapons and have an active duty military strength of 1.5 million and a civilian force of 750,000. By 2000 a continuation of the present trends in international relations would permit elimination of an additional 5 divisions, 6 wings, 100 ships, and 3,000 nuclear weapons and an additional 750,000 military and civilian personnel. Real spending in all the categories except research and development would fall as the active force structure declines, readiness is lowered, procurement slows, and emphasis shifts to protecting the U.S. technology base.

As regards the military risks and obligations of the United States, the nation has clearly entered a new era. The Bush budget has not crossed

TABLE 4-7. Defense Budget Authority for Fiscal Year 1990
and Author's Proposal for Fiscal Years 1995 and 2000
Amounts in billions of 1990 dollars

	1990		1995		2000		Change, 1990–2000	
Item	Amount	Percent	Amount	Percent	Amount	Percent	Amount	Percent
Military personnel	79	27	63	28	40	26	−39	−49
Operations and maintenance	87	30	66ᵃ	29	43ᵃ	28	−44	−51
Procurement	83	28	56ᵇ	25	37ᵇ	24	−46	−53
Research, development, test, and evaluation	37	13	36	16	28	18	−9	−24
Otherᶜ	8	2	6	2	4	3	−4	−50
TOTAL	291	100	227	100	152ᵈ	100	−140	−48

SOURCES: For 1990, *Department of Defense Annual Report, Fiscal Year 1990*, p. 69; for 1995 and 2000, author's estimates. Figures are rounded.
a. The amount for operations and maintenance assumes a readiness rate approximately 25 percent below current levels.
b. The amount spent on procurement assumes not only that there are smaller forces but also that they live off some other inventory built up during the Reagan expansion.
c. Includes construction of family housing and offsetting receipts.
d. If readiness and modernization stayed at their present rates, this figure would rise to about $200 billion.

the threshold psychologically or fiscally. Its defense program is basically flawed. The latest defense guidance, issued on January 24, 1990, continues to dwell on a Soviet threat to the third world that is no longer credible.[33] Because the fear of a Soviet threat, in an era when the Soviet empire and even the Soviet Union itself are crumbling, cannot keep sustaining a robust military posture, the problem is not that the defense budget will remain too high but that it will drop too fast. As Representative Les Aspin has noted, the defense budget is in a political free-fall.[34] The formidable and important challenge to the Bush administration is to explain to the American people that even without the specter of the "evil empire" a substantial military force remains vital to U.S. security. It must be a military appropriate for a great power dependent for its economic well-being on the smooth working of the international political system, which has always needed military power in the background.

The coming reductions in defense spending will also require some economic adjustments at home. Overall, reducing defense spending by

33. Barbara Amouyal, "Defense Plan Gives Broad Latitude," *Defense News*, February 12, 1990, p. 1; and Patrick E. Tyler, "New Pentagon Guidance Cites Soviet Threat in Third World," *Washington Post*, February 13, 1990, p. A1.
34. His remarks are quoted in *Aerospace Daily*, December 8, 1989, p. 388.

25 percent by 1995 and 50 percent by 2000, and reducing it by 2 to 3 percent of GNP, will have a positive effect on the U.S. economy. But some communities will need short-term assistance to deal with base or plant closings. If a comprehensive plan is not developed, the 1991–95 period will replay the events of 1989, when members of the military-industrial complex, scrambling for scarce defense dollars, persuaded Congress to stretch out rather than cancel programs. A shrinking military force will narrow the opportunities for upward mobility used by many members of the lower socioeconomic classes. Alternative educational programs need to be developed for them. In short, the Bush administration should develop a strategy to deal with the end of the cold war rather than try to preserve the military structure that won it. The 1991 defense budget does not do that job.

TABLE 4A-1. Defense Budget Authority for Fiscal Years 1984–91, by Program and Function

Millions of dollars

Item	1984	1985	1986[a]	1987	1988	1989	1990	1991
Current dollars								
Military personnel	48,363	67,773 [b]	67,794 [b]	74,010 [b]	76,584 [b]	78,477 [b]	78,548 [b]	79,054 [b]
Retired pay	16,503							
Operations and maintenance	70,950	77,803	74,888	79,607	81,629	86,221	86,761	90,092
Procurement	86,161	96,842	92,506	80,234	80,053	79,390	82,561	77,855
Research, development, test and evaluation (RDT&E)	26,867	31,327	33,609	35,644	36,521	37,530	36,809	37,972
Military construction	4,510	5,517	5,281	5,093	5,349	5,738	5,266	5,578
Family housing	2,669	2,890	2,803	3,075	3,199	3,276	3,221	3,458
Special foreign currency program	3	9	2	4	...	...	...	...
Defense-wide contingency	...	...	...	...	...	...	...	−300
Revolving and management funds	2,774	5,088	5,235	2,612	1,246	897	−769	2,228
Trust and receipts	−628	−426	−707	−781	−801	−668	−999	−776
Intragovernmental receipts	−22	−21	−22	−28	−26	−25	−28	−29
TOTAL	258,150	286,802	281,390	279,469	283,755	290,837	291,369	295,131
Constant 1991 dollars								
Military personnel	63,155	80,110 [b]	77,261 [b]	82,442 [b]	82,100 [b]	81,460 [b]	81,142 [b]	79,054 [b]
Retired pay	20,872							
Operations and maintenance	88,314	94,934	90,434	93,034	92,451	93,680	90,885	90,092

Procurement	110,696	120,712	111,707	93,481	89,698	85,559	85,627	77,855
RDT&E	34,311	38,819	40,562	41,706	41,198	40,653	38,306	37,972
Military construction	5,820	6,905	6,423	5,973	6,021	6,203	5,469	5,578
Family housing	3,355	3,535	3,349	3,576	3,604	3,546	3,356	3,458
Special foreign currency program	4	11	2	4	...	...	...	...
Defense-wide contingency	...	...	...	...	...	...	...	-300
Revolving and management funds	3,522	6,248	6,253	3,037	1,407	972	-801	2,228
Trust and receipts	-798	-523	-844	-908	-904	-723	-1,041	-776
Governmental receipts	-28	-26	-26	-33	-30	-28	-30	-29
TOTAL	329,224	350,724	335,123	322,311	315,546	311,324	302,915	295,131
Percent real growth								
Military personnel	1.2	26.8	-3.6	6.7	-0.4	-0.8	-0.4	-2.6
Retired pay	-1.2	-100.0	0.0	0.0	0.0	0.0	0.0	0.0
Operations and maintenance	5.2	7.5	-4.7	2.9	-0.6	1.3	-3.0	-0.9
Procurement	3.8	9.0	-7.5	-16.3	-4.0	-4.6	0.1	-9.1
RDT&E	13.6	13.1	4.5	2.8	-1.2	-1.3	-5.8	-0.9
Military construction	-3.2	18.6	-7.0	-7.0	0.8	3.0	-11.8	2.0
Family housing	-4.4	5.4	-5.2	6.8	0.8	-1.6	-5.4	3.0
TOTAL	4.6	6.5	-4.4	-3.8	-2.1	-1.3	-2.7	-2.6

SOURCE: *Department of Defense Annual Report, Fiscal Year 1991*, p. 69. Figures are rounded.
a. Lower budget authority in the military personnel accounts in 1986 reflects the congressional direction to finance $4.5 billion for the military pay raise and retirement accrual costs by transfers from prior year unobligated balances.
b. Retired pay accrual included in military personnel appropriation.

FIGURE 4A-1. Defense Spending as a Share of Federal Outlays, Fiscal Years 1950–95

Percent

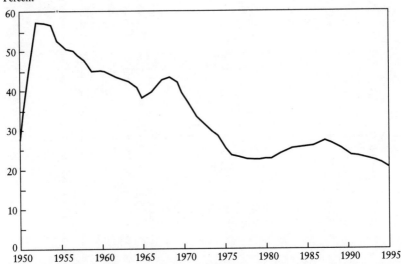

SOURCE: Office of Assistant Secretary of Defense (Public Affairs), "FY 1991 Department of Defense Budget Request," News Release 29-90 (January 29, 1990).

FIGURE 4A-2. Defense Outlays as a Share of Gross National Product, Fiscal Years 1950–95

Percent

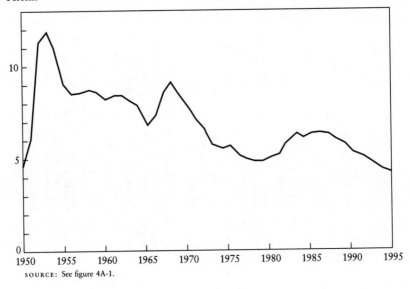

SOURCE: See figure 4A-1.

FIGURE 4A-3. Defense-Related Employment as a Share of the Total
Labor Force, Fiscal Years 1950–95

Percent

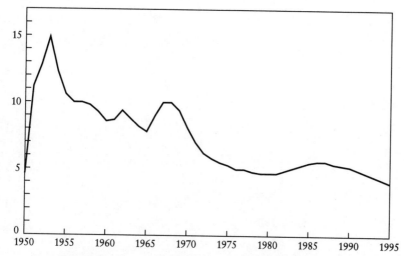

SOURCES: Office of the Assistant Secretary of Defense (Comptroller), *National Defense Budget Estimates for FY 1988/1989* (April 1988), pp. 120–21; and *Department of Defense Annual Report, Fiscal Year 1990*, p. 72.

5

ROBERT Z. LAWRENCE

Innovation and Trade: Meeting the Foreign Challenge

FOR MOST of the postwar period the United States pursued free trade with almost religious zeal. Even though it did so for reasons of self-interest, other nations greatly benefited from this strategy. Lately, U.S. policy has begun to embrace increased governmental participation in trade and technical development, allegedly to defend against similar actions abroad. Is this shift in policy in the American interest? And what policies should the United States adopt to deal with its changed international position?

The United States no longer falls neatly into the category of either leader or follower. In the past the U.S. strategy was clear. As the world's technological leader, the United States wanted free markets at home and open markets for its products abroad. As the free world's leader, it wanted to contain Soviet expansion with a strong military at home and prosperity abroad. But today U.S. policies reflect the growing pressures of its changed global status; the U.S. technological position has changed to "first among equals." The concern of the technological leader, to achieve unrestricted access to foreign markets, has been tempered by the concern of the follower, to nurture domestic firms. As U.S. conflicts with the Soviet Union have become less threatening, the concern of the superpower, to contain Soviet aggression, has been tempered by concerns about commercial rivalries with allies and an eroding industrial base.

The challenge for U.S. policies in this new environment is to steer between two extremes. On the one hand, the United States can no longer take its commercial innovation for granted, nor can it ignore those foreign policies that damage its living standards. On the other hand, the

This paper reflects work in progress on my study of U.S. manufacturing, financed by the Ford Foundation. I am indebted to Sheryl D. Nowitz for research assistance and Evelyn Taylor for text processing. I received helpful comments from Henry J. Aaron, Martin N. Baily, Claude Barfield, Theodore H. Moran, Pietro S. Nivola, and Charles L. Schultze.

United States must avoid nationalistic, protectionist intervention through sectoral industrial policies at home and managed trade abroad. U.S. policies should stimulate innovation and diffusion within the United States. They should also allow the United States to take full advantage of global markets through access to foreign markets, products, and technology.

Before discussing policy options aimed at meeting this challenge, I review the recent history of U.S. policies and consider the best approach to encourage innovation, first for a single economy and then for an economy with foreign rivals.

Postwar Trade and Innovation Policies

The 1990s provide a new competitive environment for the United States. The postwar era, marked by U.S. technological dominance and geopolitical rivalry with the Soviet Union, is coming to a close.

The Era of Confidence

In the 1950s and 1960s U.S. firms and the U.S. government took America's technological preeminence for granted. The main goal of U.S. foreign policy, to contain Soviet expansion, was achieved through policies that enhanced U.S. military power and promoted economic growth and a liberal trading order in countries outside the Soviet bloc. The United States sacrificed narrower economic advantages for strategic geopolitical goals. It restricted exports of some advanced products to prevent diffusion of high technology to unfriendly countries, and in arms sales to allies it readily transferred defense technology in so-called offset programs.[1]

More generally, the United States refused to exploit its power to restrict technological diffusion through inhibitions on foreign trade, investment, or licensing. Instead, it gave its multinational companies free rein to exploit their technologies, including transfer of technology to overseas affiliates. It implemented policies designed to facilitate company operations by opening foreign markets and insured foreign direct investment against expropriation. Even where foreign markets were kept closed for U.S. exports, U.S. firms were allowed to invest; and even where markets were closed both to U.S. exports and investment, as in

1. See Bernard Udis and Keith E. Maskus, "Offsets as Trade Policy: Some Motivations and Consequences for the Aerospace Industry," University of Colorado, Department of Economics, May 1988.

Japan, U.S. companies were allowed to license their technology to foreign producers.

The United States sought a liberal global trading order. Its policies aimed to open foreign markets not only for U.S. products but also for products of all nations. With U.S. leadership a series of multilateral negotiations under the General Agreement on Tariffs and Trade (GATT) diffused reductions in trade barriers through the principle of most favored nation treatment. If any GATT member granted another member a lower tariff, all GATT members were entitled to similar treatment.

At home, the United States relied on market forces to develop commercial technology. The emphasis was on preserving competition through antitrust policies rather than on providing incentives for innovation. Within this framework the government confined its financial support for innovation either to sectors with a clear public purpose, such as national defense, space, health, and basic research, or to activities in which commercial support seemed inadequate for social needs, such as synthetic fuels, breeder nuclear reactors, and "Project Breakthrough" to improve methods for residential construction.

Except in defense, the United States allowed foreigners to participate in its research and to share its fruits. For example, as a regulated government monopoly, American Telephone and Telegraph Company was required by U.S. antitrust law to license its inventions to all comers, foreign and domestic. When AT&T invented the transistor, Japan's Sony Corporation was among the first to be licensed.

To be sure, not all U.S. policies were so self-abnegating. The government supported commercial research and development (R&D) ventures in such sectors as agriculture and synthetic fuels, and it financed the rescue of private corporations like Lockheed and Chrysler. It also protected domestic industries such as textiles, steel, and automobiles and discriminated against foreign firms in government procurement. Nonetheless, the general thrust of policies toward liberalism was clear.

From Preeminence to First among Equals

These policies were remarkably successful. They lowered global trade barriers and diffused U.S. technologies and products internationally. But although the United States remained the world's most productive major economy, by the 1980s foreign productivity levels had converged close to those in the United States (table 5-1). Indeed, in some sectors foreign productivity exceeded U.S. productivity. During the 1950s and 1960s

TABLE 5-1. Relative Levels of Gross Domestic Product,
"Group of Seven" Countries, Selected Years, 1950–88
U.S. GDP = 100

| Country | Gross domestic product per employed person | | | | | |
	1950	1960	1970	1980	1987	1988
United States	100.0	100.0	100.0	100.0	100.0	100.0
Canada	76.8	79.7	83.8	92.5	95.4	94.6
Japan	15.2	23.3	45.7	62.7	70.3	71.5
France	38.1	47.6	63.8	80.2	85.0	85.6
West Germany	34.5	49.1	61.9	77.5	80.4	81.0
Italy	29.3	41.7	63.0	81.8	84.9	85.1
United Kingdom	53.7	54.5	58.2	66.4	72.6	71.6

SOURCE: U.S. Department of Labor, Bureau of Labor Statistics, Office of Productivity and Technology, "Comparative Real Gross Domestic Product, Real GDP per Capita, and Real GDP per Employed Person: Thirteen Countries, 1950–1988," August 1989, pp. 14–15.

economists described a product cycle in which new products were introduced in the United States and later diffused abroad.[2] By the 1980s, however, the product cycle operated in both directions across the Atlantic and the Pacific.[3] Earlier, reflecting their technological and managerial advantages, U.S. firms had found opportunities to set up manufacturing and marketing operations abroad, and U.S. direct foreign investment abroad had expanded rapidly. But by the late 1970s foreign firms found that the U.S. market provided an increasingly attractive location for investment to exploit their advantages. Previously, U.S. firms had dominated innovation; by the 1980s they had been joined by firms from other countries. In 1970, for example, U.S. inventors accounted for 73 percent of the patents granted in the United States; in 1986 they accounted for 54 percent.[4]

A New Competitive Environment

In the 1980s the budget deficits and restrictive monetary policy associated with President Ronald Reagan's supply-side economics led to

2. Raymond Vernon, "International Investment and International Trade in the Product Cycle," *Quarterly Journal of Economics,* vol. 80 (May 1966), pp. 190–207.

3. Raymond Vernon, "The Product Cycle Hypothesis in a New International Environment," *Oxford Bulletin of Economics and Statistics,* vol. 41 (November 1979), pp. 255–67.

4. National Science Board, *Science and Engineering Indicators–1987* (Washington: National Science Foundation, 1987), p. 302.

high interest rates that pushed up the exchange value of the dollar. With their technological lead declining and their products overpriced by the strong dollar, U.S. firms increasingly complained about the government aid received by their foreign competitors.

Unlike the United States, both Japan and Europe have had extensive programs aimed at improving commercial performance. The Japanese challenge is particularly important. In a series of plans the Ministry of International Trade and Industry (MITI) laid out the sectoral priorities of Japanese economic development. It then helped priority sectors with a wide range of measures, some financial (such as accelerated depreciation allowances; special R&D funding, often through an industry association; tax benefits; and government loans), some organizational (such as encouragement of mergers), and some protectionist (such as administrative guidance and selective government procurement and other export promotion). Increasingly, the Japanese have targeted areas in which the United States has displayed particular technological strength: semiconductors, computers, aerospace, and biotechnology.[5]

The contribution of Japanese industrial policy to Japan's economic performance is unclear, as is the applicability of Japanese methods to an economy like that of the United States, which has very different political institutions and a different global economic position.[6] Nonetheless, Japanese trade and industrial performance have strengthened the position of those who believe the Japanese strategy should be emulated.

As Japan has emerged as the principal competitor of the United States, attention has focused on the asymmetries between the two countries in market entry. The United States is by and large an open market for foreign products: U.S. capital markets permit foreigners ready access to U.S. technology and companies, and the government has given U.S. firms free rein to sell technology. By contrast, the Japanese market remains difficult for foreigners to crack, particularly in high-technology sectors

5. See, for example, Daniel I. Okimoto, *Between MITI and the Market: Japanese Industrial Policy for High Technology* (Stanford University Press, 1989); Hugh Patrick, ed., *Japan's High Technology Industries: Lessons and Limitations of Industrial Policy* (University of Washington Press, 1986); and Ryutaro Komiya, Masahiro Okuno, and Kotaro Suzumura, eds., *Industrial Policy of Japan* (San Diego: Academic Press, 1988).

6. For a serious econometric study that finds a positive effect, see Marcus Noland, "Industrial Policy and Japan's Trade Pattern," Institute for International Economics, Washington, 1989. For a persuasive statement of the opposite case, see Gary R. Saxonhouse, "What Is All This about 'Industrial Targeting' in Japan?" *World Economy*, vol. 6 (September 1983), pp. 253–74; and Phillip H. Tresize, "Industrial Policy Is Not the Major Reason for Japan's Success," *Brookings Review*, vol. 1 (Spring 1983), pp. 13–18.

that have been targeted for development. Although the nature of barriers to entry has engendered considerable academic debate, the data suggest that Japanese imports of manufactured goods and the share of foreign firms in Japanese domestic sales are unusually low.[7]

These increased competitive pressures and the challenge from Japan have changed the attitude of U.S. high-technology firms. Once, these firms disdained government intervention to aid their industries and staunchly advocated liberal trade. Today they have adopted increasingly complex positions.[8] Some now seek government support at home and assistance in securing access to, and even in guaranteeing shares of, markets abroad.[9]

Besides these competitive pressures from foreign firms, two other new features of innovation are important. First, the United States has long relied on commercial spillovers from defense to stimulate technology in private industry. Increasingly, however, commercial innovations are moving much faster than at the fairly sluggish pace with which the Department of Defense adopts new technologies. So the department relies on commercial innovations in designing new weapons systems. But U.S. firms are no longer always technological leaders, and as foreign investment grows in the United States the share of firms eligible for defense contracts shrinks. Thus the effect of reduced commercial competitiveness on defense technology has become a matter of growing concern.[10]

Second, the nature of technological development is changing. Companies are increasingly dependent on others for technology. The growing

7. See, for example, Robert Z. Lawrence, "Imports in Japan: Closed Markets or Minds?" *Brookings Papers on Economic Activity* 2:1987, pp. 517–54 (hereafter *BPEA*); and Robert Z. Lawrence, "How Open Is Japan?" paper presented to the National Bureau of Economic Research Conference on "The U.S. and Japan: Trade and Investment," October 11, 1989.

8. Helen V. Milner and David B. Yoffie, "Between Free Trade and Protectionism: Strategic Trade Policy and a Theory of Corporate Trade Demands," *International Organization*, vol. 43 (Spring 1989), pp. 239–72.

9. See, for example, *A Strategic Industry at Risk*, Report to the President and the Congress from the National Advisory Committee on Semiconductors, November 1989; and Advisory Committee on Trade Policy Negotiations, "Analysis of the U.S.-Japan Trade Problem," Report to Carla Hills, Washington, February 1989.

10. Defense Science Board, *Final Report of the Defense Science Board 1988 Summer Study on the Defense Industrial and Technology Base* (Office of the Undersecretary of Defense for Acquisitions, October 1988); and Office of Technology Assessment, *Holding the Edge: Maintaining the Defense Technology Base*, OTA-ISC-420 (April 1989).

use of basic science and integrated knowledge from several disciplines, the need for developing complex systems, and the rise in development costs have all led to greater interfirm cooperation.[11] Moreover, the speed with which new products are brought to market puts a premium on the rapid adoption of innovations made by others.

Today, therefore, innovation is marked by system development that lends itself to cooperative research and joint ventures of many kinds. Even without government assistance, U.S. firms have formed cooperative ventures with one another (for example, the Microelectronics and Computer Corporation, MCC, which includes many firms) or in association with academic institutions (for example, the Semiconductor Research Corporation, the Microelectronics Center of North Carolina, and the Stanford University Center for Integrated Systems). Joint ventures, alliances, and other collaborative efforts have also proliferated. Firms that compete in some areas now often cooperate in others.

Furthermore, the international convergence of technological capabilities has made technical cooperation global. Corporate alliances increasingly span national boundaries, often making it difficult to identify the national origins of products.[12] Even though people compare the American Boeing with the European Airbus, the Boeing is often equipped with a Rolls-Royce engine and the Airbus with an engine built by the U.S.-owned General Electric Company. Indeed, when Pan American purchased the Airbus, it listed almost 500 U.S. companies that produced parts for the aircraft, claiming the sale would generate 37,000 American jobs in thirty-five states.[13] Likewise, technology is increasingly being developed in international alliances.[14] American microchip makers, for example, agreed in November 1989 to work with Japanese companies in building components for high-definition television. IBM has agreed to work with Siemens on a DRAM (dynamic random access memory) of sixty-four megabits; Motorola is producing memory chips with Toshiba Corporation; Texas Instruments is cooperating with Hitachi; the Intel Corporation will sell memory chips made by NMB Semiconductor; and

11. Francois Chesnais, "Technical Co-operation Agreements between Firms," OECD, *STI Review,* no. 4 (December 1988), pp. 52–119.

12. See, for example, John M. Kline, "Inter-MNC Arrangements: Shaping the Options for U.S. Trade Policy," *Washington Quarterly,* vol. 8 (Fall 1985), pp. 57–71.

13. Kline, "Inter-MNC Arrangements," p. 62.

14. Michael L. Katz and Janusz A. Ordover, "R&D Cooperation and Competition," *BPEA* (forthcoming), provide an extensive list of domestic and international alliances in semiconductors.

Advanced Micro Devices will acquire advanced semiconductor manufacturing technology in an alliance with Sony.[15]

Taken together, these developments have made the environment for
U.S. technology policy extremely complex. On the one hand, the growing
international competitive pressures on U.S. firms, the need to respond
to foreign industrial policies, the increased importance of commercial
technology for national defense, and the need for increased collaboration
among firms have all created demands for U.S. government aid and
protection. On the other hand, the proliferation of corporate inter-
penetration and joint production among multinational corporations of
differing national ownership has made it increasingly difficult for governments to know exactly which interventions do and which do not
advance the interests of their own firms, workers, and citizens. This
latter consequence is often less appreciated than the former.[16]

New Policies

In the 1980s, despite the rhetorical embrace of economic liberalism
by Republican administrations, U.S. policies were affected by all the new
pressures. The nation, which was once secure in its technological
superiority and enacted antitrust laws to ensure competition among its
firms, developed concern about the inability of its firms to collaborate
to meet foreign competition.[17] The technological leader that claimed all
nations should enjoy unrestricted access to foreign markets is now the
follower, anxious to nurture domestic companies.[18] The world's largest

15. Andrew Pollock, "Sony to Share Data at U.S. Plant," *New York Times,* February
21, 1990, p. D1.

16. For a perceptive discussion, see Robert B. Reich, "Who Is Us?" *Harvard Business
Review,* vol. 68 (January–February 1990), pp. 53–64.

17. Legislation has tilted away from an extreme concern over the potential for
monopoly of firm cooperation. In 1982 the Export Trading Company Act immunized
joint export activities from antitrust concerns. In 1984 the National Cooperative Research
Act reduced the exposure to private antitrust action of firms engaging in joint R&D. In
1989 and 1990 legislative consideration has been given to permit joint manufacturing and
marketing.

18. For example, government support has been provided to research programs with
commercial goals for semiconductor equipment (Sematech), high-temperature supercon-
ductivity, and high-definition television. Under the aegis of the National Science Foundation,
engineering and science research centers at universities have been established to perform
commercially relevant generic research in such areas as robotics and biotechnology processes
and materials. A special tax credit for commercial R&D has been in effect since 1981.
Some of these U.S. commercial programs are now limiting or excluding foreign participa-

direct foreign investor is increasingly worried about foreign investment in the United States.[19] The superpower, which, confident in its technological superiority, sought to raise defense capabilities abroad, is now concerned that its policies might reduce its commercial advantages.[20] Finally, the unchallenged world economic leader, which sought a liberal trading order through multilateral approaches, increases quota protection at home,[21] organizes a global cartel in semiconductors,[22] and pursues many bilateral initiatives abroad.[23]

Because of these actions, U.S. policies are in danger of becoming increasingly inconsistent and contradictory. The long-standing U.S. opposition to trade barriers is coupled with increasing quotas at home.[24] In its multilateral negotiations, the United States calls for countries to treat foreign and domestic companies alike, for "national treatment," but at home it funds research programs that exclude foreign-owned firms. It insists that developing countries honor GATT rules on copyrights

---

tion. See David C. Mowery and Nathan Rosenberg, "New Developments in U.S. Technology Policy: Implications for Competitiveness and International Trade Policy," *California Management Review*, vol. 32 (Fall 1989), pp. 107–24.

19. The Department of Commerce informally discouraged the takeover of Fairchild Semiconductor by Fujitsu. In 1988 Congress set up a more extensive surveillance mechanism for foreign investment in the United States in the Exon-Florio Act.

20. The Omnibus Trade Act of 1988 contains measures designed to rationalize export controls. After being challenged, the initial agreement between Japan and the United States over production of the FSX fighter was changed to provide increased protection for U.S. technologies.

21. In the 1980s quota protection was renewed for U.S. textiles and extended to U.S. automobiles, steel, and machine tools.

22. In 1986 the United States and Japan concluded a semiconductor agreement providing higher prices for Japanese semiconductors sold in both the United States and third countries. In a confidential and controversial letter of understanding, the Japanese government agreed that sales of foreign-owned companies could achieve a 20 percent share of the Japanese market by 1991. In April 1987, dissatisfied by the results, the Reagan administration imposed 100 percent tariffs on $300 million of imported Japanese electronics. This move caused the Japanese government to organize production and export controls and led to higher DRAM prices worldwide.

23. In the 1980s bilateral negotiations with Israel and Canada led to free trade agreements. Between 1986 and 1988 eleven cases were initiated under section 301 of the trade law against foreign barriers to U.S. exports, including pharmaceutical practices in Brazil and mobile telephones in Japan. Prompted by congressional legislation in the "super 301" clause of the Trade Act of 1988, the Bush administration initiated negotiations with Japan, India, and Brazil over practices that, if not satisfactorily changed, could lead to U.S. retaliation with tariffs. Many bilateral market-opening initiatives have been conducted with Japan including the Structural Impediments Initiative in 1989–90.

24. For a discussion of the two-faced nature of U.S. trade policy, see Jagdish N. Bhagwati, "U.S. Trade Policy at Crossroads" *World Economy*, vol. 12 (December 1989).

TABLE 5-2. Federal Spending for Research and Development, by Selected Agency, 1989

Millions of dollars

Item	Total, all agencies	Department of Defense	Department of Energy	National Institutes of Health	National Aeronautics and Space Administra-tion	National Science Foundation	All other agencies
Total R&D	60,323	37,505	5,182	6,233	5,416	1,827	4,161[a]
Basic research	10,299	947	1,267	3,964	1,374	1,708	1,039
Applied research	9,412	2,407	959	1,789	1,700	119	2,439
Development	40,611	34,151	2,956	480	2,342	0	682

SOURCE: National Science Board, *Science and Engineering Indicators, 1989* (Washington: National Science Foundation, 1989), p. 278.

a. Of this amount, $118 million is spent on commercial applications (National Bureau of Standards) and $4,043 million on noncommercial applications (Departments of Agriculture, Education, Interior, Housing and Urban Development, Justice, Labor, State, Transportation, and Treasury, the Environmental Protection Agency, Nuclear Regulatory Commission, and Veterans Administration). National Science Foundation, *National Patterns of R&D Resources, 1989*, Final Report, NSF 89-308 (Washington, 1989), p. 56.

of intellectual properties and pay royalties for the use of such properties, but it unilaterally violates other GATT rules, such as imposing tariff measures against Brazil. Even though the Bush administration professes to believe in open markets and to oppose managed trade, it actively promotes a global semiconductor cartel and managed trade in Japanese semiconductor imports.

It would be inaccurate, however, to interpret these actions as an abandonment of the postwar goals of an open trading system. So far, they represent positions given up in a rearguard action rather than an abandonment of the field. The Bush administration has continued to place its highest priority on achieving progress in the multilateral trade negotiations, scheduled to end in 1990, and has committed itself to removing the restraints on U.S. steel imports by 1992. It has emphasized rules-based negotiations with Japan and, as of early 1990, apparently rejected the notion of a large government-backed industrial policy initiative to support a national program in high-definition television. The 1990 *Economic Report of the President* rejects industrial policy and managed trade and, to stimulate innovation, advocates such traditional measures as secure intellectual property rights and a capital gains tax reduction.[25]

The U.S. budget continues to reflect the lack of government support for commercial R&D. Although the federal government spends about $60 billion on R&D, it is heavily concentrated in defense, health, and space (table 5-2). Virtually none is explicitly devoted to commercial technology. While support has been granted, through a tax credit, to incremental R&D spending, it involves relatively small expenditures, and over the 1980s the rate was reduced from 25 to 20 percent.

Nonetheless, the debate over U.S. policies is not over. Large sections of Congress favor various forms of protectionism or managed trade. In the end, I reject these calls for industrial policies and managed trade. But I also suggest that the traditional U.S. approach to innovation needs to be changed.

Innovation in One Country

The innovation policies best suited for a single economy in isolation would be the policies a fully integrated world economy should adopt multilaterally. In a single private market, too little innovation will occur

25. *Economic Report of the President, February 1990*, pp. 114–18.

because the social benefits of innovation usually differ from the private benefits. Consumers and other companies often derive benefits from innovation that are not captured by the innovating firm. Competition often forces innovating companies to lower prices, which enables all consumers who are willing to pay a price that covers costs of production to buy the commodity. Other companies benefit from being able to copy innovations, and workers carry specialized know-how and skills to other companies. More generally, knowledge, once produced, costs nothing to use and therefore should be freely available.

Indeed, as Joseph Schumpeter emphasized, the essential challenge for innovation policy is how to balance the appropriately high private returns necessary to stimulate a socially optimal amount of innovation with the imperative that, once produced, knowledge has a zero social cost and should therefore be freely available.[26] Monopoly profits may have a role in inducing and encouraging the development of knowledge but none in diffusing it. Thus innovation policies must first stimulate innovation and then diffusion. Patents exemplify both elements; they give innovators monopoly rights for a time, but after the patent expires all are free to use the innovation.

Creation

Innovation can be promoted by research, not only by grants of monopoly rights but also by grants of money (for example, National Science Foundation grants to individual companies or to groups) or by indirect subsidies (for example, through tax credits that permit decentralized decisionmaking).

Although the principle is clear that research should be carried out until that last dollar spent yields one dollar of benefits to society as a whole (not just to the innovator), implementing this principle is extremely difficult for many reasons. Two are of great practical significance. First, public support should be focused on projects in which social benefits greatly exceed private benefits, but identifying such projects is hard. Second, public resources should be used to induce additional R&D, not to pay for research that private companies would have undertaken anyway. These two problems are closely related.

Commercial versus basic research. Some economists argue that gov-

---

26. Joseph A. Schumpeter, *The Theory of Economic Development: An Inquiry into Profits, Capital, Credit Interest, and the Business Cycle* (Harvard University Press, 1934).

ernment should support only basic research because proprietary rights over the results of such research are so weak that innovators are often unable to capture any benefits for themselves and also because the need for diffusion is greatest in that area.[27] To be sure, basic research merits government support. But the social benefits of applied research and development also greatly exceed private returns. Several studies have found social rates of return of between 50 and 100 percent, compared with private returns of between 20 and 30 percent.[28]

Grants versus credits. There is no reason to think that grant administrators can identify applied research projects that have both a large excess of social over private benefits and market potential. Private companies themselves should be instrumental in determining the nature of applied research. R&D tax credits or decentralized subsidies achieve this goal automatically. Companies decide what to investigate, the government pays part of the cost through the tax system, and companies put some of their own resources at risk.

Indeed, Japanese research projects are distinguished by relatively limited government financial support. The Japanese government typically accounts for just a quarter of all Japanese spending on R&D.[29] Because private participants are unlikely to provide funds unless they see potential commercial benefit, private funding of such research tends to result in marketable products.

Additionality. Research grants will increase total useful research only if the grantor can pick out good projects that applicants would not otherwise have funded. But grant applicants will tend to submit their best projects; that is, those they would have undertaken in any case. Insofar as applicants shift their own funds to some purpose other than research, the grant merely shifts payment from private to public budgets. A tax credit, however, will lower the marginal cost of R&D and thus affect decisions at the margin throughout the economy.

27. Robert Eisner, "The R&D Tax Credit: A Flawed Tool," *Issues in Science and Technology,* vol. 1, no. 4 (1985), pp. 79–86.

28. Edwin Mansfield and others, "Social and Private Rates of Return from Industrial Innovation," *Quarterly Journal of Economics,* vol. 91 (May 1977), pp. 221–40; John Beyer, "Net Rates of Return on Innovations," submitted to the National Science Foundation by Robert R. Nathan Associates, Washington, 1978; and J. G. Tewksbury, "A Survey on Net Rates of Return on Innovations," submitted to the National Science Foundation by Foster Associates, Washington, 1978.

29. Daniel Okimoto, "The Japanese Challenge in High Technology," in Ralph Landau and Nathan Rosenberg, eds., *The Positive Sum Strategy* (Washington: National Academy Press, 1986), p. 551.

R&D grant programs lend themselves well to mission-oriented "big bang" achievements in technology. But growth of national productivity rests not just on actions of a few large companies or R&D for a few big projects but also on the much broader innovative actions of businesses throughout the economy. And grants are hard to apply so as to encourage the many small incremental innovations by thousands of companies that adapt more fundamental breakthroughs to a wide variety of uses. These activities will be stimulated more by a system of diffused subsidies through R&D tax credits than by centralized grants.

These considerations suggest the following policy: small grants to provide partial support for projects, the social benefits from which greatly exceed private benefits; and widely available tax credits, to encourage large numbers of commercially relevant R&D activities.

Diffusion

It is not enough simply to invent a technology; it is equally important to ensure that its commercial potential is fully exploited through rapid diffusion and commercial application.[30] In certain areas, for example, the United States is weak even though it took the dramatic first-step measures of invention. Products that today are important Japanese exports, such as the semiconductor and the VCR, were invented in the United States. Moreover, in several case studies of U.S. industries, Martin Baily and Alok Chakrabarti found that "productivity slowdowns took place . . . because . . . industries failed to take advantage of technology that was potentially available."[31] It is also not enough for the United States just to have the leading scientists and engineers who make the breakthroughs. Innovative American scientists and engineers should not end up working in effect for foreign manufacturers because the United States lacks the vigorous management and technically competent work force to exploit the breakthroughs.

Competition promotes diffusion; monopolies inhibit it. Monopolists

30. For a perceptive discussion and further references, see Paul A. David, "Technology Diffusion, Public Policy and Industrial Competitiveness," in Landau and Rosenberg, eds., *Positive Sum Strategy,* pp. 373–91.

31. Martin Neil Baily and Alok K. Chakrabarti, *Innovation and the Productivity Crisis* (Brookings, 1988), p. 105. See also Nathan Rosenberg and W. Edward Steinmueller, "Why Are Americans Such Poor Imitators?" *American Economic Review,* vol. 78 (May 1988, *Papers and Proceedings, 1987*), pp. 229–34.

with a vested interest in one innovation may try to slow or limit further innovation or prevent others from using their technology. Policies such as antitrust and other measures to remove entry barriers are critical in encouraging diffusion.

Industrial policies in Switzerland, Germany, and Sweden have placed great stress on diffusion.[32] These countries have emphasized vocational training and extensive programs of worker retraining, with employers and trade unions strongly involved; extensive systems of industrial standardization that enhance quality and aid compatibility; and cooperative research on innovation through close industry-university links and industrywide cooperative research laboratories. Henry Ergas argues that these policies have been particularly effective in maintaining the competitiveness of the three countries in traditional mechanical engineering.

The United States has focused too much attention on Japanese projects for achieving technological breakthroughs and too little on the role of Japanese policies and practices in promoting diffusion. The Japanese have deliberately promoted the rapid adoption of innovations in machine tools and robotics, and they have encouraged increased collaboration between suppliers and producers. Japanese policies have not sacrificed the benefits of competition and have been carefully designed to encourage the development of more than one or two firms. Even in sectors targeted for promotion, companies have been urged to collaborate in the generic, precompetitive phases of research but forced to compete in manufacturing and marketing. By speeding up diffusion through collaboration, policies focus competition on these later phases. Similarly, administrative guidance and import barriers have protected domestic industries from foreign competition in the domestic market, but particular firms have rarely been granted a secure share of the domestic market. Japanese companies in favored sectors continue to compete strongly with one another at home and abroad. By contrast, French industrial policies have often promoted national "champions," single firms granted preferred status and protected from competitive pressures. This approach stifles competition. Where one firm is granted such status, frequently other domestic firms may be discouraged from competition.

---

32. Henry Ergas, "Does Technology Policy Matter?" in Bruce R. Guile and Harvey Brooks, eds., *Technology and Global Industry: Companies and Nations in the World Economy* (Washington: National Academy Press, 1987), pp. 191–245.

Collaboration

Policies to encourage collaborative ventures can raise the returns to research by dividing its fixed costs, making all potential beneficiaries of research pay for it, and reducing socially wasteful and duplicative expenditures.[33] They can also accelerate diffusion and increase competition by ensuring that several companies have access to precompetitive know-how.

Since cooperation is difficult to achieve between competitors and may foster monopolistic practices, it is best encouraged in generic and precompetitive research and development. The closer firms are to the production of generic scientific knowledge, the easier it is for them to negotiate and organize cooperation between many partners.[34]

Successful innovation often spans industries. Japanese innovation is marked by its success in achieving effective coordination between producers and their suppliers; for example, between automakers and steelmakers rather than among automakers. Four-fifths of all Japanese cooperative research is conducted by firms in different lines of business.[35]

Summary

The government should encourage technological innovation and diffusion, not just basic research. It should make grants to partially support precompetitive research by individual companies as well as collaborative ventures, and it should provide tax credits to encourage widespread research and development. It should also stimulate the rapid diffusion of best-practice technology by ensuring vigorous competition, supporting education and training, setting standards, and promoting other ventures to raise national technical competence.

The Foreign Challenge

The case for innovation policies made thus far has ignored foreign rivalry. But it is concern about foreign competition that lies behind the current U.S. interest in industrial policy at home and managed trade

33. For an extensive discussion, see Katz and Ordover, "R&D Cooperation and Competition."

34. Chenais, "Technical Co-operation Agreements between Firms," p. 59.

35. Richard J. Samuels, "Research Collaboration in Japan," MIT Japan Program, WP-87-02 (1987), p. 22.

abroad. Indeed, proponents of such measures concede that the United States is not ideally equipped to implement industrial policies, but they argue that it has no alternative but to adopt them because of the foreign challenge.

Deindustrialization

Some observers fear that if foreigners subsidize and promote their industries while the United States does not, U.S. export growth will be stifled, U.S. import growth will increase, and a permanent trade deficit will result in the erosion of the U.S. industrial base. But this argument assumes, implicitly and falsely, that a debtor nation can permanently sustain large and growing trade deficits.[36] As a country runs deficits, it accumulates debt on which it eventually must make payments that in turn create pressures that reduce the trade deficit. As interest obligations build up on the debt, for example, they set up outflows that first weaken the currency and then lower the trade deficit and increase the industrial base.

In any case, the trade balance is determined largely by domestic saving and investment behavior, not by the underlying competitiveness of the nation's industries. If domestic saving falls short of domestic investment, the result will be net foreign borrowing, or a trade deficit. Thus the cure for the deindustrialization caused by a trade deficit is to raise saving relative to investment.

The converse position is the mercantilist fallacy, the notion that a country could increase without limit its share of production in world markets with an ever-growing balance of trade. Eventually countries that run large trade surpluses accumulate large volumes of assets abroad. Income from these assets gives rise to a reverse inflow of payments to the creditor country that raises the demand for its currency, causing a decline in its trade balance. A net creditor country may permanently be lending to the rest of the world, but that will entail a trade deficit offset by a surplus in interest earnings.

36. Trade deficits in manufactured goods do not necessarily lead to a shrinkage in the domestic industrial base. The causes of the trade deficit must be analyzed. A trade deficit implies that the nation exports less than it imports. If the domestic demand for manufactured goods rises, both imports and domestic production could increase. The response could be both a bigger deficit and a larger industrial base. But if the deficit increased because exports fall or domestic purchasers shifted to imports, the manufacturing base could shrink.

Terms of Trade

Although foreign industrial policies cannot permanently saddle the United States with a trade deficit and a reduced industrial base, they can affect U.S. terms of trade—the quantity of foreign goods the United States can buy with its exports. If, for example, foreigners subsidize aircraft exports, U.S. exporters have to charge lower prices to match the competition.[37] Similarly, if foreigners erect barriers against some U.S. exports, then to achieve a given U.S. export level, more exports of other products will be required. To induce greater sales of those exports, they will have to be more attractively priced.

But not all foreign subsidies damage the U.S. terms of trade. If foreigners improve their relative ability to make products that the U.S. imports, Americans will benefit. If imports are sold in competitive markets, U.S. consumers will derive benefits that outweigh the losses that accrue to U.S. producers. To be sure, in the short run, some of the adjustment costs incurred in moving factors of production to alternative uses must be added, but over time foreign policies that make U.S. imports cheaper will raise American living standards.

In short, the policies of foreign countries to induce innovation or subsidize exports are not necessarily bad for the United States, but they can be. Those directed at lowering the costs of goods the United States can import will raise American living standards. But those directed at U.S. export industries could hurt.

As long as Japan and other nations helped companies that produced goods the United States imported, such as textiles and steel, the United States was likely to gain. But the United States was hurt as countries started to subsidize products that competed with U.S. exports, such as aircraft, satellites, and computers. Targeting by foreign countries must be taken more seriously as they become competitive with the United States.[38]

---

37. Although this argument may imply lower U.S. living standards, it does not imply a smaller traded-goods base. On the contrary, it implies that for any given level of the trade balance, the United States must produce a greater number of products—that is, more resources must be used rather than fewer.

38. Foreign countries could, however, follow policies that tax rather than subsidize their exports. Here the argument is reversed. The United States will benefit if foreign countries tax products that compete with U.S. exports and will lose if they tax products that compete with U.S. imports. Indeed, traditional trade theory has pointed to the benefits a large nation might enjoy by exploiting its monopoly power to optimize its terms of

While it is difficult to ascribe all the effects to targeting, in fact terms of trade have had to decline for many years to achieve any given trade balance. But the shift has had only small effects, depressing U.S. gross national product (GNP) less than one-tenth of a percent a year.[39]

Key Industries

Proponents of industrial policies argue that some industries are more important than others. They voice concern that foreign industrial policies will drive U.S. producers out of these key sectors and thus lower U.S. living standards. Why are all industries not created equal? If the market system is operating perfectly, it will automatically allocate resources to their highest marginal use. The next dollar invested in making hamburgers will yield the same social benefits as the next dollar invested in computers. However, if there are market failures, there is a case for favoring some industries over others. These failures can occur in three cases: (a) if some industries provide firms with surplus profits (rents) higher than is strictly necessary to induce investment in the sector; (b) if they pay workers premium wages that are higher than is necessary to induce them to work; or (c) if an increase in the industries' output provides benefits to others in the economy, for which producers in the sector receive no payments, that is, spillovers. I consider each case in turn.

Profits. The traditional case for free trade presumes highly competitive markets. It shows that from a global standpoint free trade maximizes global welfare. If a single country has monopoly power over a single good, however, it can improve its welfare, at the expense of others, by imposing tariffs or taxing its exports. But if other countries retaliate with tariffs or taxes of their own, *all* nations will be worse off. In recent years the analysis has moved beyond the assumption that competition is perfect, to take account of the economies of scale (the tendency of average production costs to fall as the scale of production rises) and of the widespread reality of imperfect competition.[40]

---

trade. The danger in such behavior, however, has always been that of foreign retaliation. See Harry G. Johnson, *International Trade and Economic Growth* (Harvard University Press, 1967), pp. 31–55.

39. For a more extensive analysis, see Robert Z. Lawrence, "The International Dimension" in Robert E. Litan, Robert Z. Lawrence, and Charles L. Schultze, eds., *American Living Standards: Threats and Challenges* (Brookings, 1988), pp. 23–65.

40. For excellent introductions, see Elhanan Helpman and Paul R. Krugman, *Market*

Taking into account these factors usually *strengthens* the case for free trade, because the gains from trade are larger when larger markets allow fixed costs to be spread and a greater variety of products to be available.[41] It underscores the importance of having access to large foreign markets and increases estimates of the costs of protection. But the new analysis also suggests how government policies can affect competition and improve national welfare at the expense of other nations.[42] In particular, if companies can earn monopoly profits from sales in foreign markets, successful efforts to boost the share of domestic companies in those markets can raise national income.

Export subsidies can deter foreign firms from competing at all.[43] In the presence of scale economies, protection of the domestic market for a firm could act like a subsidy, deterring foreign firms from expanding and increasing the returns of domestic firms.[44]

Some observers use these analyses as a basis for seeking increased government intervention in trade. But the conclusions of these analyses are often sensitive to the exact way companies and consumers are assumed to behave, and the assumptions are not verifiable. Given one set of assumptions, export subsidies help; given another set, the same policies backfire.[45] Moreover, empirical studies suggest that even where

---

Structure and Foreign Trade: Increasing Returns, Imperfect Competition, and the International Economy (MIT Press, 1985); and Helpman and Krugman, *Trade Policy and Market Structure* (MIT Press, 1989).

41. See J. David Richardson, "Empirical Research on Trade Liberalization with Imperfect Competition: A Survey," OECD, Department of Economics and Statistics, Working Paper 58 (November 8, 1989).

42. The novelty of the results derived from this analysis is often exaggerated. On this point see Jagdish Bhagwati, "Is Free Trade Passé after All?" *Weltwirtschaftliches Archiv*, vol. 125 (1989), pp. 17–44.

43. Barbara J. Spencer and James A. Brander, "International R&D Rivalry and Industrial Strategy," *Review of Economic Studies*, vol. 50 (October 1983), pp. 707–22.

44. See Paul R. Krugman, "Import Protection as Export Promotion: International Competition in the Presence of Oligopoly and Economies of Scale," in Henryk Kierzkowski, ed., *Monopolistic Competition and International Trade* (Clarendon Press, 1984), pp. 180–93; and Krugman, "Is Free Trade Passé?" *Journal of Economic Perspectives*, vol. 1 (Fall 1987), pp. 131–44.

45. Thus Eaton and Grossman have shown that in the same duopoly used by Spencer and Brander, if firms react to prices rather than quantities, an export subsidy will hurt the country that provides it, and in fact the country is better off taxing its exports. See Jonathan Eaton and Gene M. Grossman, "Optimal Trade Policy under Oligopoly," *Quarterly Journal of Economics*, vol. 101 (May 1986), pp. 383–406. Although subsidies may drive foreigners out of the market, they could also induce entry by domestic firms. This, as Horstmann and Markusen have emphasized, could ultimately dissipate the rent

they are successful, national gains from strategic rent-shifting policies at best are small, in part because profits usually constitute a small share of total value—typically less than 10 percent. Lawrence Katz and Lawrence Summers have found, for example, that "shareholders in American firms receive only very small monopoly rents. The weak available evidence suggests that the same situation holds for Japan."[46] The empirical studies also show that the nature of the optimal policy can be very sensitive to minor changes in behavioral parameters. Avinash Dixit studied the U.S. automobile industry and concluded that the optimal policy for the United States was a tariff on imports and a subsidy to domestic production.[47] Kala Krishna, Kathleen Hogan, and Phillip Swagel demonstrated that with quite minor changes in specifying the industry demand curve, the optimal policy became a subsidy on imports and production.[48]

Premium-wage jobs. Workers with the same skill and educational levels often earn far more in some industries than in others.[49] Some analysts have argued that it is appropriate to subsidize production in such activities. But that approach has several drawbacks. First, where unions have monopoly power, they may prefer to capture such subsidies through higher wages rather than increased employment.[50] Second, the distributional effect of using taxes to support high-wage sectors is regressive. Third, it is difficult to distinguish between rents and payments

---

to foreign consumers. Ignatius J. Horstmann and James R. Markusen, "Up the Average Cost Curve: Inefficient Entry and the New Protectionism," *Journal of International Economics*, vol. 20 (May 1986), pp. 225–48. Drawing scarce scientific and engineering resources into a particular sector could create losses elsewhere in the economy that outweigh the gains in the sector being promoted. Avinash K. Dixit and Gene M. Grossman, "Targeted Export Promotion with Several Oligopolistic Industries," *Journal of International Economics,* vol. 21 (November 1986), pp. 233–50.

46. Lawrence F. Katz and Lawrence H. Summers, "Industry Rents: Evidence and Implications," in *BPEA: Microeconomics 1989*, p. 269.

47. See Avinash Dixit, "Optimal Trade and Industrial Policy for the U.S. Automobile Industry," in Robert C. Feenstra, ed., *Empirical Methods for International Trade* (MIT Press, 1988), pp. 141–65.

48. Kala Krishna, Kathleen Hogan, and Phillip Swagel, "The Non-Optimality of Optimal Trade Policies: The U.S. Automobile Industry Revisited, 1979–1985," National Bureau of Economic Research Working Paper 3118 (Cambridge, Mass., September 1989).

49. See William T. Dickens and Kevin Lang, "Why It Matters What We Trade: A Case for Active Policy," in Laura D'Andrea Tyson, William T. Dickens, and John Zysman, eds., *The Dynamics of Trade and Employment* (Ballinger, 1988), pp. 87–122; and Katz and Summers, "Industry Rents," pp. 209–90.

50. See, for example, the comments on Victor Norman, "Imperfect Competition and General Equilibrium Aspects of Trade," in *Centre for Economic Policy Research Bulletin,* October 1989, pp. 5–6.

that reflect skills and other costs such as the disutility of certain types of labor. Since wage premiums seem to be higher in U.S. export-producing sectors than in import-competing sectors, the U.S. interest is in actions to expand rather than contract trade. In any event, the total benefits to be captured from broad measures to raise subsidies to sectors with premium wages are rather small.[51]

Many have suggested that U.S. national income has been reduced through foreign trade in the 1980s, because trade has induced significant losses of manufacturing jobs. Yet a study by Dickens and Lang shows, in fact, that the effect due to loss of labor rents is small. Eliminating the *entire* 1984 trade deficit by increasing exports and providing employment opportunities in import-competing industries for workers with average earnings, given their age, education, and experience, would have raised national output by less than 0.2 percent of GNP.[52]

Spillovers. Living standards will be enhanced by encouraging sectors that provide large spillover benefits to the economy. Policies abroad that discourage U.S. domestic production in such sectors could deprive the United States of the benefits from production. But it is important to be clear on the nature of these benefits. Spillovers need not be confined to a single economy. Innovations by a foreign company could allow U.S. companies to improve their technologies through reverse engineering. Similarly, U.S. consumers could benefit from intensified competition. These examples highlight the possibility that policies of foreign governments to promote innovation need not harm the United States.

As is well recognized, spillovers to consumers are strong in a single economy. It is striking, for example, that the wages of workers in high-technology industries rise at the same rate as the wages of workers in the rest of the economy (table 5-3). What matters for living standards is the overall rate of innovation, not the rate in the sector in which a worker is employed. The real buying power of barbers, whose productivity has shown almost no improvement, will rise at the same rate as that of people producing semiconductor chips, because the benefits of innovation in chips are passed on to *all* consumers through lower prices.

---

51. Although Katz and Summers find that taking account of labor rents suggests that the Airbus A300 program raises European welfare, it does so by between 0.86 and 1.80 billion (1985) dollars over a twenty-year period. That is between 5.6 and 11.7 percent of the total present discounted value of shipments. Katz and Summers, "Industry Rents," p. 258.

52. Author's calculations based on Dickens and Lang, "Why It Matters What We Trade," table 3-2.

TABLE 5-3. Average Hourly Wages of High-Technology Workers as Percentage of Manufacturing Wages, by Country, Selected Years, 1961–85[a]

Manufacturing wage = 100

Country	1961	1970	1985
United States	110	107	107
Japan	n.a.	105	106
West Germany	105	108	111
Canada	114	109	102

SOURCE: Author's calculations from Arthur Neef, "An International Comparison of Manufacturing Productivity and Unit Labor Cost Trends," paper prepared for October 1988 Social Science Research Council Conference on International Productivity and Competitiveness.

n.a. Not available.

a. Chemicals, engineering, instruments, and aerospace industries.

In fact, the main explanation for the convergence in incomes among developed economies in the world economy over the postwar period is precisely that U.S. innovations spilled over to the rest of the world. Moreover, the fact that incomes in small countries (such as Switzerland, Sweden, Austria, and Denmark) with incomplete industrial structures are no lower than incomes in large countries suggests that global spillovers are powerful. What is important for living standards, therefore, is not only what a country produces itself but also the access it has to the innovations of others.

Nonetheless, the tendency of companies from the same industry to locate near one another—for example, Silicon Valley—does suggest *some* role for geographically confined spillovers. In principle, therefore, these market imperfections could deprive a country of important benefits.[53]

To deal with this problem, the best policy for the United States might sometimes be to support an industry, sometimes to support a single company, and sometimes to do nothing. In general, the benefits from the spillovers must be weighed against the distortionary effects of the policies required to follow such a promotion measure. The most precise method of support would be production subsidies to activities with high, geographically specific industries. But as will be discussed, the implementation problems are difficult.

53. As Paul Krugman has pointed out, even where there are external economies, "If additional resources of capital and labor are supplied elastically to the industry, the external benefits of larger production will not be confined to the promoting country. Instead they will be passed on to the consumers around the world." Krugman, "Is Free Trade Passé?" p. 140.

Summary

The theoretical analysis suggests that there are circumstances in which interventionist policies of foreign governments could lower U.S. living standards. The U.S. terms of trade could be reduced if entry into foreign markets is hindered or products that compete with U.S. exports are subsidized. U.S. capital could lose profits, U.S. labor could lose premium-wage jobs, and the U.S. economy could be deprived of beneficial spillovers through foreign targeting. But the overall magnitude of these effects should not be exaggerated. In many cases, foreign policies could actually improve U.S. welfare; and without adequate information, adopting similar policies could make the United States even worse off. Although the United States should not ignore those practices, it should not feel driven to adopt similar policies on the assumption it has no alternatives.

Policy Options

The discussion so far has suggested that the United States should steer a course between extreme laissez-faire on the one hand and interventionism through industrial policies and managed trade on the other. Here I examine these various positions in greater detail.

Laissez-Faire

The extreme laissez-faire approach is inappropriate for current U.S. circumstances. Because of the large difference between private and social rates of return in commercial research, government support needs to go beyond basic research and the protection of intellectual property rights. Moreover, the doctrine of free trade "always and everywhere" does not withstand scrutiny. First, no matter how committed to free trade governments may be, in practice they will sometimes be forced politically to protect their domestic industries. It is far better to have a strategy for approaching those problems than simply to cave in to the loudest political voices.[54] Second, foreign protection can damage the United States. Unilateral free trade denies the United States the ability to retaliate and to bargain for lower barriers abroad by providing reciprocal access to the United States.

54. For a more extensive discussion, see Robert Z. Lawrence and Robert E. Litan, *Saving Free Trade: A Pragmatic Approach* (Brookings, 1986).

Industrial Policies

The interventionist approach would use industrial policies to aggressively promote U.S. firms and industries at home and managed trade to enhance exports and restrict imports. Key industries would be singled out and a wide variety of measures used to promote their commercial performance. Thus, for example, some believe that the U.S. consumer electronics industry should be promoted, starting with a program for high-definition television. Advocates of HDTV project it will be a prime determinant of technology, employment, and trade flows over the next twenty years.[55] They seek to combine financial support, antitrust exemptions, selective government procurement products, standards, and trade protection to promote a domestic HDTV industry. At the same time, they advocate a shift toward managed trade to ensure that U.S. companies negotiate shares in markets abroad.[56]

However, HDTV is just one of many sectors that are ready to make claims on the government purse. Industries lobbying Washington are like children in Lake Woebegon—they are all above average. If no consistent set of principles exists to determine which industries the government should support, who will decide? An industry committee with a vested interest in cheap financing is scarcely the appropriate arbiter of how society's scarce resources should be spent. To decide on the areas to support, the government would need (a) a consistent and defensible set of principles to choose among claims for help; (b) adequate information to determine if claims are justified; and (c) adequate restraint to avoid political pressures to provide aid where it is not justified. Indeed, one of the principal advantages of a basically free trade approach is that it provides politicians with a convenient reason to say "no" to special interest practitioners. Proponents of an industrial policy, for example, have advocated support for sectors that are high tech, pay high wages, have high value added, are intensive in R&D, have strong links to other

55. See Robert B. Cohen and Kenneth Donow, *Telecommunications Policy, High Definition Television, and U.S. Competitiveness* (Washington: Economic Policy Institute, 1989). For a rebuttal see Congressional Budget Office, "The Scope of the High-Definition Television Market and Its Implications for Competitiveness," Staff Working Paper, July 1989.

56. The American Electronics Association, for example, proposed a package of federal support for HDTV that would include $1.0 billion in loans and loan guarantees for manufacturing facilities, $300 million over three years to expand the Defense Advanced Research Project Agency's (DARPA's) HDTV research, and $50 million to develop product standards.

industries, or show rapid growth in productivity. Almost any industry can make a claim under one or another of these headings. Basically the proponents ignore the principle that intervention and the associated costs are worthwhile only if those measures yield a higher return than would other uses of the same resources; people often forget that in a fully employed economy, resources redirected by the government into HDTV or steel or any other favored industry will reduce output elsewhere in the economy. Nor is there any reason to think government officials can predict market outcomes better than private businesses can. If private entrepreneurs are able to capture the benefits from investing in sectors with high R&D intensity and rapid growth, it is unlikely the government will be able to do better.

Furthermore, the case for industrial policies requires that assistance be carefully targeted. Industries usually produce many products, some with significant spillovers, others without. But in practice this won't happen. The broader the government program, the more it will disperse benefits to all comers. Trade protection, for example, that was intended to help small clothing producers has been extended to sophisticated, highly competitive chemical companies that manufacture synthetic textiles.

Finally, globalization makes these problems particularly difficult. The links between product development and production in a global economy are uncertain. Simply because a product is developed abroad does not imply it will be manufactured abroad. Indeed, even though there is just one U.S.-owned company producing television sets in the United States—Zenith—most large TVs sold in the United States are built in this country. Conversely, simply because a product is developed in the United States does not imply it will be built in the United States or use U.S. components.

In a globalized economy it is not even clear which companies the U.S. government should assist. Should the U.S. HDTV program be directed toward U.S.-based companies or U.S.-owned companies?[57] By insisting on U.S. ownership as a condition for firms in such a program, the United States may exclude leading participants and reduce its ability to achieve the best product. Even defining which firms are U.S.-owned is not easy, particularly since ownership changes constantly. Although the MCC cooperative venture, for example, was confined initially to U.S.-owned firms, Honeywell, a substantial participant, was later sold to the French firm Bull.

---

57. For a persuasive answer, see Reich, "Who Is Us?"

The broader the array of measures used to promote a particular sector, the more difficult it is to confine benefits to U.S.-owned firms. Thus, allowing foreign firms to produce in the United States behind a trade barrier, for example, might increase domestic employment opportunities and spillovers but not necessarily increase the ability of U.S.-owned companies to compete.

The adoption of strongly nationalistic U.S. industrial policies would also have serious reverberations abroad. The United States retains a large global presence. U.S. discrimination against foreign-owned firms and products would undoubtedly be met by retaliation. Small countries may be able to support protection at home and free trade abroad simultaneously; an economy as large as that of the United States cannot.

Managed Trade

Proponents of domestic industrial policies sometimes argue that such policies should be complemented by managed trade. Mistrustful in particular of Japan's adherence to international trading rules, they argue that trade should be managed to ensure results satisfactory to all participants. Some advocate setting ceilings for imports of specific products; others seek floors for U.S. exports.

Imports. One group seeks to protect U.S. firms at home from competition. A favored policy would allot shares of U.S. imports. These so-called voluntary export restraints have been imposed on textiles, steel, TVs, and automobiles. Typically the restraints are initially imposed on Japan and then extended to other countries.

Advocates of these quotas often claim they are needed to preserve jobs in particular industries. But quotas are an outrageously expensive way to save jobs. They raise the costs to consumers of imported goods and the domestically produced goods with which they compete. American consumers in 1980 paid an estimated $74,155 per job saved through quotas on imported TV sets; through tariffs and quotas on footwear, $77,155 per job; and through tariffs and quotas on carbon steel, $85,272 per job.[58] These measures do not even ensure that jobs of current workers will be saved. By boosting profits that attract investment, quotas may

58. Murray L. Weidenbaum and Michael C. Munger, "Protection at Any Price?" *Regulation*, vol. 7 (July–August 1983), p. 17. See also Gary Clyde Hufbauer, Diane T. Berliner, and Kimberly Ann Elliot, *Trade Protection in the United States: 31 Case Studies* (Washington: Institute for International Economics, 1986).

cause a change in plant location or the purchase of more automated machinery. Insofar as protection encourages such a response, it can exacerbate dislocation and reduce employment. Quotas on textile imports probably increased rather than reduced dislocation by encouraging U.S. textile firms to move from New England to the South. Protecting commodities early in the chain of production causes further problems. By raising domestic prices for steel, for example, quota protection undermined the competitiveness of the heavy users of steel, such as the auto industry, which is now also protected by "voluntary" agreements that curtail auto imports.

So protection is a very costly, unpredictable, and inefficient device for saving jobs. By encouraging relocation and automation, screening domestic producers from competition, and raising production costs, it may actually reduce jobs in the protected industries. And even if protection temporarily preserves jobs, the effects wane with time. Meanwhile workers elsewhere in the economy may be harmed and, as noted, consumers pay an unreasonable price.

Protectionists claim that with a brief period of shelter, import-damaged industries can recuperate, modernize, and return to profitability. This line of argument raises an important issue. If an industry can be profitable with modest aid, what prevents it from borrowing enough to tide itself over until it is profitable? Why cannot lenders recognize the opportunities that industries claim as justification for protection?

This issue is most salient for the United States, since it has the world's best-developed capital market. Given so many sophisticated investors and a highly developed system of financial intermediaries, why would the government have a systematic advantage over the market in recognizing industries that have good prospects in the international marketplace? In short, those industries that cannot find help except from the government probably deserve to fail.

Quotas on imports may help foreign companies even more than the domestic industry. The "voluntary" restraints on imports of Japanese cars, for example, raised car prices throughout the American market. U.S. car manufacturers enjoyed an increase in profits, but so did their major foreign competitors, which could perpetuate, if not widen, their cost advantage over American producers.

To be sure, trade can conceivably impair a nation's defense by harming key domestic industries. But trade protection is a needlessly inefficient way to preserve an industry deemed essential to national defense. A far cheaper way is to pay for the capacity or to build enough stockpiles to defend the nation.[59]

In sum, managing U.S. imports is a costly and relatively inefficient way to achieve the goals of saving jobs, restoring competitiveness, and preserving the production capacity needed for national defense.

Exports. Increasingly, U.S. attention has shifted from protecting firms at home toward ensuring sales abroad. Many suggest that the Japanese economy operates under radically different rules from those in the United States. Efforts to open the market through changes in rules will fail. Instead, the United States should negotiate to ensure a minimum share of the Japanese market.

The 1986 Semiconductor Trade Agreement (STA) is an effort to manage foreign sales in the Japanese market. The agreement sets minimum prices for Japanese chip exports and requires Japan to boost its purchases of foreign semiconductor chips.[60] Defenders of this agreement argue that without it the U.S. economy will lose a strategic sector. But it is illuminating to examine the specifics of the agreement and how it operates.

The agreement calls for the products of foreign-owned companies to achieve 20 percent of domestic sales in Japan by 1991. It says nothing about where the chips should be produced. Indeed, it reflects the concerns of non–Japanese-owned companies rather than concerns about U.S.-based economic activity. The semiconductors that Texas Instruments produces in Japan or Korea, with Japanese or Korean labor and spillovers, qualify for this quota; the semiconductors that Nippon Electric or Fujitsu produce in the United States, with U.S. labor and spillovers, do not. As implemented, therefore, this initiative is not framed to affect the U.S. structure of production directly.

Japanese semiconductor firms allegedly gain an important advantage because their home market is protected; they can therefore enjoy rents not available to U.S. firms. The STA settles for giving foreign-owned firms 20 percent of those rents, but it does not undermine the basis of

59. For an excellent discussion of options, see Theodore H. Moran, "The Globalization of America's Defense Industries: What Is the Threat? How Can It Be Managed?" *Industrial Organization* (forthcoming).

60. Laura D'Andrea Tyson, "Managed Trade: Making the Best of the 'Second Best,' " in Robert Z. Lawrence and Charles L. Schultze, eds., *An American Trade Strategy: Three Options for the 1990s* (Brookings, forthcoming). For a defense of mandatory import requirements, see Michael G. Borrus, *Competing for Control: America's Stake in Micro-electronics* (Ballinger, 1988).

those rents. Indeed, because the STA has cartelized the global market for DRAMs, it has dramatically increased the profitability of Japanese chip firms. The agreement has done much more to boost the profits of Japanese firms that dominate world production than to raise the profits of its U.S. competitors. Moreover, the STA has thus far not been successful in raising the share of foreign chips in Japanese consumption close to its target. So Japanese firms continue to enjoy the scale economies arising from their strong domestic position.

One serious problem with sector-specific managed-trade solutions is that they will be dominated by industry participants whose interests do not necessarily coincide with those of the United States as a whole. This is particularly true in a key linkage sector like semiconductors. The cartelization of the global market for DRAM chips is certainly not in the interests of U.S. computer firms, which are not vertically integrated. Instead of favoring so-called linkage industries for these arrangements, the United States should be particularly reluctant to include them. The STA is thus a clear demonstration of the pitfalls of the managed-trade approach to strategically important sectors.[61] When results are being managed, the devil lies in the details. Unless a clear rationale for the policy exists, the specifics can make the results disappointing. For some purposes, such as enhancing the welfare of U.S. workers, it may be enough to emphasize greater U.S. exports; for other purposes, such as enhancing the profits of U.S. firms, it may be enough to seek increased participation by U.S. firms in Japan. But these approaches should not be confused with policies that aim at maximizing global welfare by achieving a true open market—namely, one that can be readily contested by new firms, both foreign and domestic, that choose to supply products made at home and abroad.

Finally, sector-specific agreements are always justified as transitional measures. But their history suggests that, once established, they expand, become institutionalized, and are extremely difficult to eliminate. Thus the voluntary export restraint in cotton textile exports from Japan to the United States in 1955 became the multilateral Short-Term Arrangement in cotton textiles in 1960, then the Long-Term Cotton Arrangement

---

61. For further discussion, see Kenneth Flamm, "Industry and Politics in the International Semiconductor Industry," paper presented to the SEMI ISS Seminar, Newport Beach, California, January 1989; and Flamm, "Semiconductors," in Gary Hufbauer, ed., *Europe 1992: An American Perspective* (Brookings, 1990).

in 1962, and eventually the Multifiber Arrangement in 1973, which, renewed and tightened, is still in force today.[62] Many developing countries that objected to its establishment have acquired a vested interest in its perpetuation.

By the same token, the U.S. firms that are given managed access to a market will be unwilling to give up their guaranteed market shares. Although a managed-trade arrangement may make the numbers look better in the short run, it is likely to be a step back from, rather than toward, the open, free trade regime the United States would like to see established.

Bilateralism

It is tempting for the United States to try to solve its trade problems with particular trading partners on a bilateral basis. As the world's largest economy, the United States seems in a particularly strong position when it confronts smaller and weaker economies one-on-one. Bilateralism allows the United States to present its case forcefully.

But bilateralism has many disadvantages.[63] It may be particularly costly politically. In many countries the notion of submitting to American economic influence is not popular. U.S. actions under section 301 of the Trade Act of 1974 have caused Koreans to burn the U.S. flag and a Thai cabinet to resign. Mexico, which joined the GATT recently, found it was easier to open up multilaterally, in the name of *reducing* its dependence on the United States, than to agree on a free trade area with the United States. Bilateral approaches may also increase friction with excluded third parties. The improvements in trade with some countries could come at the expense of broader relations with others.

Multilateral approaches may also be more persuasive. If the discussions about the closed nature of Japan were held multilaterally, for example, they would not turn into a debate about the problems of U.S. competi-

62. See William R. Cline, *The Future of World Trade in Textiles and Apparel* (Washington: Institute for International Economics, 1987), chap. 6.

63. For excellent discussions of the problems of bilateralism, see Jeffrey J. Schott, "More Free Trade Areas?" in Schott, ed., *Free Trade Areas and U.S. Trade Policy* (Washington: Institute for International Economics, 1989), pp. 1–58; and C. Michael Aho and Sylvia Ostry, "Regional Trading Blocs: Pragmatic or Problematic Policy?" in William E. Brock and Robert D. Hormats, eds., *The Global Economy: America's Role in the Decade Ahead* (Norton for the American Assembly, 1990), pp. 147–73.

tiveness. They would focus on the problem *all* foreigners have in selling in Japan.

Bilateralism also many not lead to the best economic results. In an interdependent global economy many problems simply cannot be solved bilaterally. Take, for example, the issues of subsidies to agriculture in the U.S.-Canada free trade agreement. Although both Canada and the United States had a real interest in reducing these subsidies, they could not achieve a meaningful result in their bilateral negotiations, for neither could see itself without the subsidies in third-country competition.

A multilateral deal brings all interested parties to the table simultaneously. This is a great simplifying device compared with piecemeal discussions that occur under much greater uncertainty when a series of bilateral negotiations are implemented. The value of a benefit to a particular country depends on who is party to the deal. Countries will object if they conclude a special deal for free access to the U.S. market, and in a later agreement the United States reduces the value of this concession by concluding a similar agreement with their main competitor. A sequence of bilateral deals may not be readily transformed into a multilateral system. The danger exists that proceeding piecemeal will result in a complex, crazy-quilt system in which U.S. trade with different partners is subject to different regulatory regimes.

All these problems created by bilateral approaches suggest that the United States should give its highest priority to multilateral approaches. The GATT should be used wherever possible to settle bilateral disputes and to negotiate new trade rules.

Preferable Options

The U.S. political system is likely to face major problems in trying to carry out a strategy that is not fairly simple and clear. The overall philosophy should reflect two main principles. First, government intervention should be confined to the well-known cases where private markets are inefficient; in particular, problems of monopoly and spillovers. It should deal with such failures across the economy rather than on a sector-specific basis. Second, U.S. responses to foreign practices should be based on rules. With regard to foreign-firm behavior in the United States, the principal instruments should be U.S. trade and antitrust rules. To change practices abroad, the emphasis should be rules-based, multilateral negotiations.

Innovation

All countries should encourage innovation with a variety of instruments, including government grants and tax benefits for privately financed basic and applied research. Support should be given to government laboratories in applied R&D patterned, for example, after Bell Laboratories. Research subsidies should include three features. First, they should include government grants to partially fund projects by firms and consortiums provided through a civilian technology agency. If grants are provided to single firms, their financial participation should be extensive. If they are provided to joint projects, a somewhat larger government commitment might be justified. But in no case should government funds account for more than a third of the funds. Second, research subsidies should include tax benefits for private grants to basic and applied research institutions, and third, an enhanced and permanent R&D tax credit. The government should aid, and certainly not stand in the way of, firm efforts at collaboration, in precompetitive generic research; that is, research into technologies that have a wide variety of applications.

The grant programs to stimulate specific technologies should be adminstered by a civilian technology agency that would complement the roles of the National Science Foundation in developing basic research and the Defense Advanced Research Project Agency in developing defense technology. These agencies might cooperate from time to time, but their missions should be kept separate. In particular, to ensure an efficient allocation of resources, the United States should continue to keep spending on technology for national defense purposes separate from spending for commercial goals.[64]

There is a danger that by relying on defense spending for commercial technological development, the United States will get neither the specific investment related to military missions and requirements nor the breadth of investment needed for commercial applications. Spillovers from defense to commercial technologies should not be the rationale for defense R&D.[65]

64. As Eads and Nelson note, "In the French case, the commercially oriented aspects of the R&D support program got tangled with the objective of establishing or preserving a French capability to design and produce military equipment. As a result, clear commercial targets were not pursued, but industry was given shelter and subsidy simply to keep it operating." George C. Eads and Richard R. Nelson, "Japanese High Technology Policy: What Lessons for the United States?" in Patrick, ed., *Japan's High Technology Industries*, p. 267.

65. For a more extensive treatment of the Defense Department's technology policy,

Open Markets

U.S. companies and their workers need open global markets. The United States has seldom used trade policies to protect its high-technology products, and it should continue this restraint. But as long as the United States provides foreigners with the opportunity to profit from sales here, it is justified in demanding similar access for its firms to markets abroad. Because scale economies are critical in the development of high-technology products, a protected home market can give domestic firms an unfair advantage. A protected home market can also provide domestic firms with excess profits they can use to accelerate their technological development. The United States must insist that mature industrial economies do not implement the protectionist measures appropriate to infant industries.

Specifically, the United States should demand that all countries treat high-technology companies of all nations identically. If programs for R&D development are organized in the European Community, Japan, or the United States, foreign-owned firms should be allowed to participate. The United States should make participation in U.S. government-funded research programs and institutions contingent on reciprocal access for U.S. firms abroad.

If foreigners protect their high-technology sectors and refuse to accord U.S. companies equal treatment, the United States should impose tariffs on the sale of products developed in that way. The key lies in putting foreign countries on notice during the development phase of such programs, rather than in waiting until U.S. importers have become dependent on such products. To do so requires the use of actions under section 301 that are directed at targeted programs in their initial stages.

U.S. antidumping laws should be enforced, vigorously and early, to ensure that foreign markets are not used to subsidize exports to the United States. However, the rules should be limited to classical dumping— that is, selling at lower costs abroad than at home as opposed to selling below an arbitrary fair market value. As Michael Borrus has argued, antidumping laws have no teeth, since the remedy is only to restore a fair market value.[66] A more severe penalty for discriminatory dumping should be applied.

see Kenneth Flamm and Thomas L. McNaugher, "Rationalizing Technology Investments," in John D. Steinbruner, ed., *Restructuring American Foreign Policy* (Brookings, 1989), pp. 119–57.

66. Borrus, *Competing for Control*, p. 247.

The United States should not succumb to the temptation to negotiate a market share for its firms. That approach will not solve the essential problem, which stems from the fact that the foreign market is not open. Indeed, it is likely to reinforce foreign monopoly powers.

Antitrust Measures

The United States is likely to become dependent on foreign supplies for some important high-technology products. The government will be tempted to subsidize domestic production on the grounds that dependence on foreign suppliers (and owners) renders the United States vulnerable to foreign pressures.

In some instances this argument may be compelling, but not all dependence is bad. If foreign suppliers are geographically diverse and compete vigorously, the United States has little to fear from dependence on foreign ownership or supplies. Where foreign takeovers threaten undue concentration of the global market, they should be stopped. Similarly, antitrust authorities must be vigilant if the United States is relying on a few foreign suppliers for a vital input. It is not necessarily efficient for the United States to respond to fears about foreign monopoly power by financing domestically owned production. Antitrust policies should be used to ensure the rapid diffusion of foreign products to the United States. If, for example, a small number of foreign firms in control of the market for DRAM semiconductors were to engage in monopolistic practices denying access to U.S. users or engaging in price fixing, U.S. antitrust policies should be invoked. Those damaged by these practices should be entitled to the normal treble-damages compensation.[67]

Diffusion

Technological diffusion requires support for training and educational institutions to improve management and worker skills, as well as vigorous antitrust policies to ensure adequate competition. Manufacturing and marketing ventures should not receive immunity from antitrust laws. Nor should policy aim to create national champion firms or ventures. Diffusion policies should use standards not to provide protection but to ensure relatively easy entry by newcomers and to facilitate collaboration between users and suppliers.

67. For an application of the antitrust principles to the issue of foreign inputs for defense, see Moran, "Globalization of America's Defense Industries."

As other nations attain technical equality, the United States needs to increase its ability to learn from them. The U.S. government should sponsor exchanges and frequent visits by American managers to examine foreign programs and practices. The diffusion of foreign technologies to the United States must also be encouraged, not by governmental regulation of diffusion through performance requirements on foreign firms, but by making the United States an increasingly attractive location for production. Foreign investment in the United States should be welcomed and encouraged by ensuring that the U.S. labor force is highly skilled and by establishing a regulatory and tax regime that does not discourage production. The evidence suggests that foreign firms do not, by and large, set up production in the United States to perform low value-added tasks. Indeed, to do so would make no sense given the level of U.S. wage rates.[68]

The experience of the U.S. automobile industry demonstrates how foreign investment facilitates the diffusion of technology. Ever since Japanese-affiliated automakers brought production technology and skills to the United States, they have shown that the cost advantages Japanese auto manufacturers enjoyed in the early 1980s were not based on attributes unique to Japan. Nor were the higher costs of U.S. automakers traceable to U.S. workers or to unions; Japanese methods can be applied with American labor and suppliers. The operations of the Japanese and the responses of some U.S. automakers have restored competitiveness to an industry in which it had seriously eroded.

The new approaches to production technology, buyer-supplier relations, and labor-management practices introduced by the foreign-affiliated automakers into their own operations are being diffused to their "big three" U.S. competitors. By engaging in joint ventures, U.S. producers have learned valuable lessons not only about building small cars but also about labor-management relations.

Global Harmonization

In the early postwar period, tariffs and quotas obstructed trade, and capital movements were severely restricted. When economic interde-

---

68. Graham and Krugman conclude: "U.S. affiliates of foreign firms look quite similar to U.S. firms in the same industries in terms of value added per worker, rates of compensation, and research and development." Edward M. Graham and Paul R. Krugman, *Foreign Direct Investment in the United States* (Washington: Institute for International Economics, 1989), p. 3.

pendence was limited, trade policy could deal only with policies, such as tariffs and quotas, that affected goods trade directly.

Economic interdependence has now expanded so much that major differences and inconsistencies among the policies of different governments can no longer be readily tolerated. As border barriers have been eliminated, national differences in antitrust, regulation, tax, and technology policies can now hamper trade and investment flows. Critics are correct, therefore, when they argue that the GATT must extend its purview beyond tariffs and quotas. Indeed, the agenda of the current GATT negotiations, which includes such areas as services, agriculture, intellectual property rights, trade-related investment measures, and subsidies, shows that most GATT members feel the need for improvements in the global rules on these issues. Better mechanisms for surveillance and dispute settlement are also needed.

In 1990, in particular, with negotiations reaching a critical point, U.S. trade policy should place its highest priority in achieving progress through GATT reform. Unilateral policy measures that might conflict with this goal should be strictly avoided. Over the medium term, U.S. trade policy should strive for an open global trading system governed by a common set of rules. This regime should be implemented through a vastly strengthened and extended GATT apparatus. Once the GATT negotiations are concluded and the mechanisms for achieving a single internal European market are reached in 1992, the next step should be a multilateral effort to achieve a single OECD (Organization for Economic Cooperation and Development) market for goods, services, and capital by the year 2010.[69]

The approach should use the example of the initiative for Europe 1992. The European governments decided they needed to complete the internal European market by 1992 by removing all remaining obstacles to the free movement of goods, labor, and capital within the European Community. In a 1985 White Paper, they laid out the 300 measures required to achieve that goal. In a similar way, the OECD should be given the task of formulating measures to create an integrated market.

Of course it would be impossible and undesirable to obtain identical practices across all nations. But that should not be necessary; some competition among regulatory regimes could actually be beneficial. The difficult task will be to determine those issues on which harmonization

69. For a similar proposal, see Gary Clyde Hufbauer, *The Free Trade Debate*, background paper for a report of the Twentieth Century Fund Task Force on the Future of American Trade Policy (New York: Priority Press, 1989).

will be essential and those in which such principles as national treatment and mutual recognition of technical standards will suffice. Ideally, participating countries would agree to common procedures for handling allegations of unfair trade as well as safeguards. They would also agree to a set of rules to encourage innovation. These would include provisions for nondiscriminatory government procurement and national treatment for foreign firms. Similarly, an international entity would supplement national antitrust policies.

It is striking that most proponents of bilateralism and managed trade still believe a single world market with a rules-based regime should ultimately be established. They claim that their approaches are the more effective means for achieving that objective. As Lenin once said, it is sometimes necessary to take two steps backward to take one step forward. But in this instance, the steps toward bilateralism and managed trade are steps in the wrong direction.

Conclusions

U.S. innovation policies and trade must respond to America's changed international position. On the one hand, the United States remains the world's largest economic power, and its policies reverberate in other countries. Therefore, its policies at home should be compatible with its demands on others. On the other hand, the United States is no longer technologically preeminent. In some industries American firms continue to lead, in some they have parity, and in others Japanese and European firms now lead. U.S. policies should therefore be designed both to open markets abroad and to encourage diffusion of foreign technologies to the United States.

The United States has also become heavily integrated into the world economy. While it remains the world's largest direct foreign investor, it has also become home to a large number of foreign-owned companies. Moreover, multinational companies operate in so many places and international alliances between U.S.- and foreign-owned companies have become so numerous that determining the national origin of firms, products, and technologies is growing more difficult. U.S. policies should not discriminate against foreign-owned firms in the United States and should aim at national treatment for U.S. firms abroad.

There is a theoretical case for government intervention to stimulate innovation. It rests on the excess of social over private rates of return. Empirical studies confirm that the difference is large and exists both for basic research and commercial R&D. The generally poor U.S. productivity performance over the past two decades strengthens the rationale for increased government support. Private markets may also prevent the optimal diffusion of technology. Thus policies to hasten technological diffusion should not be overlooked.

Promoting innovation can increase, not merely redistribute, welfare around the world. The United States can gain from foreign innovation by emulating foreign discoveries and buying imports at lower cost and in greater variety than would otherwise be possible. However, some foreign innovation policies could lower U.S. living standards—in particular, foreign programs targeted on U.S. export industries and on industries with imperfect competition, in which U.S. producers could lose profits and worker rents and in which the U.S. economy could lose geographically specific spillovers.

These principles suggest that the United States should steer a course between extreme laissez-faire and excessive interventionism. In particular, domestic programs that target entire sectors for promotion should be avoided. The United States should have a general grant program to provide partial funding for precompetitive, generic commercial research. It should also stimulate research through an enhanced permanent R&D credit. But extensive programs designed to promote firms or sectors should be avoided. There are no easy principles for selecting sectors to be favored, and there are great dangers such programs will be captured by interests that will serve their own, rather than the nation's, goals. Moreover, in a global economy the links between product development and production are uncertain.

The United States should improve the mechanisms for diffusing technology. The most important is to ensure competition. Antitrust laws can be relaxed to encourage collaborative ventures in basic and precompetitive research. But they should be vigorously applied at the global level to prevent unwarranted exercise of potential monopoly powers. Speedy provision of standards, and programs to improve worker training and managerial competence, will also increase diffusion.

Managed-trade arrangements to limit imports or promote exports should be avoided. They usually have unintended consequences and are often counterproductive. The United States does, however, need policies to ensure open foreign markets. In particular, there must be an international agreement that mature countries not be permitted to take infant industry protection measures. Products benefiting directly from foreign subsidies should be subject to countervailing duties. Foreign exports benefiting from indirect subsidies through a protected home market should be subject to antidumping actions. Products developed under protectionist, targeting programs in other developed countries should be declared ineligible for sale in the United States.

U.S. policies should take advantage of superior foreign technologies. Their diffusion to the United States should be encouraged, not through local-content programs but through policies that make the United States an attractive location for investment. U.S. dependence on imported products and foreign takeovers in the United States should not be viewed through the prism of economic nationalism; rather, antitrust considerations should be taken into account.

Ultimately, increased globalization requires a single global market. Patterned after the program for a single European market in 1992, the principal developed economies should set out a vision of a single OECD market by 2010. Another need is to develop a global-level antitrust agency and a common set of rules that extend far beyond the removal of trade barriers at the borders.

6

WILLIAM D. NORDHAUS

Global Warming: Slowing the Greenhouse Express

POLICYMAKERS WHO yearn for the familiar will undoubtedly have the opportunity to struggle with perennial problems such as recessions, inflation, and government deficits. As if traditional ills are not enough, in the late 1980s governments were confronted with yet another issue: the deterioration of the global environment. Recent studies have identified four major global environmental concerns: widespread damage from acid rain; the appearance of the Antarctic "ozone hole," interpreted by some as the harbinger of global ozone depletion that threatens to remove the shield from harmful ultraviolet radiation; deforestation, especially in the tropical rain forests, which may upset the global ecological balance and deplete genetic resources; and the "greenhouse effect," which threatens global warming and major climatic changes in the decades to come.

Although all four issues concern policymakers, this chapter concentrates on global warming, both because it is likely to have the most important economic impact and because it has been the source of the greatest controversy. The discussion covers the scientific theory and evidence of global warming; the economic effects of climatic change; the kinds of policy responses that might be available; and policy recommendations for the near term.

Scientific Theory and Evidence of Global Warming

For almost two centuries scientists have suspected that climate could be affected by changes in the chemical composition of the earth's atmosphere. The first analysis of this idea was carried out in 1896 by S. A. Arrhenius, who estimated that a doubling of the atmospheric con-

Helpful comments were provided by Jesse Ausubel, Garry Brewer, Clark Bullard, Robert Chen, William Clark, John Perry, Thomas Schelling, and Aaron Wildavsky.

TABLE 6-1. Estimated Atmospheric Concentrations of Important
Greenhouse Gases, Selected Years, 1850–2100

	Level (parts per billion)			Growth (percent per year)	
Greenhouse gas	1850	1986	2100ª	1850–1986	1986–2100
Carbon dioxide	290,000	348,000	630,000	0.16	0.52
Methane	880,000	1,675,000	3,100,000	0.56	0.54
Nitrogen oxides	285,000	340,000	380,000	0.15	0.10
Chlorofluorocarbonsᵇ	0	0.62	2.90	...	1.37

SOURCES: Donald J. Wuebbels and Jae Edwards, *A Primer on Greenhouse Gases,* prepared for Department of
Energy, DOE/NBB0083, March 1988; and Environmental Protection Agency, *Policy Options for Stabilizing Global
Climate* (February 1989), vol. 1: chaps. 1–6.
  a. Projected from EPA, *Policy Options.*
  b. Includes only major sources, CFC-11 and CFC-12.

centration of carbon dioxide (CO_2) would increase global mean temperature by 4° to 6° centigrade (C).[1] What causes the greenhouse effect?
The atmosphere is composed of a number of "radiatively active" gases
that absorb radiation at different points of the spectrum. Those known
as the "greenhouse gases" (GHGs) are transparent to incoming solar
radiation but absorb significant amounts of outgoing radiation. The net
result is an increase in the earth's temperature of about 33°C (59°F).
The greenhouse effect helps explain the hot temperatures on Venus along
with the frigid conditions of Mars.

Human activities are raising atmospheric concentrations of greenhouse
gases significantly and thus pose a threat to the climate. GHGs of greatest
concern are carbon dioxide, methane, nitrogen oxides, and chlorofluorocarbons (CFCs). Scientific monitoring has firmly established that these
GHG concentrations are increasing (see table 6-1).

Not all greenhouse gases are created equal. GHGs have different
radiative properties and different lifetimes. Table 6-2 shows the important
greenhouse gases, their "instantaneous" and "total" contribution to
global warming, and the industries in which the emissions originate.[2]

1. A short history of scientific concerns about the greenhouse effect can be found in
Jesse H. Ausubel, "Historical Note," in National Research Council, *Changing Climate:
Report of the Carbon Dioxide Assessment Committee* (Washington: National Academy
Press, 1983), pp. 488–91.
2. Traditionally, the relative effect of greenhouse gases is measured by their *instantaneous* contribution to global warming (in °C). The problem with this method is that GHGs
differ in their lifetimes and chemical transformations. In order to calculate the *total*
contribution of each GHG, I have estimated the sum of the instantaneous contributions
over the indefinite future (in ° C-years).

TABLE 6-2. Estimated Contribution of Different Greenhouse Gases
to Global Warming for Concentration Changes, 1985–2100

Greenhouse gas	Relative contribution (percent)		Source of emission
	Instan-taneous[a]	Total[b]	
Sources by chemical compound			
CO_2	76.1	94.7	Largely from combustion of fossil fuels
Methane	9.6	0.8	Poorly understood; from a wide variety of biological and agricultural activities
CFCs	11.6	3.3	Wholly industrial, including solvents and refrigerants
Nitrous oxides	2.7	1.2	From fertilizers and energy use
Sources by economic activity			
Energy	62.8	76.2	CO_2 emissions, nitrous oxides, methane[c]
Agriculture	20.6	19.8	CO_2, methane, nitrous oxides[c]
Industry	0.7	0.1	Methane[c]
Natural	4.3	0.7	Methane, nitrous oxides[c]
Other	11.6	3.3	Chlorofluorocarbons

SOURCES: For chemical compounds, see William D. Nordhaus, "Contribution of Different Greenhouse Gases to Global Warming: A New Technique for Measuring Impact," Yale University, Department of Economics, February 1990; for economic activity, see William D. Nordhaus, "To Slow or Not to Slow: The Economics of the Greenhouse Effect," paper prepared for the 1990 annual meeting of the American Association for the Advancement of Science. Estimates of emission sources are from EPA, *Policy Options*, vol. 1, chap. 2.
a. The effect of concentration change at the instant of release.
b. The relative contribution to global warming over indefinite future.
c. Sources highly uncertain for methane and nitrous oxides.

CO_2 is the principal contributor to global warming, and most of it comes from the combustion of fossil fuels. Of the fossil fuels, natural gas emits 58 percent as much CO_2 per unit of energy as coal, and petroleum 81 percent as much. Next in importance are the chlorofluorocarbons (CFCs), which are small in volume but have a warming potential almost 20,000 times as powerful as CO_2 per unit of volume.

One difficulty in estimating the economic and environmental damage from climatic change and the costs of slowing it is to find an index that can apply to both. In this discussion, I use the "CO_2 equivalent" of GHG emissions, which can provide a unit of measurement for the cost effectiveness of policies in different sectors.

Climate Models and Forecasted Climatic Change

No one disputes the buildup of greenhouse gases. The question is, how can one predict the climatic changes this buildup will cause many years into the future? Today, mathematical models are used to trace the effect of changes in the radiative balance on climatic variables such as temperature, humidity, winds, soil moisture, and sea ice. Because these changes are unprecedented in recorded history, the models cannot rely on historical experience, but must extrapolate beyond current observations.

Large general-circulation models (GCMs) simulate changes in the weather over a century or more. The largest models take average conditions in 500-kilometer-square grids through several layers of the atmosphere. Such models are extremely expensive to run, and a single CO_2 scenario might take a supercomputer up to a calendar year to calculate.

Interestingly, the basic estimates of the effect of a CO_2-equivalent doubling on *equilibrium* appear to have changed little since the earliest calculations. A National Academy of Sciences panel concluded in 1983: "When it is assumed that the CO_2 content of the atmosphere is doubled and statistical thermal equilibrium is achieved, all models predict a global surface warming. . . . [GCMs] indicate global warming [from CO_2 doubling] to be in the range between about 1.5 and 4.5° C."[3] Even with improvements in models and faster computers, there has been no significant narrowing of this estimate since 1983. The current range of scientific opinion is shown in table 6-3. Most experts believe that mean temperature will rise and that precipitation and runoff will increase as a result of the warmer climate. Some models predict hotter and drier climates in midcontinental regions, such as the U.S. Midwest. Few modelers expect to be able to forecast regional climatic changes over smaller areas, and not many modelers expect to do so with any degree of accuracy in the foreseeable future.

Temperature Records

There are several possible ways to test the climate models, but they can only be fully validated when and if global temperatures actually begin to rise. According to available historical records, which have very inadequate coverage for much of the globe, global mean temperature

---

3. Carbon Dioxide Assessment Committee, "Synthesis," in NRC, *Changing Climate,* p. 28.

TABLE 6-3. Range of Estimates from Climate Models: Equilibrium
Effect of Doubling of CO_2 Equivalent on Main Variables

Variable	Projection of probable global average change	Distribution of regional change	Confidence in prediction[a] Global average	Confidence in prediction[a] Regional average
Temperature	+2 to +5° C	−3 to +10° C	High	Medium
Sea level	+10 to +100 cm	...[b]	High	...[b]
Precipitation	+7 to +15 percent	−20 to +20 percent	High	Low
Soil moisture	???[c]	−50 to +50 percent	???[c]	Medium
Runoff	Increase	−50 to +50 percent	Medium	Low
Severe storms	???[c]	???[c]	???[c]	???[c]

SOURCE: Adopted from L. Mearns, P. H. Gleick, and S. H. Schneider, "Prospects for Climate Change," in Paul Waggoner, ed., *Climate Change and U.S. Water Resources* (Wiley, 1990).

a. The "confidence in prediction" is a subjective estimate of experts of their confidence that the range of estimates provided is accurate. These estimates are based on formal models, historical analogy, and other experience.

b. Increases in sea level are the average of the global rate. Sea-level rise in particular locations will be higher or lower than this figure, depending on local geological conditions.

c. No basis for forecast of this variable.

has increased about 0.5° C since the 1880s. Whether the increases observed in the temperature record are consistent with the predictions of climate models is a hotly debated question. Some authors have used statistical techniques to test for the presence of a "greenhouse signal" in this upward trend over the past century. The statistical hypothesis that the global mean temperature follows a trendless process can be rejected at a high level of confidence.

Still, a great deal of evidence suggests that climatic variables fluctuate over periods of a century or more. Unfortunately, there is not enough known about the background trends and cycles to determine whether the warming in recent years is a normal fluctuation or something new and different.[4] Although statistical analysis of the historical record has lagged far behind the construction of new and more refined GCMs, this record is an important, independent source of evidence about the pace of global warming.

4. The eminent climatologist James Hansen has stated that he is "99 percent" confident that the warming of the 1980s was associated with the greenhouse effect. See James Hansen, testimony before the Senate Energy Committee, June 23, 1988. According to other respected scientists, however, "No conclusion about the magnitude of the greenhouse effect in the next century can be drawn from the 0.5° C warming that has occurred in the last 100 years." See George C. Marshall Institute, *Scientific Perspectives on the Greenhouse Problem* (Washington, 1989), p. 29.

Uncertainties about Future Climatic Change

A particularly nettlesome aspect of this subject is the chain of uncertainties about the magnitude, timing, and effects of climatic change. Uncertainties include the rate of economic growth over the next century and the rate of emission of GHGs per unit of economic activity, not to mention the rate of atmospheric retention of different GHGs, the equilibrium relationship between increased concentrations in GHGs and climate change, the speed with which actual climate will move to the new equilibrium, and the extent to which climate would change were humans influences absent.

A rational response to climatic change must take these uncertainties into account. I have combined estimates of uncertainty about future climate change from a number of sources.[5] The assumed effect of rising GHGs follows the consensus of modelers that a doubling of CO_2 would in equilibrium raise global temperatures by 3° C (with a standard deviation of 1° C). I have derived an estimate of the lag of actual temperature behind the equilibrium temperature using evidence from GCMs and the historical record.

Figure 6-1 presents my estimated range of greenhouse warming over the period from 1850 to 2000 and an index of actual mean surface temperature over the past century.[6] The median estimate of realized warming from 1800 to 1990 is about 0.7° C, and about 0.6° C from the beginning of the temperature record in 1880. This estimate approximates reasonably well the actual temperature increase of 0.5° C shown by the highly volatile series in figure 6-1.

Figure 6-2 shows the estimated range of greenhouse warming over the next century. My projection of the most likely global temperature rise is 1.8° C from 1800 to 2050 and 3.3° C from 1800 to 2100. According to this calculation, the chances are one in four that the

5. Estimates of the distribution of emissions of some GHGs are derived from William D. Nordhaus and Gary W. Yohe, "Future Carbon Dioxide Emissions from Fossil Fuels," in NRC, *Changing Climate*, pp. 87–153. Estimates of emissions and concentrations of CFCs, methane, and other GHGs are from Environmental Protection Agency, *Policy Options for Stabilizing Global Climate* (February 1989), vol. 1: chaps. 1–6.

6. A description of the procedure for calculating the uncertainties is outlined in William D. Nordhaus, "Uncertainty about Future Climate Change: Estimates of Probable Likely Paths," Yale University, Department of Economics, January 1990.

FIGURE 6-1. Actual Global Mean Surface Temperature
and Estimated Distribution of Greenhouse Warming, 1850–2000[a]

Degrees centigrade (1880-90 = 0)

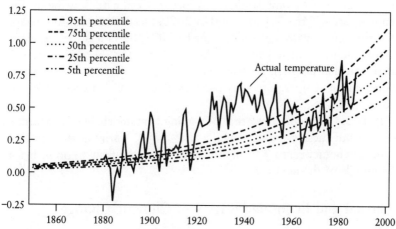

FIGURE 6-2. Calculated Change in Temperature, 1800–2100[a]

Degrees centigrade (1800 = 0)

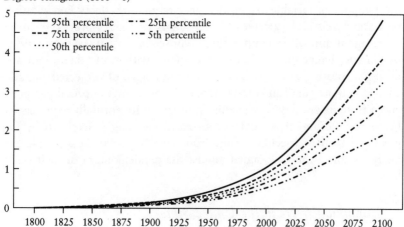

a. Percentiles represent distribution of estimated future greenhouse warming. The range spanned by 25th and 75th percentiles represents a range of temperature increases in which warming has a one-in-two chance of lying.

temperature change from 1800 to 2050 will be less than 1.5° C or greater than 2.2° C.

Another important question to ask is when the canonical 3° warming, used in many economic studies, will occur. I estimate that the average temperature will rise 3° from 1800 by 2090; there is a one-in-four chance that this much warming could occur by 2075, but a less than a one-in-twenty chance that it will occur before 2050. On the optimistic side, these calculations suggest that there is almost one chance in two that global mean temperature will rise less than 3° C between 1800 and 2100.

It should be emphasized that projecting climatic change is hazardous at best. But these estimates suggest that a 3° C warming is most likely to occur about a century from now and is quite unlikely to occur before the middle of the next century.

Social and Economic Effects of Climatic Change

Technological change has made it possible for human societies to thrive in a wide variety of climatic zones, with the result that variables such as temperature or humidity have little effect on economic activity in advanced countries. Indeed, since the development of air conditioning, migration patterns in the United States have favored warmer regions.

At the same time, globally averaged surface temperature is not the most important variable to consider when estimating effects. Precipitation or water levels and extremes like droughts or freezes are likely to be more significant. Mean temperature is chosen because it is a useful *index* of climatic change that tends to be associated with most other important changes. Another point to note is that the degree of projected climatic change is quite small in comparison with the changes normally experienced from day to day. The change in temperature normally experienced between 8:00 and 9:00 A.M. on an April morning is likely to be far greater than the expected change from 1990 to 2090. Few people are likely to notice the CO_2 signal amidst the pandemonium of their daily lives.

Economic Effects in the United States

Climatic change is likely to have different effects on different sectors of the economy.[7] In general, those sectors that interact with unmanaged

7. I concentrate on the United States because the most careful studies of the impact

ecosystems—in other words, that are heavily dependent on naturally occurring rainfall, runoff, or temperatures—may be hit the hardest. Agriculture, forestry, and coastal activities fall into this category. Most parts of the U.S. economy have little *direct* interaction with climate, and the effects of climatic change are likely to be very small in these sectors. For example, climatic change is not likely to pose a direct threat to activities performed in a carefully controlled environment, such as cardiovascular surgery or the manufacture of microprocessors.

Table 6-4 presents a breakdown of U.S. national income, organized by the sensitivity of the sector to greenhouse warming.[8] Approximately 3 percent of U.S. national output originates in climate-sensitive sectors and another 10 percent in sectors modestly sensitive to climatic change. About 87 percent of national output comes from sectors that are negligibly affected by climatic change. These measures of output may understate the impact of climatic change on well-being because they omit important nonmarket activities—especially leisure activities—that may be more sensitive to climatic change than measured output.

Information from recent studies can be used to speculate on the likely economic effects of climatic change. Of the sectors for which numerical estimates are available, agriculture is the most climate-sensitive. Some studies suggest that greenhouse warming will reduce the yields of many crops, but the higher CO_2 concentrations will have a fertilization effect and will tend to raise yields. A National Academy of Sciences panel concluded that "we do not regard the hypothesized CO_2-induced climate changes as a major direct threat to *American* agriculture *over the next few decades*."[9] The Environmental Protection Agency (EPA) has estimated that a CO_2 doubling may lead to a rise or fall in the value of U.S. agricultural output by as much as $10 billion annually, depending on the magnitude of the climate change.[10] The forest products industry may also benefit from CO_2 fertilization.[11] Water systems (such as runoff in

---

of greenhouse warming have been conducted for this country. See Environmental Protection Agency, *The Potential Effects of Global Climate Change on the United States* (December 1989). Although the studies reviewed here use different assumptions, one should envisage the estimated effects as occurring in the second half of the next century.

8. "National income" is total national output measured at factor costs. It equals GNP less indirect business taxes and depreciation.

9. Carbon Dioxide Assessment Committee, "Synthesis," in NRC, *Changing Climate*, p. 45 (emphasis in original).

10. EPA, *Potential Effects of Global Climate Change on the United States*, p. 45.

11. Clark S. Binkley, "A Case Study of the Effects of CO_2-Induced Climatic Warming on Forest Growth and the Forest Sector: B. Economic Effects on the World's Forest

TABLE 6-4. Breakdown of Economic Activity by Vulnerability to Climatic Change, 1981

| | National income | |
| | Value (billions of dollars) | Percentage of total |
Sector		
Total national income	2,414.1	100.0
Potentially severe effect	**74.8**	**3.1**
Farms	67.1	2.8
Forestry, fisheries, other	7.7	0.3
Moderate potential effect	**243.6**	**10.1**
Construction	109.1	4.5
Water transportation	6.3	0.3
Energy and utilities[a]		
Energy (electric, gas, oil)	45.9	1.9
Water and sanitary	5.7	0.2
Real estate		
Land-rent component[b]	51.2	2.1
Hotels, lodging, recreation	25.4	1.1
Negligible effect	**2,095.7**	**86.8**
Mining	45.1	1.9
Manufacturing	581.3	24.1
Other transportation and communication	132.6	5.5
Finance, insurance, and balance real estate	274.8	11.4
Trade	349.4	14.5
Other services	325.2	13.5
Government services	337.0	14.0
Rest of world	50.3	2.1

SOURCE: Based on U.S. National Accounts, *Survey of Current Business,* July 1984, pp. 70–71.
a. National income in electric, gas, sanitary industry is subdivided on the basis of consumption of major components.
b. Estimate of land-rent component is drawn from two sources: national balance sheet data on values of land and structures and surveys of housing prices. Estimate assumes that 25 percent of nonlabor income in real estate industry is from land rents.

rivers or the length of ice-free periods in lakes and rivers) may be affected, but the costs are likely to be determined more by the rate of climatic change than by the new equilibrium climate. Construction in temperate climates will be favorably affected because of a longer period of warm weather.

The effect on recreation and water transportation will be mixed,

Sector," in M. L. Parry, T. R. Carter, and N. T. Konijn, eds., *The Impact of Climatic Variations on Agriculture,* vol. 1 (Dordrecht, Netherlands: Kluwer Academic Publishers, 1988), pp. 197–218.

depending on the initial climate. Cold regions may gain while hot regions may lose; investments in water skiing will appreciate, whereas those in snow skiing will depreciate. But for the much of the economy—manufacturing, mining, utilities, finance, trade, and most service industries—it is difficult to estimate the direct effects of the projected climatic changes over the next fifty to seventy-five years.

Most studies indicate a gradual rise in average sea level over the next century. The consensus until recently was that sea level might rise 70 centimeters in the next century, but recent evidence has cut this estimate sharply. Using the estimate of 70 centimeters, the EPA projects the costs of sea-level rise to be about 6,000 square miles in land lost; a total capital outlay on the order of $100 billion for the protection of high-value property (by levies and dikes); and costs of protecting open coasts.[12] Total costs are approximately 0.1 percent of cumulative gross private domestic investment over the period 1985–2050.

Greenhouse warming will also increase the demand for space cooling and decrease the demand for space heating. The net impact of CO_2 doubling on energy use is estimated to be less than $1 billion at 1981 levels of national income.

The fact that many valuable goods and services are not captured in the net of the national income accounts might affect the calculations. The most notable ones are human health, biological diversity, amenity values of everyday life and leisure, and environmental quality. Some people will place a high moral, aesthetic, or environmental value on preventing climate change, but I know of no comprehensive estimates of what people are willing to pay to stop greenhouse warming.[13] I am aware of no studies that point to major nonmarket costs, but further analysis will be required to determine whether these omitted sectors will affect the overall assessment of the cost of greenhouse warming.

In sum, the climatic changes induced by a doubling of CO_2 concentrations are likely to have only a small effect on the U.S. economy. The best guess today is that the impact, in terms of those variables that have been quantified, is likely to be around one-fourth of 1 percent of national income. However, current studies omit a number of potentially important effects, so this estimate has a large margin of error.

12. But see National Research Council, *International Perspectives on the Study of Climate and Society: Report of the International Workshop on Climate Issues* (Washington: National Academy Press, 1978).
13. EPA, *Potential Effects of Global Climate Change on the United States.*

Economic Effects outside the United States

Only a few preliminary studies have been completed for other countries, so no general conclusions can be drawn at this time.[14] Existing evidence suggests that other advanced industrial countries are likely to experience modest effects, similar to those in the United States. Detailed studies for the Netherlands and a less comprehensive study for six large regions (the United States, Europe, Brazil, China, Australia, and the Soviet Union) found that the overall impact of a CO_2-equivalent doubling will be small and probably difficult to detect over the next half-century or more.[15]

Small countries that are heavily dependent on coastal activities or that experience a significant climatic change may be severely affected. It has been suggested that low-lying areas in Bangladesh may be inundated and that the Maldives may eventually disappear, but the timing of these impacts is conjectural. Particular concerns arise where people or activities cannot easily migrate in response to climate change. Such situations include natural reserves (like Yosemite) or populations limited to small areas (like South Sea islanders).

Developing countries are probably more vulnerable to greenhouse warming than are industrialized countries, particularly those poor countries with few resources to divert to problems connected with climatic change. However, most of these countries depend on agriculture, and the benefits of CO_2 fertilization might offset the damages.

In summary, I conclude that CO_2-induced climatic change is likely to produce a combination of gains and losses of uncertain magnitude and distribution with no strong presumption of substantial net economic damages. This conclusion applies especially to large, wealthy, and geographically diverse countries, with many unanswered questions about small, poor countries. This statement should not be interpreted as being a brief *in favor of* climatic change. Rather, it suggests that those who paint a bleak picture of desert Earth devoid of fruitful economic activity may be exaggerating the injuries and neglecting the benefits of climatic change.

14. Remember that the studies referred to here represent "best-guess" scenarios of climatic change. They omit uncertainties and possible nonlinearities, which are covered later in the chapter.

15. See National Oceanic and Atmospheric Administration, National Climate Program Office, *Climate Impact Response Functions: Report of a Workshop Held at Coolfont, West Virginia* (GPO, 1989).

Possible Responses to the Threat

A wide variety of responses have been suggested to deal with the threat of global warming (see figure 6-3). The option that has received the greatest public attention is to slow or prevent the warming itself. Most policy discussion of this option has focused on reducing energy consumption, switching to nonfossil fuels, and undertaking reforestation to remove CO_2 from the atmosphere. Whatever the final choice, the policy should be structured to obtain the maximum reduction in harmful climatic change for a given level of expenditure.

Second, greenhouse warming could be offset through climatic engineering, for example, by shooting particulate matter into the stratosphere to cool the earth or changing cultivation patterns in agriculture. Although these proposals have not been fully investigated, many environmentalists are opposed to them because "you shouldn't fool with Mother Nature."

Third, an effort could be made to adapt to the warmer climate. As the climate changes and the oceans rise, adaptation can take place gradually on a decentralized basis through the automatic response of people and institutions or through markets. In addition, governments can prevent harmful effects by introducing land-use regulations or investing in research on living in a warmer climate.

Preventive Measures

The most important question policymakers face at present, however, is whether major steps should be taken in the near term to prevent global warming. The answer depends on the costs of reducing GHG emissions relative to the damage that they would cause if they continued unchecked.

The little work that has been done on estimating the costs of slowing greenhouse warming has concentrated on reduction of emissions and atmospheric concentrations of greenhouse gases (the first strategy in figure 6-3). These examples—reducing CFC emissions, reducing CO_2 emissions, and reforestation—are not the only options, but they have been studied most intensively.

In my calculations, I measured the cost of preventive measures in tons of CO_2 equivalent. Measures that cost up to $5 per ton of CO_2 equivalent are considered inexpensive; at this cost, global warming could be stopped dead in its tracks at a total cost of less than $40 billion per year (about 0.2 percent of global income). Costs approaching $10 to $50 per ton CO_2 equivalent are expensive but manageable (costing ½ to 2½ percent

FIGURE 6-3. Alternative Responses to the Threat
of Greenhouse Warming

---

*Slow or prevent greenhouse warming: reduce emissions and concentrations of
greenhouse gases*
Reduce energy consumption
Reduce GHG emissions per unit of energy consumption or GNP
    Shift to no-CO_2 or low-CO_2
    Divert CO_2 from entering atmosphere
    Shift to substitutes for CFCs
Remove greenhouse gases from atmosphere
    Grow and "pickle" trees

Offset climatic effects
Climatic engineering
    Put particles into stratosphere
    Species selection and cultivation patterns

Adapt to warmer climate
Decentralized/market adaptations
    Population and capital move to new temperate zones
    Corn belt migrates toward Canada and Siberia
Central/governmental policies
    Build dikes to prevent ocean's invasion
    Regulate land use
    Conduct research on drought-tolerant crops

---

of global income). Measures costing more than \$100 per ton of CO_2 are
extremely expensive.

Reducing CFC emissions. Reducing emissions of chlorofluorocarbons
into the atmosphere should probably be the first strategy to consider
because they are extremely powerful greenhouse gases. Scientists believe
that new chemical substitutes for the two most important CFCs can be
found that will significantly reduce greenhouse warming. A rough estimate
is that these substitutes can reduce warming at a cost of less than \$5
per ton of CO_2 equivalent. This approach would bring a significant
reduction in warming at a modest cost.

Reducing CO_2 emissions. More than 95 percent of CO_2 emissions
come from the energy sector and deforestation. These emissions can be
reduced by increasing energy efficiency, decreasing final energy services,
substituting less GHG-intensive fossil fuels for more GHG-intensive fossil
fuels, substituting nonfossil fuels for fossil fuels, and developing new
techniques of production along with new products and services.

Because energy interacts with the economy in so many ways, complex
models of the energy system are required to estimate the costs of reducing
CO_2 emissions. These models must take into account the behavior of

both producers and consumers as well as possible future technological changes. A number of studies have employed such models to provide estimates of the long-run costs of reducing CO_2 emissions.[16] The results point to two main conclusions.

First, small reductions incur low costs. Reductions of up to 10 percent of CO_2 emissions from the energy sector can be attained over the long run at an average cost of less than $10 per ton of CO_2 reduced. At the current global level of emissions (about 6.5 billion tons of CO_2 a year), a 10 percent reduction would cost around $6 billion a year.

Second, the cost of reducing CO_2 emissions increases rapidly and becomes extreme when the reductions are substantial. I estimate that in the long run, but with today's energy technologies, the marginal cost of a 50 percent reduction in CO_2 emissions is approximately $130 per ton of CO_2. In other words, to induce producers and consumers to reduce their CO_2 emissions by one-half, policymakers would have to impose a carbon tax (or the regulatory equivalent thereof) of $130 per ton of CO_2, which would generate tax revenues totaling about $400 billion a year. The *total* resource cost of a 50 percent reduction in CO_2 emissions is about $180 billion a year, which is slightly less than 1 percent of world output at current price and output levels.

The incremental costs of reducing CO_2 emissions rise rapidly because no substitutes currently exist for many uses of fossil fuels. For example, transportation uses could achieve a large reduction in CO_2 emissions only if people traveled less or fewer goods were transported. Both of these solutions would be quite costly.

Forestry options. Several studies have proposed using trees to remove carbon from the atmosphere. Four interesting suggestions are to slow the deforestation of tropical forests; reforest open land, and thereby increase the amount of carbon locked into the biosphere; introduce a "tree bounty" to subsidize the sequestration of wood in durable products; and store trees indefinitely, in a "tree pickling" program.

16. The studies reviewed for this discussion included estimates based on specific technologies (such as CO_2 scrubbing and substitution of methane for oil and coal); econometric or elasticity analysis (often using highly aggregated models); and mathematical programming or optimization approaches (which often use activity-analysis specifications of energy technologies). For all three of these approaches, one can estimate the cost of reducing CO_2 emissions as a function of the *penalty* or *tax* imposed on those who emit CO_2. Note that all these estimates refer to the long-run cost—that is, the cost after the capital stock has fully adjusted. Attempts to reduce CO_2 emissions in the short run would be much more expensive. These costs do not include any adjustments for unmeasured or external environmental, health, or economic effects.

FIGURE 6-4. Total Global Cost of Greenhouse Gas Reduction[a]

Billions of U.S. dollars

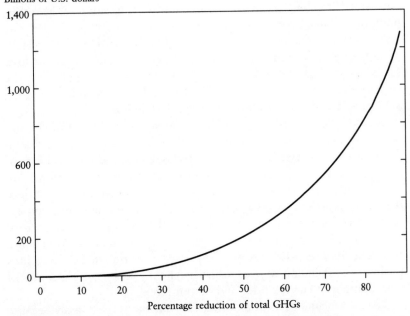

Percentage reduction of total GHGs

a. The calculations assume 1989 levels of world output and prices and 1989 levels of GHG emissions per unit output. Details of the calculations are provided in William D. Nordhaus, "Uncertainty about Future Climate Change: Estimates of Probable Likely Paths," Yale University, Department of Economics, January 1990.

It has been estimated that deforestation in tropical forests adds 0.5 billion to 3 billion tons of carbon per year to CO_2 emissions (this amounts to 5 to 30 percent of total GHG emissions). Much deforestation is uneconomic in tropical regions even without the greenhouse effect. Therefore, if uneconomical deforestation was stopped, greenhouse warming could probably be slowed down significantly at little cost. The other three options would entail modest costs, but would only be marginally successful in reducing atmospheric concentrations of carbon.

Overall costs of prevention. It appears that a significant fraction of GHG emissions—perhaps one-sixth—can be eliminated at relatively low cost (figure 6-4). The most cost-effective way to slow greenhouse warming would be to curb CFC production and prevent uneconomic deforestation. Putting all the low-cost options together, I estimate that about one-sixth of CO_2-equivalent emissions can be reduced at an average cost of $4 per ton of CO_2 equivalent, for a total cost of about $6 billion a year.

To achieve further reductions in GHG emissions after the low-cost options have been exhausted, it will be necessary to curb CO_2 emissions, say, through taxes or regulations on the carbon content of fuels. But a sharp reduction of GHGs quickly hits diminishing returns: a 50 percent reduction in GHG emissions in the long run will cost about $200 billion a year, which is about 1 percent of global output; attempts to restrict GHG emissions severely in the short run would be even more expensive.

It will be useful to compare these costs with historical events or regulatory programs. A low-cost program for slowing global warming (say one associated with the low-tax proposal in table 6-5 below) would impose a burden equivalent to a major U.S. regulation, such as those on drinking water, noise, or surface mining.[17]

The more stringent program to cut GHG emissions by half (associated with the high-tax scenario in table 6-5) would impose annual costs of around 1 percent of world output. This can be compared with the costs of *all* environmental, health, and safety regulations in the United States, which were estimated to cost 1 to 3 percent of GNP.[18] Another parallel is with the impact of the energy price increases of the 1970s. Dale Jorgenson estimates that the energy price increase lowered U.S. output growth by 0.2 percent a year, or a total of about 3 percent, between 1974 and 1980.[19] Charles Schultze found similar estimates for the effect of the first oil shock.[20]

Adaptive Measures

Faced with the prospect of a changing climate, societies may decide to adapt. The key adaptions are by private agents—such as consumers and businesses. Decentralized adaptations—population migration, capital relocation, land reclamation, and technological change—will occur more or less automatically in response to changing relative incomes, prices, and environmental conditions.

Governments can also play an important role by ensuring that the legal and economic structure is conducive to adaptation. In particular, they can make sure that the environmental or climatic changes are reliably translated into the price and income signals that will induce

---

17. See Robert E. Litan and William D. Nordhaus, *Reforming Federal Regulation* (Yale University Press, 1983), chap. 2.

18. Litan and Nordhaus, *Reforming Federal Regulation*.

19. Verbal communication from Dale Jorgenson.

20. Edward R. Fried and Charles L. Schultze, eds., *Higher Oil Prices and the World Economy: The Adjustment Problem* (Brookings, 1975).

private adaptation. This may be difficult to do because markets do not set appropriate prices on most of the effects of climatic change. For example, greenhouse warming may alter the runoff patterns of major rivers, but water is allocated in such an archaic way that there is no guarantee of efficient allocation when water availability changes.[21] Governments can improve adaptation by introducing general allocational devices (such as water auctions) that will channel resources to their highest-value uses. Similar issues will arise over the use of land near sea coasts and in floodplains.

Although adaptation and prevention are often treated as though they were the same solutions, they differ in one crucial respect: whereas preventive policies must generally precede global warming, adaptive policies will be taken as warming occurs. This point is crucial since cause precedes effect by a half-century or more. Immediate action is necessary to stabilize climate, while adaptations can wait for decades.

Although many people recognize that climate changes slowly, they often make the mistake of thinking about future climatic changes in the framework of today's world and ignore the inevitable social and economic evolution that will also take place in the coming decades.[22] If, as suggested earlier, it takes eighty years or more for CO_2 to double, adaptations will be spread over a similar period. Yet social and economic structures will change enormously over that time. Think of how much the world has changed since 1910. That was the age of empires, when the Ottoman, Austrian, and Czarist regimes ruled much of Eurasia. The map of Europe has been redrawn three times since 1910 and is being restructured again. The power density of the United States was about 1½ horsepower per capita as opposed to 130 horsepower per capita today; one-sixth of the horsepower was produced by the 21 million horses in use, which were the leading polluters of the time. Air conditioning, nuclear power, electronics, and computers were unheard of.

Consequently, it would be foolish to prescribe adaptive steps *now* to smooth the transition to climatic changes over the next century. The time scale of most adaptations is much shorter than the time scale of climatic change. CO_2 doubling will take place over the next century, whereas financial markets adjust in minutes, product prices in weeks,

21. See Roger R. Ravelle and Paul E. Waggoner, "Effects of a Carbon Dioxide-Induced Climatic Change on Water Supplies in the Western United States," in NRC, *Changing Climate*, pp. 419–32.

22. These issues are discussed at length by Thomas C. Schelling, in "Climatic Change: Implications for Welfare and Policy," in NRC, *Changing Climate*, pp. 449–82.

labor markets in a few years, and the economic "long run" is usually reckoned at no more than two decades. To adapt now would be akin to building a Maginot Line in 1935 to cope with the military threats of the 1990s.

When adaptation is viewed in this light, it seems unwise to undertake costly adaptive policies unless (a) they have such long lead times that they must be undertaken now to be effective; (b) they would clearly be economical even in the absence of climatic change; or (c) the penalty for delay is extremely high. By these criteria, the only effective adaptive measures that surely can be taken now are to promote a healthy economy, strive to internalize most external effects to ensure an appropriate response to changing climatic signals, and raise the national saving rate to provide the investments needed for changing infrastructure.

Policies to Slow Global Warming

The discussion up to now suggests that it is difficult to find large economic costs of climatic change. Even so, the prospect of a catastrophic change might justify taking steps to slow global warming. What should the United States do now to respond to the threat of global warming over the next century?

A Cost-Benefit Approach

On economic grounds alone, any policies that promise incremental benefits worth more than their incremental costs are worth undertaking.[23] As I mentioned earlier, it is useful to define policies as carbon taxes that penalize emissions of greenhouse gases in proportion to their global warming potential. These "taxes" are in a sense a metaphor for explicit steps the government might take to reduce GHG emissions through energy or gasoline taxes, CFC bans or regulatory limits, prohibitions on tree cutting, taxes on carbon emissions, or energy-efficiency standards.

Using the damage estimates outlined above and assuming a low

23. The analysis that follows ignores any relationship or "tie-in" between policies to slow global warming and policies to correct other economic or environmental problems. In fact, these relationships are often quite sigificant. For example, reducing CFCs is aimed primarily at countering ozone depletion, reducing oil consumption will improve the trade balance, and reducing coal consumption will reduce acid precipitation and other kinds of air pollution. These reinforcing effects are omitted here because the analysis examines appropriate policies to combat global warming; any further effects should be analyzed separately and added to or subtracted from the appropriate policies discussed here.

TABLE 6-5. Measures of Effects of Different Carbon Taxes[a]

Dollars unless otherwise specified

	Level of stringency of GHG reductions	
Sector of effect	*Low tax*	*High tax*
Tax effect		
Tax on CO_2 equivalent (per metric ton carbon)	5.00	100
Effect on fossil-fuel prices (1989 prices)		
Coal price		
Per metric ton	3.50	70
Percentage increase	10	205
Oil price		
Per barrel	0.58	11.65
Percentage increase	2.8	55
Gasoline price		
Per gallon	0.014	0.28
Percentage increase	1.2	23.3
Overall effects		
Estimated percentage reduction of GHG emissions (CO_2 equivalent)	13	45
Total tax revenues, U.S. (billions)	10	196
Estimated global net economic benefits ($+$) or costs ($-$), billions of dollars per year, 1989 global economy[b]	12	-96

SOURCE: Nordhaus, "To Slow or Not to Slow."

a. Figures do not take into account the reduction in GHG emissions in response to carbon tax; that is, they are "without feedback."

b. Assumes a discount rate equal to 1 percent in excess of the growth of output and damages from a CO_2 doubling equal to 1 percent of global output.

discount rate on future damages from climatic change, I calculate that an efficient policy would impose a penalty on GHG emissions of about $5 per ton of CO_2 equivalent.[24] This tax or penalty would lead to a total reduction in GHG emissions of about 13 percent, which would include a large reduction in CFCs and a small reduction in CO_2 emissions. Such a tax would amount to $3.50 on a ton of coal, 58 cents on a barrel on oil, and 1.4 cents on a gallon of gasoline (table 6-5). U.S. revenues from a carbon tax of $5 per ton would amount to about $10 billion annually. I also show the impact of a more severe restraint—$100 per ton of CO_2—which would be close to the tax required to reduce CO_2

24. The estimate of the "efficient" policy or tax is obtained by combining the estimated costs of reducing GHG emissions and the estimated damages from climate change. The best policy is a tax or restraint on GHGs beyond which the incremental costs of further restraints exceed the incremental benefits of reducing damages from climate change.

emissions by one-half. The high-tax strategy would clearly have a major impact on the U.S. and global economies.[25]

Realistic Complications

A simple economic cost-benefit analysis is a useful way to start assessing possible actions, but it overlooks two practical questions that complicate policy enormously: how to discount future costs and how to allow for uncertainty.

Discounting future climate damages. The question of how to discount the costs of future climatic change in making current decisions is a particularly thorny one because the atmospheric residence time of CO_2 is hundreds of years. In part, discounting involves an ethical question about the relative valuation of the well-being of current and future generations. But a discount rate on climatic change cannot be chosen arbitrarily and without regard to other decisions. A rate close to the return on capital in most countries—say, 8 percent a year or more— would imply that one should forget about climatic change for a few decades.

In contrast, a low discount rate—say, 4 percent a year or less—would give considerable weight today to climate changes in the late twenty-first century. But such a low discount rate implies that other investment opportunities have been exhausted—hardly an attractive assumption in a capital-starved world. A low discount rate on climatic change along with a high return on capital is simply inconsistent. Faced with the dilemma of a low social discount rate and a high return on capital, the efficient policy would be to invest heavily in high-return capital now and then use the fruits of those investments to slow climate change in the future.

Uncertainty. Clearly, the debate on global warming is rife with uncertainty—about future emissions paths, about the GHG-climate linkage, about the timing of climatic change, about the impact on flora and fauna, about the costs of reducing emissions, and even about the

25. See William D. Nordhaus, "To Slow or Not to Slow: The Economics of the Greenhouse Effect," paper prepared for the 1990 annual meeting of the American Association for the Advancement of Science. This analysis assumes that the discount rate on goods and services exceeds the growth rate of the economy by 1 percent a year. If the damage from a doubling of CO_2 is ¼ percent of total output, then the efficient CO_2 tax is $3.20 per ton of CO_2 equivalent; if the damage is 1 percent of output, the efficient tax is $12.70 per ton. I choose $5 as an illustrative intermediate figure.

William D. Nordhaus

speed with which the uncertainties can be reduced. How should decisionmakers proceed in the face of such uncertainty: like generals or environmentalists who assume the worst case, or like cigarette manufacturers who assert that unproved is untrue?

One answer would be to take a "certainty equivalent" or "best guess" approach, ignore uncertainty and the costs of decisionmaking, and plunge ahead. The cost-benefit analysis performed above represents this approach. It is appropriate as long as the risks are symmetrical and the uncertainties are unlikely to be resolved in the foreseeable future. Unfortunately, neither of these conditions is likely to be satisfied for the greenhouse effect.

Risk asymmetry. Virtually all observers agree that the uncertainties of climatic change are asymmetrical; people are likely to be increasingly averse to climatic change the larger the change. To go from a 2° to a 4° warming is much more alarming than to move from a 0° to a 2° warming. The greater the warming, the further the climate moves from its current state and the greater the potential for unforeseen events. Moreover, it is the extreme events—droughts and hurricanes, heat waves and freezes, river flooding and lake freezing—that produce serious economic losses. As probability distributions shift, the frequency of extreme events increases (or decreases) proportionately more than the change in the mean. Whether the increases in unpleasant extremes (like droughts in the corn belt) will be greater or less than the increases in pleasant extremes (like frost-free winters in the citrus belt) is, like most questions about climatic change, unanswered.

In addition, most climatologists think that the chance of unpleasant surprises rises as the magnitude and pace of climatic change increases. One must go back 5 million to 15 million years to find a climate equivalent to what is likely to occur over the next one hundred years; the concentrations of GHGs in the next century will exceed levels previously observed. Climate systems are complex, and it is not known whether they have multiple locally stable equilibria. It is sobering to remember that the Antarctic "ozone hole" was a complete surprise.

Among the kinds of physical effects that have been suggested and cannot be ruled out by scientists today are extensive shifts of glaciers and a subsequent rise in sea level of twenty feet or more in a few centuries; drastic changes in ocean currents, such as the displacement of the Gulf Stream, that would alter the climates of Atlantic coastal communities; and large-scale desertification of the grain belts of the world. Climatic changes might also upset the delicate balance of bugs, viruses, and humans as the tropical climates that are so hospitable to spawning and spreading new diseases move poleward. No one has demonstrated that these effects *will* occur. Rather, it seems likely that unexpected and unwelcome phenomena, like the Antarctic ozone hole, will occur more frequently under conditions of more rapid climatic change.

Learning. The threat of an unforeseen calamity argues for more aggressive action than a plain-vanilla cost-benefit analysis would suggest. However, the possibility that uncertainties about climatic change might soon be resolved argues for postponing action until knowledge is more sound. Most scientists believe that research can improve understanding of the timing, extent, and impact of climatic change and thus sharpen the ability to identify appropriate policies. The best investment today may be in *learning* about climatic change rather than in *preventing* it.

In attempting to prevent climatic change, decisionmakers could easily make some serious mistakes. Imagine that a massive nuclear power program had been mandated for twenty years, only to find that the technology was expensive and unacceptable. Learning to cope with the threat of climatic change includes not only improving the estimates of its consequences, but also performing research to develop inexpensive and reliable ways of slowing climatic change.

A Framework for Policy

In designing policies to slow global warming, government must first recognize that this is a *global* issue. Efficient policies cannot be devised unless all countries take steps to restrict GHG emissions. In order to induce international cooperation, the United States and other high-income nations may need to subsidize the actions of poor nations (say, to slow deforestation or to phase out CFC use). Unilateral action may be better than nothing, but concerted action is better still.

In view of the costs of global warming that have been identified, the world would be well advised to take three modest steps to slow the process and at the same time avoid any precipitous and ill-designed actions that it may later regret. First, a concerted effort should be made to improve understanding of the climate by better monitoring of the global environment; analyzing past climatic records, as well as the environmental and economic effects of past and future climatic change; and evaluating the steps that might be taken to slow climatic change. Great strides have already been made in this direction in the past two decades, but further research is required to sharpen pencils for the tough decisions that will have to be made in the future.

Second, the United States should support research and development (R&D) efforts aimed at finding new technologies to slow climatic change—particularly energy technologies that have low-GHG emissions per unit of output. Very little is invested in such work at present because of a "double externality": private returns are less than social returns, both because the fruits of R&D are available to those who spend nothing on research and because the benefits of GHG reductions are currently worth nothing in the marketplace. More government support should also go toward developing replacements for fossil fuels. Inherently safe nuclear power, solar energy, genetic engineering, and breeding of better biofuels, as well as energy conservation, are particularly promising areas of research.

Third, policymakers should try to identify and accelerate the myriad sensible measures that would tend to slow global warming, often at little or no economic cost. For example, they could strengthen international agreements that severely restrict CFCs, take steps to slow or curb uneconomic deforestation, and try to slow the growth of the uneconomic use of fossil fuels, say, through higher taxes on gasoline, on hydrocarbons, or on all fossil fuels.

These three steps would suffice for today, but should it be desirable to press further, one more step might be worth taking. Global environmental taxes could be imposed on the CO_2-equivalent emissions of greenhouse gases, particularly on CO_2 emissions from the combustion of fossil fuels. A GHG tax on the order of $5 per ton of CO_2 equivalent would be a reasonable response to the future costs of climatic change. A carbon tax would be preferable to regulatory interventions because taxes provide incentives to minimize the costs of attaining a given level of GHG reduction, whereas regulations often do not. To reap the maximum advantage, a carbon tax should be part of an international agreement implementing a tax or restraint in all the major countries of the world.

Some would argue that carbon taxes in particular would be a sensible economic policy. The consumption of fossil fuels has many negative spillovers beside the greenhouse effect, such as local pollution, traffic congestion, wear and tear on roads, and accidents. In addition to slowing global warming, carbon taxes would discourage the consumption of fossil fuels, encourage R&D on nonfossil fuels, favor fuel switching to low-GHG fuels like methane, lower oil imports, reduce the trade and budget deficits, and raise the national saving rate. Indeed, in the tax kingdom, a carbon tax is the rara avis that increases rather than reduces economic efficiency.

Although the arguments for a carbon tax are persuasive, I hesitate to recommend it at the present time. Negotiating a global carbon tax would be a daunting task even for a president who likes taxes. Reducing the risks of climatic change is a worthwhile objective, but humanity faces many other risks and worthy goals. In providing for the future, in allocating investment resources, there is a long list of important targets— factories and equipment, training and education, health and hospitals, transportation and communications, research and development, housing and environmental protection, population control, and curing drug dependency. Reducing GHG emissions is yet another investment, the goal of which is to prevent the damages from climatic change. Given the numerous urgent economic problems around the world today, it is difficult to justify devoting a much larger share of investment to this area than the amount proposed above.

Current Policy Initiatives

How does this framework for policy compare with the approach taken by the Bush administration? The current political concern about greenhouse warming can be traced in part to the unusual heat wave of the summer of 1988, which coincided with a growing scientific consensus that greenhouse warming indeed posed a serious threat. Candidate George Bush promised to move ahead vigorously on environmental issues and endorsed action to slow global warming. Other heads of government joined President Bush at the Paris summit in July 1989 in recognizing the need for international cooperation to solve global environmental problems.

The administration's policy on global warming was finally unveiled in February 1990.[26] In terms of the four sets of policy measures discussed above, the policies are as follows:

1. Expand knowledge. The administration proposes a large expansion in its funding of studies of "global climate change." The programs it

26. The central political statement is found in President Bush's speech to the Intergovernmental Panel on Climate Change at Georgetown University on February 5, 1990. The 1990 *Economic Report of the President* contains an extensive discussion of the scientific, economic, and policy issues. The details of the budget changes are contained in the budget for fiscal 1991.

TABLE 6-6. Energy Research and Development Funds in Fiscal Year
1991 Budget, Budget Authority

Budget category	Amount (millions of dollars)		Percentage change
	Fiscal 1990	Fiscal 1991	
Total Department of Energy budget	16,423	17,480	6.4
Total, civilian applied research and development	1,298	1,057	−18.6
R&D on technologies with low-GHG emissions	415	436	5.2
Conservation	194	183	−5.9
Solar, renewables, geothermal, other	138	175	27.3
Nuclear (reactor programs only)	83	79	−5.6
R&D on technologies with high-GHG emissions	883	621	−29.7
Coal	829	566	−31.7
"Clean coal"	554	456	−17.7
Other coal	275	110	−59.9
Oil and gas	54	54	0.5
Basic research	2,399	2,680	11.7
Basic physics	872	952	9.2
Superconducting super collider	219	318	45.4
Biological and environmental	418	436	4.4
Basic energy sciences			
Magnetic fusion	320	325	1.6
Other	570	649	13.8
National Science Foundation, basic research	1,651	1,853	12.2

SOURCE: *Department of Energy Posture Statement and Fiscal Year 1991 Budget Overview,* January 1990; and *Budget of the United States Government, Fiscal Year 1991.*

recommends are largely scientific and, at $1.03 billion for fiscal 1991, they represent a 57 percent increase in outlays over the prior year.

2. Reorient energy research and development. Table 6-6 shows a breakdown of the administration's energy R&D budget for fiscal 1991. Although the overall budget of the Department of Energy is designated for a modest increase, civilian R&D programs will decline sharply; there will also be a large cut in fossil energy programs, but little change in low-GHG technologies after correcting for inflation. The reduction in conservation is puzzling given the importance of increasing energy efficiency.

3. Phase out the most powerful CFCs. The U.S. government has taken the lead in this important initiative, which is contained in the Montreal

Protocol of 1987 that commits signatories to cut production in half by 1998. (Note that the decision to phase out CFCs was made in order to prevent ozone depletion; the impact on global warming is a welcome but serendipitous side effect.) Even with the Montreal Protocol in place, however, the climatic impact of CFC emissions is expected to rise over the next century.

4. Plant trees. The Bush administration also proposes a "plant-a-tree" program, with proposed outlays of $175 million annually, to plant a billion trees each year. I estimate this program will reduce annual global emissions of GHGs by about 0.01 percent.

On the whole, the government's policy to date represents a reasonable response to the threat of global warming. The Bush administration has recommended a cautious approach and avoided measures that would set the economy on a path that could not respond flexibly to new information or emerging technologies. If only all national priorities were addressed this well!

Final Thoughts

The United States and other large industrial countries would be well served by continuing to pursue the first three goals outlined above—improving knowledge, investing in R&D in new technologies, and tilting away from greenhouse gases. This approach would prepare the world for whatever developments might unfold in the future—for a tightening of the screws if the threat of global warming accelerates or for a relaxation of policy if science or technology alleviates concerns.

But above all, I would leave policymakers with the following advice: The threat of climate change is uncertain. It may be large, and might conceivably be devastating. But we face many threats. And don't forget that humans have the capacity to do great harm through ill-designed schemes, as the communist experiment clearly shows. Gather information, move cautiously, and fashion policies efficiently and flexibly so that you can respond quickly as new information becomes available on the gravity of greenhouse warming.

7

JOHN E. CHUBB &
ERIC A. HANUSHEK

Reforming Educational Reform

THE FAILURE of the U.S. school system to educate American children has become a cliché fanned by television, newspapers, and magazines. Unfortunately, the widespread message that schools are doing a bad job is not a product of inflamed journalism. American children, in fact, are learning less and appear less prepared to enter the labor market than they did in the past.

It would be comforting if this problem could be solved by simply doing more of what has customarily been done—spending more money, hiring teachers with more training, reducing the size of classes, and reforming the curriculum. It would be comforting because a great deal of traditional reform activity is already well under way. In our view, however, most of this activity does not amount to reform at all. Improving the achievement of American school children requires the more difficult and radical step of reforming the entire organization of American schools. The federal government, which has never played much of a role in elementary and secondary education, can play a limited, if crucial, part in this process by helping to smooth the road to reorganization.

A More Serious Problem Than People Think

The decline of American education is evident in a wide variety of performance measures. Some of these measures are imperfect, to be sure. But all available measures point in the same direction.

Standardized Tests

The drop in scores on the scholastic aptitude test (SAT), administered to more than one-third of all high school graduates each year, has done more to advertise the drop in educational achievement than any other indicator (figure 7-1). For various reasons, this trend is neither a complete

The authors wish to thank Vida Megahed for her secretarial assistance.

213

FIGURE 7-1. Scholastic Aptitude Test Scores, 1966–88

Average SAT score

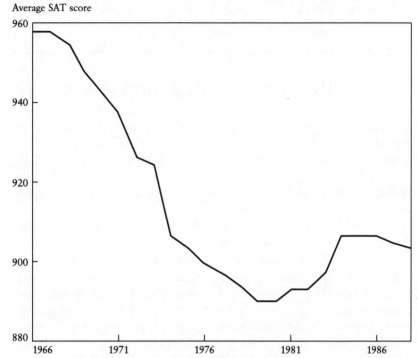

SOURCE: National Center for Education Statistics, Office of Educational Research and Improvement, *Digest of Education Statistics, 1988* (Department of Education, 1988), table 88.

nor an entirely fair report card on the performance of students and schools. The SAT is not taken by a representative population; the mix of students taking it has changed over time; and many factors other than schools affect scores.[1] Nevertheless, the trend is sobering.

Other measures confirm that student performance fell after the mid-1960s.[2] Although performance seems to have recovered modestly during the later 1970s and 1980s, it remains generally below the previous peak.

1. The proportion of high school graduates taking the scholastic aptitude test (SAT) has changed over the past two decades, contributing to aggregate score changes. Analysis suggests, however, that selection factors explain only a fraction—perhaps only a quarter—of the overall trend.

2. Congressional Budget Office (CBO), *Trends in Educational Achievement* (Washington, 1986); and CBO, *Educational Achievement: Explanations and Implications of Recent Trends* (Washington, 1987).

More ominously, however, the recent improvement seems to have come in rote learning, computation, and basic skills, rather than in problem solving and other higher-order skills.[3]

The results of international tests are also chilling. In science and mathematics, U.S. students place below the middle of a broad comparison group that includes developed and less developed countries. In mathematics the average U.S. seventeen-year-old in 1982 performed worse than did students from nearly all of the fifteen other countries surveyed; and the best U.S. students fared no better.[4]

The trends in test scores are imperfect measures of changes in student capabilities. Some are poor indicators of subsequent performance in the job market, for example. "Overtesting" is eroding the reliability of tests as measures of ability and casts doubt on the value of comparing test results over time. Finally, as noted previously, the trends in aggregate test scores may mask more serious losses in higher-order skills. Despite these problems, the message is clear: educational performance over the last two or three decades has dropped or stagnated.

Other evidence suggests the same conclusion. High school completion rates reached 75 percent in the 1960s and have not increased since. The dropout rate nationwide is stuck at roughly 25 percent. Dropout rates in some large cities average 50 percent. Moreover, college enrollment rates have been stuck at about half of all high school graduates for two decades.[5]

3. CBO, *Trends in Educational Achievement*; and Robert Rothman, "NAEP Results in Reading, Writing Show Few Gains," *Education Week,* January 17, 1990, p. 1.

4. D. F. Robitaille and R. A. Garden, ed., *The IEA Study of Mathematics II: Contexts and Outcomes of School Mathematics* (Oxford: Pergamon Press, 1989). Comparisons are given for eighteen countries for thirteen- and seventeen-year-olds. In general, U.S. thirteen-year-olds do relatively better than the older age group, but that group's best ranking in specific fields was tenth. Some care should be used in interpreting these results, however, since earlier tests, before the decline in U.S. test scores, showed similar rankings. See Torsten Husén, ed., *International Study of Achievement in Mathematics: A Comparison of Twelve Countries,* vols. 1 and 2 (John Wiley, 1967). For more recent data see Barbara Wobejda, "Survey of Math, Science Skills Puts U.S. Students at Bottom," *Washington Post,* February 1, 1989, pp. A1, 14.

5. The Department of Education stopped producing estimates of high school graduation rates in the 1980s. Graduation percentages stayed close to 75 percent between 1965 and 1980. Completion rates for people aged twenty-five to twenty-nine reported in the Current Population Survey have hovered around 85 percent during the 1980s. The higher rates may reflect students returning to complete high school or may reflect survey errors. Bureau of the Census, *Statistical Abstract of the United States: 1970,* 91st ed.; *1982–83,* 103d ed.; *1989,* 109th ed. (Department of Commerce, 1970, 1982, 1989), tables 188, 253, 211, respectively.

Productivity and Competitiveness

Two developments external to education reinforce the concerns aroused by trends in standardized tests. Growth of economic productivity slowed dramatically during the 1970s and has not recovered. During roughly the same time, the competitiveness of the American economy in world markets declined and trade deficits grew. Although most evidence has been interpreted to suggest that other factors have been much more important than educational achievement in explaining these developments, particularly the international ones, the case is not conclusive.[6]

Slow productivity growth portends slow increases in the standard of living. Productivity growth between 1948 and 1965 averaged 2 percent a year, but fell to 1 percent between 1965 and 1973, and almost stopped thereafter.[7] Although past research viewed educational achievement as only a minor component of productivity growth,[8] the slowdown in that growth occurred soon enough after the decline in school performance to raise new questions about education's economic role.[9]

The Disadvantaged

The drop in average performance is bad enough. The consequences for disadvantaged students are even more disturbing. A large gap persists between the completion rates and achievement scores of minorities and disadvantaged students on the one hand and the rest of the country's students on the other. On the SAT tests, where the gap is largest, the average black student in the mid-1980s is one standard deviation below

6. The U.S. balance of trade deficit is traceable largely to low U.S. national savings, relative to domestic investment opportunities. See chap. 2 in this volume. The loss of world market shares in certain commodities may reveal something about the skill of the American work force in producing high-quality or high-technology products. But the success of managers of foreign-owned companies in achieving quality and productivity equivalent to that achieved abroad suggests that in this area as well the role of education may be exaggerated. See chap. 5 in this volume.

7. John H. Bishop, "Is the Test Score Decline Responsible for the Productivity Growth Decline?" *American Economic Review*, vol. 79 (March 1989), pp. 178–97, cited on p. 178.

8. Edward F. Denison, *Trends in American Economic Growth, 1929–1982* (Brookings, 1985); Martin Neil Baily, "What Has Happened to Productivity Growth?" *Science*, vol. 234 (October 1986), pp. 443–51; and CBO, *Economic and Budget Outlook: Fiscal Years 1988–1992* (Washington, 1987).

9. Bishop, "Is the Test Score Decline Responsible?"

the average white student, which translates into the average black student falling into the sixteenth percentile of the white distribution.[10] The gap has narrowed modestly from around 1.2 standard deviations in the mid-1970s, but it remains unacceptably large. Poor performance is concentrated in central city school systems populated disproportionately by black, Hispanic, and other minority students. The concentration of minorities in these schools, attributable in part to white flight from desegregation, injects a racial and ethnic element into these educational problems.

Taking Stock

All of this is reason for serious concern. A nation that led the world in the introduction of mass education for all residents and that has been accustomed to strong and steady improvements in educational and economic performance has been living for twenty years now with considerably less.

The educational problem, however, is even more sobering than dismal outcome trends suggest. Despite a national commitment to keep output high, educational output has fallen. For more than three decades, since the Soviets launched the world's first satellite, *Sputnik,* successive U.S. governments have striven, sometimes quite vigorously, to improve education. Real expenditures per student rose at an annual rate of 3¾ percent, nearly tripling between 1960 and 1988 (table 7-1). Moreover, the added spending bought just what many advocates of increased educational spending sought: smaller class sizes and more experienced and educated teachers (table 7-2).[11] During the past quarter century, the average pupil-teacher ratio in public schools fell from more than twenty-five to less than eighteen, a 30 percent reduction. More than half of current teachers have a master's degree or higher. And, by 1986, half of the teachers had at least fifteen years of teaching experience.

These data taken together indicate the true magnitude of the problem. Spending has nearly tripled and performance has dropped. The added resources have clearly made the school system more expensive than in

10. CBO, *Trends in Educational Achievement;* and National Center for Education Statistics (NCES), Office of Educational Research and Improvement, *Digest of Education Statistics, 1988* (Department of Education, 1988), p. 151.

11. Part of the drop in class size resulted not from hiring more teachers but from declining enrollments in the 1970s. Whether or not the decline resulted from "active policy," the data are still relevant for assessing the efficacy of such policies.

TABLE 7-1. Public School Expenditures per Student in Average
Daily Attendance (ADA), 1960–88

Expenditures	1960	1966	1970	1975	1980	1985	1988
Current expenditures/ADA[a]							
Nominal dollars	375	537	816	1,286	2,230	3,486	4,209
1988 dollars	1,499	1,961	2,488	2,828	3,202	3,833	4,209
Total expenditures/ADA							
Nominal dollars	472	654	955	1,503	2,502	3,813	4,626
1988 dollars	1,886	2,388	2,912	3,305	3,592	4,192	4,626

SOURCES: Authors' calculations based on data from Bureau of the Census, *Statistical Abstract of the United States: 1970*, 91st ed.; *1981*, 102d ed.; *1985*, 105th ed.; *1989*, 109th ed. (Department of Commerce, 1970, 1981, 1984, 1989); and *Economic Report of the President, 1990*, table C-58.

a. Includes all spending except that for capital outlays and interest on debt.

the past but do not seem to have made it better.[12] The United States cannot hope to reverse trends in education just by spending more money. In our view, it must undertake reform that profoundly changes how money is spent. The nation must overhaul education organization.

Why "More" Has Not Meant "Better"

Educators agree on many of the ingredients of a good education: highly motivated students, involved and supportive parents, skilled and sensitive teachers, strong leadership from principals, and ambitious and focused academic programs. The problem is how to put these ingredients in place. On this practical question, educators disagree.

Inputs

Education policy is usually seen as a problem of selecting the correct inputs—teachers, principals, books, and buildings—and combining them

12. Attention has focused recently on whether the United States spends more or less per student than do other countries when compared with the size of GNP. See M. Edith Rasell and Lawrence Mishel, "Shortchanging Education: How U.S. Spending on Grades K-12 Lags Behind Other Industrial Nations," Washington, Economic Policy Institute, 1990. Because we think that expenditures do not indicate quality in the United States, we think that such international comparisons are uninformative. Shares of GNP are also ambiguous comparative indicators of national educational efforts. See Department of Education, "Statement by Charles E. M. Kolb, Deputy Under Secretary for Planning, Budget, and Evaluation on International Expenditures on Education," February 27, 1990; and John Hood, "Education: Is America Spending Too Much?" Washington, Cato Institute, 1990.

TABLE 7-2. Characteristics of Public School Teachers, 1961–86

Characteristic	1961	1966	1971	1976	1981	1986
Pupil-teacher ratio	25.6	24.1	22.3	20.3	18.9	17.8
Median years of experience	11	8	8	8	12	15
Percent with master's degree or greater	23.5	23.3	27.5	37.5	49.6	51.4
Average nominal salary (dollars)	5,515	6,952[a]	9,705	13,354	19,274	26,551
Average real salary (1988 dollars)	21,820	25,383	28,348	27,764	25,084	28,659
Ratio to average worker pay[b]	1.28	1.35	1.47	1.46	1.45	1.67

SOURCES: Authors' calculations based on data from National Center for Education Statistics, Office of Educational Research and Improvement, *Digest of Education Statistics, 1988* (Department of Education, 1988), tables 51, 54, 57; and *Economic Report of the President, 1990*, tables C-58, C-44.

a. Estimated.

b. Ratio of average teacher salary to annualized average weekly earnings of private nonagricultural employees in the United States.

in the best way—designing a proper curriculum, organizing staff and students in an effective way, and so forth. At different levels of government, policy addresses different educational problems. But the approach to various problems is typically the same: select the right mix of inputs.

There is a fundamental problem with this approach, however. It presumes that policymakers and administrators know the inputs that determine educational outcomes and that they know the best way to combine these inputs for all students under their jurisdiction. The evidence we have just reviewed suggests these assumptions are wrong. If the educational process were understood, one would expect increased resources to have a direct impact on performance. In fact, expenditures on schooling have increased dramatically, but performance has not increased commensurately—indeed, it has not increased at all.

Admittedly, this aggregate evidence could be misleading. It is possible that educational inputs, despite appearances, are directly related to educational achievement. If factors outside of schools—families, or societal attitudes, for example—deteriorated enough to offset the positive influence of increased inputs on school performance, trends in achievement might look like those just described. To be certain that more inputs are not the answer to current educational woes, one must look in more detail at the relationship of educational inputs to outcomes.

TABLE 7-3. Results of 187 Studies of the Effects of School Inputs on Student Achievement

| | | Statistically significant | | | Statistically insignificant | | |
Input	Number of studies	Increases achieve-ment	Decreases achieve-ment	Total	Increases achieve-ment	Decreases achieve-ment	Un-known effect
Teacher-pupil ratio	152	14	13	125	34	46	45
Teacher education	113	8	5	100	31	32	37
Teacher experience	140	40	10	90	44	31	15
Teacher salary	69	11	4	54	16	14	24
Expenditures per pupil	65	13	3	49	25	13	11

SOURCE: Eric A. Hanushek, "The Impact of Differential Expenditures on School Performance," *Educational Researcher*, vol. 18 (May 1989), pp. 45–51.

This relationship has been extensively investigated. For more than two decades—since the massive government study, *Equality of Educational Opportunity,* was conducted in the mid-1960s—researchers have tried to identify inputs that are reliably associated with student achievement and school performance.[13] The bottom line is, they have not found any. Researchers have found no systematic relationship between student achievement and the inputs that reformers (and researchers) always assumed matter: class size, teacher education, teacher experience, teacher salaries, and expenditures. Table 7-3 summarizes available statistical evidence about the effects of each factor on performance.[14] The research shows clearly that policymakers can have no confidence in policies built on conventional assumptions.

To be sure, research finds substantial differences in the effectiveness of individual teachers. But research has not been able to identify a set of specific teacher characteristics that are systematically linked to higher student performance. All we know for sure is that teacher effectiveness

13. James S. Coleman and others, *Equality of Educational Opportunity* (Department of Health, Education, and Welfare, 1966), often referred to as the Coleman Report.

14. These results are discussed in detail in Eric A. Hanushek, "The Economics of Schooling: Production and Efficiency in Public Schools," *Journal of Economic Literature,* vol. 24 (September 1986), pp. 1141–77, and Hanushek, "The Impact of Differential Expenditures on School Performance," *Educational Researcher*, vol. 18 (May 1989), pp. 45–51. They come from an exhaustive review of 187 separate estimates of input-output, or production function, studies. The results of these separate investigations are tabulated to identify the direction of effect (whether, for example, more educated teachers produce higher or lower student performance) and the statistical significance of the estimated relationships. The underlying studies all investigate the independent influence of specific characteristics of teachers and schools after allowing for the influence of family background and other individual attributes on performance.

is not correlated with the experience and education of the teacher or with the size of classes that teachers teach.

Organization

A new line of research, however, has been more promising. It has concentrated on what is special about schools identified as performing well.[15] This research has shifted its focus from educational inputs to the educational process—or how schools are organized. Unlike input-output research, it is often based on close observation of small numbers of schools. Although there is much less of this research than research on education inputs, evidence is mounting that effective school organizations are distinguished by such things as a clear sense of academic purpose, strong educational leadership, and genuine professionalism among teachers.[16]

Policymakers, however, do not know how to train or select people who have the necessary leadership skills or professionalism. They do not know how to instill in schools a sense of mission or how to foster commitment and teamwork among the school staff. In short, they do not know any more about how to impose effective organizational characteristics on schools than they do about how to specify effective inputs.

Consider the policies typically implemented or suggested to improve school organization. State rules about certification and personnel dictate the background, preparation, and in-service training of teachers and principals. Other rules specify the curriculum and the organization of schools and classrooms. But these are simply a form of "input policies" that stipulate which kinds of people will work with which resources. They do not ensure that people will commit themselves to coherent school objectives, or that principals will trust teachers as well as lead them, or that teachers will work cooperatively and as colleagues, or that the school will take responsibility for its performance. Effective organi-

15. For a review of this evidence, see Stuart C. Purkey and Marshall S. Smith, "Effective Schools: A Review," *Elementary School Journal*, vol. 83 (March 1983), pp. 427–52.

16. John E. Chubb and Terry M. Moe, *Politics, Markets, and America's Schools* (Brookings, 1990); John I. Goodlad, *A Place Called School: Prospects for the Future* (McGraw-Hill, 1984); Theodore R. Sizer, *Horace's Compromise: The Dilemma of the American High School* (Houghton, Mifflin, 1984); Michael Rutter and others, *Fifteen Thousand Hours: Secondary Schools and Their Effects on Children* (Harvard University Press, 1979); and Wilbur Brookover and others, *School Social Systems and Student Achievement: Schools Can Make a Difference* (Praeger, 1979).

zation, like an effective mix of resources, is very difficult to specify and mandate.

Policy Implications

The evidence of the past three decades is unequivocal. Government manipulation of educational inputs has not worked.

Research has not proved that an input strategy could never work under any circumstances. But research does indicate that such a happy outcome is extremely unlikely. Some analysts argue, for example, that higher salaries will improve the pool of teachers. This argument, with which few would disagree, does not, however, establish that the quality of teaching will improve, because it is still necessary to select and to retain the better people from any enlarged pool. The research on performance indicates that schools have not developed effective salary policies. The exact mechanism leading to this result is not really known; it could be poor selection, poor promotion, or poor retention. But the outcome is clear. Why should the future be different from the past?

A similar analysis could be applied to many other policy options in contemporary "reform" packages. The current institutional structure and incentives in schools do not ensure any success through added resources. Moreover, even if success is achieved (and identified), there is no mechanism ensuring that it will be replicated. Educators simply do not know how to make intelligent "input policies." Continuing this approach to educational policy will lead to disappointment and waste resources.

The Problem of Bureaucracy

Organizing teachers, students, and other educational inputs into a well-functioning school is not just a technical exercise. It is also a complex problem of implementation and control. Even if elected officials and their administrators knew exactly what good schools look like, they would still have to know how to institute good schools, and their plans would have to be faithfully carried out.

America's public schools are currently run by bureaucracies trying to carry out the wishes of elected officials at various levels of government. Over time these bureaucracies have become larger and more influential. School reformers have long held that schools are best run by professional educators who can design curricula, select the best instructional materials, identify competent teachers, and generally rescue schools from the narrow and unenlightened demands of parents and politicians.[17]

But the growth of bureaucratic influence is also a response to educational politics.[18] Public schools are controlled directly by elected officials—local school boards, state governments, and to some extent, the federal government. These bodies are the arenas for battles among teachers' unions, administrators, advocacy groups for students with special needs, business interests, textbook publishers, and others, each of whom has a different idea about how to run schools. However the battles go, some groups are pleased while others are not. Bureaucracy is the winners' instrument for getting the losers in educational politics to comply. Rules, regulations, and reporting requirements make sure that schools do what higher authorities want.

Less obviously, the interaction of politics with the administrative hierarchies that govern schools tends to create serious impediments to effective education. In particular, the characteristics of effective schools that we just identified—strong on-site administration, collegiality, and wide discretion for teachers and principals—are undermined by the constraints that bureaucracies inevitably place on educators.[19]

This problem is particularly serious in the United States because three separate levels of government have a hand in setting educational policy. Because federal officials, for example, cannot choose state and local education officials to carry out policy set in Washington, they rely on prescriptive programs to see that their wishes are fulfilled.[20] State officials face similar problems with local administrators. When local regulation is added to state and federal regulation, the confusion and constraints faced by schools can cripple virtually all initiative.

The problem of bureaucracy has grown as responsibility for supporting

17. On this influential perspective on school reform, see Raymond E. Callahan, *Education and the Cult of Efficiency: A Study of the Social Forces That Have Shaped the Administration of the Public Schools* (University of Chicago Press, 1962). On the influence of the progressives, see David B. Tyack, *The One Best System: A History of American Urban Education* (Harvard University Press, 1974).

18. Chubb and Moe, *Politics, Markets, and America's Schools*, chap. 2.

19. Chubb and Moe, *Politics, Markets, and America's Schools*, chap. 2.

20. This is one reason why federal education policy is implemented through scores of narrow categorical grant programs and why these programs have grown from simple statutes into excruciatingly detailed laws occasionally running a hundred or more pages. See John E. Chubb, "The Political Economy of Federalism," *American Political Science Review*, vol. 79 (December 1985), pp. 994–1015. On the proliferation of education regulation, see John E. Chubb, "Excessive Regulation: The Case of Federal Aid to Education," *Political Science Quarterly*, vol. 100 (Summer 1985), pp. 287–311.

schools has moved up from localities to the states and as federal regulation has grown.[21] Most of the increase in federal regulation stems from the rise of federal grant programs as instruments of national policy. With increased state funding, state regulation has also expanded.[22] Decisions by state and federal courts, primarily on issues of financial equity and racial segregation, have also contributed to the trend.

Increased regulation has contributed to the declining proportion of instruction in current educational expenditures, falling from 68 percent in 1960 to 61 percent by 1980.[23] Moreover, between 1960 and 1984 the number of nonclassroom instructional personnel grew 400 percent, nearly seven times the rate of growth in the number of classroom teachers.[24] In 1983 full-time classroom teachers represented half (54 percent) of all local school employment; administrators represented 13 percent.[25]

The bureaucratization of schools has also contributed to the development of unions, which in turn have further rigidified the schools. In part to protect themselves from political and administrative impositions (and in part to improve their economic position), teachers have increasingly organized and bargained over the rules by which schools operate. Combined with expanded federal, state, and local rules, union rules have reinforced bureaucratic constraint. Even though teachers want and need more freedom from bureaucracy—more opportunity to work as professionals—teachers' unions are part of the bureaucracy problem.

The Need for Output Policies

To improve performance, the U.S. public education system must focus on educational outcomes. It should desist from telling schools in detail what inputs they must use and how they must use them. It should instead offer resources to schools (or take resources away) based on school performance. The central idea of this proposal is simple: resources should

21. At President George Bush's Education Summit in September 1989, the key commitment that the governors extracted from the White House was an effort to cut back on federal education regulation.

22. The state share in school budgets rose from 39.1 percent in 1960 to 49.4 percent in 1985. NCES, *Digest, 1988,* table 107.

23. NCES, *Digest, 1988,* table 110.

24. William J. Bennett, *American Education: Making It Work* (Department of Education, 1988), p. 46.

25. NCES, *Digest of Education Statistics, 1985–86* (Department of Education, 1986), table 47.

flow to schools that are performing well and away from schools that are performing poorly. Such a system does not require anyone to specify just what makes a "better teacher" or a "better school." Indeed, it recognizes that there are many different ways to produce high performance.

The only big problem with this proposal is that running schools based on performance is relatively untried. The United States has little experience with assessing performance or with running an educational system this way. This does not mean, however, that reformers must fly blind. A variety of performance-based systems have been proposed, and several have received a fair amount of theoretical and empirical analysis. We shall discuss a number of different proposals. But generally, we distinguish two broad approaches to reform: administrative reforms of the existing system of politically controlled schools, and new systems of school control modeled after economic markets. Because market, or "choice," systems represent greater departures from conventional administrative practice, we devote most of our attention to them.

Administrative Reforms

The introduction of merit pay is the most frequently discussed proposal within the current system of education. Teachers' pay would be based on their success in lifting student achievement. The appeal of merit pay, aside from long-time familiarity, is that it promises to help in retaining the best teachers while discouraging the worst. Despite its familiarity, few merit pay systems have survived for very long. The only systems that survive are ones that do not sharply differentiate pay by performance—in short, that do not apply the principle on which merit pay is based.[26] This is partly because teachers' unions have vigorously resisted merit pay.

Three arguments are frequently made against the use of merit pay. First, because no objective measuring system for student performance exists, the distribution of salaries, it is alleged, will be set arbitrarily or decided on extraneous grounds such as politics. Second, teachers' performance ratings would tend to reflect things beyond their control, such as family inputs—thus discouraging teachers from taking on difficult students and classes. Third, because of the nature of teaching within

26. Richard J. Murnane and David K. Cohen, "Merit Pay and the Evaluation Problem: Why Most Merit Pay Plans Fail and a Few Survive," *Harvard Educational Review*, vol. 56 (February 1986), pp. 1–17.

schools, teamwork is very important, and the competition introduced by merit pay might be counterproductive.

Because experience with merit pay is meager, these arguments are hard to assess. Nevertheless, merit pay is used successfully in a wide range of nonschool settings that face similar problems in measuring outputs. Standardized tests might well encourage abuse and distortions (for example, "teaching to the test") if they were used to set teacher pay. But research does suggest that evaluation by principals is technically feasible and that evaluations of performance need not rely solely on test scores.[27] These studies also confirm that it is possible to differentiate between performance of the teacher and the effect of families and other factors. Only the effect of merit pay on teamwork is truly unknown.

Under a variant of merit pay the performance of entire schools would be evaluated. This approach—call it "merit schools"—is designed to encourage cooperation among teachers and staff by promising increased resources for good schoolwide performance. One of the most important issues in this approach concerns whether increased resources are used to reward teachers and other staff with higher pay for good performance or to advance other objectives, that is, whether altered resources provide substantial incentives to the teachers and administrators. It also seems unlikely that any such scheme would do much to alter the stock of teachers unless individual school administrators are given considerable flexibility in choosing teachers and staff. Finally, evaluating schools may be harder than evaluating individual teachers. Certainly, there would be a strong need to rely on highly aggregated test score information, which would make it difficult to adjust fully for differences in student populations and would increase the chances of misusing test scores.

Despite these uncertainties, it is possible to think of various merit plans that could have beneficial effects. The key to any plan is that it relate resources to performance more directly than the two are related

---

27. Two studies have employed sophisticated statistical models to estimate the "value-added" by individual teachers and then have compared these estimates with evaluations of teachers by the principals. This research indicates that principals, who did not evaluate teachers on the basis of student test scores, developed ratings that were consistent with the test-based measures. See David Armor and others, *Analysis of the School Preferred Reading Program in Selected Los Angeles Minority Schools*, R-2007-LAUSD (Santa Monica: Rand Corporation, 1976); and Richard J. Murnane, *The Impact of School Resources on the Learning of Inner City Children* (Ballinger, 1975). These results did not come, however, from school systems that employed evaluations for purposes of deciding pay. It seems likely that other teachers could also provide good evaluations of teaching performance.

now. The main problem is that current regulations, personnel contracts, and other policies obstruct this outcome. As long as teachers, principals, administrators, and schools are protected against adverse consequences for poor performances, plans to reward or punish school performance have little chance of succeeding.

Such plans have one other problem as well. Merit pay or merit schools would not alter the system of management under which U.S. schools have operated for the last hundred years. Top-down management would try to hold schools accountable for output rather than attempting to control inputs. This difference is important, but schools would still face the political and technical problems associated with centralized public control. The success of merit plans depends on circumventing past bureaucratic operating principles while still working within the existing administrative structure. This is clearly difficult.

Market-Oriented Reforms

A fundamentally different approach is to hold schools accountable through decentralized evaluation in educational "markets" that involve parents and students in deciding which school to attend. If parents choose schools that are performing well, and resources follow consumer choices, this arrangement should result in the gradual improvement of the school system.

In educational markets, as in other markets, consumers cannot command suppliers to produce what they want, but through voluntary exchanges with producers, they can effectively, if indirectly, control what is produced. Indeed, no way has been found to meet demands for most private goods and services that is more efficient than free economic markets.

Of course, education is not an ordinary private good. Education has consequences for the quality and equality of political and economic life that extend far beyond the individual student or the student's family. But even if the social ramifications of education are far more important than the private ramifications, by providing parents and students with the financial resources and legal authority to select the schools they want to attend and by giving schools the opportunity to compete for the financial support of families, society can take advantage of the power of individual decisions to shape schools to its ends. The government retains the capacity to ensure social objectives by maintaining control of the level and distribution of financial support and by writing the ground rules within which schools can compete.

The Case for Market-Oriented School Reforms

Market-oriented school reform rests on the proposition that social as well as private objectives will be advanced if schools are driven more directly than they are now by the interests and judgments of parents and students as they are expressed in the choice of schools. As a necessary complement to parental choice, schools would be given greater latitude in deciding how they would operate—what they would teach, who their teachers and principals would be, and how they would attract parents and students. School resources would also be related directly to consumer evaluations of performance. What market-oriented reform would achieve depends on how reform is implemented. But certain gains can be expected from almost any variant.

Reduced bureaucratization. Market mechanisms would likely lead to a reversal of the trend toward the bureaucratization of schools. This effect flows directly from the "technology" of education, which depends for its success or failure largely on such factors as the personal relationships and interactions among teachers, students, and parents, and on the skillful application of knowledge and expertise by teachers.[28] Large administrative systems obstruct, rather than facilitate, these relationships. A properly designed market should reward them.

In addition, the administrative requirements of controlling schools effectively from above are daunting. Because evaluating teacher effectiveness or school performance on a mass basis in an objective, quantifiable manner, is so difficult, the process of devising generalizable bureaucratic rules for rewarding truly effective performance has proved impossible.

Centralized bureaucracy would be expected to atrophy if schools are given the power to respond to the demands of students and parents, as they must if the marketplace for schools is permitted to operate freely. People in schools are in a much better position to know the needs of their clients and to know how to respond to them than are administrators removed from the scene.

Better school organization. By shifting management away from bur-

28. See especially, Sizer, *Horace's Compromise*; and James P. Comer, "Educating Poor Minority Children," *Scientific American*, vol. 259 (November 1988), pp. 42–48.

eaucracies and toward schools, markets would promote more effective school organization. Mission-oriented, strongly led, professional schools, while incompatible with strong bureaucratic control, are quite compatible with market control.[29]

Politically controlled hierarchies tend to discourage the development of clear purposes in subordinate organizations because of the continual need for political compromises. Bureaucratic organizations tend to discourage strong leadership, collegiality, shared decisionmaking, and professionalism in teachers. In short, bureaucracy discourages effective school organization.

Markets, in contrast, reward effective school organization, encourage clear goals, high expectations, strong leadership, and true professionalism—characteristics that translate into successful schooling. Successful schooling, in turn, earns its own reward by attracting parents seeking schools that offer better achievement and the added resources that increased attendance brings.[30]

Closer relationships between families and schools. As bureaucratic influence wanes and market control increases, schools are encouraged to shift their attention from bureaucratic superiors to their clients. This shift of allegiance, which is likely to strengthen relationships among schools, parents, and students, is crucial because a close and mutually supportive relationship among the child, the family, and the school is central to sustained learning.[31]

The bureaucratic control under which many public schools operate offers schools little authority to accommodate parental objections to course content, teacher assignments, or textbooks, even if they believe the objections are valid. In such cases, schools run a serious risk of breeding conflict, rather than fostering support, if they seek parent involvement. Schools that must compete for the allegiance of parents and children have strong incentives not only to seek parental involvement but to respond to parental objections. By reaching out to parents, a

29. For statistical estimates of the relationship among markets, bureaucracy, and school organization, see Chubb and Moe, *Politics, Markets, and America's Schools,* chap. 5. The observations that follow are developed in the book.

30. It is little wonder that all else being equal—when parents and students are fully comparable—private schools in the United States are more likely than public schools to be effectively organized. John E. Chubb and Terry M. Moe, "Politics, Markets, and the Organization of Schools," *American Political Science Review,* vol. 82 (December 1988), pp. 1065–87; and Chubb and Moe, *Politics, Markets, and America's Schools,* chap. 5.

31. See especially Comer, "Educating Poor Minority Children."

school can increase its knowledge of what parents want and improve understanding among parents about the school's goals.

Parents have independent incentives to intensify their involvement in their children's education. The opportunity to choose the schools their children will attend encourages parents to learn more about what different schools have to offer—an incentive that is almost completely suppressed in conventional public school systems once the family has chosen where to live.

The voluntary nature of the school-family relationship should also increase the interest that children take in their schools and the interest that schools take in their students. In a market setting, students will seek schools responsive to their interests and needs and in which they want to be enrolled. Students will consequently tend to be better motivated than they are when their schools are not to their liking. Schools will tend to reinforce the benefits of self-selection by recruiting staff and developing programs that fit distinctive missions and appeal to distinctive clienteles.

Summary. The case for market control of schools rests on three propositions. First, if public education is governed more by markets than by politics, the relationship between schools and democratic authorities will become much less bureaucratic and much less prone to the problems of excessive regulation and inadequate accountability that now plague our school systems. Second, freed from bureaucratic constraint but subject to competition and choice, schools should organize themselves more effectively. Third, competition and choice should promote closer and more cooperative relationships among schools, students, and parents. The overall effect of these developments should, in turn, be greater student achievement.

The Case against Market Control

Markets are prone to various problems or "failures," such as monopoly, deceptive advertising, and barriers to new market entrants, that can hamper competition and reduce consumer welfare. Markets efficiently satisfy demands backed by money but do not automatically address such societal goals as equality or the elimination of poverty. They also fail to provide adequate supplies of "public goods," such as urban streets or national defense.[32] Consequently, the efficient operation of an economy

32. A free market will underinvest in public goods—items that are shared by all, such

based on private property and markets requires governmental involvement in many functions, including education, where goals other than pure efficiency have been central. Although society may express its concerns about education better through markets than through direct management and bureaucratic control, market control of education, like private economic markets, is potentially subject to a variety of market failures. As we shall explain, the seriousness of these shortcomings will depend on how education markets are structured.

Inadequate information. This concern is the one most frequently voiced and least likely to cause real problems. Forcing schools to compete for students would strengthen their incentives to provide parents with information about programs, personnel, and performance and to explain why they are the best possible institutions for particular students and families. Parents would also have strengthened incentives to seek out information from schools and from other parents. Parents do not need to assess all schools. Parents can use subjective information, garnered in part from conversations with one another, to form judgments about the appropriateness of various schools for their children. Not all parents will make optimal choices. But the standard of appropriateness that would have to be met to outperform current arrangements is not high.

The greatest informational concern for the government is likely to be related not to the quantity, but to the quality, of information. The government already tries to ensure truth in advertising. It would be even more important for government to prohibit false claims by schools than by appliance manufacturers.

Monopoly. An education market may support too few competitors to realize the advantages of markets. Currently, individual school districts determine the number of schools, and parents have little or no choice about which school their children will attend. Realizing the full advantages of competition would require that school districts be stripped of their current status as sole providers of public education. This does not require, as we discuss below, that private suppliers be permitted. It does require, though, that choice be broad enough and that resources flows based on choice be large enough to sustain a multiplicity of schools. In areas where student populations are very sparse, this may be difficult. But for the vast majority of students, competition among schools would be practical.

---

as national defense—because each individual has an incentive to free ride on the expenditures of others.

Inequality. Public education in the United States today exhibits gross inequalities. The affluent find superior schools for their children either by paying private school tuition or by buying homes in communities with good public schools. Those without economic means must often settle for less. The federal and state governments have attempted to compensate for this inequality by putting extra money into schools that the poor attend or that localities underfund. But these efforts, for the reasons discussed previously, have reduced differences in educational outcomes only marginally.

In a system of public education based on market principles, poor and middle-class families could enjoy the same leverage over schools that only upper-income families enjoy now. In its most complete form, markets would give poor and middle-class families the power to leave schools that are not satisfactory, and schools would be compelled to improve or to lose families to schools that were doing better. Schools that lost many families would be allowed to close—to be replaced or reopened as new schools with different principals, teachers, and programs. As we have said, there are good reasons to expect this process to improve school performance and to boost student achievement, including the achievement of typical poor and middle-class students.

This is no small accomplishment. Nevertheless, it does not ensure a reduction in inequality. Parents who are well educated or deeply committed to education are likely to make better choices than other families do. (This source of inequality, of course, exists now because some parents pay much more attention to local schools than do other parents in deciding where to reside.) Government can reduce, but not eliminate, this source of inequality by helping certain parents—the economically disadvantaged, for example—make their educational choices. Moreover, even those participants in a market who do not try to make informed choices—those who automatically choose the school closest to their homes, for example—will benefit from the improved schools that the informed choices of others bring about.

There is another possible source of inequity, however. Inequality also may result if children who are academically gifted or come from wealthy families are able to get into the best schools. If the relationship between schools and students is entirely voluntary, children who seem easier to educate or who can pay more for their education may be selected by schools over children who lack these "virtues."

But this source of inequality is easy to exaggerate and conceptually straightforward to alleviate. Not all schools can compete for the wealthiest and most gifted and survive. To prosper, schools would have to carve out market niches where they can specialize and be competitive. More important, the government can help to minimize such inequality. It could guarantee all children the same financial resources with which to shop for a school. It could even provide extra resources for children who are more expensive or more challenging to educate, thus rendering them more attractive to schools. It could also require that each school select some portion of the student body on the basis of educational disadvantages or by lottery. Ultimately, inequality in a market-controlled system of education, as under current arrangements, will depend on how much effort society makes to reduce it.

Values. Many fear that market-driven education will support undesirable values. Parents may not be sufficiently interested in academic achievement to support good enough schools. Parents may encourage different schools to teach values antithetical to national unity or democracy. They may seek racially homogeneous schools and thereby perpetuate racial intolerance and injustice. Although there is little reason to believe that parents as a group hold very different educational values than society as a whole, there are nevertheless some reasons for concern.

Some parents may simply give little weight to academic quality in selecting schools. Parents might choose, for example, to send their children to a "football high school," where athletics are promoted at the expense of academics. Although variations would exist, we doubt that academically unacceptable choices would be very common, even in a completely unregulated market. As long as most parents prefer schools that offer their children better rather than worse prospects of high school graduation, gainful employment, college admission, and other outcomes dependent on academic achievement, schools will be encouraged to aim for quality. Schools that provide students with no future, or a relatively poor one, should find it hard to attract many families, even if they field winning sports teams. Nevertheless, some government regulation might well be necessary and appropriate to curb excessive school specialization in socially less desirable endeavors.

Another concern is that without trading off academic performance, some parents might select schools that teach or support ideas or values that society as a whole could never agree should be taught—for example, detailed sex education or no sex education at all, creationism, or particular religious principles. Society could, of course, continue to limit or prescribe what is taught, but in so doing it would risk perpetuating the bureaucratic ossification that market-oriented reforms are intended to counter.

If society decides to avoid this risk and to accept the teaching of alternative values in publicly funded schools, would it not run additional risks, however? Would it risk the aggravation of intolerance and social cleavage? Would it jeopardize democratic values? We doubt it for several reasons. First, some of the concerns about intolerance, cleavage, and ignorance that were reasonable fears in the last century, when the "common school" was established, are not reasonable fears today.[33] The United States is no longer a young and fragile nation trying to unify a population made up mostly of recent immigrants. Furthermore, respect for democracy can result not only through a common curriculum in democratic values, but also by displaying tolerance and acceptance of a diversity of schools.[34] Finally, there is no evidence whatsoever that private school students currently turn out to be systematically worse citizens than their counterparts who have learned their democratic lessons in public schools. For all of these reasons we believe that market approaches are unlikely to impair the transmission of democratic values.

Even so, some values may be too important to be left to parental choice. One is racial equality, or integration, a value that has not historically enjoyed the strong support of either parents or the broader public. Parents might choose schools based on racial composition, out of sheer bigotry, or as a proxy for school quality or safety. To forestall such behavior, society might insist that all publicly supported schools do more than adhere to nondiscrimination laws in student admissions (and in the hiring of staff). Society might want to impose racial quotas or to insist that enrollments satisfy desegregation plans.

Whether such steps are necessary to promote desegregation is an open question, however. Recent history suggests that parental choice, properly structured, does not produce resegregation. Given the opportunity, parents tend to choose schools that are safe and excellent regardless of their racial makeup. This is the idea behind magnet schools, which have had considerable success in promoting voluntary desegregation.[35] More

33. See Charles Leslie Glenn, Jr., *The Myth of the Common School* (University of Massachusetts Press, 1988); and James S. Coleman, "Choice, Community, and Future Schools," paper prepared for the Conference on Choice and Control in American Education, University of Wisconsin, 1989.

34. See John E. Coons and Stephen D. Sugarman, *Education by Choice: The Case for Family Control* (University of California Press, 1978).

35. See Rolf K. Blank, "Educational Effects of Magnet Schools," paper prepared for the Conference on Choice and Control in American Education, University of Wisconsin, 1989; M. H. Metz, *Different by Design: The Context and Character of Three Magnet Schools* (Routledge and Kegan, 1986); Mary Anne Raywid, "The Mounting Case for

important, if poor racial minorities were given the resources to choose and be chosen by better schools, the chances of resegregation are further diminished. Finally, private schools, especially inner-city Catholic schools that serve poor racial minorities, are often more racially integrated than public schools are.[36]

Alternative Market Mechanisms

Among the many ways in which a market approach to schooling can be implemented, four have received the most attention: magnet schools, open-enrollment (or public school choice), tuition tax credits, and vouchers (or all-school choice).

Magnet Schools

Virtually all urban school districts have introduced magnet schools over the last two decades, especially during the 1980s. The use of magnet schools varies widely but is rising. Among high school students, enrollment in magnet schools may now be 20 percent in urban districts.[37] Growth has been inspired by the desire to desegregate voluntarily and to improve educational outcomes. Magnet schools have attempted to satisfy these desires by offering specialized curricula, by using especially interested faculty, by opening their doors to students outside of normal attendance zones, and by building student bodies based on the choices of parents and (sometimes) of schools.

Magnet schools nevertheless introduce choice into school systems while maintaining much of the current structure of organization, finance, and management. Although rules vary, the school system typically allows students to choose between a magnet school and a traditional school. Beyond this freedom, the school system may do little else to emulate a market or to permit performance to drive school organization and improvement. In particular, there is no assurance that resources follow school performance and parent-student choice, or that schools have the

---

Schools of Choice," in Joe Nathan, ed., *Public Schools by Choice: Expanding Opportunities for Parents, Students, and Teachers* (St. Paul, Minn.: Institute for Learning and Teaching, 1989); and Robert S. Peterkin and Dorothy S. Jones, "Schools of Choice in Cambridge, Massachusetts," in Nathan, *Public Schools by Choice.*

36. See James S. Coleman, Thomas Hoffer, and Sally Kilgore, *High School Achievement: Public, Catholic, and Private Schools Compared* (Basic Books, 1982).

37. Blank, "Educational Effects," p. 4.

authority and flexibility to respond effectively to competition and demand.

In important respects, though, magnet schools have succeeded. They appear to have promoted desegregation and to have raised the achievement of students enrolled in magnets.[38] Their major failure is that they have done little to help students in traditional schools—students who do not get into the magnets. Indeed, if magnet schools take the best students and teachers from throughout the system, traditional schools can be made worse. Their net effects on school systems as a whole may therefore be zero.

It would also be a mistake to regard all or even most magnet schools as successes in their own right. Magnet schools have struggled in many instances to create the kind of organizational climate necessary for improvement.[39] Principals have not been routinely given the power to control their teaching staffs (union contracts, for example, are still in force), and teachers have often had to work with all of the usual constraints. The problem is that magnet schools do little to change the patterns of control of the supply of public schools by political authorities. The system does not inherently dictate that the desires of parents and students drive the finance, organization, and performance of schools. Magnet schools are a step toward market control of schools but only a step.

Open-Enrollment Plans

The next logical step toward greater market influence over public schools is, in a sense, to make all schools magnets. In the extreme, parents could choose from all existing public schools with no assigned attendance areas.

Public school choice, as such arrangements are now most frequently called, comes in two basic forms: intradistrict open enrollment, which permits families to choose any public school within a particular school district, and interdistrict open enrollment, which permits families to choose public schools in any number of districts—at the extreme, any public school district in a state. Experience with both forms is rapidly growing. A good number of school districts—most notably, New York City's District 4 in East Harlem, and Cambridge, Massachusetts—have

38. Blank, "Educational Effects," pp. 9–13.
39. Blank, "Educational Effects," p. 8.

been utilizing intradistrict choice for ten or more years.[40] Seven states—Arkansas, Idaho, Iowa, Minnesota, Nebraska, Ohio, and Utah—have recently adopted or begun to implement statewide interdistrict choice.

Experiences with choice programs have been mostly positive. Most students have been able to enroll in the school that is their top choice, and fears that choice would be an administrative nightmare have proved unfounded. Parents have generally been satisfied. Principals and teachers in some cases have acquired increased control over their schools and work. And student performance has improved. In Cambridge, Massachusetts, the choice system won many families back from private schools. In East Harlem test scores rose from last among the city's thirty-two community school districts to sixteenth.[41]

But, equally as clearly, not all results have been positive. Some students have been left behind in poorly performing schools that too few students have chosen. Some parents have chosen schools primarily because they are close to their place of work. Many choice programs, especially those operating statewide, are too new to judge. And definitive evaluations have been conducted on none.

The greatest problem, though, is that public authorities have yet to permit market forces to supplant the political and bureaucratic forces that have undermined school performance. They have yet to permit resources to flow freely to schools based on parent and student choices. As a result, many of the improvements expected to follow from market-oriented reform have not been realized.

The supply of schools remains firmly under the control of central authorities—not under the control of schools and their clients. Intradistrict choice plans have typically imposed tight controls on admissions, thus constraining student choice. In only one district, New York's District 4, did authorities cede authority to open, close, and reorganize schools and to change personnel to the schools themselves, or to the market. So far, interdistrict choice plans permit students who cross district lines to transfer only the share of educational costs guaranteed by the state.[42] When the incremental costs of education exceed this amount, departing

40. Several of these experiences are described in Nathan, *Public Schools by Choice.*

41. See Raymond J. Domanico, "A Model for Choice: A Report on Manhattan's District 4," Education Policy Paper 1, Center for Education Innovation, Manhattan Institute for Policy Research, June 1989; and Robert S. Peterkin and Dorothy S. Jones, "Schools of Choice in Cambridge, Massachusetts," in Nathan, *Public Schools by Choice,* chap. 7.

42. The amount transferred differs from state to state. In Minnesota, the state-guaranteed minimum or foundation includes some local money.

students bestow a "profit" on the districts they leave and inflict a loss on the districts they enter—just the opposite of the resource incentives that are desired. The combined impact of the existing plans is opening up more of the schools to parental evaluation of performance but stopping far short of a full market system.

Open-enrollment plans, as they currently exist, are innovative attempts to move toward the introduction of market discipline, but the current structure needs to be modified if public school choice is to live up to its potential. Most important, ineffective schools and teachers cannot be fully insured against "lack of choice" by parents. Excellent schools and teachers—those that are frequently chosen—cannot go unrewarded. School resources need to follow more closely the decisions of students and parents and less closely the judgments of public authorities.

Tuition Tax Credits

One way to loosen the control of public authorities over the supply of schools is to provide parents with the financial means to choose schools that public authorities do not control, namely, private schools. Giving parents a credit against their federal or state income taxes for some portion of school tuition is the way most often proposed to this end. The government helps parents afford private schools by paying part of the bill. Because more parents would be able to afford private schools, more competitive pressure would be exerted on all schools, public and private. The education of those who take advantage of the credit and find an appropriately matched private school would almost certainly be improved.[43] The education of those who remain in public school might, by virtue of private school competition, also be improved.

Most proposed tax credits would, however, limit support to an amount too small to make private schools generally accessible. In practice, tuition tax credits would provide only $500 to $1,000 per child a year, or only a small part of typical private school tuition. Furthermore, unless the tax credit were refundable to tax filers with liabilities less than the credit, it would be unavailable to parents with low income. Such credits would provide tax relief to relatively well-to-do parents, many of whom

43. There is some dispute about the relative performance of existing private schools. See especially Coleman, Hoffer, and Kilgore, *High School Achievement*; and James S. Coleman and Thomas Hoffer, *Public and Private High Schools: The Impact of Communities* (Basic Books, 1987). See entire *Sociology of Education*, vol. 55 (April–July 1982).

would have sent their children to private schools even without the credit. They would do little to improve schools for other children.

Despite the flaws of actual proposals, the principle embodied in tuition tax credits represents an important step in the direction of market improvements. In contrast to magnet schools and open enrollment schemes, tuition tax credits move toward the elimination of the exclusive control that public school districts now exercise over the supply of publicly supported education. Credits also ensure some minimum resource flows based on performance. Both of these developments, as we have argued, would represent fundamental improvements in the current organization of public education. The key problem with tax credits is that because of their very limited size, they do not permit these developments to proceed very far, and thereby deny most parents, especially the economically disadvantaged, the potential benefits of true market-oriented reform.

Voucher Plans

The obvious way to overcome the main limitations of tax credits— to provide all parents with effective market power, and to thereby change the incentive structure governing the supply of schools—is to provide parents with full subsidies, vouchers, or scholarships. These could then be used to obtain education at any public or publicly approved private school. Full subsidies would afford every family the kind of market influence now exerted only by the rich. All parents would have the authority and resources to seek an education for their children at any school that meets public standards. School revenue would depend on the number and kind of students attracted to the school.

By opening up private schools to a larger potential clientele, or by permitting alternative suppliers of public schools, a system of broad educational choice would change existing public schools significantly. Public schools would be encouraged to decentralize their administration, make their organizations more professional, and revise their relationships with authorities and clients. All schools would be encouraged to try to stay ahead of their competition, creating direct forces for improving school performance. Schools that did not improve would lose large numbers of students who would find better alternatives elsewhere—and their revenues would be directly affected.

A system of public-private competition, or a system of autonomous public schools, faces the potential problems we discussed before, and virtually everybody favoring such systems also favors some government regulation to ensure that public objectives are achieved.[44] The government could give parents information about schools and ensure the accuracy of information provided by schools. It could minimize inequality by providing the educationally disadvantaged with larger-than-average vouchers, which would make these students attractive candidates to schools that might otherwise not want them. It could require all participating private schools to accept vouchers as full payment, in other words to become completely publicly funded. The government could also set desegregation goals and regulate admissions consistent with them. Finally, the government would have final authority to set eligibility rules, graduation requirements, teacher certification requirements, admission rules, financial constraints, and anything else it believes important for participating private as well as public schools.

Obviously, the more government regulation, the further the plan deviates from the concept of an educational market. Nevertheless, the government has the authority to create any kind of market it likes and to pursue whatever mix of quality and equality goals it likes. With little experience it is impossible to describe the "right" balance of market forces and government regulation, and investigating this balance would be an important aspect of any initial implementation.

Trade-offs and Uncertainties

The alternative market plans we have just discussed, and the within-system merit schemes we discussed previously, represent a continuum of possible changes. Full voucher plans are the most radical and, from a perspective that argues the need for market-oriented reform, the most conceptually appealing. They also have the least support of the education establishment and hence the least potential of being adopted. In addition, they come with the greatest uncertainty, since they have never really been tried. Other plans require less alteration of the current system and, in part because of this, hold less potential for improvement. They do, however, have better chances of being adopted and are more predictable in their consequences.

Policymakers must make these trade-offs and weigh the associated risks. One thing, however, is perfectly clear. Policymakers must move toward *some* system based on school performance.

44. For a description of a system of public school choice based on autonomous public schools, see Chubb and Moe, *Politics, Markets, and America's Schools,* chap. 6.

The Role of Federal Policy

If the performance of America's schools is to improve, schools must in some fundamental way be held accountable for their performance.[45] Without performance accountability, schools are likely to absorb any increase in spending or to accommodate higher standards, new curricula, and alternative forms of management without changing the way they operate. The inertia of business as usual will muffle reforms, so that they yield positive results in some places, negative results in others, and make no difference in most schools and, on balance, in the nation as a whole. The reason is that the organization and operation of an effective school are inherently difficult, if not impossible, to specify and to mandate. Politics tends to complicate this problem with layers of bureaucratic control. Collectively bargained work rules further hamper improvements in school operations. Money is lavished on efforts to hire particular kinds of teachers, to develop and offer new courses and programs, and to follow publicly agreed methods and procedures, in the vain hope that more will produce better educational outcomes.

Policymakers need to recognize that this approach has not worked in the past and is quite unlikely to work in the future and that improved educational output does not follow predictably from increased educational input. If policymakers want better educational outcomes, they must hold schools accountable for achieving them.

This lesson presents a problem for federal policymakers. They cannot hold schools accountable directly. The federal government does not operate schools. It does not hire teachers. The federal government cannot require schools to pay teachers based on merit or to fund schools based on performance. The federal government cannot give parents the right to choose their public schools. It cannot authorize alternative suppliers of public education. Only state governments and their local agents have the constitutional power to do these things directly. The federal government can encourage fundamental improvements in America's public schools, but it cannot make them. Until state and local governments take the major steps necessary to restructure the finance and governance of schools, additional federal support for public education is likely to make little difference.

---

45. The term accountability is used in widely different ways in educational discussions. We use the term specifically to mean that rewards, most commonly defined by resources, are directly related to performance.

Consider the fiscal year 1991 budget. President George Bush is proposing a 2 percent increase ($508 million) in budget authority for the Department of Education. Democrats and most education interest groups have roundly criticized this proposal as a pitiful commitment, especially from a self-professed "education president." For the sake of argument, imagine that the president proposed a 10 percent increase—five times the current proposal. Imagine further that the president were to commit all of the increase to elementary and secondary education (not half, as proportional increases would require), and that every cent of the increase was devoted to higher salaries for teachers. The result of such a historic commitment would be a salary increase of roughly $1,000 a year for every public school teacher. While teachers may in some sense deserve such a reward, awarding modest increases to every teacher, regardless of merit, is unlikely to affect the performance of existing teachers or to attract substantially more talented people into the teaching pool. Indeed, during the 1980s teachers received salary increases averaging nearly $1,000 *every* year.[46]

The federal government need not wait idly for state and local innovation, however. The federal government can encourage state and local governments to restructure their educational systems. It can promote school accountability. Doing so, however, requires the president and Congress to alter their approach by as much as we believe local schools must be changed.

Grants-in-Aid

By offering grants to states or school districts that adopt reforms to make schools accountable for performance, the federal government could promote such changes. Such programs could promote accountability within the current structure by covering part of the cost of merit-pay or merit school programs. The Bush administration has proposed to give financial rewards directly to merit schools. To encourage alteration of the basic system of accountability, the federal government could aid states or school districts that establish systems of educational choice. The Department of Education now spends roughly $12 billion annually— half its budget—on elementary and secondary education, most of it

46. NCES, *Digest, 1988*, table 57. See also data on teacher salaries compiled by the Educational Research Service and cited in Pat Ordovensky, "Average Teacher's Pay Tops $30,000," *USA Today*, February 27, 1990, p. D1.

implemented through seventy or so categorical grant programs.[47] Only a sliver of the budget—one program running a little over $100 million a year—is devoted to promoting accountability for school performance. Even that effort, to promote magnet schools, encourages only magnet schools created for desegregation and not those created to pursue academic excellence.

To date, the federal government has not made much of its aid contingent on school performance or on innovations that state and local officials might not want to undertake. For obvious political reasons, the government has instead offered educational assistance that can be enjoyed universally.[48] It has imposed utilization and reporting requirements, but they add to the bureaucratization of public education without changing its form or increasing attention to performance.

Grants to Individuals

The federal government could also make grants to individuals rather than to state and local governments. It could base such grants on need, thereby targeting expenditures rather than providing them universally. It could offer the grants to eligible households only in districts that allowed parents some choice in selecting schools or that instituted systems of merit pay. It could accomplish these goals at no added cost to the federal budget by converting institutional grants for the disadvantaged, the handicapped, and perhaps for vocational education into need-based entitlements for students. The entitlements could then be used by students to purchase supplementary educational services, subject to federal restrictions, at any school of their choosing.

Grants to students rather than institutions could spark significant school improvement because they would act like partial vouchers. The

47. The elementary and secondary total includes $7.6 billion spent by the Office of Elementary and Secondary Education, $0.2 billion by the Office of Bilingual Education and Minority Language Affairs, $3.8 billion by the Office of Special Education and Rehabilitative Services (excluding grants for special institutions for the handicapped), and $0.9 billion for the Office of Vocational and Adult Education (excluding adult education). The remainder of the Department of Education budget is spent on the Office of Postsecondary Education ($10.7 billion), the Office of Educational Research and Improvement ($0.2 billion), and department management ($0.3 billion), for a Department of Education total of $24.1 billion. These figures are estimated actual expenditures for fiscal year 1990. *Education Reports,* vol. 11 (January 29, 1990), pp. 1–4.

48. See, among many sources, John E. Chubb, "Federalism and the Bias for Centralization," in John E. Chubb and Paul E. Peterson, eds., *The New Direction in American Politics* (Brookings, 1985), chap. 10.

formula could be designed to ensure that more money would reach truly needy students than reaches them now.[49] Furthermore, the current compensatory education program, which purports to help at-risk students by requiring schools to provide them with supplementary services (a couple of sessions with a reading tutor every week, for example), does nothing to improve the disastrously bad schools in which many of those students spend the rest of their week. Sufficiently generous student-based grants that could be used in alternative public schools or in private schools might enable at-risk children to get out of their miserable schools and into more effective ones. In states or districts with functioning choice programs, federal grants could give at-risk students the financial leverage they need to get a decent education in decent schools, not just a couple of hours of special services in educational disaster areas. In states currently without choice programs, such grants could give school officials who support market accountability but are legitimately concerned about the welfare of the disadvantaged the reassurance they require and the financial leverage they need to support and implement choice plans.

Improved Data on Performance

Data on performance is an important element of any system that rewards performance. When the U.S. Office of Education was created in 1867, its purpose was to collect education statistics. Over time, however, other activities have eclipsed this function. As recently as the 1960s, the federal government systematically gathered data on expenditures, enrollments, and little else. Data on student achievement have only been routinely gathered, through the National Assessment of Educational Progress (NAEP), since the early 1970s. Today, the statistical arm of the Department of Education is one of its smallest components, receiving about $40 million annually.

This meager effort provides only national data on performance. No data on school performance at the state or district level will be gathered until 1992, when the NAEP will permit interstate comparisons, but only for fourth grade reading and math.[50] Occasional independent studies or efforts by school systems themselves provide some additional subnational data. But the results are dubious, as suggested by the amusing fact that

49. See Denis P. Doyle and Bruce S. Cooper, eds., *Federal Aid to the Disadvantaged: What Future for Chapter 1?* (Philadelphia: Falmer Press, 1988).

50. Chester E. Finn, Jr., "The Need for Better Data on Education," *Education Week,* February 7, 1990, p. 36.

all states recently claimed that their students were performing above average.[51] By carrying out nationwide tests or paying for them, the federal government could give lower levels of government the information they need to hold schools accountable for their performance and could encourage parents to make informed choices among schools.

By developing improved tests, the federal government could also reduce the tendency of tests to distort schooling. Currently available standardized tests emphasize lower-level skills heavily dependent on recall, rather than higher-level ones demanding problem-solving ability and creativity. They also give too little attention to the acquisition of advanced knowledge.[52] If tests are going to be used to promote accountability, they must measure what effective schools should be teaching. The federal government is in a better position than any other entity to underwrite the development of such tests.

The collection of data should not be limited to just student performance. Because the suggested federal policies and the reorientation of general school policies are novel, more must be learned about the implementation of alternatives. This aim, in part, means promoting research on the performance of reorganized school systems. Naturally, the federal government would be important in the development and dissemination of knowledge about the implementation of performance-based educational reforms. Past efforts at educational research by the federal government have been frequently criticized, most importantly because of the lack of competition—and hence quality—in the federal research effort. To be effective, the government must therefore ensure that its research effort is disciplined by competition or some other mechanism that ensures better research.

Goals

The federal government can encourage state and local officials who are trying to convince their colleagues that better accountability is necessary by specifying what American students should achieve. Goals

51. John Jacob Cannell, "Nationally Normed Elementary Achievement Testing in America's Public Schools: How All 50 States Are Above the National Average," *Educational Measurement: Issues and Practice,* vol. 7 (Summer 1988), pp. 5–9, and Cannell, "The Lake Wobegon Effect Revisited," *Educational Measurement: Issues and Practice,* vol. 7 (Winter 1988), pp. 12–15.

52. Finn, "Need for Better Data"; and Richard J. Murnane, "Improving Education Indicators and Economic Indicators: The Same Problems?" *Educational Evaluation and Policy Analysis,* vol. 9 (Summer 1987), pp. 101–16.

should include not only targets for high school graduation or college attendance rates but also qualitative standards for proficiency in such areas as math, science, English, and history. Goals should also include proficiency in skills—problem solving and reasoning, for example—that are linked to performance in an increasingly dynamic labor market.[53] By regularly measuring state and local progress toward these objectives and by publicizing its assessments, the federal government can convey that it is serious about accountability.

The White House and the National Governors' Association are currently negotiating such an arrangement. But, given the current state of performance testing, the process may not prove especially useful. If the federal government relies on currently available test data—for example, SAT scores—to offer annual assessments, the states will object that the assessment process has been unfair.[54] If the national government instead relies on nontest measures—for example, graduation rates, course enrollments, and improvements in teacher education or school requirements—the states may be better satisfied, but performance will not have been adequately measured. For all parties to be satisfied and for meaningful assessment to take place, the federal government simply must have better data.

Conclusion

We have set out a menu of "output-based" options ranging from small intrusions on the current structure of school systems to a thoroughgoing revision of system structure. Each has advantages and disadvantages. Because each is substantially or totally new, each is also fraught with risk and uncertainty.

If the nation waits until all doubts about these options have been

---

53. Goals specifically related to the labor market should probably not be set until the relationship between schooling and labor market performance is better understood—something federally supported research could promote. In any case, goals should not be so specific that economic change quickly renders mandated skills obsolete.

54. State mean levels in SAT scores can be misleading indicators of the performance of schools because they do not consider other factors that explain differences in test scores. Unfortunately, common statistical corrections to SAT scores based on state income levels, percentage of test takers, and the like are insufficient. Accurate assessment of state differences must employ longitudinal information about performance. See Eric A. Hanushek and Lori L. Taylor, "Alternative Assessments of the Performance of Schools: Measurement of State Variations in Achievement," *Journal of Human Resources*, vol. 25 (Spring 1990), pp. 179–201.

eliminated, more generations of American children will be exposed to schools that are not just sub par but are seriously deficient. We are convinced that little progress can be made in improving education under current institutional arrangements. Simply throwing money at schools is certain to raise budgets, but it is not likely to do more unless fundamental changes occur in the way these resources are applied. U.S. educational policy over the past three decades has been a massive experiment that has tested whether spending more money within the traditional educational structure will result in better-educated students. The results are in. The experiment has failed.

The fundamental change we urge means linking school expenditures to performance. Schools and teachers who boost student performance should be directly rewarded. Schools and teachers who do a poor job should be replaced. Because this approach has been used sparingly, recommendations that it be used widely must rest heavily on conceptual arguments. We cannot guarantee that it will succeed, though we clearly believe it will bring improvement. We think we can guarantee that business as usual, even if more richly financed, will fail.

8

HENRY J. AARON

A Prescription for Health Care

THE U.S. health care system is marked by paradox. This country spends 38 percent more per capita on health care than does Canada, which has the world's second most costly health care system. The quality of the care most Americans receive for acute illness is unsurpassed anywhere in the world. Yet millions of Americans cannot afford, and are thereby denied, care that every other industrialized country treats as a routine right guaranteed to all residents. Although Americans are hospitalized less than residents of many other industrialized countries and their hospital stays are shorter than anywhere else in the world, the American hospital system is the world's most costly one. Despite this prodigious outlay, U.S. infant mortality is higher than in most other industrialized countries and life expectancy at birth is no better than average.

Two major problems confront the U.S. health care system in the 1990s. First, many Americans suffer from insufficient health insurance. Roughly one nonelderly American in seven lacks any insurance against the cost of care for acute illness. Millions of others are covered by plans that incompletely protect them against the cost of serious illness or particular risks. Few people are insured against the costs of long-term care, other than the very poor who are covered in varying degrees by the state-federal medicaid program. Second, the cost of health care is not only high, but rising as a share of national output, despite repeated cost-control efforts by corporations, unions, and the government.

Although the 1991 budget contains no hint of a departure from established policy, President Bush opened the door to such a departure in his 1990 State of the Union message to Congress. Several major studies of health care financing are now under way. The quadrennial Advisory Council on Social Security is developing a plan to reform not

I wish to thank Robert Ball, Jack Meyer, Joseph Newhouse, Robert Reischauer, and Charles L. Schultze for helpful comments. Maria Kefalas provided valuable research assistance, and Kathleen Elliott Yinug provided secretarial assistance.

only medicare but also other programs to pay for health care. A congressional commission, chaired by Senator John D. Rockefeller IV, has designed a plan to cover most Americans for the costs of acute illnesses and long-term care.[1] President Bush directed Secretary of Health and Human Services Louis Sullivan to lead a review of the recommendations of these and other groups and to suggest what federal actions are indicated. The significance of this directive will depend on what Secretary Sullivan recommends and how the president chooses to respond. But, like President Reagan's similar call in the 1986 State of the Union address for a careful review of welfare policy, this presidential announcement could stimulate sufficient interest in an acknowledged problem to lead to new federal policy.

Health Care Expenditures

Health care outlays have been growing rapidly for four decades. Real spending per capita has risen at an annual rate of 4.1 percent. Total spending rose from $69.9 billion in 1950 to $380.9 billion in 1980, and is projected at $661 billion in 1990.[2]

Several factors contributed to the increase in per capita spending. First, the range of diagnostic and therapeutic interventions has expanded rapidly for several decades. This process promises to continue.[3] Second, the spread of private insurance for hospital and physician expenses, especially during the 1950s and 1960s, reduced the price of care and increased demand for it.[4] Third, the relative cost of health care services has increased, in part because of improved quality and in part because productivity has not grown as fast as wages in the provision of large parts of hospital care, such as feeding, space rent, and routine nursing care.[5]

1. This group is called the "Pepper commission" after its initial chairman, the late representative from Florida, Claude Pepper.
2. "Health Spending Continues to Rise," *Medicine and Health*, vol. 44 (January 15, 1990), p. 1. All dollar totals in this chapter are expressed in 1990 dollars.
3. Louise B. Russell, *Technology in Hospitals: Medical Advances and Their Diffusion* (Brookings, 1979); and Henry J. Aaron and William B. Schwartz, "Rationing Health Care: The Choice before Us," *Science*, vol. 247 (January 26, 1990), pp. 418–22.
4. On the sensitivity of the demand for care to the cost patients face, see Joseph P. Newhouse and others, "Some Interim Results from a Controlled Trial of Cost Sharing in Health Insurance," *New England Journal of Medicine*, vol. 305 (December 17, 1981), pp. 1501–07.
5. One measure of this increase in the cost of hospital care is the growth in the number

The source of payment varies widely among medical services (see table 8-1). Some form of "third-party" payment (payment to the provider by someone other than the patient) accounted for more than 90 percent of hospital revenues in 1987, and the federal government was the source of more than half. In contrast, direct payments by patients accounted for about one-fourth of physicians' income. Individuals are heavily insured against the costs of hospitalization, but bear much of the cost of routine care.

International Comparisons

The United States spent more on health care in 1987 than any other country in the world, and expenditures have risen more rapidly than in most other major countries (see table 8-2).

Analysts are not sure how much of this difference is explained by more intensive use of services, how much by higher physicians' fees and other medical prices, and how much by such other factors as the age of the population and efficiency in the health care system. Nor are analysts certain how much of the difference, if any, is due to the relatively restricted role of the U.S. government in paying for health care, compared with governments in other countries.[6]

Although the United States spends more on health care than other countries do, the health of its citizens is no better, and by some indicators worse, than that in other countries. Among countries in the Organization for Economic Cooperation and Development, U.S. life expectancy is about average and infant mortality is slightly below average.[7] The

---

of employees per 100 patients, from 272 in 1971 to 392 in 1986. See Department of Health and Human Services, *Health U.S., 1988* (Washington, 1987), p. 104. As the general wage level rises, the cost of services rises if productivity in those sectors rises less rapidly than elsewhere in the economy. See William J. Baumol and William G. Bowen, *Performing Arts: An Economic Dilemma* (MIT Press, 1966).

6. Among twenty-three Organization for Economic Cooperation and Development countries, governments are the source of all hospital revenues in fifteen and at least 87 percent of the budget in seven others. The 40 percent of hospital budgets paid by governments in the United States is less than half that of any other OECD country. The absence of market prices for hospital care in most countries hinders distinctions between changes in real output and changes in prices. See Organization for Economic Cooperation and Development, *Financing and Delivering Health Care: A Comparative Analysis of OECD Countries* (Paris, 1987), table 19.

7. Among twenty-four OECD countries (including such relatively poor countries as Turkey, Greece, Portugal, and Spain), U.S. life expectancy at birth is fifteenth for males and eleventh for females; at age 40, thirteenth for males and eleventh for females; and at

TABLE 8-1. Sources of Payment for Personal Health Care Services, 1987
Amounts in billions of dollars

| | Direct payment | | Third-party payment | | | | | | Total | |
| | | | Private insurance | | Government | | Other | | | |
Source	Amount	Percent	Amount	Percent	Amount	Percent	Amount	Percent	Amount	Percent
Hospital care	18.5	9.4	71.9	36.9	102.2	52.5	2.2	2.7	194.8	100.0
Physicians	26.3	25.6	44.6	43.4	31.8	31.0	0.1	0.0	102.8	100.0
Pharmaceuticals	25.5	75.0	4.7	13.8	3.9	11.5	0.0	0.0	34.1	100.0
Nursing homes	20.0	49.3	0.4	1.0	19.9	49.0	0.3	0.7	40.6	100.0
Dental services	20.0	61.0	12.1	36.9	0.7	2.1	0.0	0.0	32.8	100.0
Other[a]	12.7	33.7	5.4	14.3	16.9	44.8	2.7	7.2	37.7	100.0
TOTAL	123.0	...	139.1	...	175.4	...	5.3	...	442.8	...

SOURCE: "National Health Expenditures, 1980–87" (with updated tables), *Health Care Financing Review*, vol. 10 (Summer 1987), p. 115, table 3.
a. Includes expenditures on other professional services, eyeglasses and appliances, and other personal care.

TABLE 8-2. Health Care Expenditures in Eight Industrialized Countries, 1987

Percent

Country	Per capita expenditures as percent of U.S. outlays, 1987	Change in real health expenditures as percent of 1987 GNP, 1970–87[a]
Australia	46	4.2
Canada	72	4.9
France	54	4.9
Germany	53	4.1
Japan	45	4.6
Sweden	60	3.8
United Kingdom	37	3.0
United States	100	6.6

SOURCE: George J. Schieber and Jean-Pierre Poullier, "Data Watch: International Health Care Expenditure Trends: 1987," *Health Affairs*, vol. 8 (Fall 1989), pp. 170–72.

a. Based on the product of gross domestic product (in constant domestic currency units) multiplied by the share of health expenditures in gross domestic product (measured in current domestic currency units). This measure reflects not only increases in real spending but also changes in the relative price of health care.

coincidence of mediocre health outcomes and high outlays has led some observers to conclude that the United States misdirects health care spending. While the conclusion may be correct, these statistics do not prove it. Health care services play a much smaller part in determining health than do public health measures, income and attendant amenities, consumption and eating patterns, environmental hazards, and, perhaps, genetic differences.[8] Even if health services were optimally distributed, health care spending might be either negatively or positively related to measures of public health: negatively related if countries facing adverse health conditions spent heavily to offset these risks, or positively if the beneficial effects of differences in health care spending dominated other influences on health outcomes.

Nevertheless, persuasive evidence suggests that the well-being of the American population could be improved in important ways if health services were redistributed or increased for those who are underserved. For example, pregnant women who see physicians early and regularly

age 65, fifth for males and fourth for females. Infant mortality rates in the United States are fifteenth among twenty-two OECD countries for whom data are reported. OECD, *Financing and Delivering Health Care*, tables 8, 9, 10, 11.

8. Victor R. Fuchs, *Who Shall Live?* (Basic Books, 1974); and *A New Perspective on Health of Canadians: A Working Document* (Ottawa: Information Canada, 1975).

during pregnancy give birth to underweight babies less frequently than do women who do not.[9] More generally, health care not only affects the course of illnesses but also serves as assurance to the sick that they are receiving attention and care.

Why Are Rising Health Expenditures a Problem?

Rising sales, which signal success for most industries, are a problem for the health care industry because, many observers believe, some part of health care expenditures goes for low-benefit care provided at needlessly high cost. Fully insured patients have little incentive to stint on care, because payments, by private companies or government programs, insulate them from most of the cost of illness. If physicians selflessly implement the wishes of such patients, they will make sure that all beneficial care is rendered, regardless of cost. If physicians allow the added income that more care generates to influence decisions, they might even provide care that produces no benefits at all. In the absence of clear and widely understood standards for care, they might inadvertently provide harmful services. In short, strong incentives exist for the provision of care that costs more than it is worth, and the incentives for efficiency are weak.[10] Moreover, as research expands the menu of beneficial diagnostic and therapeutic interventions, the bill for high-cost, low-benefit medicine is almost certain to grow.

Every developed country faces this problem because all have decided, through public decisions or private actions, to insulate patients from the cost of care when ill. The challenge of modern health care policy is how to reduce the incentives to produce wastefully large quantities of health care at unnecessarily high cost without directly imposing excessively burdensome costs on people when they are sick.

Health Insurance

Who has health insurance—and, by inference, who does not? How do they get it? And why does it matter?

Americans typically derive some form of health insurance in one of

9. Underweight babies are prone to developmental disabilities and various illnesses and are less likely to survive than are other newborns.

10. If physicians strove consistently to maximize net incomes, incentives for efficient production would remain intact. But a large body of literature suggests that the behavior of physicians is driven by many motives other than the maximization of income.

three ways.[11] Three in five receive health insurance as an element of compensation for work, their own or that of a relative. Governments provide insurance to their own civilian and military employees, to some of the poor, and to the aged and disabled who have worked in jobs covered by medicare. And some people buy insurance for themselves and their dependents. Approximately 31 million people lack insurance of any kind.

Employer-sponsored coverage for workers is popular because group insurance is less costly than individual insurance and, in contrast to cash wages, it is not subject to personal income tax.[12] This exclusion lowers federal revenues—by $29.8 billion in 1990 and an estimated $33.5 billion in 1991.[13] Individuals seeking health insurance can get it at much lower cost through work than on their own.

The lack of insurance can be related either to incomplete coverage of people who work or to lack of employment.[14] The tax system encourages but does not require employers to offer health insurance. Furthermore, certain aspects of the market for private insurance—notably the high cost of insurance for small groups—cause low rates of coverage among workers employed by small companies. The current system also permits employers to require employees to pay for part or all of the cost of insurance for themselves or their dependents, causing some employees to refuse coverage even when it is offered.[15] The relatively high cost of individual insurance means that a large fraction of those who are not

11. I shall use the term *health insurance* in the broadest sense, to encompass not only conventional insurance, but any form of payment for health services by someone other than the patient, whether payments are made to providers by some third party or providers are hired by someone other than the patient to provide care.

12. Group insurance minimizes "adverse selection"—the tendency of those who use more health care than average to buy more insurance than average. To avoid losses from adverse selection, insurance companies must charge individuals or small groups much higher premiums per person than they charge large groups. Furthermore, per capita selling and billing costs are lower for large groups than for individuals or small groups.

13. If the government provided equivalent insurance and taxed the benefits, the cost of the insurance would be $36.5 billion in 1990 and $40.9 billion in 1991. See *Budget of the United States Government, Fiscal Year 1991*, table C-1, p. A-72.

14. This method of examining the lack of health insurance would make no sense in countries such as Canada and Great Britain where coverage under a national health plan is an incident of citizenship or residence.

15. Some employees (and their dependents) who refuse insurance may be covered under the policy of a spouse, other relative, or third party. And workers or nonworking dependents may be covered by public programs; for example, workers over the age of 65 typically are covered by medicare.

employed and do not reside in households in which someone works are insured only if covered under some government program.

The results of refusal by employers to offer insurance or by employees to accept it are not random across socioeconomic groups. In some industries and occupations insurance is the norm; in others it is not (see table 8-3). In general, insurance is most common in industries with high wages and large companies and in all industries with heavy unionization. It is less pervasive in industries characterized by small companies, low average wages, and self-employment. Three factors explain this pattern: the high price of individual and small-group plans caused by administrative and selling costs and adverse selection; the high cost of health insurance relative to the compensation of low-wage workers; and the use of collective bargaining by unions to obtain generous health insurance.

The importance of the incompleteness of employer-sponsored insurance is underscored by a simple fact: if all workers, their spouses, and their children were covered by employer-sponsored health insurance or equivalent coverage for the self-employed, the number of uninsured would be cut by about 85 percent.[16]

The Uninsured

Only a minority of almost every demographic and economic group lacks health insurance. Nearly all of the elderly are insured for hospital services under part A of medicare, and 98.9 percent of those eligible for part A elect coverage under part B, which reimburses most of the costs of covered physician services. Among the nonelderly, low-income households are less likely to be insured than higher-income households, but more than six in ten of the nonelderly poor have insurance of some kind, most through government programs, notably medicaid. Even among the unemployed, nearly two-thirds have insurance. Although most members of these groups have insurance, disproportionate numbers are uninsured. Nearly half the uninsured in 1986 had incomes less than 150 percent of official poverty thresholds. And nearly half are children or young adults under 25 years old. The uninsured are concentrated in these groups in part because poor, female-headed families are unlikely

16. *Cost and Effects of Extending Health Insurance Coverage*, Committee Print, Subcommittee on Labor-Management Relations and Subcommittee on Labor Standards of House Committee on Education and Labor, Subcommittee on Health and the Environment of House Committee on Energy and Commerce, and Senate Special Committee on Aging, 100 Cong. 2 sess. (Government Printing Office, October 1988), p. 73.

TABLE 8-3. Characteristics of Groups without Health Insurance, 1987

Characteristic	Population uninsured (millions)	Proportion of group without insurance (percent)
Employment experience		
None (workers only)	7.7	11.1
Full-time, full-year		
Workers only	7.7	10.0
Workers and families	13.0	n.a.
Less than full-time, full-year		
Workers only	8.9	21.1
Workers and families	12.1	n.a.
Income		
Less than 150 percent of official poverty threshold[a]	15.0	27.5
150–184 percent	3.3	20.9
185 percent or more	12.8	7.5
Family type		
Two or more adults, with or without children	17.1	10.3
Single, with or without children	14.0	19.0
Race and ethnicity		
White	10.5	11.1
African-American	2.6	21.7
Hispanic	3.5	28.8
Size of employer[b]		
1–24	7.2	23.4
25–99	2.4	16.6
100–499	1.8	11.7
500 or more	3.3	7.2
Industry		
Agriculture, construction, or retail trade	7.2	22.8
Services	4.7	13.0
Manufacturing and other	4.7	9.3

SOURCE: M. Eugene Moyer, "A Revised Look at the Number of Uninsured Americans," *Health Affairs*, Summer 1989, pp. 102–10.
n.a. Not available.
a. The official poverty threshold estimated to be $11,611 for a family of four in 1987.
b. Number of employees.

to have employment-based coverage and in part because young adults are more likely than other groups to work in jobs without coverage, to reject coverage when it is available, or to be in the process of changing jobs. Extending insurance only to certain groups—children or the unemployed, for example—would leave many uninsured.

An estimated 31.1 million people—roughly one nonelderly American in seven—were uninsured for health costs by any private or public program in 1988. Although a considerable shadow of uncertainty surrounds this estimate, the number of uninsured appears to have risen in the early 1980s.[17] Various forces contributed to the loss of coverage. Young adults, among whom insurance is less frequent than among older groups, came to account for an increased share of the population. Many employers, smarting under rising insurance costs, shifted premiums to employees, some of whom dropped coverage. Other employers simply dropped plans. Employment shifted to economic sectors in which health insurance has been relatively uncommon. In 1981 Congress approved President Reagan's request to narrow eligibility for welfare assistance and thereby excluded many from medicaid. In the late 1980s Congress reversed this process by extending medicaid coverage to previously ineligible groups.

Millions of people change health insurance because they change work status or shift plans.[18] Consequently, many people who now have insurance can expect to lose it, and many who now lack it can be expected to gain it. If medical expenses can be deferred, the lack of insurance may be less serious than suggested by the snapshot statistic that 31.1 million people lack insurance. If medical expenses are not postponable, incomplete insurance is a more serious problem than survey statistics suggest, because far more than 31.1 million people will be uninsured at some time during an interval of a few years. To point up what is at stake, although the uninsured report that their health status

17. Virtually all the elderly are classified as insured because they are covered by medicare. An estimated 28.4 million people were uninsured in 1979, but this number rose to just over 37 million in the mid-1980s. Nothing happened in the market for health insurance in 1988 to explain the drop to 31.1 million. Changes in the wording of questions on health insurance in census survey instruments and in the Census Bureau's methods of adjusting responses to remove apparent inconsistencies may explain much of the difference. The increase in the numbers of uninsured from the late 1970s to the mid-1980s seems to have been real, but the decrease since 1987 may be largely an artifact of measurement procedures.

18. See Alan C. Monheit and Claudia L. Schur, "The Dynamics of Health Insurance Loss: A Tale of Two Cohorts," *Inquiry*, vol. 25 (Fall 1988), pp. 315–27.

is somewhat worse than that of the insured, they have fewer contacts with physicians and spend fewer days in hospitals.[19]

The Nature of Insurance Coverage

Nearly 650 companies (including 78 Blue Cross and Blue Shield plans) sell health insurance in the United States, and they typically offer several distinct plans. The completeness of health insurance varies enormously. Because each insurance plan has its own limits and many employers offer more than one plan, the American population is covered by a bewildering variety of health insurance policies (table 8-4). Almost all plans cover hospitalization and associated physician services, although benefits vary widely; preexisting conditions, for example, may be uninsured.[20] But plans differ in the amounts they will pay physicians; whether physicians may bill patients for charges in addition to those covered by insurance; the proportion of the premium that employees must pay for their own or their family's coverage; and whether coverage extends to nursing homes, home health care, inpatient mental health benefits, outpatient mental health benefits, treatment of alcohol and other drug abuse, and the services of such providers as podiatrists, chiropractors, optometrists, and Christian Science practitioners. Moreover, insurance coverage changes, often in rather fundamental ways, for many of those who change jobs or move from one community to another.

A recent innovation combines limits on cost sharing with limits on providers. Some plans reimburse patients at a higher rate for care from "preferred providers," who promise reduced prices, than for care given by other providers who make no such commitment. Health maintenance organizations (HMOs) normally insure members for a wide range of services with little or no cost sharing if patients accept care from an approved list of approved physicians and other providers.

To an increasing extent, U.S. insurance companies do not function as

19. Differences in self-reported health status may understate actual differences, as contact with physicians may heighten awareness of and sensitivity to illnesses.

20. Some health maintenance organizations (HMOs) and indemnity insurance plans provide virtually unlimited hospital and physician benefits. In contrast, medicaid in Lousiana pays for only ten days of hospitalization per year and ten in-patient physician visits per year. Several other medicaid programs have similar, if somewhat less stringent, limits. Most states have no limits on hospitalization or physician visits. *Medicaid Source Book: Background Data and Analysis*, Committee Print, Subcommittee on Health and Environment of House Committee on Energy and Commerce, 100 Cong. 2 sess. (GPO, November 1988), tables III-3, III-4.

TABLE 8-4. Limits on Coverage among Health Insurance Plans

Limit	Percent of employer-sponsored plans	Medicare	Medicaid
Particular benefits			
Hospitalization and medical care	100	Yes	Yes[a]
Dental care	87	No	Varies[a]
Physical examinations	71	Yes	Yes[a]
Vision care	21	No	Varies[a]
Separate prescription drug plan	12	No	No
Deductible for covered services			
$50 or less	6	First day in	No deductible
$100	47	hospital	
$150	20	$560 (part A);	
$200	20	$85 (part B)	
More than $200	7		
Lifetime limits on benefits for covered services			
Under $250,000	3	90 days of	No limit
$250,000	11	hospitalization[b]	
$250,000–$750,000	16	No limit on	
$1 million and over	44	physician	
No maximum	26	services	
Maximum patient expense for covered services			
$500 or less	23	No maximum	0
$501–999	12		
$1,000–2,000	36		
Over $2,000	4		
No provision	17		
Total monthly premiums			
Individual			
Under $50	7	$31.90	0
$50–69	35		
$70–89	34		
$90–119	19		
$120 or over	5		
Family			
Under $130	6		
$130–189	40		
$190–219	19		
$220–280	27		
Over $280	8		

SOURCE: *Health Insurance and the Uninsured: Background Data and Analysis,* Committee Print, Subcommittee on Labor-Management Relations and Subcommittee on Labor Standards of House Committee on Education and Labor, Subcommittee on Health and the Environment of House Committee on Energy and Commerce, and Senate Special Committee on Aging, 100 Cong. 2 sess. (Government Printing Office, May 1988), tables 2.6, 2.9, 2.11, 2.12 and charts 2.3, 2.5.

a. Limits on benefits vary from state to state.

b. See footnote 28.

insurers in the operation of health insurance. A growing proportion of U.S. businesses "self-insure," by paying whatever approved health costs their employees and their families incur. Only one-third of the 694 plans covered in a major survey were "fully insured," in the sense that the premiums an employer faced were fixed prospectively for a definite period.[21] And even under most of these plans insurance companies periodically adjust premiums to reflect actual claims of the insured group. The enormous diversity of American health insurance entails major costs and confers significant benefits.

Costs. Multiple insurers generate administrative costs in their competition to maintain or expand their share of the market. Employers who offer more than one health plan pay to provide information and to help employees choose among these plans. Hospitals and physicians must cope with many payers who follow different rules and require different information. And employees must bear still other costs to master the various systems. Each of these costs would be reduced significantly if insurance were uniform and providers dealt with one payer. They would be reduced still further if hospitals operated on fixed budgets that did not require separate billing for individual patients.[22]

In addition, the exclusion of certain preexisting conditions and waiting periods before new employees are covered under private plans cause some people to be uninsured. Some private plans provide few or no benefits for certain risks, thereby leaving some who are ostensibly "insured" effectively without protection against part of their medical costs. The potential importance of this problem is growing with the emergence of techniques to screen people for predispositions to a wide range of diseases.

Finally, the existence of large numbers of payers, each of whom is typically responsible for only a minority of the revenue of any provider,

---

21. *Health Insurance and the Uninsured: Background Data and Analysis,* Committee Print, Subcommittee on Labor-Management Relations and Subcommittee on Labor Standards of House Committee on Education and Labor, Subcommittee on Health and the Environment of House Committee on Energy and Commerce, and Senate Special Committee on Aging, 100 Cong. 2 sess. (GPO, May 1988), p. 85.

22. One study placed the extra costs of the U.S. system relative to one with a single payer at $29.3 billion in 1983, or 12 percent of the combined outlay on hospitals, physicians, and nursing homes. The corresponding cost for 1990 would be just over $50 billion if the relative costs of administration were unchanged since 1983. See David U. Himmelstein and Steffie Woolhandler, "Cost without Benefit: Administrative Waste in U.S. Health Care," *New England Journal of Medicine,* vol. 314 (February 13, 1986), pp. 441–45.

means that no payer has as much leverage over providers as would a single buyer. While cooperative action to curtail growth of costs is possible, it is costly to organize and seldom happens. Furthermore, coordinated efforts by private payers to control costs may violate antitrust laws.

Benefits. Diversity of insurance plans and providers also brings significant benefits. First, Americans can match insurance to preferences by selecting among plans of equivalent cost but with different features. This advantage is realized fully only for workers whose employers offer a wide range of plans.

Second, the same competition among insurers that raises administrative costs may improve service and foster innovation. For example, insurance companies have encouraged groups of physicians to form "independent practice associations" that provide a stipulated range of services to patients for a fee fixed at the start of each year. They have promoted measures to reduce costs, including "managed care" under which reimbursement for some services is denied if they have not been approved in advance by someone designated by the insurer. They have cooperated in organization of hospitals or physicians into preferred provider organizations (PPOs).[23]

Insurance for Long-term Care

Private insurance for long-term care remains a rarity: in 1989 only 1.3 million long-term care insurance policies had been sold and only 3 percent of these were employer-sponsored.[24] Roughly half the cost of nursing home services is paid by the medicaid program described below and roughly half by individuals.

Long-term care encompasses both home health services and nursing home care. Use of these services rises sharply with age, and the population over age 85 is projected to more than double over the next three decades.[25] The number of people suffering from severe dementia, a

23. It is doubtful that PPOs or managed care will be effective in counteracting the incentives under insurance for the provision of low-benefit, high-cost care, but sufficient data for their evaluation are not yet available.

24. Joshua M. Wiener and Raymond J. Hanley, testimony on the "Federal Employees Long-Term Care Insurance Act of 1989, S.38," presented to Subcommittee on Federal Services, Post Office, and Civil Service of Senate Committee on Governmental Affairs, Washington, November 2, 1989.

25. The proportion of the population aged 85 or older living in nursing homes in

problem disproportionately afflicting the very old, is projected to more than double between 1980 and 2020 and to more than double again by 2040.[26] In short, demand for nursing home care and home health services is projected to increase rapidly in the United States.

The current methods of paying for long-term care are unsatisfactory for several reasons. Most elderly people cannot afford long-term care for very long without assistance.[27] Only the wealthy or those poor enough to qualify for medicaid can afford nursing home care. Others can gain access to nursing home services only by paying fees they cannot afford and running down their assets until they qualify for medicaid. The absence of insurance for long-term care thereby burdens the children or other heirs of the elderly, through either reduced inheritances or the obligation to care for the elderly themselves.

Similar problems arise with respect to home health care, except that publicly financed home health benefits are negligible in most communities. Furthermore, the range of services that enables people with limitations on activities of daily living to remain in their own homes is diverse, and costs may approximate those of nursing homes.

The Role of Governments In Health Care

Although the federal government directly accounts for only 29 percent of total health care spending, its policies have shaped the development of the U.S. health care system. In addition to sponsoring research, the federal government directly provides services, manages tax policy, and, along with state governments, regulates health insurance and providers.

Direct Government Spending

The federal government and, to a lesser extent, state and local governments directly pay for health care for their 18 million employees

---

1985 was more than eight times as large as the proportion of those aged 65 to 84. Among the younger group, 19.7 percent had some form of disability; among the latter group, 62.8 percent. Kenneth G. Manton, "Epidemiological, Demographic, and Social Correlates of Disability among the Elderly," *Milbank Quarterly*, vol. 67, supp. 2, pt. 1 (1989), p. 30.

26. Robert M. Ball with Thomas N. Bethell, *Because We're All in This Together* (Washington: Families U.S.A. Foundation, 1989), p. 21.

27. The median family with a head aged 85 or older had financial assets of $6,425 in the last half of the 1980s; the average annual cost of nursing home care averaged $25,000 in 1988. Ball, *Because We're All in This Together*, p. 13.

and selected groups, principally the elderly, the poor, veterans, merchant seamen, and Native Americans.

Medicare. Medicare, the largest government health program, pays for hospital care and limited nursing home benefits under part A for 33.2 million elderly and disabled beneficiaries who have worked in employment covered by social security or railroad retirement.[28] The same population is eligible to buy insurance for physicians' charges under part B at an annually adjusted premium ($382.80 in 1989).[29] The premium covers about one-fourth of program costs; appropriations from general revenues cover the rest. The heavy subsidy helps explain why almost everyone who is eligible voluntarily buys part B coverage.

A payroll tax of 2.9 percent of earnings taxable under social security (earnings of up to $51,300 in 1990) pays for part A of medicare. The proceeds of this tax are deposited in a trust fund from which part A benefits are paid. According to current projections, this tax and accumulated trust fund reserves will cover currently legislated benefits only until 2005.[30]

28. Part A pays the full cost of up to sixty days of hospitalization per illness and three-fourths of the cost of the next thirty days per illness after the patient has paid a deductible ($560 in 1989). Medicare will pay half the cost of an additional sixty days of hospitalization that can be used at any time (a "life-time reserve"). In addition, medicare pays for dialysis for patients with end-stage renal (kidney) disease. The catastrophic health bill, enacted in 1988 and repealed in 1989, would have waived all cost sharing, other than the deductible, and placed no limit on the number of covered days. Medicare part A also covers posthospitalization care in skilled nursing facilities and hospice care, with limited cost sharing. The actuarial value of medicare benefits in 1989 was estimated at $3,130 a year. House Committee on Ways and Means, *Background Material and Data on Programs within the Jurisdiction of the Committee on Ways and Means, 1989 Edition*, 101 Cong. 1 sess. (GPO, 1989), p. 98.

29. Part B pays 80 percent of allowed charges for physicians' services over an annual $75 deductible. Physicians may bill patients for the other 20 percent of charges that medicare deems reasonable and for additional amounts if the physicians wish. On 76 percent of claims representing 79 percent of covered charges in 1988, physicians elected to "take assignment," thereby agreeing not to bill patients for any balance. House Committee on Ways and Means, *Background Material*, pp. 137, 393–95.

30. This statement refers to projection IIB prepared for the 1988 *Trustees Report on the Federal Hospital Insurance Trust Fund* by the actuaries of the Health Care Financing Administration. More optimistic projections indicate revenues will be adequate until 2008; more pessimistic projections indicate the trust fund will be depleted as early as 1999. The 1989 projections were somewhat less optimistic than those of 1988, but did not extend beyond 1991 because of computational difficulties introduced by repeal of the Medicare Catastrophic Coverage Act of 1988. Exactly when additional revenues will be required, from payroll taxes or some other source, will depend on whether and how much Congress or the administration cuts costs and on whether economic or demographic conditions turn out to be more or less favorable than those assumed in the projections.

Because medicare covers only a portion of personal health care costs of the elderly—75 percent of hospital bills and 58 percent of physicians' costs in 1984—most elect to buy supplementary insurance through "medigap" insurance.[31] The best of these plans have well-controlled selling and administrative costs, but some plans pay out less than half of premiums as benefits.[32]

Medicaid. Although grouped under a single name, the federal-state medicaid program is actually a collection of programs diverse within and among states. In particular, medicaid pays for acute-care services and for long-term care, but the mix and generosity vary enormously.

To participate in the program and qualify for federal matching grants, states must offer hospital care, physicians' services, and certain other benefits to specified populations; they may offer additional benefits or cover additional groups.[33] Some states cap the numbers of hospital days and physician visits, and many pay medicaid providers much less than customary fees.[34]

Health care services—some mandated by the federal government and others provided at state option—are available to two classes of recipients. States *must* provide mandatory benefits to welfare recipients (and selected other groups) and *may* serve the "medically needy" if they wish.[35] The

31. Daniel R. Waldo and Helen C. Lazenby, "Demographic Characteristics and Health Care Use and Expenditures by the Aged in the United States: 1977-1984," *Health Care Financing Review,* vol. 6 (Fall 1984), pp. 8, 13.

32. Medigap plans never cover nursing home care, the area where medicare provides only negligible coverage, but they do fill in gaps in coverage for hospital and physician costs. The Medicare Catastrophic Coverage Act of 1988 would have extended medicare to cover most of the costs covered by medigap policies.

33. Other mandatory services include outpatient hospital benefits; laboratory and X-ray services; skilled nursing facility care for people over age 21; home health care for those eligible for skilled nursing care; early periodic screening, diagnosis, and treatment for those under age 21; family planning services and supplies; and nurse-midwife services. In fact, states may offer virtually all other health care services (excluding abortions where the life of the mother is not at risk). House Committee on Ways and Means, *Background Material,* pp. 1151–52. The federal government pays from 50 percent to 79.8 percent of program costs; states with below-average incomes get the larger matching rates.

34. In 1986 the medicaid fee for a brief follow-up office visit averaged 67 percent of the medicare fee and was less than half in ten states, including such large states as California, New York, Michigan, and Illinois. As a result, significant minorities of physicians in various specialties—32 percent of cardiologists, 42 percent of psychiatrists, and 22 percent of primary care physicians—refused to accept medicaid patients in the late 1970s. As might be expected, participation varies widely from state to state. *Medicaid Source Book,* Committee Print, pp. 446, 450–52.

35. Welfare recipients consist mostly of recipients of aid to families with dependent

medically needy include the near poor and others whose large medical bills have impoverished them.[36]

The cost of a state's program depends on the range of medical services and the generosity of reimbursement; the breadth of eligibility; the number of poor people resident in the state; and the proportion of recipients who are mentally retarded and elderly and who use costly long-term care. As a result, medicaid expenditures vary enormously around the nationwide average of $169 per resident in 1986, from $462 per resident in New York to $63 in Wyoming.

Taxation

The Internal Revenue Code provides several benefits to encourage health insurance and to support other aspects of the health care industry. Shown below are the revenue losses for 1990 (in billions of dollars) of several tax benefits.

Provision	Revenue reduction
Exclusion of employer-financed health insurance	29.8
Exclusion of medicare benefits	6.3
Interest exclusion for state and local debt of nonprofit facilities	2.4

The exclusion of employer-sponsored health insurance from federal personal income and payroll taxes was noted above. Medicare benefits greater than tax payments represent a form of income for recipients, but

---

children (AFDC) and supplemental security income (SSI), a cash assistance program serving the poor aged, blind, and disabled. States must also cover pregnant women and young children in families with income and assets low enough to qualify for AFDC and must provide limited benefits to pregnant women and mandatory benefits to children under age 1 from families with incomes below federal poverty thresholds by July 1, 1989. The categorically needy also include people excluded from AFDC for reasons prohibited by medicaid, former AFDC recipients for twelve months after termination of benefits, and, starting on October 1, 1990, two-parent families where the principal breadwinner is unemployed. House Committee on Ways and Means, *Background Material*, pp. 1127, 29.

36. Actual health outlays are subtracted from income in determining whether households qualify. Thus a family with income well above the maximum for eligibility will qualify for medicaid if medical expenses are sufficiently large.

unlike most other income they are not taxed.[37] These tax provisions undergird the system of employer-sponsored insurance that forms the basis of the U.S. health insurance system. Although not treated as expenditures, they contribute as much to the federal deficit as would equivalent expenditures.

A major issue in tax and health care policy concerns the desirability of retaining unlimited exclusion of employer-sponsored health insurance from the personal income tax. It violates the income tax principle that all income in cash or in kind should be taxed.[38] While the exclusion has been broadly successful in encouraging the voluntary provision of insurance in private markets, coverage remains well short of universal. Furthermore, the exclusion encourages the provision of excessive insurance and numbs awareness of the cost of various insurance plans.

Because of concern about these issues, President Reagan proposed in 1982 capping the exemption of health insurance from the personal income tax at $175 a month for families ($70 for individuals). Representatives of both business and labor opposed the proposal, and Congress did not act on it. The Treasury Department suggested the same cap in its initial proposals for tax reform in 1984. This time the White House backed away, omitting the proposal from its 1985 tax reform plan. The Congressional Budget Office estimates that including in personal and payroll tax bases the value of employer-financed health insurance above $250 a month for families and $100 a month for individuals would increase tax collections by $5.4 billion in 1990 and by an average of $10.3 billion a year from 1991 through 1995.[39]

---

37. These exclusions, together with the exemption from tax of income from bonds issued by state and local governments for private nonprofit health facilities, produce the same effect on the budget as would direct government expenditures on services whose value was subject to income tax. In addition, individuals are allowed to deduct unreimbursed medical costs to the extent that these costs exceed 7 1/2 percent of income, a provision whose outlay equivalent in 1990 is $2.3 billion. This deduction for extraordinary medical outlays, like deductions for casualty losses, is justified under an income tax because the expense is a surprise loss equivalent to a destruction of income. In contrast, deduction of routine costs is not justified under an income tax, because such outlays represent ordinary consumption.

38. See Mark V. Pauly, "Taxation, Health Insurance, and Market Failure in the Medical Economy," *Journal of Economic Literature,* vol. 24 (June 1986), pp. 625–75; and Martin Holmer, "Tax Policy and the Demand for Health Insurance," *Journal of Health Economics,* vol. 3 (December 1984), pp. 203–21.

39. Congressional Budget Office, *Reducing the Deficit: Spending and Revenue Options* (February 1990), p. 144.

Regulation

The federal and state governments have ample power to enforce any health care regulations they may impose, by threatening to withhold reimbursement under medicare or medicaid. Since medicare and medicaid supply more than one-third (36.5 percent in 1987) of the revenues of hospitals and more than one-fourth (26 percent in 1987) of the revenues of physicians, few providers can lightly flout federal rules. The federal and state governments can restrict the insurance that companies can sell or employers purchase, and the federal government can deny employers the right to deduct the costs of plans that violate federal rules in computing business taxes.[40]

Much of the debate over how best to slow the rapid growth of health care spending centers on how the federal government, acting alone or in concert with states, should use these regulatory powers toward that end. Two recent modifications of the medicare program illustrate the issue.

Diagnosis related groups. In 1984 the Health Care Financing Administration (HCFA) introduced a new system of paying part A hospital benefits according to diagnosis related groups (DRGs), a set of fixed fees based on the patient's primary and secondary diagnosis at time of admission.[41] This system, which replaced reimbursement based on cost of care, was to reduce costs and slow future growth by changing incentives. Under cost-based reimbursement, hospitals had few incentives to economize because they could count on payment for all reasonable expenditures. Because the DRG fee is the same regardless of the patient's length of stay, hospitals, it was hoped, would try harder to cut costs because they, rather than the government, would reap the savings.

Some evidence suggests that the DRG system has slightly slowed the growth of hospital spending.[42] Furthermore, regardless of the costs

40. The Tax Reform Act of 1986 underscored this power. It strengthened the "nondiscrimination" regulations by tightening limits on the proportion of cost of employer-sponsored fringe benefits that can be paid to high-paid employees. Employers who did not meet these standards would have lost deductibility for the cost of these benefits, but Congress repealed these provisions in 1989 because business objected that the requirements were too stringent. Still, no one doubted the power of federal instruments to compel compliance.

41. The DRGs provide some extra payment for extraordinarily lengthy or costly stays.

42. Hospital expenditures equal the product of admissions, cost per day, and length of stay. Many observers expected admissions to increase after introduction of the DRG system, as hospitals sought to make profits by admitting relatively low-cost patients who

hospitals actually incurred, the DRG system permits HCFA to directly restrict what it pays by limiting growth of payments and thereby to control the rate at which budget outlays for medicare benefits rise. HCFA has used this power, raising DRG prices by less than the average increase in wages and the price of commodities hospitals buy.

Relative value scales. HCFA has customarily paid physicians 80 percent of "reasonable" charges.[43] These charges vary widely among communities and specialties in ways that variations in practice costs or in training cannot explain. In 1989 Congress enacted a fee schedule based on the relative costs of services performed by physicians, slated to take effect in 1992. This schedule, inexactly named a "relative value scale" (RVS), is based on differences in office expense, other practice costs, and training required to provide various services. In addition, Congress took steps to prevent physicians from offsetting the effects of any cuts in fees by increasing the number of patient visits. If costs exceed targets for total spending, HCFA is authorized to reduce fees in subsequent years to recapture the excess.

The RVS system could profoundly change the cost and composition of physicians' services in several ways. It can be used to restrain the growth of medicare spending on physicians' services. Because of reductions in relative fees for surgery and other invasive procedures, the RVS may change current medical practice and the fields of medicine that students choose to enter. But the RVS would have its greatest effect if it acted as a model for changes in payments by other insurers.

Strategies for Reform

Proposals for correcting the U.S. health care system's major problems have proliferated in recent years. They differ primarily in the relative roles assigned to government or private organizations and the compre-

---

previously might have been treated on an outpatient basis. Admissions in fact declined, not only for medicare patients, but for others who were not covered by the DRG system. It appears that hospitals were reacting to influences other than the new DRG system. See Judith Feder, Jack Hadley, and Stephen Zuckerman, "How Did Medicare's Prospective Payment System Affect Hospitals?" *New England Journal of Medicine*, vol. 317 (October 1, 1987), pp. 867–73; and Louise B. Russell and Carrie Lynn Manning, "The Effect of Prospective Payment on Medicare Expenditures," *New England Journal of Medicine*, vol. 320 (February 16, 1989), pp. 439–44.

43. Defined as the smaller of (a) the physician's actual charge, (b) the physician's median charge during a preceding time period for similar services, or (c) the seventy-fifth percentile of the customary charge by physicians for that service in the community.

hensiveness of the proposed changes. Some plans focus on acute care and its costs, while others encompass both acute and long-term care.

All plans must come to terms with a fundamental dilemma. The U.S. system is based on employer-sponsored health insurance for the non-elderly. Expanding that system to areas where coverage is particularly spotty—small companies and the self-employed—could raise employment costs and discourage hiring, especially of low-wage workers, and it would perpetuate the lack of leverage that a single payer (other than the federal government) has on health care spending. However, providing large subsidies or direct public insurance to reduce or avoid the increases in employment costs would sharply increase government budgets and might induce many employers to drop current health insurance plans.

Voluntary Incrementalism

Voluntary incrementalism would remove imperfections in the market for private insurance that restrict availability of work-based health insurance. It would rely on private insurance to help people pay for long-term care. It would increase eligibility for medicaid or other publicly subsidized care. And it would rely on competition among insurers and health care providers to slow the growth of outlays. This approach minimizes the role of government and of mandates on private action.

Risk pools. A centerpiece of voluntary incrementalism is a set of proposals to increase the appeal of private health insurance to managers of companies that do not now offer it to workers. The development of "risk pools"—treating several small companies as one large group for the purpose of setting premiums—would reduce or eliminate the surcharges that insurance companies add to premiums for small groups out of concern for adverse selection.[44] Public subsidies could be provided to such pools when the actual loss experience indicates abnormally high costs.

Experience to date offers little hope that such measures would make much of a dent in the ranks of the uninsured unless the government provided large subsidies.[45] Such subsidies run a significant risk. If large

44. See Randall R. Bovbjerg, "Insuring the Uninsured through Private Action: Ideas and Initiatives," *Inquiry*, vol. 23 (Winter 1986), pp. 403–18.

45. Bovbjerg, "Insuring the Uninsured"; Katherine Swartz, "Strategies for Assisting the Medically Indigent and People without Health Insurance," Urban Institute Working Paper 3789-02 (Washington, January 1989); and Katherine Swartz with the assistance of

enough to induce substantially universal coverage of workers and their families, they would tempt employers who currently offer insurance to drop it and join the pools, thus greatly boosting budgetary costs and defeating the private-market focus of the approach.

Medicaid extension. A second element of this approach is the extension of medicaid eligibility to some groups not now covered by the program. States might be required to extend eligibility to certain groups—all children with incomes below some fraction or multiple of official poverty thresholds, for example. Medicaid could underwrite subsidies to enable individuals or employers to buy medicaid benefits at a price scaled to family income. This approach completely circumvents the administrative difficulties and added costs of forming risk pools for low-wage workers and incorporates an individually tailored subsidy.

Medicaid "buy-ins" would court the same risk as subsidies to risk pools. If the price of buying in is unsubsidized, few are likely to buy coverage; if the subsidy is large, employers will be tempted to drop plans they currently sponsor and transfer to medicaid, transferring some current costs of health care from private to public budgets. Furthermore, the cost of extending medicaid is high: the Congressional Research Service estimated that extension of only medicaid mandatory benefits (excluding long-term care) to everyone living in families with incomes below official poverty thresholds would have increased government expenditures by $11.3 billion in 1986.[46]

Long-term care. Voluntary incrementalism would count on private insurers to develop long-term care insurance policies that would appeal to individuals and businesses. Such insurance has attracted little interest among young workers for whom the prospects of disability are remote and uncertain. Only about 40 percent of the people who reach age 65 will ever enter a nursing home, and only half of them can expect to stay more than one year. That young workers find insurance against such an unpleasant and remote risk less appealing than cash wages or other fringe benefits is hardly surprising. For older people, the risk is more immediate, but the cost of good insurance is high—$800 to $1,100 a

---

Debra Lipson, "Strategies for Assisting the Medically Uninsured," Urban Institute Working Paper 3785-02 (Washington, January 1989).

46. This total is the result of increases in state and federal medicaid spending of $5.5 billion and $7.8 billion, respectively, offset by reductions in federal spending on other programs of $2 billion. Including long-term care, optional services, or more stringent minimum standards for state programs would have added to costs. See *Costs and Effects of Extending Health Insurance Coverage,* Committee Print, pp. 134, 136.

year for a 65-year-old and over $1,500 for a 70-year-old.[47] Because no one can accurately forecast inflation and real costs of care, insurance companies must restrict benefits in ways that reduce the appeal of insurance. Despite these problems, the large potential size of the market for long-term care insurance has led companies to devote considerable resources to designing and marketing new plans. It seems unlikely that private insurance could ever provide anything approaching universal coverage for long-term care, and it certainly cannot do so for many years.[48]

Competition. Another component of voluntary incrementalism is emphasis on heightened competition to help control cost increases at various stages in the financing and purchase of health care. Promoting price consciousness in the purchase of both health insurance and medical care is one way to foster competition. Because people must pay taxes on earnings used for other kinds of consumption, but not on employer-financed health insurance, tax rules boost the amount of health insurance people prefer to buy, and increased insurance in turn raises consumption of health services. For this reason, capping the exclusion of employer-financed health insurance from personal income tax, which would encourage cost sharing and other devices to sensitize patients to the cost of treatment, is a key element of voluntary incrementalism.

Improved information about the quality of services offered by providers and the prices they charge can also promote competition. HCFA has begun to publish information on mortality rates and other data on hospital performance. The publication of similar data on physicians is under discussion. The practical question is whether such data can offer a reliable index of the quality of care and whether businesses and individuals will be able to use such information to buy care of a given quality at least cost.

The Department of Health and Human Services has also initiated a research program to improve knowledge about the efficacy of various medical interventions. Surprisingly few clinical procedures have been

47. For particularly comprehensive coverage, providing reimbursement for up to $100 per day for home care (after a twenty-day deductible) and nursing home care, the Travellers Insurance Company in 1989 charged a premium of $2,892 at age 70 and $5,958 at age 76 for a plan that covers both types of care. Ball, *Because We're All in This Together*, pp. 38, 56.

48. Ball, *Because We're All in This Together*; and Alice M. Rivlin and Joshua M. Wiener, with Raymond J. Hanley and Denise A. Spence, *Caring for the Disabled Elderly: Who Will Pay?* (Brookings, 1988).

subjected to rigorous evaluation. Furthermore, the incidence of various types of surgery varies widely across geographical areas.[49]

In 1989 Congress initiated studies of treatments of lower-back pain, myocardial infarctions, cataracts, and prostatic hypertrophy and cancer. This research promises to improve care by identifying what procedures work best. Many observers also think that this research will perceptibly slow growth of medical expenditures by curtailing or eliminating care found to produce little or no benefit.[50] This hope is not likely to be realized for three reasons. Some therapies will have to be provided in place of those found to be ineffective. Research is likely to identify some procedures that are underused. And any savings that the research will generate will be realized over many years. While effectiveness research deserves a high priority in the federal budget, because it can improve the quality of care and it may yield savings many times its cost, the effect will be small relative to the strong upward trend in health care spending.

Increased competition is also likely to reduce cost. Once again, the question is: how much? Advocates of increased competition predict large continuing savings. However, the effects on the long-term growth of outlays will be slight, because the primary force behind the rise in health care outlays has been the development of new methods of diagnosis and treatment. Increased competition would discourage patients from seeking some fraction of low-benefit care. It would also encourage providers to produce services with heightened efficiency. But these are one-shot savings; once realized, they cannot be continually repeated.[51] Moreover, patients who are insured almost completely for hospital care and heavily insured for other medical services would have no financial reason to forgo care that promises any benefits whatsoever. Physicians and other providers would continue to have every incentive to make such care available. Unless the stream of innovations is slowed or their use rationed by means other than physician and patient choice, the principal force

49. No one has successfully explained those differences using such factors as age or disease incidence. Mark Chassin and others, "Variations in the Use of Medical and Surgical Services by the Medicare Population," *New England Journal of Medicine*, vol. 314 (January 30, 1986), pp. 285–90; and John Wennberg and Alan Gittlesohn, "Variations in Medical Care among Small Areas," *Scientific American*, vol. 246 (April 1982), pp. 120–34.

50. National Leadership Commission on Health Care, *For the Health of a Nation: A Shared Responsibility* (Ann Arbor, Mich.: Health Administration Press Perspectives, 1989).

51. William B. Schwartz, "The Inevitable Failure of Current Cost-Containment Strategies: Why They Can Provide Only Temporary Relief," *Journal of the American Medical Association*, vol. 257 (January 9, 1987), pp. 220–24.

behind the long-run increase in outlays would persist. Of course, any
constraint on the demand for health care will slow innovation to the
extent that research outlays are based on expected revenues.[52] However,
no major savings from reduced innovation will be felt soon because the
gestation period of most medical innovations is long and many costly
medical advances are on the verge of introduction.[53]

Advantages and disadvantages. Voluntary incrementalism would require no major breaks with current policy. This is its strength and its
weakness. Improvements in the operation of insurance markets would
extend insurance to some who now lack it. Increased competition would
reduce spending somewhat. Vigorous marketing of long-term care
insurance will increase sales.

But this strategy holds out little hope for closing the gaps in insurance
for acute or long-term care or for controlling the growth of costs. Risk
pools have enjoyed little success in spreading employer-sponsored insurance for acute care. Medicaid extensions would reduce the uninsured
population by only about one-sixth if they reach everyone officially
designated as poor. If they are extended further up the income scale,
they reduce incentives for private employers to offer or to retain ordinary
plans. Private insurance for long-term care will not appeal to employees
and employers. Increased competition and effectiveness research will
reduce health care spending, but the savings will accrue too gradually
to be noticed against the rising trend in health care costs.[54]

Mandatory Employment-Based Insurance

Mandatory employment-based insurance, like voluntary incrementalism, would build upon, rather than replace, the current system of

52. On this subject, see Joseph P. Newhouse, "The Structure of Health Insurance and
the Erosion of Competition in the Medical Marketplace," in Warren Greenberg, ed.,
Competition in the Health Care Sector: Past, Present, and Future, Proceedings of a
Conference Sponsored by the Bureau of Economics (Federal Trade Commission, March
1978), pp. 270–87; and Newhouse, "Has the Erosion of the Medical Marketplace Ended?"
Journal of Health Politics, Policy, and Law, vol. 13 (Summer 1988), pp. 263–77.

53. For a short list of already developed high-cost innovations, see Aaron and Schwartz,
"Rationing Health Care," pp. 418–22.

54. If competition and effectiveness research cut personal health care spending by 10
percent, outlays would be cut by roughly $50 billion in 1990 dollars, an enormous
dividend. But if the savings were spread over, say, fifteen years, the annual saving would
be 0.7 percent, an amount that would be hard to detect if the underlying trend rate of
growth of per capita spending continues to oscillate around an annual rate of more than
4 percent a year.

insurance. Under this approach employers would be required to offer a specified minimum program of acute-care health insurance to all employees who work more than a minimum number of hours and to their dependents. The plans typically limit the proportion of the total premium that employees can be required to pay. In some variants employers could excuse themselves from this obligation by paying a tax set high enough to cause most employers to offer insurance, but low enough to permit those for whom insurance costs would be unusually high relative to payroll to pay the tax instead. This approach requires a backup plan for those out of the labor force, for many of the self-employed, and for employees of companies that choose not to offer insurance. The proceeds of the tax, along with other revenues, would pay for such coverage.

Underlying this approach is the conviction that in the absence of a mandate many employers will refuse to offer acute-care medical insurance. While this approach could be linked to the competitive strategy for holding down costs and to reliance on private long-term care insurance, mandatory acute-care coverage could also be combined with direct government regulation of provider payments and with a prominent role for government in assuring coverage for long-term care.

Among the large number of additional issues mandatory employment-based insurance plans must resolve are the following:[55]

—What benefits should be included in the mandatory plan? Should any limits be placed on negotiated supplemental benefits?

—Which employers should be required to participate? For example, should small companies or the self-employed be included?

—Should premiums be uniform regionally or reflect the actual claims experience of each group?

—Should only full-time workers be included, and if so, how many hours per week could be considered full time?

—Should employees' participation be voluntary or mandatory for themselves and for their dependents? If mandatory, should employees be required to pay a part of the premium?

—How much cost sharing should be imposed on those who are insured?

55. For an exhaustive and informative examination of these issues, see *Insuring the Uninsured: Options and Analysis*, Committee Print, Subcommittee on Labor-Management Relations and Subcommittee on Labor Standards of House Committee on Education and Labor, Subcommittee on Health and the Environment of House Committee on Energy and Commerce, and Senate Special Committee on Aging, 100 Cong. 2 sess (GPO, October 1988).

—What agency should be charged with enforcing the mandate—a federal or a state agency or some newly constituted organization?

Illustrative plans. The National Leadership Commission on Health Care has proposed that all employers should be required to pay at least three-quarters of the premium cost of a basic health insurance plan that would cover every employee 18 years of age or older who worked more than twenty-five hours a week and that employee's dependents.[56] Companies that failed to offer such a plan would be required to pay a tax of about 9 percent of earnings up to a maximum ($45,000 in 1988). The plan would require cost sharing by patients up to a maximum annual liability of $1,000 per patient ($3,000 per family). Employers could offer more generous plans if they wished. The 9 percent tax would also have to be paid on behalf of uncovered part-time employees. Everyone not covered by an employment-based plan (including those eligible for medicaid acute-care benefits) would be covered by a new universal access program offering the same benefits as the employment-based plan. People with incomes above 150 percent of official poverty thresholds would be required to pay a tax of about 2 to 2½ percent of earnings for coverage, whether or not they had employment-based coverage. The proceeds of this tax, together with current government expenditures on medicaid, would finance insurance for everyone not covered under employment-based plans.

Massachusetts has adopted an alternative approach. Beginning in 1992, employers of more than five workers will have to pay a tax of 12 percent on the first $14,000 of each worker's wages. Employers will be given a credit against this tax for the cost of any health insurance they provide for their employees. The proceeds of the tax are to be placed in a state pool from which anyone without insurance can purchase health insurance on a sliding scale related to income. The plan provides for insurance pools to reduce premiums for small businesses and direct subsidies that could reduce the net cost to employers to 5 percent of gross revenue. The state pool would also reimburse hospitals for uncompensated care and support expansions of medicaid coverage.[57]

Both the National Leadership Commission and the Massachusetts plans would provide nearly universal coverage. These plans or others of

56. National Leadership Commission on Health Care, *For the Health of a Nation.*
57. National Governors Association, Center for Policy Research, *Capital Ideas* (Washington, December 1, 1988); and Gail R. Wilensky, *The "Pay or Play" Insurance Gamble: Massachusetts' Plan for Universal Health Coverage* (Washington: The House Wednesday Group, September 26, 1988).

the same genre would sharply reduce the number of gaps in the current system—waiting periods for new employees, exclusions for previous conditions, and holes in coverage.

Cost control. Mandatory insurance heightens the importance of measures to control costs because the increased demand from broadened coverage would add to the already rapid increase of health costs. Proposals to mandate employment-based coverage and to cover others through a backup plan are consistent with virtually any approach to the problem of rising medical costs. The National Leadership Commission, for example, advocated that state agencies responsible for those not covered by employer plans should negotiate with providers over fees. But it left open the question of whether these agencies should also be empowered to set fees used under employment-based insurance. The commission suggested that the state agencies might wish to use PPOs or HMOs, apparently believing that these organizations hold down costs, but it recommended no structural change in the fee-for-service method of paying physicians and hospitals now used to pay most providers. The controls proposed by the National Leadership Commission would not be effective in holding down costs unless they were supplemented with direct limits on hospital budgets and restrictions on the range of services that can be provided outside the hospital setting (and hence outside the budget limits).

Massachusetts already has in operation a general system of controlling hospital spending. The effects of these controls have not yet been evaluated. The central problem is that the extension of health insurance compounds the problem of any insurance plan: namely, that patients and providers have the incentive to seek and to provide services whose benefits are small relative to cost.

Long-term care. While it would be possible to mandate that employers offer long-term care insurance to their workers and pay for some part of the premium cost, no such proposal has been advanced. The reason is quite straightforward. To keep premiums down, contributions must start early in workers' lives to cumulate with interest into a fund sufficient to pay for anticipated costs. But long-term care insurance has not ranked high on the wish lists of either workers or their employers because it insures against a contingency that lies in the distant future for most workers. Accordingly, legislation mandating such benefits has had little political appeal.

Conceivably employer-sponsored insurance for long-term care might become more attractive if it were subsidized, perhaps through tax-free reinvestment of income earned on the accumulation. Such subsidies decrease government revenues, however, and like direct expenditures, increase the budget deficit. They would have to be weighed against other measures to extend coverage for long-term care or to provide other health benefits. In particular, unless all employees were included in such a plan or strict measures assured that coverage would be extended to low- and moderate-income households, much of the lost revenue would simply be a tax cut for upper-income households who would be able to pay for long-term care anyway.

Advantages and disadvantages. Mandatory employment-based insurance could extend health insurance to as many as five out of six of currently uninsured Americans. In combination with liberalization of medicaid, it could achieve virtually universal coverage. But, unless it were combined with administrative controls over total payments to physicians and hospitals, it would increase health care costs not only by the value of the added services consumed by those who are now uninsured, but also by some additional amount through inflation in health care costs for all.

Making employer-sponsored insurance mandatory would add a fixed sum—the mandated premium—to the cost of hiring workers. Standard economic theory holds that worker compensation adjusts over time to approximate the worker's contribution to the company's revenues. An increase in wage costs could cause other elements of compensation— cash wages, for example—to fall. Some reduction in employment of low-wage workers would be likely, because the minimum wage sets a floor under their compensation. Furthermore, the adjustment in prices and wages would proceed gradually and unevenly, threatening losses and even survival for some businesses forced to add insurance. For these reasons, most programs for requiring employer-sponsored insurance allow companies to elect to pay a tax instead of offering insurance and include transitional subsidies to help employers, especially small businesses, whose costs may be seriously increased by the requirement.

A more fundamental problem is that mandating health benefits represents further extension of government rules into the operation of private businesses. Many such rules now exist, requiring employers to pay taxes for social security, medicare, and unemployment insurance; to buy workers' compensation insurance for employment-related injuries; and to maintain a safe and healthful working environment. The introduction of each set of rules has met considerable resistance, and one might dismiss resistance to mandatory health insurance as just another rearguard action by employers in the war to maintain as much control over their businesses as possible. But opponents of such mandates counter that if health insurance is a national priority, government should collect taxes and provide such services, rather than mandating employers to act in its stead.

Comprehensive Restructuring

Comprehensive restructuring of health insurance can follow either of two courses: replacing employer-sponsored health insurance with government-sponsored insurance, or modifying employer-sponsored insurance to achieve both universal coverage and effective budget control over health care providers.

Government-sponsored insurance. In the 1960s and 1970s some plans called for health insurance as an attribute of citizenship or residence.[58] Under these plans each citizen or resident would have been provided with a health card or assured access in some other way to a specified list of services. Such services would have been supported by taxes on individuals and businesses and by funds reallocated from existing programs to be replaced by the new plan. A few advocates of such plans called for the employment of physicians by the plan on a salaried or capitated basis.

The replacement of the current system by a wholly new one promised important benefits of truly universal coverage and maximum governmental leverage over health costs, since a single authority would determine physicians' fees and hospital budgets. Whether the promise would have been realized was debated but never settled. Among many unresolved questions was whether the political system would control providers or providers would capture the political regulatory system for their own ends.[59]

58. Karen Davis, *National Health Insurance: Benefits, Costs, and Consequences* (Brookings, 1975). The most sweeping of these plans, the proposed Health Security Act cosponsored by Senator Edward M. Kennedy and former Representative Martha Griffiths, would have provided tax-financed health care to everyone without cost sharing.

59. Sam Peltzman, "The Economic Theory of Regulation after a Decade of Deregulation," *Brookings Papers on Economic Activity, Microeconomics, 1989*, pp. 1–41. Governments of other countries play a much larger part in the management of the health care system than is true in the United States, and they have experienced slower growth of health care spending, as noted above. But slower growth in medical spending abroad may be attributable to factors other than governmental involvement. And even if governments abroad have been instrumental in slowing growth of expenditures, the United States might not realize similar economies because the U.S. political system differs from those abroad.

In recent years, the Canadian system of paying for health care has become an object of considerable interest. The various Canadian provinces operate separate plans for paying for health care. All must meet certain national standards, but they differ in detail. In general, patients receive care without charge, hospitals operate under fixed budgets, and physicians are paid on a fee-for-service basis according to a fee schedule set by the province. If total outlays exceed targets, the fees are reduced to bring total spending to the desired level. Physicians must accept these fees as total payment. Attempts to control rising costs have led to complaints about the deterioration of services—queues, insufficient equipment, and denial of care.[60] Despite these difficulties, public opinion polls indicate that the Canadians think their system superior to either the U.S. or British systems and that Americans also think the Canadian system compares favorably with their own.[61]

Two characteristics of plans to shift financing of health care away from the workplace prevented them from ever being taken seriously in Congress. First, they would have shifted hundreds of billions of dollars of expenditures from private to public budgets, with associated increases in taxes. To be sure, reduced private spending on health insurance and health care would have fully or partially offset increased taxes; advocates even claimed that net savings would eventually be achieved from enhanced cost control. But many groups—physicians, hospitals, and pharmaceutical companies, for example—were threatened by such proposals. Even more fundamentally, a direct government role of the magnitude implied by this approach was inconsistent with traditional American distrust of government power.

Second, a fully national health plan would end the jobs of thousands of health insurance administrators in private businesses and insurance companies, require massive reorganization of methods of payment, and reduce private control over health insurance plans. Such an upheaval

60. John K. Igelhart, "Canada's Health System," *New England Journal of Medicine*, vol. 315 (July 17, September 18, and December 18, 1986), pp. 202–08, 778–841, 1623–28; and Igelhart, "Canada's Health Care System Faces Its Problems," *New England Journal of Medicine*, vol. 322 (February 22, 1990), pp. 562–68.

61. Only 8 percent of Canadians indicated that they would prefer the British or U.S. systems of paying for health care to their own; 40 percent of British respondents thought that they would prefer the U.S. or Canadian systems to their own; but 61 percent of U.S. respondents indicated that they would prefer the Canadian system and 29 percent said they would prefer the British system to their own. See Robert J. Blendon and Humphrey Taylor, "Views on Health Care: Public Opinion in Three Nations," *Health Affairs*, vol. 8 (Spring 1989), p. 153.

seemed to many too high a price to pay for extending insurance to the minority of uninsured Americans and for the speculative gains in cost control.

Universal coverage plus new payment systems. None of the principal current proposals for extending health insurance would replace employment as the primary source of health insurance for workers and their families. They differ from proposals simply to mandate employer-sponsored coverage by including new intermediaries between insurance companies and providers of care, thus transforming the character of insurance and the payment system.

The Department of Health of the State of New York published a draft plan in 1989 that would have established mandatory employment-based health insurance but would have gone beyond simple mandates in two key respects.[62] It proposed to create a state-managed "single-payer authority" between all payers and providers. This authority would set rates of reimbursement and presumably determine whether providers should be reimbursed on a fee-for-service basis, under a fixed budget, or by capitation. Such a system of payment, it was claimed, would achieve a one-time reduction in administrative costs by establishing uniform payment rules and make possible additional savings by providing leverage for slowing the rate of growth of costs.

The New York plan also would have limited private insurance liability to $25,000 a person annually. A state plan would cover annual costs above $25,000 for those with private insurance and all costs for everyone else (except for those eligible under medicare). This cap on private liability would have given the state immediate leverage over management of very high-cost illnesses, which account for a surprising fraction of health care expenditures.[63] If kept fixed, the cap would gradually shift responsibility for medical costs from private, employment-based insurance to a single state plan.

---

62. New York State Department of Health, *Universal New York Health Care, UNY*Care* (September 1, 1989). Governor Mario Cuomo embraced the plan in principle, but did not ask for legislation.

63. One percent of the general population accounted for 29 percent of all health expenditures in 1980, and charges incurred averaged $8,744. One percent of the aged accounted for 21 percent of outlays by the aged, and charges incurred averaged $16,701. With inflation the average charges in 1990 could be $27,160 for the most costly 1 percent of the general population and $51,800 for the most costly 1 percent of the elderly. For data on 1980, see Steven A. Garfinkel, Gerald F. Riley, and Vincent G. Iannacchione, "High-cost Users of Medical Care," *Health Care Financing Review*, vol. 9 (Summer 1988), pp. 41–52.

The feature of the proposal that represents fundamental restructuring is the introduction of the state agency as the single payer for all health care. Effective cost control cannot rely on fee limits or improved efficiency. It can succeed in the long run only if some authority can decide under what circumstances care will be denied because the cost exceeds the expected benefits. To an increasing degree such decisions revolve around high-technology medicine and high-cost illnesses. The $25,000 cap would have gradually given the state agency the power to engage in this kind of rationing. The question is whether it would enjoy the political support to use this power.

A health plan developed by Alain Enthoven and Richard Kronick would restructure the health care system along different lines. It would require employers to offer health insurance, but it is predicated on a recognition that unregulated competition in health insurance and health care makes universal coverage impossible and needlessly expensive.[64] To deal with this problem, they propose the creation of financial agents who would stand between employers and individuals, on the one hand, and providers of health care, on the other. These "sponsors" would act as regulators of competition among health insurers and providers. For example, the sponsors would evaluate the expected medical outlays for various groups of people and tag such groups with premiums that vary with risk, thereby reducing or eliminating the incentive of insurers to seek low-cost patients and reject high-cost patients. The sponsors would commission studies to evaluate the quality and cost of various physicians and hospitals and publish the results so that employers or individuals could buy services from relatively efficient providers.[65]

The Enthoven-Kronick plan raises an issue that lies at the heart of private, employment-based insurance: is it desirable for premiums charged employers to vary with the risk characteristics or average health outlays of their employees? In most cases, the answer seems to be "no." If workplace risks or hazards vary by company, charging companies health

64. Alain Enthoven and Richard Kronick, "A Consumer-Choice Health Plan for the 1990s: Universal Health Insurance in a System Designed to Promote Quality and Economy," *New England Journal of Medicine*, vol. 320 (January 5 and 12, 1989), pp. 29–37, 94–101.

65. Enthoven and Kronick are not explicit about how the sponsors would be organized, who would pay them, and what their powers would be. Some critics have questioned whether organizations with sufficient power could be sustained that would, in effect, free the market for health insurance and health care from the myriad imperfections now present. See Stanley B. Jones, "Can Multiple Choice Be Managed to Constrain Health Care Costs?" *Health Affairs*, vol. 8 (Fall 1989), pp. 51–59.

insurance premiums that reflect these risks is economically efficient, because it requires purchasers of that company's products to pay prices sufficient to cover these costs as well as other expenses of production. But variations in the cost of health care that are associated with the age, race, sex, or health status of workers should not be allowed to affect relative prices of various commodities.[66] It is hard to see the social or economic gain from requiring that the costs of pregnancy associated with hiring premenopausal women be charged against the firm or from permitting the wages of such women to be reduced by the expected cost of pregnancy benefits. Whatever the source, risk rating causes premiums for equivalent benefits to vary widely, with given plans twice as costly for some companies as for others.[67] This line of argument raises the question of whether risk rating, so essential for the operation of private insurance, is desirable in a national health plan, except possibly to help incorporate the costs of unsafe production into product prices or to penalize gross overuse of services by some groups.[68]

A 1990s Agenda for Health Care Financing

The U.S. health insurance system has done a splendid job of providing access to high-quality health care for the vast majority of Americans. But it has failed to provide coverage for more than 31 million people. It has failed conspicuously to control rising costs. And it has provided meager coverage for the expenses of long-term home care or nursing home care. Prospects are slight that it will do materially better during the 1990s, and it may do worse unless it undergoes major changes.

The U.S. system rests on three pillars: employer-financed health

66. They would not do so if money wages just offset variations among these and other groups in health costs, but public law prohibits variations in wages based on these characteristics. Few people would argue, for example, that a company that hires the handicapped or the elderly should have to bear higher costs than do competitors who fail to hire such workers.

67. This issue has become critical in recent years because the Employee Retirement Income Security Act of 1974 exempted from state insurance regulation employers who self-insure (that is, pay all health insurance costs themselves, using insurance companies, if all, only as agents for processing bills). See Jones, "Can Multiple Choice Be Managed to Constrain Health Care Costs?" p. 53.

68. The advance of biomedical science promises to test the acceptability of risk rating in a more fundamental way. Advances are making it increasingly possible to identify individuals prone to various illnesses and to pick out those for whom various workplace environments pose particular risks. To what extent should insurers or employers be permitted to use such tests or to act on their results?

insurance voluntarily provided as a fringe benefit of employment; government-sponsored health insurance available for the elderly and disabled as a right based on prior employment; and income- or means-tested benefits available to the poor. A favorable view sees the system as diverse and flexible; seen less charitably, it is fragmented and uncoordinated. Either way, providers of health care in the United States receive income from more separate and independent payers than do providers in any other developed country.

Because so many separate groups pay for U.S. health care, providers have successfully resisted efforts to slow the growth of spending. As cost consciousness has grown, each payer has sought to make certain that it pays only for the costs generated by patients for whom it is responsible. Medicare payments have been reduced in a variety of ways—most notably through DRGs, but also through other adjustments designed to hold down spending. Private companies have been seeking negotiated discounts from hospitals and physicians. Because of all these efforts, some hospitals, particularly those with caseloads consisting disproportionately of the uninsured or medicaid recipients, are reporting deficits or sharply reduced profits.

As noted earlier, these efforts promise some savings by encouraging the elimination of purely wasteful expenditures. But they offer no effective barrier to continued medical cost inflation based on the proliferation of beneficial diagnostic and therapeutic interventions for patients who are well insured. And as insurance companies respond by charging each group or individual the full cost of expected medical outlays, they encourage employers to limit or to discontinue insurance plans, employees facing increased premiums to reject optional coverage, and providers to reject uninsured patients.

In short, the effort to control health care costs is now at war with the objective of extending coverage to the uninsured and even of maintaining current coverage. Extension of insurance would add to overall costs, but the increase would be less than proportional to the numbers of people newly insured. According to one estimate, increasing the proportion of the American population with health insurance by 13.1 percent would directly raise health care spending by 4.6 percent.[69] Furthermore, some parts of the U.S. health care system have excess supply. Hospital occupancy rates, for example, fell from an annual

69. *Cost and Effects of Extending Health Insurance Coverage,* Committee Print, pp. 73, 82.

average of 77.9 percent in 1981 to 69.2 percent in 1988, signifying a considerable excess of beds nationally. Nevertheless, specific communities have high occupancy rates; and inflationary pressures in these localities might be pronounced. Extending insurance coverage would boost real consumption of medical services, Even a modest increase in the price of care for those already insured would sharply boost the total cost of extending coverage.

Thus a major challenge for health policy during the 1990s is to extend health insurance without fueling inflation. Voluntary incrementalism will not achieve a sufficient extension of insurance. Mandatory employer-based insurance will not fundamentally alter the current payment structure that precludes effective control of costs. To achieve both goals simultaneously will require some form of comprehensive restructuring. This approach should not abandon the enormous achievement embodied in the current system of employer-sponsored health insurance. Because of the huge investment in that system, the plans sketched above would build on, rather than replace, that system. They would mandate employer-sponsored coverage for all workers employed more than a minimum number of hours per week, but lodge control over spending in entities designed to control physician reimbursement.

Developing protections against the costs of long-term care poses rather different problems. So few long-term care insurance policies have been sold, despite vigorous efforts by private insurers, that sales could multiply many times and still leave most Americans without protection. And prospects are nil that those too poor to pay directly for long-term care but too rich to qualify for medicaid will be covered unless the government offers large subsidies.

The President's Program and Budget for Health Care

President Bush's budget for fiscal year 1991 requests no significant changes in current policies, other than intensified efforts to reduce federal medicare outlays. The budget calls for reductions in medicare spending that would save a claimed $5.5 billion in 1991 and $15.2 billion in 1995.[70] Most savings would result from cuts in payments for given services. For example, the budget would reduce payments for new capital and medical education, it would lower fees for radiologists and anesthe-

70. Of these savings, $3.3 billion of 1991 spending and $5.2 billion in 1995 are in hospital insurance (part A). The rest would accrue in supplemental medical insurance (part B). *Budget of the United States Government, Fiscal Year 1991*, pp. 210–11.

siologists, and it would hold down the annual increase in DRG payments. In past years, Congress has refused to accept many similar recommendations to cut medicare spending.

The budget emphasizes the encouragement of managed care in medicare and medicaid. It would offer medicare patients "medicare plus," an option that would spare patients some cost sharing if they enroll in a preferred provider organization. It would gradually alter the fee structure for medicare patients to encourage managed care and increase the incentives of HMOs to enroll medicare patients. The matching formula under medicaid would also be changed to encourage states to offer services in managed-care settings. In addition, the budget calls for $52 million to be spent in fiscal year 1991 on research to determine the effectiveness of various medical procedures. The budget contains no proposals to extend coverage for health care, other than exhortation to the states to extend optional medicaid coverage to pregnant women and infants residing in families with incomes between 133 percent and 185 percent of official poverty thresholds.

For reasons presented earlier, a cost-control strategy based on encouragement of managed care and research on effectiveness of health interventions promises small savings at best. The president has not reintroduced proposals to limit the exclusion of employer-financed health insurance from personal taxable income, which is a key element not only of the voluntary incrementalist strategy but also of many agendas for tax reform, since it would heighten taxpayers' awareness of the rising cost of health insurance.

The budget advances no proposals for improving access to long-term care. In this case both political considerations and budgetary exigencies coincide. The administration and Congress are no doubt loath to revisit extension of health services for the elderly, in part because of last year's debacle over the catastrophic health bill, in part because of a widespread sense that other groups are in greater need than the elderly, and in part because any conceivable federal action to increase support for long-term care would be costly.

A Health Program for the Nineties

This chapter concludes with a proposed approach to dealing with the various health problems confronting the nation.[71] It rests on five

71. This program is similar to one outlined in Henry Aaron, "How to Combine

propositions. First, in common with all the approaches sketched earlier in this chapter, it presumes continued reliance on a system of employer-sponsored health insurance for working people and their families. Second, it presupposes that this system can never provide coverage for people with little or no connection to the work force—the elderly and disabled, the unskilled and long-term unemployed. Coverage for these groups must come from government action. Third, in common with the proposals for fundamental restructuring, it posits that reducing the number of payers—to one, if possible—is a necessary condition for slowing growth of health care spending. Fourth, it recognizes that in a country as large and diverse as the United States many aspects of the health care system are likely to differ from one region to another. While allowing for this diversity, the federal government can still use its regulatory powers, including tax rules, to achieve substantially universal coverage of working people and their families through private, employer-sponsored insurance. But it will have to use its spending powers to assure coverage of people who cannot secure insurance through work. Finally, in light of the vital importance to the long-term health of the U.S. economy of sharply reducing or eliminating the federal budget deficit, the approach is designed to advance that goal.

To achieve universal coverage, the federal government would first mandate coverage for workers with significant attachment to the labor force and for their immediate families. Companies could initially remain outside this system if they pay a payroll tax at a rate sufficient to pay for all covered employees. While premiums for employer-sponsored coverage would initially reflect group experience, the plan would shift gradually to fees based on local community averages ("community rating"), except to the extent that variations in costs were shown to be related to workplace hazards. Companies would be required to come into the plan by the time community rating was fully in place.

Second, a backup plan providing the same benefits required of employer-sponsored plans would be provided for all those not covered at work. This plan would cover the elderly and disabled who are currently covered by medicare and everyone else not covered by an employer-sponsored plan.

Program Reform and Deficit Reduction: An Application to Federal Expenditures on Health Care," National Economic Commission Briefing, October 19, 1988; and in Robert D. Reischauer, "Thinking Systematically about the Budget Deficit Decisions Facing the Next President," in Reischauer, ed., *The Federal Deficit: Where Do We Go From Here?* (Syracuse University Press, 1988), pp. 127–50.

Third, the burden of controlling costs would rest with regional, state, or local organizations ("finance agents") charged with negotiating physicians' fees and hospital budgets for all payers, private as well as public. These agents would be responsible to state (or possibly multistate or regional) authorities. This arrangement for a single payer would create the capacity to control costs, contrasting sharply with current arrangements under which millions of individuals and groups have been largely ineffectual in slowing the growth of spending.

To strengthen the hand of the finance agents in cost control, an annual limit on private insurer liability should be set, along the lines proposed in the New York plan sketched above. In that way, the finance agents would be responsible for high-cost episodes of care. As overall prices rise, the proportion of care for which the finance agents are responsible would increase. But the principal initial insurance responsibility of the finance agents would be to pay for acute health care for all people not covered under employer-sponsored insurance, along the lines proposed by the National Leadership Commission on Health Care and other proposals to mandate workplace coverage.

The finance agents would also serve as the channel for financing long-term home care and nursing home care. They could do so in either of two ways. They could be the administrative agent for a social insurance program, in which long-term care would be provided as a matter of right to each person suffering from stipulated limitations on activities of daily living.[72] Alternatively, they could administer federally or state-financed grants to local governments or nonprofit organizations that would operate under limited budgets and would provide such care up to the limits of available funds. The latter approach would not establish an entitlement to care, thereby reducing the risk of much larger than anticipated costs. The grant mechanism would also create an instrument, absent from the social insurance approach, for controlling costs of providers.

These activities of the financial agents would encompass all current health activities of the federal government under medicare, medicaid, federal employee health benefits, and certain other health programs,[73] as well as state expenditures on medicaid, which would be maintained. Outlays under current policy for these activities are projected to reach $206.7 billion in 1991. But the approach indicated here would entail

72. For illustrations of such plans, see Ball, *Because We're All in This Together;* and Rivlin and Weiner, *Caring for the Disabled Elderly.*
73. Those under budget account 551 and 553.

additional responsibilities: subsidies to some private companies that offer health insurance; coverage for workers in private companies that might elect initially not to offer coverage but to pay a tax instead; acute-care coverage of individuals not currently provided benefits under a public program; and any additional long-term care benefits.

The total budget of the federal health care agency would exceed the current budget of any other federal department, except the Department of Defense and the Social Security Administration.[74] Because expenditures on health care are not only large but certain to grow—as technological change increases the number of beneficial interventions and as the elderly population increases—it would be sound budgetary procedure to house these functions in an independent cabinet department and to finance federal expenditures on health care, like those on social security pensions and medicare hospital benefits, through earmarked revenues. Revenues to the trust fund would include the current 2.9 percent medicare tax on earnings up to the social security maximum; state medicaid payments; proceeds from the imposition of personal income tax on the value of employer-financed health insurance above $250 a month for families ($100 a month for individuals); premiums now paid by individuals for part B medicare coverage; and a dedicated value-added tax (VAT) of 6 percent.

Table 8-5 illustrates such a plan as if it were in full operation in 1991. Total spending of the new department would be approximately $272 billion in 1991. This total includes a crude allowance for added expenditures to support acute care directly through public programs, to pay transitional subsidies to new private insurance plans, and for the cost of additional long-term care services. Although expressed in 1991 dollars, any new program would take several years to become fully effective.

The additional revenues from employer payments, personal income tax collections on health insurance, and the VAT would amount to $140 billion, offset in part by additional spending of $65 billion. Thus the plan would reduce the budget deficit by $75 billion. An alternative self-financing plan that did not contribute to deficit reduction would require additional tax revenue of only $26 billion.

The role of the federal government as direct provider and manager of health insurance would be smaller under this approach than it is

74. The 1991 budget projects that health care outlays under current policy will exceed defense outlays after 1996 and social security benefits after 2009. With added responsibilities for the health department, these crossovers would occur sooner.

TABLE 8-5. Proposed Health Care Trust Fund, 1991[a]
Billions of 1991 dollars

Expenditures		Revenues	
Current activities		*Current revenues*	
Medicaid	80	Payroll tax and medicare trust fund interest	85
Medicare	104	Contributions to medicare Part B	12
Veterans' health	13		
Other	10	State medicaid outlays (estimated)	35
Subtotal	207	Subtotal	132
Additional activities[b]		*Additional revenues*[b]	
Acute care	40	Employer payments in lieu of insurance	30
Long-term care	25	Tax employer-financed health insurance above cap	9
		Value-added tax at 6 percent[c]	101
TOTAL	272	TOTAL	272
Addendum: Reduction in federal deficit relative to current policy			
Added revenue	140		
Added expenditure	65		
Deficit reduction	75		

SOURCES: *Budget of the United States Government, Fiscal Year 1991,* pp. 101–34; and *The Federal Hospital Insurance Trust Fund,* H. Doc. 101-34, 101 Cong. 2 sess. (GPO, 1990).
a. Figures are rounded.
b. Author's estimates.
c. Based on Congressional Budget office, *Reducing the Deficit: Spending and Revenue Options,* February 1989, p. 367, assuming full effectiveness by 1991. The VAT revenues assumes the CBO "narrow base" medical expenditures. The inflationary effects of the VAT on medical prices are assumed to be offset by cost-control measures.

under current law. Administration of health care plans would reside with state or regional bodies—the finance agents—rather than with federal agencies. But the financial responsibility of the federal government would be greatly expanded for raising revenues sufficient to support costs of acute-care health benefits for those not covered through work, high-outlay episodes of acute care for everyone, and long-term care.

This approach can deal with the problems sketched at the start of this chapter. It would provide essentially universal financial access to acute care. It would greatly expand access to long-term care. And by creating powerful entities to negotiate fees and hospital budgets, it would establish the basis for control over the growth of medical care costs. Whether this power would be used to hold down costs would hinge on the support for cost control that the finance agents received from states and localities and ultimately from the American people. It is vital to recognize that slowing the growth of spending on health care for more than a brief period will be impossible unless Americans are prepared to forgo some beneficial care—in plain language, to endure health care rationing. If rationing is to prove acceptable, it is necessary to fashion acceptable rules for deciding which medical interventions in which circumstances are not worth what they cost. Whether sick Americans and their families, who are renowned for their insistence that everything possible be done, will accept such decisions is not assured. But people in other countries have done so.

9

THOMAS E. MANN

Breaking the Political Impasse

THE MOST STRIKING and unsettling feature of American politics at the dawn of the 1990s is the stark contrast between the extraordinary pace and scope of change occurring outside the country and the political immobilism within. Each day brings news of yet another unanticipated, until recently unimaginable, development in Eastern Europe—but it also brings yet another example of deadlock and escapism in the U.S. government. A *Time* cover headline, "Is Government Dead?," reflected a growing sentiment among professional observers that American political institutions and leaders are no match for the domestic and international problems and opportunities facing the nation.[1] Any serious effort to reshape national priorities and identify needed policy changes must perforce grapple with the political obstacles to their adoption and implementation.

The critique that U.S. governing arrangements tend toward stalemate and inaction is hardly original. Critics have long complained that the constitutional separation of powers constrains effective government. Spasms of decisive action—in times of war or economic collapse or in the wake of an unusually clear and consistent message from the electorate—are the standard by which normal politics is judged. But it is a standard that the political system seldom meets. During the 1970s, and particularly during the Carter years, critics blamed the political stasis on the weakening of parties and the resultant fragmentation of political life. Presidents and members of Congress had separate political bases, it was alleged. And Congress, altered by reforms in the early 1970s, had incentives, resources, and opportunities to pursue its own agenda. Although in the 1980s the initial policy successes of the Reagan administration seemed to belie this analysis, a political impasse soon

The author wishes to thank Pietro S. Nivola, Bert A. Rockman, and Joseph White for their comments.

1. See Stanley W. Cloud, "The Can't Do Government," *Time*, October 23, 1989, pp. 28–32.

emerged, attributed to relatively strong and ideologically polarized parties operating within a divided government. Sharp disagreement between Democrats and Republicans on such matters as taxes, spending, and U.S. policy toward Central America ensured that the executive and legislative branches would remain at loggerheads.

Bush's First Year

The first year of the Bush presidency did little to reassure the political system's severest critics. Indeed, the year underscored the tenuous connection between what government accomplishes and how those who lead government are judged. By most objective measures, the first session of the 101st Congress was disappointing. The few significant pieces of legislation that passed were damage-control measures: the bailout of the savings and loan industry, the repeal of the insurance program to deal with catastrophic illness that was adopted by the 100th Congress, and still another effort to slow the growth of medicare costs. The budget deficit survived unscathed, and the long-term problems that beset the country's social and physical infrastructure were not addressed. President Bush's legislative record in Congress was mediocre.

Problems of ethics dominated the session, from the questionable financial dealings that led to the unprecedented resignation of House Speaker Jim Wright and Majority Whip Tony Coelho to charges that five senators who received major campaign contributions from savings and loan executive Charles Keating used improper influence with the bureaucracy on his behalf. The most substantial achievement of the new leadership in the House was the adoption at year's end of a salary and ethics package, reversing the pay raise fiasco that opened the session in January 1989.

This meager legislative output did nothing to harm George Bush's political standing. At the end of his first year in office, the public's approval ratings of him compared favorably with those received by his predecessor and other recent presidents. Through a variety of accounting devices and with the help of a temporary sequestration, the deficit reduction goals of the Gramm-Rudman-Hollings laws were technically satisfied, although almost no reduction in the deficit actually occurred. The president adhered to his campaign promise of no new taxes. His tactical positioning on domestic issues kept the Democrats in Congress off balance and unable to advance a compelling agenda of their own. With the possible exception of dispatching a delegation to China in what some regarded as unseemly haste after the Chinese government crushed student protests, he avoided serious foreign policy missteps in a rapidly changing world. By seizing the policy initiative at the NATO meeting in Brussels, in a summit with Mikhail Gorbachev at Malta, and most emphatically in the invasion of Panama, he undercut criticisms of timidity and a lack of imagination.

Bush clearly benefited from favorable domestic and international conditions. U.S. economic expansion continued into its seventh year with no persuasive evidence of recession. The palpable reduction of the Soviet military threat raised the prospect of a substantial decline in defense spending in the next decade. And the cry of freedom that rang triumphantly in Eastern Europe reinforced and legitimized the president's inclination to emphasize foreign affairs more than domestic policy.

But Bush's political success was the result of more than good luck. He fared well in spite of the incredibly low expectations for his tenure in office, expectations created by the electoral, personal, and policy circumstances of his presidency. In the 1988 elections his party had lost seats in both the House and Senate, leaving him in the weakest position with respect to Congress of any new president in this century. He seemed to lack both core beliefs to guide his administration and a public persona to inspire citizens through the mass media. And he inherited from Ronald Reagan a major imbalance between demands on government and the discretionary resources of government to meet those demands.

These constraints and others conditioned and limited the Bush administration's approach to Congress and to governance more generally. Rejected out of hand was the model of American politics based on electorally induced policy change. A deliberate pace displaced the fast start. Expectations of bold policy initiatives were dampened. This was to be a period of consolidation and adjustment, not policy reversal. Presidential leadership shifted from wholesale to retail as the rhetorical flourishes of the public presidency gave way to one-on-one politicking inside the beltway. Bush sought to be consensual rather than polarizing in his approach to Congress and to the public as well as in his strategy for dealing with such conflict-laden matters as relations with Nicaragua and South Africa. Consultation, conciliation, and bipartisanship became the preferred though not exclusive modes of operation, as occasional and successful vetoes, secret foreign policy initiatives, and staunch defense of presidential prerogatives demonstrated. The president overcame Democratic opposition in Congress more by clever positioning than by political pressure. Faced with certain defeat over aid to the contras, he embraced the position of his opponents. On protecting the environment and federal support for child care, he moved to the political center. On cuts in tax rates on capital gains, where victory seemed attainable, he picked a fight and nearly won. Strong presidential leadership was limited to the international arena where, in spite of an active and assertive Congress, the executive retains the capacity for initiative and influence.

In many respects, the Bush presidency seems well suited to the political context within which it must operate. Its approach is consistent with an interpretation of the election as a referendum on the Reagan presidency and its management of the economy. Its modest policy ambitions fit well with the fiscal legacy of the Reagan years, the relatively quiescent state of public opinion, and the political obstacles posed by divided government. Its tone of cooperation with Congress, respect for public service, accessibility to the press, active engagement in the job, and a pragmatic rather than ideological approach to problems constitutes a welcome contrast with Ronald Reagan's. Indeed, the Bush administration appears to have crafted a strategy for governance that makes a virtue of the constraints on its leadership, particularly in domestic policy.

The lack of a strong connection between performance and evaluation is by no means limited to the president. The classic case against Congress is that its words speak louder than its actions. How members advertise themselves and the credit they can claim for benefits delivered to their constituents seem more important for their political careers than the legislation they enact.[2] During the first year of the Bush presidency, Congress came under extraordinary attack, not so much from the public, which has long held a dim view of the institution, but from the reporters, columnists, and editorial writers who had in earlier years been champions of its reform and resurgence. A *Newsweek* cover story, "The World of Congress," which portrayed members as cowardly and cynical self-promoters consumed with their own reelection, was only slightly more hyperbolic than the typical outpouring against Congress in the press.[3]

Serious concerns about the institution lay beneath this onslaught—that money is suffocating politics, that House elections have become hopelessly uncompetitive, that members are increasingly risk averse, and that Congress is usurping legitimate powers of the president. What has

2. David R. Mayhew, *Congress: The Electoral Connection* (Yale University, 1974).
3. "The World of Congress," *Newsweek*, April 24, 1989, pp. 28–34.

emerged in the popular press, however, is a caricature of Congress as corrupt, insular, invulnerable, and irresponsible. Even so, the prospect is scant that this orgy of Congress bashing will adversely affect members' reelection prospects. The record and reputation of Congress may well affect the stature of its leaders and the satisfaction of its members, but it is largely irrelevant to their political fortunes.

For both the president and Congress, then, policy deadlock and inattention to long-term problems have entailed few, if any, political costs. Paradoxically, action to break the logjam and tend to the challenges the country faces would deprive the president and Congress of their ability to avoid blame for the associated short-term costs.

Sources of Immobilism

The seeming inability or unwillingness of political leaders to tackle the country's problems is rooted in a number of conditions, including the policy and political legacy of the Reagan years, the state of public opinion, a lack of consensus among policy specialists, the strength of local and special interests in the American polity, and the division of political control between a Republican president and a Democratic Congress.

The Reagan Legacy

Historians may well see more elements of continuity between the Carter and Reagan administrations than of the change that seemed so apparent to participants and contemporary observers. The defense buildup, the effort to restrain the growth in domestic spending, and a tight monetary policy were, after all, initiated during the Carter presidency. Confronted with an array of disturbing economic conditions (slow growth, high inflation, rapidly increasing outlays for social security and medicare) and public concerns about high taxes and the Soviet threat, Carter was forced to make a midcourse policy correction. Reagan responded to the same economic and political forces with brio, adding his own distinctive contributions: a massive tax cut, a more rapid defense buildup, and an attack on discretionary domestic spending. When combined with the determined effort of the Federal Reserve to break the back of inflation (which required high interest rates and a severe recession), these policies produced a dramatic increase in the budget deficit—from an average of 2 percent of GNP during the 1970s to more than 5 percent in the mid-1980s.

What followed was the fiscalization of all policy discussion and the politics of constraint. If the slogan of domestic politics in the 1960s was "What does it do for the poor?," then that of the 1980s was "What does it do for the deficit?" By 1982 the deficit seemed out of control, feeding on itself because of soaring interest payments on the debt. Measures to control expenditures and increase revenues diminished the threat of an exploding deficit, but did not remove the constraints it imposed (it has been stuck at around $150 billion, although declining as a share of national income). Federal spending for domestic programs, excluding social security and medicare, shrank as a percentage of GNP to near pre–Great Society levels. An enormous amount of energy was invested in protecting this diminishing part of the budget. Opportunities to launch new programs or expand existing ones were virtually non-existent.

Whatever their frustration over the constraints on domestic policy initiatives, politicians in both parties judged the most obvious remedies (increasing taxes, trimming social security benefits) to be more threatening than the ailment. Republicans embraced tax cuts as the touchstone of their party, the engine of economic growth and opportunity. Democrats portrayed themselves as champions of social security, repelling Republican attacks on the system. Both positions were exceedingly popular with the public. Each party consequently felt obliged to protect its most vulnerable flank—Democrats by forgoing tax increases, Republicans by opposing any cuts in social security.

At the end of the Reagan years, the federal government had left itself with vastly reduced discretion to attack the nation's most pressing problems. Its traditional tools for achieving social objectives—spending money, forgoing taxes, and issuing commands—had been blunted by a decade of change. The huge budget deficits and the shrinking share of the total budget available for discretionary use meant federal dollars would be scarce for the foreseeable future. Dramatically lower marginal income tax rates, the broadened income tax base, and the shift in the federal tax burden from income to payroll taxes all reduced the ability of the federal government to use tax credits to channel social behavior. And successive rounds of regulatory reform, however spotty the record in pushing deregulation beyond the transportation and communications industries, gave pause to politicians who would require the private sector to provide what government itself could not afford.

Public Opinion

As the Reagan era drew to a close, politicians in both parties recognized that on a broad array of domestic policy concerns—health care, drug abuse, quality education, affordable housing, availability of child care, and protection of the environment—public opinion strongly supported a more active role by government. At the same time, a willingness to pay taxes to fund more federal services was nowhere in evidence. The intensity of the tax revolt of the 1970s, symbolized by the passage of California's Proposition 13, may well have diminished, but citizens still wanted lower taxes. Ironically, despite the passion of the tax revolt and the myriad tax changes of the Reagan years, including a sharp reduction in marginal rates, the federal tax burden in 1990 is about 19.5 percent of national income, the same as it was in 1980 and slightly higher than the average in the previous two decades.[4]

The political reality is that raising taxes for general revenues is always unpopular, doubly so when it is billed as a deficit reduction exercise. Before income taxes were indexed in 1985, politicians had the luxury of seeing revenues rise through bracket creep; they could enact tax cuts and watch effective rates go up. With that option greatly curtailed, any increase in federal income taxes must be explicitly legislated. It is no wonder that in recent years politicians have looked to user fees and targeted revenues (most important, the payroll tax), which are less likely to incur public opposition. Even so, the recent repeal of the insurance program for catastrophic illness is a painful reminder of the potential explosiveness of any new tax program.

Policymakers are moved less by systematic evidence of mass opinion than by their own readings of the national mood.[5] During the late 1970s a feeling arose in Washington that the country was becoming more conservative because of concern about inflation and big government and the threat to U.S. national security posed by a truculent Soviet Union. Antigovernment sentiment with respect to domestic matters gave sustenance to politicians seeking to cut taxes, reduce domestic spending, and deregulate industry. And concerns about the Soviet Union provided the popular base for supporting a major defense buildup.

The national mood at the beginning of the 1990s lacks the clarity

4. Congressional Budget Office, *The Economic and Budget Outlook: Fiscal Years 1991–1995* (CBO, 1990), pp. xv, 125.

5. John W. Kingdon, *Agendas, Alternatives, and Public Policies* (Little, Brown, 1984), pp. 152–72.

and sense of urgency of the mood a decade ago. Eight years of economic expansion have left most Americans feeling relatively optimistic about their own personal finances and reluctant to tamper with a system that seems to be working.[6] George Bush's election in 1988 was widely seen as a successful referendum on Ronald Reagan's management of the national economy. Public concerns about the country's future—that the United States is becoming less competitive in the world economy, that deficit spending threatens the living standards of the next generation of Americans—are real, but muted and disconnected from the routines of everyday life.

Even the apparent demands for new government services lack the confidence and passion of an earlier era. The skepticism so evident in the 1970s and 1980s about the federal government's ability to ameliorate major social maladies is not yet fully spent. There is no clarion call for a major expansion of the size and role of government. The easing of the military threat from the Soviet Union has led the public to believe some resources can be reallocated from defense to domestic programs. Specific programs to deal with social problems will continue to garner nominal support from majorities of citizens. But there is little in most policymakers' reading of the national mood to suggest a demand for or even a tolerance of actions to deal with long-term problems if they entail painful short-term costs.

Policy Dissensus

A lack of consensus among policy specialists on how best to deal with the country's most serious problems is another force inhibiting action. The newfound modesty of policy analysts and policymakers matches the public's lack of confidence in the ability of government to make the United States more competitive in world markets, to improve public education, or to reduce drug-related violence in the cities.

Ideas can be powerful forces in redirecting national policy, but only when elite opinion converges around them.[7] The deregulation of the airline, trucking, and telecommunications industries between 1975 and 1980 was driven by a broad consensus in the policy community that regulation in potentially competitive markets had large costs and few

6. Times Mirror, *The People, the Press, and Economics* (Washington: Times Mirror Center for Press and Public Policy, 1989).

7. Martha Derthick and Paul J. Quirk, *The Politics of Deregulation* (Brookings, 1985), pp. 237–58.

benefits. A growing recognition among policy analysts that requiring welfare recipients to look for work would increase earnings, reduce public costs, and appeal to welfare recipients themselves contributed to the welfare reform of the late 1980s. And two decades of analysis on the economic benefits of reducing tax rates by broadening the tax base played a key role in the Tax Reform Act of 1986. In each instance a consensus among policy specialists provided a necessary, though certainly not sufficient, condition for substantial change.

One strains to find comparable agreement on how best to deal with the problems confronting the United States in the 1990s. Economists spoke as one to condemn federal budget deficits that were increasing sharply relative to national income in the 1980s, but current and projected deficit levels elicit less uniform concern. Although most economists probably agree that continuing large budget deficits will depress national saving and future U.S. living standards, some prominent members of the policy community hold that the costs of cutting the deficit (through tax increases and expenditure cuts) vastly outweigh the potential benefits. Politicians exhausted and frustrated by the decade-long deficit battles can find plenty of intellectual support for declaring an armistice in this war and moving on.

Similarly, there are conflicting signals on trade policy. New economic theories have challenged the theoretical orthodoxy that a country can seldom use strategic trade policy to increase its national income at the expense of other countries. Advocates of bilateral and managed trade strategies have seized these theories to justify their calls for abandonment of multilateral neutrality. Most trade analysts, however, remain deeply skeptical of the new ideas on both theoretical and practical grounds. The debate among specialists fuels rather than resolves the conflict on trade policy.

Much the same can be said about current thinking on social policy. While most people recognize that the public schools are performing dismally despite toughened standards and a sharp increase in spending, specialists engage in ideologically charged disagreements over what new policy course should be charted by federal, state, and local authorities. Similarly, the uneasy sense that family structure and individual character underlie such contemporary social maladies as poverty, drug abuse, and crime has produced nothing approaching a consensus on how public policy can best respond.

The uncertainty among analysts is mirrored by politicians. Neither party shows any signs of having developed a coherent and credible approach to dealing with problems of public finance, U.S. international competitiveness, national security, public education, or the underclass. Democrats appear particularly uncomfortable with the obvious mismatch between their pronouncements on the severity of the problems and their inability to agree on what to do about them.

Special Interests

All democratic governments have difficulty advancing general, long-term objectives of society through measures that impose immediate and focused costs. The U.S. system is especially sensitive to organized interests because its power is fragmented. And notwithstanding James Madison's injunction in the *Federalist* number 10 that Congress should "refine and enlarge the public views," representation ordinarily takes precedence over governing.

The independent electoral bases of legislators and the internal structure of the House and Senate naturally push members of Congress to serve organized interests and seek benefits for their own constituents. The changes that swept through the political system during the 1960s and 1970s—the increase in split-ticket voting, the growing cost of campaigns and reliance on contributions from special interests, the rise of television, the expansion and growing political sophistication of interest groups in Washington, and the democratization and decentralization of Congress— may well have weakened the classic iron triangles, but they also heightened the sensitivity of politicians to all forms of outside pressure. Moreover, the nation's declining economic fortunes forced a more explicit trade-off between special and general interests and between present and future benefits. Insofar as they inflict temporary relative disadvantage on some groups, policies designed to promote long-term interests are much harder to undertake in a sluggish economy than in a robust one.

It is one thing to argue that Congress is prone to particularism; it is quite another to conclude that this impulse overwhelms the public interest in most instances or that it is in evidence at only one end of Pennsylvania Avenue. Congress sometimes acts on behalf of general, unorganized interests in spite of the opposition of special interests, and presidents are often responsive to the same concentrated interests that flex their muscles so visibly on Capitol Hill. The way in which issues are framed and alternatives structured can have a profound influence on whether Congress opts for particularism or the public interest.[8] Ideas, leadership,

8. Derthick and Quirk, *Politics of Deregulation*, pp. 140–46.

institutional mechanisms, and policy entrepreneurship can be used effectively to support diffuse interests against concentrated ones. The past decade has been a period of unusual experimentation with institutional devices such as leadership summits, reconciliation, and bipartisan commissions that are designed to counterbalance the power of interest groups.

Nonetheless, when effective action on the country's most pressing problems requires the imposition of losses on organized interests, with benefits all on the distant horizon, the odds of success in the U.S. political system are not very high.

Divided Government

A central feature of governance in the U.S. system is the difficulty of reaching and enforcing agreements across separated institutions sharing power. The tensions and rivalries between the president and Congress are not merely by-products of the political system; they are essential elements of the constitutional order. Yet very early in American history, political parties emerged to join what the Framers had separated. The political party became "the indispensable instrument that brought cohesion and unity, and hence effectiveness, to the government as a whole by linking the executive and legislative branches in a bond of common interest."[9] While unified control of the national government by one political party did not guarantee cooperation between the branches, it gave presidents a powerful means of seeking support in Congress.

Unified government is no longer the norm in American politics. From Andrew Jackson's time until the second election of Dwight Eisenhower, only three presidents took office to face even one house of Congress not controlled by their party.[10] Five of the last six presidents have faced this problem. The Republicans have become the party of the presidency, Democrats the party of Congress. Political parties now are positioned best to reinforce and heighten conflict between the branches. The task of governing, especially when fiscal pressures require the imposition of losses more than the distribution of benefits, is made all the more difficult.

This is not to say that significant action is impossible under divided

9. James L. Sundquist, "Needed: A Political Theory for the New Era of Coalition Government in the United States," *Political Science Quarterly*, vol. 103 (Winter 1988–89), p. 614.

10. James L. Sundquist, "Strengthening the National Parties," in A. James Reichley, ed., *Elections American Style* (Brookings, 1987), pp. 202–03.

government. Indeed, a careful review of important measures enacted since World War II reveals little difference in legislative productivity between periods of unified and divided party control.[11] Presidents rarely build large-scale legislative victories on the basis of unified control of the government (FDR's one hundred days and LBJ's Great Society are the exceptions). More typically, policy is fashioned in response to events, shifts in the national mood, and extended efforts at problem solving, individual entrepreneurship, and broad coalition building. Under some circumstances, divided government can even facilitate bipartisan cooperation by diffusing responsibility for painful actions.

These important qualifications aside, divided government almost certainly contributes to this country's difficulty in looking out for its long-term interests. Control of the executive and legislative branches by different parties mirrors and reinforces the ambivalence in public attitudes (the desire for both low taxes and high benefits) that contributes to political paralysis. Republican presidents cut taxes or block increases while Democratic Congresses maintain the flow of benefits. With neither party fully responsible or accountable for fiscal policy, the incentive to pass the buck for the failure to balance the budget often proves irresistible. Neither party has the interest in or feels the necessity of forcing the public to reconcile its incompatible preferences.

The nearly permanent division of the national government between the parties, and the growing acceptance by each that it is unlikely to win control of the other branch, reinforces the risk-averse quality of contemporary American politics.[12] Each party seeks first to preserve its own base in national politics by adhering to the principles that have proven successful in winning control of its branch, servicing those interests whose support has been essential, and avoiding controversial positions that might prove damaging politically, especially in an era of sophisticated negative campaigns. The Democrats in particular are torn between their roles as the party of government and the party of opposition.

Given these political constraints and perverse incentives, it is not surprising to see President Bush adopt a tactical and defensive presidency and the Democratic leadership in Congress struggle to formulate an

11. David R. Mayhew, "Does it Make a Difference Whether Party Control of the American National Government is Unified or Divided?" paper prepared for the 1989 annual meeting of the American Political Science Association.

12. Charles O. Jones, "Presidents and Agenda Politics: Sustaining the Power of Office," paper prepared for the 1989 annual meeting of the American Political Science Association.

opposition strategy that responds meaningfully to the country's most critical challenges.

Prospects for Change

Is there any chance that the policy impasse will be overcome in the near future? Breakthroughs can be prompted by a variety of forces: changes in the nature of the problems, in the ideas that shape solutions, and in the balance of political forces brought to bear on them.

Problems

Often the failures of policymakers to deal effectively with problems are overcome not by better policymaking but by changes, gradual or abrupt, in the conditions that define the problems. For example, dramatic developments in the Soviet Union and Eastern Europe in 1989, and the consequent lessening of the Soviet military threat, have provided a glimmer of hope for coping with the fiscal policy deadlock. However limited the "peace dividend" may be in 1990 or 1991, the prospect of large cuts in defense spending by mid-decade certainly diminishes the size of the fiscal policy problem. Similarly, the seemingly intractable trade imbalance between the United States and Japan may be narrowed if the projected sharp rise in the number of Japanese retirees causes the high Japanese saving rate to fall. Some economists have argued that the U.S. saving rate will rise as baby-boomers enter middle age. Should these shifts occur—little evidence of either trend is yet apparent—they would relieve the pressure on the U.S. government to adopt a more disciplined fiscal policy.

But not all external developments are so benign. The *Exxon Valdez* oil spill in Alaska's Prince William Sound, revelations of mismanagement in nuclear weapons plants, predictions about global warming, and the appearance of medical wastes on East Coast beaches have all contributed to an extraordinary surge in public anxiety about the environment. Politicians in both parties have felt obliged to respond, creating a powerful counterforce to the panoply of economic and geographical interests that have stymied efforts to amend the Clean Air Act for more than a decade.

Crises are often welcomed, and sometimes even manufactured, by politicians as a way of breaking the policy logjam. Some architects of the Gramm-Rudman-Hollings deficit reduction procedures saw them as a means of generating an artificial crisis that would force a compromise between the president and Congress on taxes and spending; in practice, the threat proved less than intimidating. Unfortunately, a real economic collapse would be no more successful in moving fiscal policy in the desired direction. The stock market crash of October 1987 pushed negotiators from the White House and Congress to make some progress on deficit reduction, but a large-scale compromise remained beyond their grasp. Indeed, should recession threaten the U.S. economy, the budget and trade deficits would severely constrain use of fiscal and monetary policy to combat unemployment. An economic crisis would almost certainly worsen the fiscal policy deadlock rather than provide the political means for overcoming it.

Ideas

No one observing American politics in the early months of 1990 could fail to be impressed by the capacity of an idea to transform the policy agenda. To the utter surprise of its author, and in confirmation of the powerful role of serendipity in politics, Senator Daniel P. Moynihan's proposal to expose what he called the "real" size of the budget deficit (that is, without counting the surplus in the social security trust fund) by cutting payroll taxes has dominated the attention of policymakers and news organizations. The "man bites dog" character of the proposal—Moynihan, an architect of the 1983 agreement that raised payroll taxes, is the Senate's leading defender of social security and an outspoken advocate of balancing the budget and using the trust fund surpluses to increase the nation's productive capacity—contributed to its notoriety. Seeing a Republican administration put in the position of opposing a tax cut proposed by a prominent Democrat was perhaps too attractive as political theater to ignore.

Moynihan's success in drawing attention to fiscal deficits and social security surpluses may lead to more honesty in budgeting, but it is unlikely to be followed by other policy changes he desires. The public shows little interest in redressing the regressive dependence on payroll taxes. Instead of an adjustment through cutting payroll taxes and raising income and energy taxes, with a net increase in tax receipts, any action that results from his initiative is likely to produce a loss of revenue and a further deterioration of the budget deficit. Ideas can reshape policy but not necessarily in the preferred direction.

What is difficult to conceive of under present circumstances is the successful political marketing of the idea that the United States must reduce consumption and increase savings now in order to protect and enhance its living standards in the future. The difficulty is caused partly by a lack of demand (the public is not anxious to hear the message) but mainly by the unavailability of supply (neither party believes it can advance its political fortunes by playing this tune).

Other ideas percolating in the policy community show some promise of attracting broader support and breaking the impasse, although in each case consensus is nowhere in sight. Discussion of national health insurance has reentered polite political discourse, not solely or even primarily to extend coverage to the uninsured but as a means of controlling costs. And the idea that parents might choose which public schools their children attend may eventually unite philosophical conservatives and liberals disheartened by the colossal failure of urban school systems.

Political Forces

Some of the challenges faced by the United States may become more manageable as a result of developments beyond its control; others may be addressed through the efforts of enterprising leaders to redefine the way mass publics and elites think about them. But the chances of overcoming the most serious obstacles to reshaping national priorities rest heavily on alterations of the political environment. A sharp change in the national mood might elevate public action over private interest as the dominant force in American politics and could transform the policy debate in Washington. With or without a major shift in mood, one party might secure control of both the White House and Congress, ending the extended period of divided government and lodging authority as well as responsibility for national performance in a single party.

One explanation for the "brain-dead" quality of public discourse is that the country is in the late stages of a political cycle in which the dominant party is losing momentum but the opposition party is not yet ready to reshape its coalition by responding creatively and ambitiously to emerging new issues.[13] The idea of cycles in American politics—of

13. Kevin Phillips, "George Bush and Congress-Brain-Dead Politics of '89," *Washington Post,* October 1, 1989, p. D1.

periodic alterations between conservatism and liberalism, equity and efficiency, private interest and public action—has a distinguished pedigree in American political thought. And however skeptical one may be of any notion that smacks of determinism, of immutable swings between fixed points, the evidence of regular fluctuations in national orientation throughout the course of U.S. political history is impressive.[14]

In the twentieth century, Arthur Schlesinger, Jr., argues, eras of public purpose, inaugurated by Theodore Roosevelt in 1901, Franklin Roosevelt in 1933, and John Kennedy in 1961, have been followed by periods of conservative restoration in the 1920s, the 1950s, and the 1980s. Each phase in the cycle plants the seeds—an excess of public or private concerns—of its own destruction. Underlying his model of a thirty-year alteration between public purpose and private interest is the concept of a political generation:

> People tend to be shaped throughout their lives by the events and ideals dominating the time when they arrived at political conscious-ness. There is a feedback from the generation in power to the generation coming of political age, while in between an antagonistic generation clamors for change. Each new generation, when it attains power, tends to repudiate the work of the generation it has displaced and to reenact the ideals of its own formative days thirty years before.[15]

By Schlesinger's account, the early 1990s should see a sharp change in national mood and direction toward public purpose and action as those who grew up in the 1960s seize the reins of national power. While in theory the Bush administration, like that of Theodore Roosevelt, could harness this surge in national sentiment, Schlesinger sees the Democrats as the natural beneficiaries.

At this stage, signs of a distinctive shift in mood are at best scattered and inconclusive. A widespread indifference to national politics tempers public concerns about drug abuse, the homeless, and the deteriorating U.S. position in the world economy. President Bush's rhetorical emphasis on a "kinder, gentler nation," on the need to protect the environment, save the children, and restore excellence in public education, is a tacit acknowledgment that the public is once again turning to government

14. Arthur M. Schlesinger, Jr., *The Cycles of American History* (Houghton Mifflin, 1986), pp. 23–48.
15. Schlesinger, *Cycles of American History*, p. 30.

for unmet social needs. But his plea that "we have more will than wallet" signals an unwillingness to move far beyond rhetoric, presumably because he sees a public that is skeptical of the national government's ability to deal successfully with these major problems and unwilling to pay the costs.

If a dramatic change in national mood is to occur within the next several years, it will require a precipitating event (economic collapse, environmental disaster), a dominant issue, and an enterprising politician who succeeds in persuading the public that government can be a positive force in dealing with the nation's most pressing problems. This sequence is possible but far from inevitable. Public ambivalence about government and the nation's continuing good fortune in the economy and world affairs could sustain a Bush presidency of modest ambitions for two full terms. Moreover, the next Democratic candidate elected to the White House may look less like the charismatic liberal envisioned by Schlesinger than a problem-solving moderate like Jimmy Carter.

The other possible change that could lend some coherence to national politics and policy is the arrival of a genuine Republican majority in Washington, one that occupies both ends of Pennsylvania Avenue. The Republican dominance of presidential politics during the past two decades is irrefutable. The party has won five victories in six elections, most by landslides. The only Democratic win was Jimmy Carter's squeaker in the aftermath of Watergate. A number of factors contributed to the losses of Democrats in the White House sweepstakes, but in the end many Americans came to see the national Democratic party as "inattentive to their economic interests, indifferent if not hostile to their moral sentiments, and ineffective in defense of their national security."[16]

These liabilities in presidential elections did not, however, attach to Democratic candidates running for Congress or for state or local office. The Democrats have lost the House of Representatives only twice since 1930, most recently in 1952. The Republicans gained control of the Senate from the Democrats in the 1980 elections, the first change in party control since 1952, but they returned to their familiar minority position six years later. The partisan map of state politics reveals continuing Democratic dominance in the governorships and especially in the state legislatures.[17]

---

16. William A. Galston, "Putting a Democrat in the White House," *Brookings Review*, vol. 7 (Summer 1989), p. 21.

17. As of 1990, twenty-nine state governors are Democrats and twenty-one are

This split-level feature of American elections has become so familiar that it seems normal. Even the impressive gains made by the GOP since 1980 in closing the Democratic advantage in party identification—from a gap of over 10 percentage points to parity—did not leave a mark on voting beneath the presidential level.[18] The long-awaited party realignment appears to have fallen victim to broad social and political developments, including the weakening of political party attachments, the rise of mass media as the primary mode of political communication, and the resourcefulness of legislators in exploiting the increased advantages of incumbency.

If a return to one-party dominance at all levels of government seems unrealistic, how could Republicans break the Democratic grip on the House? Democrats win House elections for many reasons. Party diversity allows their candidates to adapt well to local political conditions. Their image as the party that provides benefits matches what the public sees as the primary job of a representative. Serious Republican challengers are nonexistent in most districts because the cost is prohibitive and the odds long against a popular incumbent. Democratic control of the redistricting process in most states limits the damage that might be done to the party by population shifts among and within states. And Democrats benefit from their party's failure to win the White House—when national conditions sour, it is the president's party that loses seats in the House.

To counter the Democratic advantages in House elections, Republicans need to support and encourage diversity among their candidates; develop a governing philosophy that provides a credible rationale for seeking election to the House; identify ways to increase the pool of able candidates and the means to finance vigorous campaigns; strengthen their position in the redistricting process; and ensure that a Democrat is sitting in the White House when the next national disaster strikes. The GOP is working hard on all but the last (another example of a party's unwillingness to take a short-term loss for long-term gain?) and pinning its hopes on the 1992 elections. The reapportionment of seats to fertile territory in the South and West, new district lines (meaning less incumbent security), a large number of open seats, continuing favorable shifts in party identi-

---

Republicans. In addition, the Democrats have control of both legislative chambers in twenty-nine states, whereas the Republicans have control over both in eight states.

18. Michael Oreskes, "Republicans Show Gains in Loyalty," *New York Times*, January 21, 1990, p. 24.

fication, a strengthened cadre of candidates, a vastly enlarged campaign budget in one hundred targeted races, a popular president seeking reelection in times of peace and prosperity, and another weak Democratic presidential nominee are the ingredients designed to produce the first Republican House in forty years.

When viewed from a historical perspective, prospects for this scenario do not appear bright. Wide swings in party strength in the House are usually associated with unfavorable conditions in the country, when a "throw the rascals out" sentiment overrides the personal popularity of incumbents. Presidents seldom strengthen their party's position in Congress after their initial election. If times are bad, the president's party is punished; if times are good, voters have little incentive to make any change. The remarkable success of House incumbents in the 1984, 1986, and 1988 elections was caused in no small part by public contentment with the economic recovery and national security.

Some changes in the rules of the game (easing the burden of raising campaign funds, limiting the effects of partisan gerrymandering) could provide marginal assistance to the Republicans in their long climb out of minority status. A more radical proposal that recently returned to the agenda—a constitutional amendment limiting congressional terms— would neutralize the Democrats' incumbency advantage, but prospects for its adoption are remote. More immediately, GOP success in 1990 in retaining the governorships of California, Florida, and Texas would increase the party's likelihood of capturing new House seats in these fast-growing states. And in time, successful Republican stewardship of the White House will pay dividends in Congress as a new generation of young Republican voters replaces an aging Democratic cohort—a trickle-down Republican realignment. Once the Republicans get within striking distance of a majority in the House, they will be better positioned to persuade conservative Democrats to follow the example of Phil Gramm and Andy Ireland by switching parties or at least to organize the House with their ideological soul mates. But without an immediate electoral boost from a failed Democratic administration, the Republicans' climb to majority status will likely be gradual and subject to setbacks as new issues arise to threaten their coalition.

The Senate offers a much more promising target for the Republican party. The volatile Senate class that produced a startling Republican majority in 1980 and a Democratic recovery in 1986 may well swing control back to the GOP in 1992. For a host of reasons (the heterogeneity of constituencies, the visibility of campaigns, the availability of candidates, and the role of issues and ideology), Senate elections are more competitive than House elections.

Neither scenario—a sharp change in the national mood that would allow the Democrats to seize the reins of government or an extension of the Republican dominance in presidential elections to the House and Senate—carries with it any certainty that the policy debate will be transformed and the political obstacles to dealing with the country's long-term problems overcome. The economic conditions favorable to the election of a Democratic president—a serious recession, for example— might severely restrict his room for policy maneuver. Bold policies will inevitably offend voters and groups with entrenched interests, who are certain to be given voice by Congress. A Republican president may find that a Congress controlled by his own party is just as skittish at cutting back on middle-class entitlements or local benefits as the present one. Yet whatever difficulties a unified Democratic or Republican government would encounter, the emergence of distinctive governing and opposition parties would clarify the problems confronting the country and the alternative policies for addressing them.

More likely than a government dominated by one party, however, is a continuation of the present situation. The waning of the cold war and the political mobilization of pro-choice abortion forces do threaten the advantage in presidential elections Republicans have enjoyed because of their positions on defense and social issues. Democrats do relish the prospect of a national debate in the 1990s on where to spend the peace dividend and how to meet the economic threats to U.S. security. But it is not at all clear that they will profit from it in presidential politics. However favorable the march of events in Eastern Europe and the Soviet Union, the public retains a skepticism and level of concern that militates against a disappearance of defense as an issue. The Republicans enjoy a commanding lead in public opinion as the party most trusted to handle responsibilities seen as presidential in character: foreign affairs, defense, and the nation's economy. To reap political benefits from a broad discussion of needed public investment in the nation's social and physical infrastructure, the Democratic party and its presidential nominee must first regain credibility on the central concerns of maintaining economic growth, providing adequate national defense, and ensuring personal security. A skillful and moderately lucky President Bush could preempt such Democratic initiatives and solidify his party's hold on executive power. But it would take considerably more luck and skill for Republicans to win a majority in the House as well.

However much one may long for an abrupt change in political forces to break the policy deadlock, the nation will probably have to get along without it.

Coping with Contemporary Political Arrangements

President Bush's budget for 1991, like the political world into which it was born, is afflicted by ambivalence. It displays soaring rhetoric about the need to tend to the country's serious long-term problems, but presents few specific proposals for beginning that effort. It does not ask the public to make any sacrifices for future benefits.

The budget is a clear and not unexpected signal that the game of fiscal policy will be played on the same terms as in recent years. Congress will impose sharper cuts in defense than the president requests. It will make fewer cuts in domestic programs than he asks. And it will spend modestly more on high-priority matters than he requests. But it will join the administration in using unrealistic forecasts and accounting deceits to meet the deficit target. The president's bargaining position will be strengthened by his willingness to absorb major cuts in defense— sequestration is now a greater threat to domestic programs, which are especially close to the hearts of Democrats, than to defense, which will be cut anyway. But both branches will continue to seek refuge in procedural reforms that avoid the unattractive choices necessary to solve the deficit problem. When the books are closed on fiscal year 1991, Congress and the president will concur in rosy forecasts of declining deficits, but in the end the deficit will change little.

Indeed, a plausible scenario for national policymaking in the 1990s, absent an abrupt shift in political conditions or change of heart by the nation's leaders, is a continuation of the escapism and deadlock of recent years, albeit with changed emphases. Under this scenario, federal deficits, while declining as a share of GNP, will be less of a drain on national savings in the 1990s than they were in the 1980s but not a substantial part of the solution for increasing productivity and improving living standards. The investment of social security surpluses to expand the nation's productive capacity and ease the burden on taxpayers of financing the retirement of the baby-boomers will never come to pass. In the short term, policymakers will try to increase private saving and improve productivity growth with tax incentives and other microeconomic adjustments, but with relatively little chance of success. As for the long term, they will be tempted to leave to the next generation the job of figuring out how to finance the bulge in social security and medicare payments.

In this scenario, the political debate in the 1990s will focus less on deficits and more on how to allocate public resources to strengthen the country's economic position in an increasingly competitive world. Congress will push for deeper and more rapid reductions in defense spending, but that exercise will be slowed by international uncertainties and the intense opposition of U.S. communities and firms threatened by closings of military bases and cancelations of procurement contracts. Parochial resistance in Congress to elements of a defense builddown will eventually be overcome, but not without substantial costs as members seek benefits for their constituencies to ease the pain of conversion.

The demands on this peace dividend will in any case greatly outpace the available resources, especially in the face of continuing budget deficits, but both parties will struggle to define priorities for its use. Democrats will seek to increase funding for existing domestic programs ranging from education, drug treatment, and child care to scientific research and replacement of physical infrastructure. Republicans will champion selected tax incentives and possibly even reductions in payroll and income tax rates. The result of this debate about national priorities, conducted under conditions of divided government, will likely be a little something for both—modest increases in domestic outlays and a reduction in tax receipts.

One can well imagine how the unavailability of federal resources for major new domestic initiatives leads policymakers at both ends of Pennsylvania Avenue to respond to demands for increased services by accelerating the use of low-cost, off-budget or deficit-neutral devices. Stricter government regulations will be a central feature of future health and environmental policy. More vigorous enforcement of existing laws will be heralded as a way to counter unfair trading practices by foreign competitors but will perhaps be adopted as a means of providing benefits to constituents. Initiatives to nurture domestic high-technology industries will rely on changes in antitrust law and modest subsidies to facilitate collaboration. User fees and targeted revenues will be sought to fund high-priority programs. And many of the most perplexing and seemingly intractable problems of social policy—including the failure of the public school system and the pathologies of the urban underclass—will be left to state and local governments. If a renaissance in social policy is to occur under present political conditions, it will almost certainly be led by governors and mayors, not presidents.

This portrait of national policymaking in the 1990s, in which the country responds belatedly and inadequately to its domestic and international challenges, is consistent with contemporary political realities but not an inevitable outcome of them. Events could conspire to redefine the central problems and reshape the political forces brought to bear on them. Or the country's leaders, frustrated by the current political and policy impasse, could cast aside their conventional approaches and emphasize long-term strategy over short-term tactics.

President Bush and his political advisers are almost certainly inclined to stay the course with a political strategy that has proven remarkably successful and, in the absence of a major economic downturn, is very likely to lead to his reelection in 1992. It is hard to imagine getting a sympathetic hearing in the White House for a more aggressive approach to the problems confronting the country and the Republican party, especially one that might offend elements of the Republican presidential coalition. And yet this is the optimal time, when his political standing is at its high water mark, for the president to move in unexpected ways to transform the policy debate.

The Republican party's unassailable reputation as the champion of low taxes and a strong national defense gives President Bush the political protection he needs to lead the debate on restructuring the nation's defense and putting its fiscal house in order. A commitment to work toward a 50 percent reduction in real defense spending by the end of the century would allow the administration to construct a sensible and coherent security posture and defense apparatus for a post–cold war world. It would also ease the nation's fiscal situation and forestall a major line of attack by the Democrats. Similarly, a willingness by President Bush to accept, as part of a package of revenue and spending proposals, a modest increase in taxes weighted toward those high-income households that reaped most of the economic benefits of the 1980s would eliminate the deficit, lower interest rates, increase investment, fuel economic growth and, not incidentally, neutralize efforts by the Democrats to mount a populist critique of the GOP.

Any damage done to Bush and the Republican party by this apparent compromise of campaign promises and party values would be more than balanced by gains from a robust economy and a perception that the country had taken steps to compete more effectively in the global economy. Moreover, the administration and the Republican party would then be in a much better position to move beyond rhetoric and pursue seriously their own brand of conservative, market-oriented solutions to the problems of health care, education, welfare, and the environment. Even tax benefits cost federal dollars.

These presidential initiatives could break the policy logjam, help the country begin to deal with its long-term challenges, and put the Republican party in a position to increase its strength at all levels of elective office. But they would be met with a storm of criticism by Republican activists and would introduce an element of uncertainty into Bush's reelection campaign. If the president were willing to offend some of his constituents and risk losing their support in pursuit of the long-term interests of his party and country, he would find the obstacles posed by divided government and ambivalent public attitudes toward taxes and spending not insurmountable. A change in the supply of political leadership emanating from the White House could well alter the nature of the demands from the public and dissipate the most serious opposition on Capitol Hill.

As the party of Congress, the Democrats are in a much weaker position to seize the political and policy initiative. Their chances of winning the 1992 presidential election are more dependent on forces beyond their control (the state of the economy, the march of events in the Soviet Union and Eastern Europe, Bush's skill in conducting his presidency) than any opposition strategy they launch from Capitol Hill. Their opportunities to enact new policies and reap political benefits from them while a Republican sits in the White House are almost nonexistent. And there is the more general problem of who speaks for the Democratic party in the absence of a presidential nominee. Nonetheless, the Democrats have a responsibility to frame a national debate, both to provide some content to accompany a party label whose meaning has been blurred in recent years and to prepare for the responsibility of governing from the White House when that opportunity next presents itself.

Democratic party strategists are currently attracted to two opposition proposals that appear to have the advantage of wedding traditional party values to new conditions. The first, economic nationalism, calls for tough, unilateral steps to deal with unfair trading practices by foreign economic competitors. The second, prompted by Senator Moynihan's call for a cut in payroll taxes to halt the regressive shift in federal taxes and expose the huge deficits in the general account, endorses a tax cut for middle- and lower-income households without a compensating increase in other federal revenues. The political appeal of each is self-evident. And yet the net effect of an opposition party strategy based on these proposals may well be to reinforce public doubts about the

Democratic party's ability to manage the nation's economy and international security. It is hard to take a party seriously when its major policy initiatives provide no credible basis for governing.

A more promising strategy (though one that poses some risk to the Democrats' congressional base) is to champion policies and programs that directly confront the party's weaknesses and the country's problems. Democrats could profitably put as much energy into defining what constitutes a strong and appropriate military and diplomatic presence in the world of the 1990s as they put into engaging in economic warfare with allies. Serious proposals to promote economic growth could complement the party's renewed concern for fairness. A commitment to increase federal resources for such pressing domestic needs as quality education could be accompanied by a willingness to entertain radical restructuring of existing programs and a decentralization of political authority. A program to ensure comprehensive health insurance coverage could be combined with a new financing mechanism such as a value-added tax. An initiative to expand federal health and education assistance for poor preschool children could be paid for by taxing more fully the social security benefits of higher-income retirees.

If the Democrats are ever again to be in a position to steer an activist government, they need to prepare the way for rearming that government. Tactical maneuvering to avoid being saddled with the responsibility for increasing taxes is self-defeating. Talking straight to the American people about what must be done to invest in the country's future—as Ways and Means Committee Chairman Dan Rostenkowski did in proposing a comprehensive deficit reduction package—is the Democrats' first step toward acting like a presidential party.

It is doubtful that either party will embrace the unconventional strategies I have outlined. But it is nonetheless reassuring to realize that an end to the current political and policy impasse lies within the grasp of the nation's leaders if they will only be so bold as to seize the opportunity.